THE CAMBRIDGE
SHAKESPEARE A

Nothing in Shakespeare's England was as important as religion. Questions of faith informed everything from history and politics to love and family, work and play, good and evil, suffering and sacrifice, and ultimately life and death. Every one of Shakespeare's plays is rich in allusions to the Bible, church rites including baptism, communion, marriage, and burial, and a host of religious beliefs. This Companion provides an essential grounding in early modern religious history and culture and the ideas that Shakespeare returns to throughout his career. Chapters dedicated to close readings of individual plays or groups of plays span both the complex and variegated Christian beliefs explored in Shakespeare's work, as well as the treatment of Judaism, Islam, and classical paganism. Authored by an international team of eminent scholars and featuring an Afterword by Rowan Williams, this Companion is the most comprehensive and incisive guide to the topic that students will find.

Hannibal Hamlin is Professor of English at The Ohio State University. He is author of *The Bible in Shakespeare* (2013) and *Psalm Culture and Early Modern English Literature* (Cambridge, 2014); and co-editor of *The King James Bible after 400 Years: Literary, Linguistic, and Cultural Influences* (Cambridge, 2010) and *The Sidney Psalter: The Psalms of Philip and Mary Sidney* (2009).

A complete list of books in the series is at the back of this book.

THE CAMBRIDGE COMPANION TO SHAKESPEARE AND RELIGION

EDITED BY
HANNIBAL HAMLIN
The Ohio State University

CAMBRIDGE
UNIVERSITY PRESS

University Printing House, Cambridge CB2 8BS, United Kingdom

One Liberty Plaza, 20th Floor, New York, NY 10006, USA

477 Williamstown Road, Port Melbourne, VIC 3207, Australia

314–321, 3rd Floor, Plot 3, Splendor Forum, Jasola District Centre, New Delhi – 110025, India

79 Anson Road, #06-04/06, Singapore 079906

Cambridge University Press is part of the University of Cambridge.

It furthers the University's mission by disseminating knowledge in the pursuit of education, learning, and research at the highest international levels of excellence.

www.cambridge.org
Information on this title: www.cambridge.org/9781107172593
DOI: 10.1017/9781316779224

First published 2019

Printed in the United Kingdom by TJ International Ltd, Padstow Cornwall

A catalogue record for this publication is available from the British Library.

Library of Congress Cataloging-in-Publication Data
Names: Hamlin, Hannibal, editor.
Title: The Cambridge companion to Shakespeare and religion / edited by Hannibal Hamlin.
Description: Cambridge, United Kingdom; New York, NY: Cambridge University Press, 2018. | Includes bibliographical references and index.
Identifiers: LCCN 2018048895 | ISBN 9781107172593 (hardback) | ISBN 9781316624234 (paperback)
Subjects: LCSH: Shakespeare, William, 1564–1616–Religion. | Religion in literature. | Religion and drama. | Drama – Religious aspects.
Classification: LCC PR3011.C285 2018 | DDC 822.3/3–dc23
LC record available at https://lccn.loc.gov/2018048895

ISBN 978-1-107-17259-3 Hardback
ISBN 978-1-316-62423-4 Paperback

CONTENTS

FIGURES

CONTRIBUTORS

THOMAS BETTERIDGE, Dean, College of Business, Arts, and Sciences, Brunel University London.

TOM BISHOP, Professor of English, University of Auckland, New Zealand.

BRIAN CUMMINGS, Anniversary Professor, English and Related Literature, University of York, UK.

ANDREW HADFIELD, Professor of English, University of Sussex, Brighton.

HANNIBAL HAMLIN, Professor of English, The Ohio State University, Columbus.

PHEBE JENSEN, Professor of English, Utah State University, Jensen.

M. LINDSAY KAPLAN, Associate Professor of English, Georgetown University, Washington, DC.

GARY KUCHAR, Professor of English, University of Victoria, Canada.

CLAIRE MCEACHERN, Professor of English, University of California, Los Angeles.

JEAN-CHRISTOPHE MAYER, Research Professor, French National Centre for Scientific Research (CNRS) and University of Montpellier.

ROBERT S. MIOLA, Gerard Manley Hopkins Professor of English and Lecturer in Classics, Loyola University Maryland, Baltimore.

KRISTEN POOLE, Blue and Gold Distinguished Professor of English Renaissance Literature, University of Delaware, Newark.

JENNIFER R. RUST, Associate Professor of English, Saint Louis University, Missouri.

HELEN SMITH, Professor of English and Department Head, University of York, UK.

ADRIAN STREETE, Senior Lecturer in English Literature 1500–1780, University of Glasgow.

DANIEL SWIFT, Senior Lecturer in English, New College of the Humanities, London.

DANIEL VITKUS, Rebeca Hickel Chair in Elizabethan Literature, University of California, San Diego.

ROWAN WILLIAMS, Master of Magdalene College and Honorary Professor of Contemporary Christian Thought, University of Cambridge.

PREFACE

A *Cambridge Companion to Shakespeare and Religion* will seem to some long overdue, since scholars have been writing on the topic for at least a couple of centuries. Those who still cling to the notion that, as the philosopher George Santayana put it, Shakespeare "is remarkable among the greater poets for being without a philosophy and without a religion" ("The Absence of Religion in Shakespeare," 1896), will find this volume puzzling. Literary scholars, however, will recognize that a substantial component of Shakespeare studies for the past several decades has been devoted to exploring religious aspects of the plays and poems and the extent to which they reflect and engage with the religious culture of Elizabethan and Jacobean England. Such scholarship is part of a larger "turn to religion" in early modern literary studies and in other periods as well.

One compelling reason for this scholarly turn is that many people living in twenty-first-century Europe and North America have experienced a similar reorientation in the world around them. With the rise of international and national conflicts based on religious differences, many people, including readers of early modern literature, have been forced to recognize that the world is not as secular as they may have formerly assumed. Of course, Americans have never really been very secular at all, if by "secular" one means unbelieving or nonreligious. Yet even in supposedly secular Great Britain, as evidenced by a 2017 British Social Attitudes survey, almost half the population describe themselves as religious, though most of these are no longer Church of England Christians. Worldwide, according to a recent Pew Research poll, the number of people who are not affiliated with a religion is still extremely small, and perhaps getting smaller. A "secular" society is not necessarily one without religion, though; it can also simply be one in which no official religion is imposed by the state. By this definition, Western nations are indeed secular, in that a citizen may choose freely to affiliate with any number of different religions, or with none at all.

Shakespeare's culture was secular in neither of these senses. Religion in Elizabethan and Jacobean England was everywhere, all the time, not just confined to Sunday worship or the practice of the particularly pious. There was only one Church, governed by the monarch and her/his bishops (who sat in Parliament as Lords Spiritual), to which all citizens automatically belonged. Attendance at Sunday and holiday services was required by law, and persistent nonattendance was punished by fines or imprisonment. Jews had been banned for centuries, Muslims largely limited to ambassadorial visits, and the remaining Catholics concealed their faith or risked discrimination and persecution. But it would be a mistake to think of religious belief and practice as imposed upon an unwilling population by an oppressive church-state. Most people needed no encouragement to go to church, and sermons were one of the most popular public entertainments – as popular as the theater. Open-air sermons at Paul's Cross or St. Mary's Spital, which no one was required to attend, nevertheless attracted audiences of several thousand, including king, court, and commoners alike. Religion pervaded every aspect of life, from government to the family, the schoolroom to the public house, geography to medicine, history to husbandry. As a member of this society, Shakespeare was naturally interested in religious ideas, biblical characters and stories, church rites, and popular practices.

The following chapters offer a variety of perspectives on Shakespeare and religion. Chapters 1–6 introduce essential contexts for thinking about religion in Shakespeare's day, including the history of the Church, the Bible, the liturgies of the Book of Common Prayer, and popular religious culture. Shakespeare's own religious beliefs and practices are explored as well, as far as they can be, though this is not actually very far. (Arguments have been made for Shakespeare as Catholic, mainstream Protestant, Puritan, skeptic, even atheist, but the actual evidence is thin and subject to diverse interpretations.) Most of these contributors focus on how Shakespeare's works represent and explore aspects of religion, and how understanding early modern religion aids in our understanding of what we see onstage or read on the page. Indeed, without understanding these contexts, some passages in Shakespeare are unintelligible. Chapters 7–10 focus on key religious ideas like love, sin, compassion, and Providence, following their appearance in plays across Shakespeare's career. Chapters 11–17 begin with the plays themselves, individually or in useful groupings, and discuss their religious language, biblical allusions, or engagement with theological dilemmas, engaging not just with Christianity but Islam and Judaism as well. Inevitably, some of the same plays will be discussed in more than one chapter, but since the contexts and contributors vary, I believe this overlap is a productive one. Nevertheless, all but three of Shakespeare's plays, and some of the poems, are addressed in this book, demonstrating how widely the religious context is imbedded in his work.

The contributors to this volume, it is perhaps worth saying, were not chosen because of any common religious beliefs. Some may consider themselves religious, some not. The only person of whose religion I am reasonably sure is Rowan Williams, the former Archbishop of Canterbury. Of the rest, I have either a limited sense or no idea at all. They are also diverse in their scholarly and theoretical interests, which can only further enrich this collection. However, it seems reasonable to say that we all concur that "religion," whatever it is, however we conceive it, is important to Shakespeare's works and to those interested in better understanding them. I am grateful to all of these scholars for their labor and their patience as this volume took shape, and of course for their insightful and stimulating contributions. The original idea for this Cambridge Companion came from Sarah Stanton, and I thank her for inviting me to edit it, as I thank her successor, Emily Hockley, for seeing it through to publication.

A NOTE ON THE TEXTS

All quotations from Shakespeare's works refer to the New Cambridge Shakespeare editions, unless otherwise specified.

All references to the Bible, unless otherwise noted, are from *The Geneva Bible: A Facsimile of the 1560 Edition*. Peabody, MA: Hendrickson, 2007, with spelling modernized.

All references to the Book of Common Prayer are from *The Book of Common Prayer: The Texts of 1549, 1559, and 1662*, ed. Brian Cummings, Oxford World's Classics. Oxford: Oxford University Press, 2013, with spelling modernized.

Quotations from other early modern works have spelling modernized and titles capitalized.

ABBREVIATIONS

BCP	Book of Common Prayer
OED	Oxford English Dictionary
ODNB	Oxford Dictionary of National Biography
KJV	King James Version (or Authorized Version) of the Bible

I

THOMAS BETTERIDGE

Shakespeare and the Elizabethan and Jacobean Church

This woodcut from John Foxe's *Acts and Monuments* (Figure 1.1) is a perfect distillation of the way that the English Church saw itself in 1600.[1] Justice stands blindfolded in the center of the picture. To the left, on the established authoritative side of the image, are idealized Protestant luminaries distinguished by their beards, which signify both masculinity and a lack of bodily vanity. Above these figures stands a church and the left-hand "Protestant" side of the picture is framed by a flourishing tree. On the right-hand side of the picture is the Roman Catholic Church; a mass of disordered clerical figures all trying to tip Justice's scales against the word of God. Rosaries, crosses, papal decrees, and Eucharist wafers (and a devil) are not enough to outweigh the Bible. Above the heads of the woodcut's parodic Roman Catholics is emptiness and the right-hand side of the picture is framed by a barren tree. The distinction that is drawn in this woodcut between ordered, flourishing Protestantism and disordered, sterile Roman Catholicism was fundamental to the self-understanding of the English Church in 1600. The visually chaotic, but also dynamic, nature of the right-hand side of this picture reflects a fear of popery but also an acknowledgment of its protean, plural, and potentially attractive nature. Roman Catholicism is sterile, it leads to blasted trees, but it is also textually and visually productive. In the place of real plenty, symbolized in the woodcut by the pastoral landscape on the left-hand side of the image, the right-hand side offers a false plenitude that is both worthless and weightless. In this woodcut it is Roman Catholicism that encourages and offers to the reader the pleasures of interpretation with its multiplicity of different images and figures. And there is nothing unintentional about this. English Protestant culture during the reigns of Elizabeth I and James VI and I is replete with self-conscious representations of this dynamic, with Edmund Spenser's "The Bower of Bliss" (*Faerie Queen*, Book 2, Canto 12) being the most obvious example. William Shakespeare's drama consistently stages, albeit tangentially, the tension embodied in the woodcut above and it consistently seeks

Figure 1.1 "A lively picture describing the weight and substance of God's most blessed word against the doctrines and vanities of man's traditions," from John Foxe, *Acts and Monuments of Matters Most Special and Memorable, Happening in the Church* (London: John Day, 1583), vol. 1, 294.
Source: Rare Books and Manuscripts, The Ohio State University.

to articulate a Protestant sensibility that at the same time does not reject the pleasures and plenitude of human reason and wit. In his drama, and in particular his late plays, Shakespeare imagines a religious space that is at once Christian and has room for fiction, storytelling, and play: a free theatrical Church in which the tensions embodied in the woodcut of Justice weighing the Bible are staged and reconciled.

The Elizabethan and Jacobean Church

The Church legislated into being by Elizabeth I's first Parliament in 1559 was a Protestant one. And by 1600 it had been established for almost fifty years. However, as John Guy has suggested, "it is a paradox that, at the time that the Elizabethan religious settlement was made, it settled little."[2]

The process by which the Church created by statute in 1559 became the largely Calvinist Protestant Church of 1600 was uneven and complex. It was partly a process of separation in which the English Church in a series of uneven steps – some brutal, as in 1559 with the rejection of papal authority, and others much slower – the demise of religious drama, separated itself from medieval Catholicism and a Roman Catholic Church invigorated by the reforms of the Council of Trent 1545–63. Peter Marshall has recently suggested that the "Reformation was a journey" and this was certainly the case in relation to the English Church, with the added complication that a number of the key figures, principally the queen and her bishops, were not only not in agreement about the eventual destination but also the length and nature of the journey.[3] There was also always a sense in which what really mattered to Elizabeth and her advisers in 1559 was to re-establish state or monarchical control over the English Church, a more "reformed" version of the Henrician Church settlement, rather than any particular form of post-Reformation Christianity. Alex Ryrie has suggested that "Elizabeth's Calvinism – without-the-consistory [local church courts] was a mirror image of Henry's Catholicism-without-the-pope."[4] In many ways Elizabeth remained throughout her reign committed to some version of a Henrician Church that was, by 1600, totally anachronistic. James VI and I, when he acceded to the English throne, did tentatively seek to clarify the nature of the English Church but appears to have relatively soon reverted to accepting the basic outlines of the Elizabethan settlement. The Church established in 1559 was Protestant and Constantinian in the sense of being ultimately under secular control but little else was decided and confirmed, and even the latter was regarded by some late Tudor and early Jacobean Christians as a matter of debate.

It was this lack of closure that led to the period between 1559 and 1625 being one in which discussion, albeit within clear constraints, about the nature of the Church, its ceremonies, structures, and some of its basic teaching, became endemic. The poet John Donne was Dean of St. Pauls from 1621 to 1631. In a poem probably written in 1620, Donne's narrator asks God to reveal the True Church – the spouse of the Lamb described in Revelation 19. During the course of the poem, however, Christ's bride becomes scandalously converted into a prostitute or at least a woman who is "open" to all men. Donne's sonnet perfectly captures this sense of the English Church's provisional, partial, even unfinished nature, the extent to which it is still on a journey navigating different possible homes:

> Show me, dear Christ, thy spouse, so bright and clear.
> What, is it she, which on the other shore

Jesus the bridegroom?

Goes richly painted? or which robbed and tore
Laments and mourns in Germany and here?
Sleeps she a thousand, then peeps up one year?
Is she self truth and errs? now new, now outwore?
Doth she, and did she, and shall she evermore
On one, on seven, or on no hill appear?
Dwells she with us, or like adventuring knights
First travail we to seek and then make love?
Betray kind husband thy spouse to our sights,
And let mine amorous soul court thy mild dove,
Who is most true, and pleasing to thee, then
When she is embraced and open to most men. (Holy Sonnet 18)[5]

Donne's Church is caught between Roman Catholicism ("seven hills"), Calvinism ("no hill"), and Jerusalem ("one hill"). But what is most significant in relation to Shakespeare's drama is the way Donne defers or rejects the option of choosing or defining which "hill" is true. Instead he uses the shocking image of the Church as a prostitute to suggest that the Church's truth is practical and provisional as opposed to absolute and fixed.[6] It took Donne's particular vision, however, to see and articulate this idea. A far more common and indeed mainstream approach, across the religious spectrum, was to regard any lack of clarity and order in the ecclesiastical field as a sign of creeping Papistry, heresy, or anarchy.

Among the groups that would have violently rejected Donne's image of an inclusive Church were the establishment of the English Church and the Godly or Puritans. The latter, while often being sharply critical of the existing ecclesiastical settlement, almost all shared to the full the desire of Elizabethan archbishops and bishops for a Church with clear and exclusionary boundaries.[7] Indeed in many ways mainstream Puritans, the vast majority of whom chose to remain within the Church despite what they regarded as its manifest imperfections, were the backbone of the Church – its most committed members and defenders. It was Puritans above all in the period 1558 to 1625 who led the process of confessionalization, the development of creeds, doctrine, and denominations, in England. It was they who took on a role of driving through the process of creating a stable Protestant and Calvinist identity for the English Church. And it is a reflection of the weakness of the English monarchy that confessionalization, which was a mainstay of emerging continental absolutism, was "privatized" in this way.[8] Elizabeth's reported desire not to "open windows into men's souls" may sound attractively tolerant but it flew in the face of early modern religious practice and it had the effect of depriving the English monarchy and state of a key political and cultural tool – one that a number of more committed

English Christians were more than prepared to pick up. Puritans did the heavy lifting in terms of the key confessional tasks of teaching, preaching, and organizing. Above all, they were the people who sought to take responsibility for defining the scope and shape of the godly English community – the English Church. In this they were reproducing a key shared element of confessionalization across early modern Europe. It is important to note that this also complicates any sense that the Puritans were a group apart from the English Church or even that they were an organized group. Neither was the case. It is far more useful to think of Puritanism as a continuum of religious and cultural practices and beliefs that were shared to different degrees by those English Protestants who wished to see further "reformation" of the English Church.

A fundamental flaw in some approaches to the relationship between Shakespeare's drama and religion is a potentially reductive emphasis on its confessional status, which can be boiled down to the question, was Shakespeare a Protestant or Roman Catholic? The key difference at a cultural level in this period was not, however, between Catholics and Protestants, but between confessional and non-confessional religion. Markus Wriedt comments that

> Calvinists, Catholics, Lutherans, and to a certain extent even Anglicans, all acted in remarkably similar ways. No wonder: each faced the same problem. Under the pressure of mutual competition the religious groups had no choice but to establish themselves as "churches," i.e. stable organisations with well-defined membership. These new "churches" had to be more rigid than the old pre-Reformation Church, where membership was self-evident and required no careful preservation.[9]

An essential element in this process of establishment was the need for clergy to teach their congregations central elements of the new Church's doctrines. This cut right across the different confessional groups. As John Bossy suggests, "In reality the consensus of Protestant and Catholic reformations converged ... on the catechising duties of the clergy."[10] The exemplary early modern clerical figure is the devout or godly Churchman, Protestant and Roman Catholic, seeking to teach his benighted parishioners the basics of confessional Christianity, and failing. The complaints of Puritan ministers about the stupidity and ignorance of their parishioners would probably have been made by the same people about the same people regardless of whether the English Church was Protestant or Roman Catholic.[11]

The English Church was committed, as were all confessional Churches, to a creation of a binary world, depicted brilliantly in the woodcut from *Acts and Monuments* (Figure 1.1), but the process of creating a fully reformed world was left by the English state to the Godly or Puritans. This created social and cultural pressures that are consistently staged in Shakespeare's drama. In particular, Shakespeare in his drama reflects on the nature of the English Church as a community while at the same time being careful to avoid directly representing the Church's ceremonies onstage. An important exception to this is the occasional portrayal of an erring or incompetent priest, such as Sir Oliver Martext from *As You Like It*. There also are a number of representations of parodic Catholic figures behaving in disreputable ways. For example, while Friar Lawrence in *Romeo and Juliet* does marry the protagonists with laudable intentions, in practice his behavior, subverting the public marriage ceremony and the authority of parents, is precisely what anti-Roman Catholic writers would expect of a friar. Shakespeare was deeply concerned about confessionalization and the kind of communities its discourses and practices produced; ones that should have been Christian and grace-full but were often marked by a violent desire to label, order, and exclude. In this chapter I will examine a number of key moments from Shakespeare's drama – *Henry VI Part 2*, *Much Ado About Nothing*, *A Midsummer Night's Tale*, *The Winter's Tale*, and *Pericles* – to illustrate Shakespeare's approach to the idea of a Church and the constitution of a Christian community of believers.

Henry VI Part 2, *A Midsummer Night's Dream*, *Much Ado About Nothing*, and Practical Protestantism

William Perkins was the doyen of Elizabethan Puritanism. From his position of influence as a fellow of Christ's College, Cambridge, and lecturer at St. Andrews Church, Perkins consistently argued for further reform of the English Church and against attempts by the government to impose uniformity of practice on clergymen. He was also, however, firmly opposed to those extreme Puritans whose desire for further reformation led them to separate themselves from the established Church. Perkins's copious writings, sermons, and treatises provided the backbone for devotional reading and a guide to leading a godly life. His work is voluminous and appears to seek to satisfy its reader's desire for spiritual comfort and guidance as much through comprehensiveness as through the actual teaching it contains. Perkins's *Exposition of Christ's Sermon on the Mount* (1606) is a very detailed interpretation and explanation of Matthew 5–7. In this work Perkins discusses the nature of the Church, arguing that "God's church is nothing else but a company of God's people, called by the doctrine of the prophets and apostles unto the state of salvation." He goes on to state that, “In the church is vocation, justification, sanctification, and the way to glorification.”[12] The relationship between these two statements hinges upon Perkins’s understanding of the phrase “a company of God’s people,” which was for him the Godly, the people dedicated to the reform of Church and society. The Godly were, like their Roman Catholic opponents, determined to reshape culture so that it reflected their version of the godly commonwealth. As Patrick Collinson writes, “the conscious thrust of the puritan doctrine was towards the redemption of the existing order.”[13] The Church as it appears in the writings of authors like Perkins is a discrete entity, the company of good men, and an image of the ideal society; the English Church as it was and also as it ought to be. The failure of the English Church as established by Elizabeth and maintained by James to live up to this ideal was a source of constant frustration and disappointment for the Godly.

In his drama Shakespeare does not represent the Church or the clergy in detail. No doubt this was largely because to do so would be to invite controversy and potential prosecution. Despite this, Shakespeare does from his earliest work produce images and moments whose meaning extends into a clearly ecclesiastical and religious direction. In *Henry VI Part 2*, possibly Shakespeare’s first play, there is a piece of Reformation drama. The royal court is visiting St. Albans when suddenly there is uproar and a miracle is proclaimed:

GLOUCESTER: What means this noise?
Fellow, what miracle dost thou proclaim?
CITIZEN: A miracle! A miracle!
SUFFOLK: Come to the king and tell him what miracle.
CITIZEN: Forsooth, a blind man at Saint Alban’s shrine,
Within this half-hour, hath received his sight –
A man that ne’er saw in his life before.
KING HENRY: Now God be praised, that to believing souls
Gives light in darkness, comfort in despair. (2.1.58–66)

Having heard about the miracle, the court party is then introduced to Simpcox, who, it transpires, has had his sight restored. King Henry, his queen, and courtiers all accept the “miracle” as real. In particular, Henry’s response is specifically religious in the sense that it locates the “miracle” within a clear pastoral context, suggesting that its meaning goes well beyond the simple restoration of Simpcox’s sight and extends to its implicit impact across Christendom.

The Duke of Gloucester, however, remains far more skeptical and through the application of some relatively simple deductive reasoning exposes Simpcox as a fraud:

GLOUCESTER: A subtle knave. But yet it shall not serve. –
Let me see thine eyes: wink now; now open them.
In my opinion, yet thou seest not well.
SIMPCOX: Yes, master, clear as day, I thank God and Saint Albones.
GLOUCESTER: Say'st thou me so? What colour is this cloak of?
SIMPCOX: Red, master, red as blood.
GLOUCESTER: Why that's well said. What colour is my gown of?
SIMPCOX: Black, forsooth, coal-black as jet. (2.1.109 –16)

Gloucester's approach to the miracle is to subject it to the kind of skeptical scrutiny that harks back to the work of earlier pre-Reformation writers and, in particular, Erasmus and later religious figures such as Samuel Harsnett. Having established that, despite claiming always to have been blind and lame, Simpcox can see and name different colors, Gloucester stages his own parodic miracle:

GLOUCESTER: My lords, Saint Alban here hath done a miracle; and would ye not think his cunning to be great that could restore this cripple to his legs again?
SIMPCOX: O master, that you could!
GLOUCESTER: My masters of Saint Albans, have you not beadles in your town, and things called whips?
MAYOR: Yes, my lord, if it please your grace.
GLOUCESTER: Then send for one presently.
MAYOR: Sirrah, go fetch the beadle hither straight.

Exit [an Attendant]

GLOUCESTER: Now fetch me a stool hither by and by. – Now, sirrah, if you mean to save yourself from whipping, leap me over this stool, and run away.
SIMPCOX: Alas, master, I am not able to stand alone: you go about to torture me in vain.

Enter a Beadle with whips

GLOUCESTER: Well, sir, we must have you find your legs. – Sirrah beadle, whip him till he leap over that same stool.
BEADLE: I will, my lord. – Come on, sirrah, off with your doublet quickly.
SIMPCOX: Alas, master, what shall I do? I am not able to stand.

After the Beadle hath hit him once, he leaps over the stool and runs away; and they follow and cry, "A Miracle!"

KING HENRY VI: O God, seest thou this, and bearest so long? (2.1.133–53)

In many ways this incident from one of Shakespeare's earliest plays encapsulates how throughout his writing Shakespeare positions his drama in a space between competing confessional absolutes. King Henry in this passage is at once a gullible believer and a committed reformer. When he thinks that the miracle is real he thanks God and when it is exposed as a fake he sees it as an example of the sinfulness of the world. Henry is a godly fool in a world of fallen humanity.

Gloucester's approach is very different. He views the miracle with skepticism and uses reason to expose it as a fraud. In the process he avoids the polarizing confessional absolutes of Henry's world. The exposure of the miracle as fake is a result not of religious or spiritual enquiry but of the correct application of the tools of social order – in this case the Beadle's whip. This is not to suggest there is anything particularly gentle about Gloucester's behavior. The command that Simpcox and his wife be whipped all the way back to Berwick, their home town, uncannily echoes the requirements of the Vagabonds Act (1572), which set down this treatment for all vagabonds including, potentially, actors; and, of course, Simpcox is indeed an actor.

Consistently in his drama Shakespeare articulates a view of the relationship between religious language and human reason, which subverts the norms of confessionalization. In the process he effectively stages a version of the Christian community, in which the Church's authority is located in the communal practice of the faithful and not in absolutist claims to scriptural or doctrinal purity.[14] The moment in *A Midsummer Night's Dream* when Bottom reflects on his night-time experience with the fairies exemplifies Shakespeare's approach to the interpretation of Scripture:

> BOTTOM: I have had a most rare vision. I have had a dream, past the wit of man to say what dream it was ... The eye of man hath not heard, the ear of man hath not seen, man's hand is not able to taste, his tongue to conceive, not his heart to report, what my dream was. I will get Peter Quince to write a ballad of this dream: it shall be called "Bottom's Dream," because it hath no bottom. (4.1.200–9)

As is well known, in this passage Bottom paraphrases 1 Corinthians 2.9. He also scrambles it so that it becomes nonsense, eyes do not hear nor do ears see and at the same time Bottom's words, as Hannibal Hamlin argues, can be seen as profoundly Pauline given their extrasensory mystical ethos.[15] The alternative to Bottom's partial and compromised understanding of what took place is articulated in Theseus's dismissal of the stories of the four Athenian lovers as the product of "seething minds." Bottom, however, not only has a better sense of what really happened but also articulates a hermeneutic approach, which in a religious context seems much more suited to the chaotic religious world of London in 1600. It is an approach to interpretation that effectively reproduces the Erasmian ideal of a textual Christian community united in and through the exchange of proverbial wisdom. "Bottom's Dream" will become a text that is exchanged, sold, and consumed, and in the process the Biblical truth it contains, its scriptural kernel, will circulate among those who buy and sing Quince's ballad.

The late Elizabethan Church was a site for constant and often heated debate over a whole range of issues. For example, the position and status of the altar was not fixed and often, particularly in London, altars would move around the church depending on the particular views of the resident clergyman and those of the engaged laity. As Kenneth Fincham and Nicholas Tyacke demonstrate in their recent study, *Altars Restored: The Changing Face of English Religious Worship*, "the altar was a vital battleground, first between Catholics and protestants, and then among protestants themselves, about conflicting beliefs on sacramental theology, imagery, sanctity, and reverence."[16] It would also be possible, however, to see the altar less as the site of a battle and more as a place where the plurality or provisional nature of the Church, as celebrated in Donne's sonnet, was played out. Shakespeare consistently portrays, arguably particularly in his late Elizabethan plays, a tension between those, usually male, characters who confidently make claims to absolute truth or the ability to discern the truth in a given situation and the distinctly different reality that the audience is presented with. In *A Midsummer Night's Dream* Theseus instructs the other characters on the fantastical nature of the events in the forest, but it is Bottom in his paraphrase of the biblical verse who gets far closer to the truth. A Church in which the altar, a central element of any Christian service, was on a constant pilgrimage around the space of the church was not one in which confident assertions of absolute truth or certainty could have much credence to anyone not committed to a particular understanding of where the altar should be.

In *Much Ado About Nothing* the tension between confessional certainty and the provisional truthfulness of humanity is played out around two key Puritan concerns, interpretation and social order. There are two pivotal moments in *Much Ado About Nothing* that rest on claims to be able to discern the truth. In the wedding scene, Claudio claims, on the basis of Don John's trick, to be able to see beyond Hero's "painted" virtue to the reality of her wantonness. There is an iconoclastic violence to the way in which Claudio exposes Hero in the most brutal way possible, tearing away, in his eyes, a mask of purity to reveal the corruption within. Hero understands the religious subtext of Claudio's actions, crying, "Oh God defend me, how am I beset! / What kind of catechising call you this?" (4.1.71–2). Claudio the Puritan enacts, within a religious space, the wedding ceremony, an act of iconoclastic "reform." He knows the truth hidden behind the painted veil of Hero's virtue. The Friar's confident assertion that Hero is chaste repeats the logic of Claudio's assertion but rejects its conclusions:

FRIAR FRANCIS: Call me a fool;
Trust not my reading nor my observations,
Which my experimental seal doth warrant
The tenor of my book: trust not my age,
My reverence, calling, nor divinity,
If this sweet lady lie not guiltless here
Under some biting error. (4.1.157–63)

The Friar, like Claudio, claims to be able to "read" Hero and discern the truth. His reference to "some biting error" suggests, given that it is made in the context of a religious ceremony, that Claudio's behavior is a form of heresy. The Church in *Much Ado About Nothing*, as represented by the wedding ceremony, has become a place in which absolutist claims to interpretative certainty clash in a way that seems to offer no possibility of resolution and conciliation.[17]

Ultimately order is restored and the wedding ceremony can be restaged:

CLAUDIO: Give me your hand before this holy friar,
I am your husband if you like of me.
HERO: And when I lived, I was your other wife,
And you when you loved, you were my other husband. (5.4.58–61)

Hero's unmasking restores grace to the space of the church, but it is also based on a number of arbitrary and highly provisional acts. There has been no serious or detailed examination of the issues. Instead, a group of incompetent watchmen, albeit figures with clear Biblical antecedents, have stumbled upon Don John's plot and exposed his lies.

Dogberry and Verges, much like Bottom, discern a truth behind the surface life of Messina that is hidden from the likes of Claudio or Don Pedro. While the latter show a particularly godly propensity to lurch from the extremes of violent repudiation, profound mortification, and Pauline revelation, the constables, through a combination of intuition and luck, restore order to the sacred space of the wedding ceremony. Dogberry and Verges are parodic but not necessarily critical agents of reform. They undoubtedly do play an important role in redeeming the crisis produced by Don John's plots, but they do so without a conscious intention. In *Much Ado About Nothing* the space of the church is restored to order, and this restoration is largely the result of the actions of an official watch, but the process is far less planned and deliberate than Elizabethan Puritans would have desired. Shakespeare consistently creates images of the Church in his plays that are sites for resolution of social and personal conflicts. The agents who produce these resolutions are, however, far from the godly male magistrates who were the driving force of confessionalization. Instead they are invariably precisely those figures – women, naive or simple artisans – who were meant to be the subjects of reform, not its drivers.

Word, Text, and London

In his later plays, *The Winter's Tale* and *Pericles*, Shakespeare works through themes of redemption, narrative, and spiritual space that consistently invoke the English Church while being careful not to transgress the limits of judicial public discourse in matters of religion. *Pericles* is a particularly provocative meditation on the place of the Church, religion, and the individual. It is a theatrical rejection of confessionalization and articulates a model of Christian living that all sides of the various debates within the early Jacobean Church would have rejected.

Shakespeare probably spent most of his adult life in London. The city was home to a bewildering array of different organized religious practices, all grouped within the official state Church. As Peter Lake suggests, "London, with its parishes crushed in on one another, its lively and scarcely regulated lecturing scene, its complex network of ecclesiastical jurisdictions and peculiars, its variegated godly community, spread widely across both the city itself and the social order, must have been a Laudian, indeed even a Bancroftian, bishop's worse nightmare."[18] Archbishop Bancroft and Archbishop Laud were two early Stuart leaders of the English Church who sought with varying degrees of success to impose uniformity on the English Church. In these terms Lake is undoubtedly right, but London was also a Puritan nightmare and for identical reasons. It was a marketplace for different forms of English Protestant practice. Indeed, in many ways London was Donne's church written large, or at least the place where a Christian could shop for whatever form of Protestant service she desired. *Pericles* in a strange way embodies both London and a particular sense of the religious past. In a world in which competing religious polemicists consistently referred to the history of the early church to justify their arguments, *Pericles* returns to the past, in the shape of the fourteenth-century poet John Gower, and to the medieval romance genre. But it also returns to earlier pre-Reformation Christian history with its invocation of medieval saints' tales, and even earlier to its restaging by Pericles of a Pauline journey across the Mediterranean in search of redemption.

One of the key moments in the play is when Marina, Pericles's lost daughter who has been sold into sexual slavery, uses her skills as a storyteller to defend her virtue against visitors to the brothel in which she is imprisoned. The brothel keepers are clear that Marina threatens their very way of life:

> BAWD: Fie, fie upon her, she's able to freeze the god Priapus and undo a whole generation. We must either get her ravished or be rid of her. When she should do for clients her fitment, and do me the kindness of our profession, she has me her quirks, her reasons, her master reasons, her prayers, her knees, that she would make a puritan of the devil if he should cheapen to kiss of her. (4.5.12–17)

Later in the play Marina's skills are demonstrated when she persuades the governor, Lysimachus, not to rape her:

> MARINA: For me that am a maid,
> Though most ungentle fortune have placed me in
> This sty, where since I came diseases have
> Been sold dearer than physic – that the gods
> Would set me free from this unhallowed place,
> Though they did change me to the meanest bird
> That flies i'th'purer air!
> LYSIMACHUS: I did not think
> Thou couldst have spoke so well, ne'er dreamed thou couldst.
> Had I brought hither a corrupted mind,
> Thy speech had altered it. (4.5.88–97)

Marina plays a role in the brothel that is instantly recognizable as coming from the medieval hagiographic tradition. And in particular Marina's plight echoes that of such figures as St. Agnes. She is also in some ways a Protestant heroine, however, since her story ends not in chastity and martyrdom but in marriage and familial reconciliation.[19] It is also noticeable the extent to which the Bawd's description of Marina's various tactics for resisting the demands of the brothel's customers has a performative quality. Marina plays the role of virgin saint, and it is this that secures her salvation. Her skills as an actor and as a storyteller bring grace to the corrupted, diseased space of the brothel.

Pericles has a pagan setting, but it is remorselessly anchored in the spiritual concerns of Jacobean Christian practice. Its sense of bricolage, of texts, characters, and places being thrown together, symbolically echoes criticisms leveled at the Jacobean Church by its critics, Puritans and Roman Catholics. What brings order out of the mess of potage that is *Pericles* is storytelling, the sense of reconciliation being produced through acceptance of a shared investment in the story as an ongoing collaborative process. Sarah Beckwith comments that "*Pericles* is a profound exploration of the resources of acknowledgement, of recognition, and of the power of stories, shown and told."[20] What is staged in *Pericles* is the emergence of a reformed, reconciled, implicitly Christian community united through their participation in a shared story that none of them own and that all of them tell. As an image of the English Church this is potentially radical and powerful. It reflects Donne's sense of the true Church being open to all and throws down a gauntlet to the confessional desire for strict boundaries and a clear separation of the godly from the reprobate.

Lancelot Andrewes in *A Sermon Preached the VI. March MDXCIIII* asks his listeners to "*Remember Lot's wife*, Christ, here; that is, To lay our actions to those, we find there, and of like doings, to look for like ends. So read stories past, as we make not our selves matter for story to come."[21] When Pericles accepts his fate he also implicitly accepts his status as a character within a story told by someone else, but this acceptance is precisely what is beyond many of Shakespeare's dominant male characters. *The Winter's Tale* is a play that is centrally concerned with the Church as an ideal Christian community, albeit in a displaced and hidden form. Indeed, the play can be read as an allegorical "history" of the English Church with Leontes in the role of Henry VIII, tearing apart the fabric of his realm and his personal life in pursuit of a mad paranoid fantasy. Leontes epitomizes the fear warned against in Andrewes's sermon of becoming the matter of stories. This is his fear above all: to become a character in ballads and stories to be handed around by all and sundry with him cast in the role of the betrayed and humiliated husband. To avoid this Leontes banishes his daughter and subjects his wife to such violent and humiliating treatment that she appears to die alongside their son. Performing a prophetic Pauline role, only Paulina among those at Leontes's court seriously resists his behavior, and she is the one who most forcibly brings home to Leontes the consequences of his behavior:

PAULINA: A thousand knees,
Ten thousand years together, naked, fasting,
Upon a barren mountain, and still winter
In storm perpetual, could not move the gods
To look that way thou wert.
LEONTES: Go on, go on.
Thou canst not speak too much; I have deserved
All tongues to talk their bitt'rest. (3.2.207–13)

Leontes, like such other male characters as Claudio in *Much Ado About Nothing*, has to learn to repent in order to restore order to his world. In the process Paulina is his guide and she continues to insist on his active repentance well after other members of Leontes's court feel he has suffered enough and advise him to marry again. The regime of prayer that Paulina imposes on Leontes is one that would have been recognized and approved of by godly English Protestants. As Alec Ryrie comments, "For early modern Protestants, prayer was a battle. To pray was to embark on spiritual warfare against a daunting array of opponents. Only the most implacable prayer-warrior could emerge victorious."[22] Paulina's lesson to Leontes is that he must fight this battle until he learns to accept his status as "matter for stories," as part of a wider, narrated spiritual community, of the kind that is sketched by Paul in his various New Testament letters and also, arguably, as is celebrated in the description of the early Christian Church in Foxe's *Acts and Monuments*.

The Winter's Tale ends with an image of reconciliation. With his daughter restored to him, Leontes is presented by Paulina with a statue of his lost wife, which then comes to life:

LEONTES: What you can make her do,
I am content to look on; what to speak
I am content to hear; for 'tis as easy
To make her speak as move.
PAULINA: It is required
You do awake your faith. Then stand still.
On! Those that think it is unlawful business
I am about, let them depart.
LEONTES: Proceed.
No foot shall stir.
PAULINA: Music, awake her, strike!
[Music]
'Tis time: descend; be stone no more; approach;
Strike all that look upon with marvel. (5.3.91–100)

Paulina here uses the magic of theater to restore order to Leontes's world. His repentance is rewarded through an act of theatrical grace. The end of *The Winter's Tale* is, like the second wedding scene in *Much Ado About Nothing*, one of those moments in his canon when Shakespeare imagines a Church that brings together repentance with popular wisdom. In the process the strictures of confessionalization are effectively rejected and an image of a Church is staged that is open to all who accept their status as the "matter of story" that is the Christian community.

Conclusion

Shakespeare's drama consistently engages with the dangers of confessional absolutism; the godly desire, invariably articulated by powerful male characters, to make the world over in its entirety, to produce one that is fully ordered, transparent, and explained. Set against these "godly" devout men are those figures, such as Bottom or Paulina, who represent a completely different ethos, one much closer to Donne's promiscuously truthful Church. An ethos that not only embraces the conversion of life into story, but regards that story as the only true basis of a Christian life. It is this that is at the center of Shakespeare's understanding of the Church. Herbert McCabe comments that "our human life consists in enacted narrative so our divine life is just our participation in the enacted narrative of God. The revelation of God to us is nothing except our being taken up into that narrative, the human story that is the sacrament or image of the unseen and unseeable, incomprehensible God."[23] Bottom understood this taking-up into the narrative of God as a moment of dream-like mysticism. Shakespeare's relationship to the Elizabethan and early Jacobean Church is one that is constantly mediated through the stories and narratives of the characters like Bottom, Paulina, or Marina, who bring the Christian community into being through the creation of a storytelling space.

Notes

1 John Foxe, *The Unabridged Acts and Monuments Online or TAMO*, 1570 edn. (Sheffield: HRI Online Publications, 2011), 795.

2 John Guy, *Tudor England* (Oxford: Oxford University Press, 1988), 290.

3 Peter Marshall, *Heretics and Believers: A History of the English Reformation* (New Haven, CT: Yale University Press, 2017), 434.

4 Alec Ryrie, "Paths Not Taken in the British Reformation," *The Historical Journal* 52 (2009): 1–22.

5 John Donne, *The Complete English Poems*, ed. A. J. Smith (London: Penguin, 1996), 316.

6 It is possible that James I and VI did share elements of Donne's vision of an inclusive English Church. Kenneth Fincham and Peter Lake comment that, "James I ... attempted to construct a unified Church based on a small number of key doctrines, in which advancement was open to a wide range of protestant opinion and from which only a minority of extreme puritans and papists were to be excluded." "The Ecclesiastical Policies of James I and Charles I," in Kenneth Fincham and Peter Lake, *The Early Stuart Church 1605–1642* (Basingstoke, UK: Macmillan, 1995), 1–32, 24.

7 There is considerable historiographical debate about the nature of Puritans and in particular whether it was a disruptive alien element in the Elizabethan and early Stuart Church or it was simply an aspect of mainstream English Protestant belief and practice.

8 Patrick Collinson comments that, "Nowhere else in early modern Europe within a legally established Church was so much collective religious consciousness and behaviour conditioned not by regulation but by a more or less spontaneous consensus of private men, the religious public themselves. That was the significance

and near uniqueness of English Puritanism." Patrick Collinson, *The Religion of Protestants: The Church in English Society 1559–1625* (Oxford: Clarendon, 1982), 247.

9 Markus Wriedt, "'Founding a New Church ...': The Early Ecclesiology of Martin Luther in the Light of the Debate about Confessionalization," in *Confessionalization in Europe, 1555–1700*, ed. John M. Headley, Hans J. Hillerbrand, and Anthony J. Papalas (Aldershot, UK: Ashgate, 2004), 51–66, 57.

10 John Bossy, *Christianity in the West* (Oxford: Oxford University Press, 1983), 118.

11 See Christopher Haigh's *The Plain Man's Pathways to Heaven: Kinds of Christianity in Post-Reformation England* (Oxford: Oxford University Press, 2007).

12 William Perkins, *The Works of William Perkins: Volume 1*, ed. J. Stephen Yuille (Grand Rapids, MI: Reformation Heritage Books, 2014), 310 and 312.

13 Collinson, *Religion of Protestants*, 179.

14 Cummings comments that one effect of the Reformation was that "A God that seemed to be immanent in language was just as much occluded by language." Certainly by 1600 the confidence of such early English Protestant writers as William Tyndale or John Foxe in the power of vernacular Scripture and print was being replaced by an anxiety about the power of text or complex language to obscure God's word. This anxiety is articulated in the work of a number of early Stuart writers, perhaps most clearly in the poetry of George Herbert. Brian Cummings, *The Literary Culture of the Reformation: Grammar and Grace* (Oxford: Oxford University Press, 2002), 417.

15 Hannibal Hamlin, *The Bible in Shakespeare* (Oxford: Oxford University Press, 2013), 109.

16 Kenneth Fincham and Nicholas Tyacke, *Altars Restored: The Changing Face of English Religious Worship* (Oxford: Oxford University Press, 2007), 1.

17 By focusing on the relationship between perception and truth, Shakespeare portrayed a deep skepticism about the power of perception, the ability of interpreted experience, and the stability of reality. Susan E. Schreiner, *Are You Alone Wise? The Search for Certainty in the Early Modern Era* (Oxford: Oxford University Press, 2011), 372.

18 Peter Lake, *The Boxmaker's Revenge: "Orthodoxy," "Heterodoxy" and the Politics of the Parish in Early Stuart London* (Stanford, CA: Stanford University Press, 2001), 395.

19 Lorraine Helms comments that, "Unlike the Prostitute Priestess and the saints, [Marina] need neither kill nor die to avoid prostitution; eloquence preserves her chastity without bloodshed." Lorraine Helms, "The Saint in the Brothel: Or, Eloquence Rewarded," *Shakespeare Quarterly* 41 (1990): 319–32, 329.

20 Sarah Beckwith, *Shakespeare and the Grammar of Forgiveness* (Ithaca, NY: Cornell University Press, 2011), 93.

21 Lancelot Andrewes, *Lancelot Andrewes: Selected Sermons and Lectures*, ed. Peter McCullough (Oxford: Oxford University Press, 2011), 112.

22 Alec Ryrie, *Being Protestant in Reformation England* (Oxford: Oxford University Press, 2013), 243.

23 Herbert McCabe, *The Good Life: Ethics and the Pursuit of Happiness* (London: Continuum, 2005), 78.

2

ANDREW HADFIELD

Shakespeare: Biography and Belief

It is not surprising that we have so much data about early modern religious belief and so little evidence of what people actually believed. The Reformation necessitated a major revision of Christian belief, as institutions and individuals had to work out where they now stood. At the same time, it became easier to be labeled a heretic, as there was no longer a unified Church to guide the faithful, and, especially in countries such as England, the authorities who determined religious policy changed at an alarming rate. Put another way, it became ever more important to think about individual salvation and equally dangerous to declare one's confessional allegiance. We owe a great debt to Alex Ryrie who has reconstructed the nature of Protestant belief in the aftermath of the Reformation.[1] Yet, while his book has enabled us to understand patterns, structures, and practices of belief, it will not always help us to determine who believed what.

If uncovering the specific beliefs of most people is hard enough, it is especially true of writers. Writing could, of course, be used as evidence against people when religious policy changed. Poets who circulated verse in manuscript might evade censorship, but work for the public stage was another matter. There were strict prohibitions, as well as checks through the office of the Master of the Revels, on the declaration of particular beliefs in plays, which is why so few are about religion and why it is almost impossible to link particular dramas to an individual's religious belief (which has not stopped some critics from trying).[2] We know very little about the religious beliefs of most Elizabethan writers, apart from those who changed confessional allegiance like Ben Jonson.[3] Even so, at the end of his long life it was hard to know which side Jonson was on. Of course, it is probably a fair assumption that Thomas Dekker (*c.*1572–1632), author of the anti-Catholic satire *The Whore of Babylon* (1607), was probably a Protestant (unless he was covering his tracks or simply wanted to take the money), and that the martyred poet, Robert Southwell (1561–95), was a Catholic. But it is very difficult to work out the religious beliefs of nearly all significant writers either from their writings or from surviving life records. Although Gabriel Harvey and Thomas Nashe insulted each other in print in a conflict that had a strong relationship to the scandalous puritan pamphlets known as the Marprelate Tracts (1588–9), we cannot easily work out what either really believed.[4] Edmund Spenser is far more enigmatic and elusive than the frequently applied label "Protestant Poet" assumes: no life records survive testifying to his religious affiliation and it is clear that both his sons were suspected of Catholicism in the mid-seventeenth century.[5] John Lyly (1554–1606) wrote for the bishops in the Marprelate conflict, alongside Nashe, but there is no clue to his religious affiliation in his life or work beyond this. Like Ben Jonson, John Donne (1573–1631) had a life defined by religious change and personal turmoil, but working out his beliefs is not a straightforward task, so shrouded are they in mystery.[6]

The dramatists who worked with Shakespeare – or who may have worked with Shakespeare, as we cannot be sure who made up the editorial team that produced the *Henry VI* plays early in his career – are equally elusive.[7] Nashe, the son of an East Anglian clergyman, has already been mentioned. George Peele (1556–96), who probably wrote at least the first act of *Titus Andronicus*, is of indeterminate Christian faith; Thomas Kyd (1558–94), who may have played a part in the *Henry VI* plays, left behind no clear sense of his religious views; the same can be said of Christopher Marlowe (1564–93), who some think was part of the same team; the rather shady George Wilkins (*c.*1576–1618), who co-wrote *Pericles*, also leaves no traces of his confessional allegiance; and Shakespeare's major later collaborator, the prolific John Fletcher (1579–1625) was the son of a bishop, but otherwise left no traces of religious activity.[8] It used to be claimed that Thomas Middleton (1580–1627), who probably wrote much of *Timon of Athens* and rather less of *Macbeth*, was a Calvinist at heart, but commentators are far less certain these days.[9]

Given this understandable lack of knowledge it should not surprise us that we have few clues about Shakespeare's religion. Vigorous cases have been made for his Catholicism, some rather more successful than others.[10] In large part these are based on particular, sometimes partial, readings of the plays (the thumb referred to by the witches in *Macbeth* referring to a famous relic of Edmund Campion's body; *The Rape of Lucrece* telling a coded story of Henry VIII's unfortunate passion for Anne Boleyn), but there are also biographical clues that require some analysis.

The most important document is the spiritual testament of John Shakespeare, William's father. This is a formulaic text, evidently distributed among Catholics, as a way for them to confirm their allegiance to true Church, which requires the faithful to insert their name in a serie propositions, written in a manner that imitates the structure of the forbidden mass. At first glance the evidence of John Shakespeare's militant Catholic faith would seem to be overwhelming. The first article begins,

> First, I here protest, and declare in the sight, & presence of Almighty God, Father, Son, and holy Ghost, three Persons, & one God; and of the B. V. Mary, and of all the holy Court of Heaven, that I will live and die obedient unto the Catholic, Roman, & Apostolic Church, firmly believing all the twelve Articles of the Faith taught by the holy Apostles, with the interpretation, & declaration made thereon by the same holy church, as taught defined & declared by her.[11]

The problem is that the provenance of the document makes it hard to judge whether it is genuine or a fake. It was discovered on April 27, 1757 in the roof of Shakespeare's house in Henley Street. The document was then passed on to the great Shakespeare scholar, Edmund Malone (1741–1812), who, although not convinced of its authenticity, published it among the "Emendations and Additions" to his edition of Shakespeare in 1790. Malone stated in 1796 that he had obtained evidence that the document could not have been written by one of Shakespeare's family and that he would publish proof in his then-forthcoming life. Unfortunately, Malone never completed this project and the document, the first leaf of which had already disappeared, was never found again, so exists only in Malone's published version of his copy.

It is, of course, possible that the lost document was genuine, and a number of similar examples survive from the seventeenth century. A letter from Dr. William Allen, rector of the English College in France, confirms that Cardinal Borromeo ordered several thousand copies of such spiritual testaments at about the same time that he met the Jesuit missionaries Robert Parsons and Edmund Campion before they traveled to England, making them an entirely plausible source of John Shakespeare's document.[12] This evidence would seem to suggest that Shakespeare grew up in an environment overseen by a Catholic father, which would surely have meant that he would have been raised in the traditional faith. However, as David Scott Kastan argues, John Shakespeare had seven children baptized in the Church of England, and a document survives that names him as the local dignitary responsible "for defacing images in the chapel," taking down the rood loft, and introducing a communion table to replace the altar.[13] If the Shakespeare household were Catholic it was clearly able to conform when necessary, and this particular fact has convinced some commentators that "the Protestants have the slightly better claim" on John Shakespeare's allegiance.[14]

There is more evidence about Shakespeare's father's faith. John Shakespeare was also twice fined for recusancy in 1592, just as his son was starting to make a name for himself in London. This may have been due to his religious convictions, and cases have been made that he was a convinced Puritan as well as a Catholic, but it is equally – if not more – likely that his long history of debt persuaded him to absent himself when he was certain to meet most of his (probably) irate creditors.[15] John was a successful businessman in many ways, but his fortunes varied and he was as often in debt as he was thriving, and, sadly, by the late 1580s he was on a downward spiral, which may have influenced William's life choices as he sought to restore the family fortunes.[16] John appears on the list of recusants as someone who did not attend church because they were too ill and infirm, or "for debt and for fear of process."[17]

The problem is that every position looks rather like special pleading. The will may be a forgery and John may have been absent from church because he had a legitimate fear of being arrested for debt. But, given how few traces there are of the thoughts and beliefs of early modern people, these two details could be seen to help in establishing a picture. Furthermore, Stratford was a town in which there was a significant presence of both Catholics and Puritans, the town taking a hard line against traveling players in the early 1600s under the influence of a Puritan-dominated council, which "must have caused a certain amount of mistrust between the council and the playwright, and surely accounted in part for his non-participation in civic affairs when he was in Stratford."[18] Whatever his own beliefs, religion clearly shaped Shakespeare's life. His family, neighbors, and associates in the local area contained a large number of Catholics. The assiduous research of Mark Eccles over fifty years ago recorded a number, including William Reynolds (1575–1632/3), a friend from Stratford named in Shakespeare's will, whose father and mother were frequently fined for non-attendance at church, and Arthur Cawdrey, who would have been at Stratford Grammar School at the same time as Shakespeare, had a brother, George, who went to the Jesuit seminary in Rheims and was later suspected of being part of the Jesuit mission in England. (John Shakespeare had to sign sureties of the peace before their father, Ralph, and other aldermen, in 1582.)[19] The Shakespeares would also have known Sir William Catesby (1547–98), who became sheriff of Warwickshire in 1577 and came from Stratford. Catesby was known as a recusant who had been imprisoned in 1581 for refusing to state whether Edmund Campion had been in his house. His son, Robert, was one of the most significant of the Gunpowder Plot conspirators who died in the final shootout in Holbeche House, Staffordshire.[20]

Such connections were probably not that unusual given the mixed religious geography of Elizabethan and Jacobean England, with Protestants and Catholics of every stripe living cheek by jowl in both harmony and discord. A list of the Protestants who Shakespeare would have known might prove just as illuminating (or misleading). More significant are Shakespeare's family connections through marriage and those through Stratford Grammar School. Shakespeare's mother, Mary, was from the Arden family and the Shakespeares acknowledged the significance of this link to the more important family in 1599 when they applied for permission to use the Arden coat of arms. The Ardens were Catholics, and the head of the family, Edward Arden (*c.*1542–83), was executed along with his son-in-law, John Somerville, when the troubled younger man was arrested after a half-baked plot to shoot the queen.[21] Was there something significant in the Shakespeares wanting to be connected to such a family in the last years of Elizabeth's reign? Could it signal the hope that the new monarch, who would probably be James VI of Scotland, the son of Mary Queen of Scots, might restore Catholicism? Edward Arden was well known enough as a zealous Catholic to be praised in Cardinal William Allen's *A True, Sincere and Modest Defence of English Catholics that Suffer for Their Faith at Home and Abroad* (1584), and John Somerville had publicly declared his hope that Mary should succeed the heretical Elizabeth. Or, given that Edward Arden was the second cousin of Mary Shakespeare, should we conclude that these links are too remote to mean a great deal and that it was the status of the Ardens, not their religion, which attracted the Shakespeares?

Shakespeare would also have come into sustained contact with John Cottom, the Stratford Schoolmaster. Cottom graduated from Oxford in 1566, so was clearly able to square whatever faith he had with swearing allegiance to the established Church, and he taught in Stratford from 1579 until he resigned in 1581.[22] Cottom's brother, Thomas, was a Jesuit who was executed alongside Edmund Campion in 1582. Shakespeare was seventeen in 1581, so he would have been taught by Cottom at the end of his school career. Ernest Honigmann has argued that Cottom is a key figure in Shakespeare's life and that it was probably through his influence that Shakespeare was persuaded to travel north to Lancashire and to enter the service of Alexander Houghton, near whose estate the Cottom family lived. Shakespeare, it is argued, is recorded in Houghton's will as "William Shakeshafte," to whom the lord asks either his brother, Thomas, or, if not him, then his friend and neighbor, Sir Thomas Hesketh, to look after Shakeshaft and Fulk Gyllome, "either to take them unto his service or else to help them to some good master."[23] Building on a comment from John Aubrey derived from William Beeston, son of the actor manager who worked with Shakespeare, that Shakespeare "had been in his younger yeares a schoolmaster in the countrey," it is claimed that Shakespeare worked either as an actor or as a schoolmaster for a leading Catholic family.[24]

Not everyone is convinced that Shakeshaft and Shakespeare are the same man.[25] Yet again the evidence seems tantalizingly balanced, not quite enough to be fully convincing, but too significant to dismiss. Many writers have large gaps in their biographies, "lost years" where evidence is lacking and speculation based on plausible inferences formed from a knowledge of the writer's work and character are brought into play. The problem with Shakespeare is that so much is at stake in every piece of information that we have about his life, so much invested in particular readings of his plays, that debates invariably generate more heat than shed light. Using the work to read the life will not necessarily help us any more than piecing together the facts and building up a picture. If the works are thought to be Catholic then the life looks Catholic; if the works look Protestant then the life looks Protestant too.

We might then wonder whether there are other clues to which we might turn. It is always a salutary maneuver to explore the lives of people connected to the writer in question or people who lived parallel lives. Writers such as Thomas Nashe and John Fletcher, as already noted, were the sons of clergymen but it is not obvious that their upbringing had any particular influence on their writing. Nashe had connections to and worked for John Whitgift (1530/1?–1604), the conservative churchman, who fought the Puritans in a series of bitter public battles.[26] Even so, it is not obvious how we might relate Nashe's presumably religious upbringing to his life and writings. The same might be suggested of John Fletcher who clearly preserved his links to the Protestant environment in which he was raised but whose work cannot be claimed to have any obvious religious affiliation.[27] Neither writer is obviously defined by their upbringing, so why should we expect Shakespeare to be any different? More significantly, perhaps, Shakespeare was evidently prepared to collaborate with both without difficulty, something we might not expect if he had been a fervent or committed Catholic. Of course, it is not always easy to tell from a significant historical distance and there may be signs that we miss. But it is hard to believe that there was literal clarity of the sort that many, eager to emphasize the distinction of the confessional divide, hope for when we know that so many authors borrowed literary tropes and features from the work of writers of different faiths.[28]

It is worth considering the case of Ben Jonson, who was openly Catholic from 1598 until 1610, as his career provides an instructive contrast to that of Shakespeare. Despite his faith, Jonson was able to find work for the public stage and, later, the court. Martin Butler has shown that issues of religious faith haunted Jonson through his long writing career, and he was clearly deeply affected when he was summoned by the Privy Council to answer for *Sejanus* because of the play's perceived parallels to the

Gunpowder Plot, the play representing the story of a doomed conspiracy against an unpopular despot.[29] The motif of the failed coup finds echoes throughout his writing, notably in the immediate aftermath in the threat of brutal torture at the conclusion of *Volpone* and a number of hostile references to conformist Catholics in *Bartholomew Fair*.[30] In *Sejanus*, he criticizes attempts to pry into the private lives of ordinary people in order to force them to conform. Jonson is obviously hostile to Robert Cecil, who had succeeded his father William, Lord Burghley, as the queen's chief minister, seeing him as an over-mighty subject who exceeds his duties, in line with a familiar Catholic critique of the Jacobean court, which accused Cecil of fostering conspiracies in order to justify his extensive persecution of non-conformists.[31] In addition, Jonson was undoubtedly more cautious in welcoming King James than more overtly Protestant dramatists such as Thomas Dekker and Thomas Middleton, and later plays such as *Catiline* and *Bartholomew Fair* represent extreme Protestants in the worst light. Jonson's plays may not be definitely Catholic in style and content but they do speak to Catholic concerns, seeming to represent a nation in which Catholics are tolerated and included rather than derided and oppressed.[32]

Much is often made of the rivalry between Shakespeare and Jonson, the different companies for whom they worked, their contrasting careers, and, in particular, the very different style of comedies they produced, Jonson writing satirical comedies of humors and Shakespeare opting for more romantic comedies in the 1590s.[33] But little is ever written about their respective religious positions. Jonson was much more openly strident in his views and bold in his self-representation as a man of principle, prepared to speak truth to power (at least in his public persona), his plays tackling the issues of contemporary London whether directly (*Bartholomew Fair* and *The Alchemist*) or through settings removed in place and time (*Volpone*, *Sejanus*). Indeed, at the start of his career Jonson collaborated with Nashe to produce the now lost *Isle of Dogs* (1597), a play that persuaded the authorities to close down all the London theaters probably because it satirized many courtiers rather too directly.[34] It is possible that Shakespeare was also in trouble soon after when *Richard II* was performed (assuming it was his play) before the failed coup by the earl of Essex, but in general he was less confrontational in life and in work than Jonson.[35] Shakespeare did not write any play with a contemporary setting, unless one counts *The Merry Wives of Windsor*, which represents contemporary suburban life even though the fictional Falstaff was a character who lived around the year 1400.[36] Plays such as *Coriolanus*, which clearly make comparisons between ancient Rome and Jacobean London, do not appear to have attracted hostile attention and are not as straightforwardly controversial as Jonson's Roman plays when they do make topical allusions.[37] Of course, many of Shakespeare's plays make pointed historical parallels, notably *Julius Caesar*, which represents the chaos of civil war at a time when Elizabeth's death and a subsequently contested succession were real and obvious fears, and *King Lear*, which imagines the break-up of ancient Britain just as James was attempting to unite the kingdoms he ruled.[38]

But there is nothing that directly alludes to current concerns of religious persecution, as there is in Jonson's work after the Gunpowder Plot. Even *Cymbeline* (1611?), a play that conspicuously unites ancient Britons and Romans in its strange ending, a maneuver that can be interpreted as a desire to encourage a rapprochement between different branches of the Christian faith, is nowhere near as easy to decode as Jonson's dramas of plots and persecutions. Shakespeare may be alluding to recent events in having the Britons triumph but agree to pay tribute to Rome in the final scene in a fantasy of religious union to end divisions, but, if so, his subtlety is hard to pin down with confidence.[39] Accordingly, his religious identity stands as another pointed contrast to that of his great rival. While Jonson leaves numerous traces of his stated beliefs, identity and allegiances, Shakespeare remains, like most Elizabethan and Jacobean writers, conspicuously elusive.

Shakespeare is also eager to stress his knowledge of the Bible in his drama, a feature that, again, we do not find in Jonson's drama.[40] Indeed, Shakespeare was the author of a play the title of which provides a direct allusion to the Bible, *Measure for Measure*. The title comes from Matthew 7:2: "For with what judgement ye judge, ye shall be judged, and with what measure ye mete, it shall be measured you again." The play invites the audience to consider whether justice is actually delivered at the end, or whether the disguised Duke does as much harm as good in attempting to reform his kingdom by passing government over to a puritanical deputy and judging events in the habit of a friar. This careful balancing of opposed religious forces is in line with the interrogative title of the play, as well as signaling the difficulty of choosing which path to follow. The Duke plans to reform the lax and wayward morals of Vienna, an aim that can be – but does not have to be – seen as akin to the larger Reformation inaugurated by Martin Luther. Despite the obviously biblical framing of the context, it is by no means clear that he succeeds, or even that we should want him to triumph.[41]

Shakespeare often adopts a particularly Biblical vocabulary, as has frequently been suggested.[42] As David Daniell has pointed out, Isabella, a novice nun, speaks in conspicuously biblical terms when she pleads with

Angelo for her brother's life against the indifferent and harsh justice that he wishes to impose:

> Alas, alas!
> Why all the souls that were, were forfeit once,
> And he that might the vantage best have took
> Found out the remedy. How would you be
> If he, which is the top of judgement, should
> But judge you as you are? Oh, think on that,
> And mercy then will breathe within your lips
> Like man new made. (2.2.74–81)[43]

Isabella's language surely alludes to the New Testament's emphasis on mercy replacing justice, as in James 2:13: "For there shall be judgement merciless to him that sheweth no mercy, and mercy rejoiceth against judgement." Here she uses the words "souls," "judge," and 'judgement," all found in biblical translations and indeed, in religious discourse more generally understood. She is reminding Angelo of the real heart of the Bible's teaching, as well as warning him of what happens to the stern, inflexible judge who inevitably commits as many sins as he enforces true justice. Her last comment that mercy acts "Like man made new" would seem to be a reference to 2 Corinthians 5:17: "Therefore if any man be in Christ let him be a new creature. Old things are passed away: behold, all things are become new," a verse that refers to the opening verse of the previous chapter, "Therefore, seeing that we have this ministry, as we have received mercy, we faint not." Christians are made new through Christ's teaching, which Protestants argued they needed to be able to read for themselves and not have the Church interpret Scripture on their behalf. Given who makes this speech, an audience must surely feel that the play is carefully poised in its religious attitudes. It is hard to detect a particular confessional sympathy here – unless a strong argument is made that Isabella is actually alluding to the specifically Protestant doctrine of the "priesthood of all believers."[44] Perhaps enclosed religious institutions do nurture virtue; but, then again, it might be better for us all if more people had access to the Bible and could read it properly.

It is also hard to avoid the conclusion that certain plays were inspired by particular books of the Bible. Steven Marx has argued that *King Lear* was written with the Book of Job in mind. Lear exclaims on the heath,

> Poor naked wretches, whereso'er you are
> That bide the pelting of this pitiless storm,
> How shall your houseless heads and unfed sides,
> Your looped and windowed raggedness defend you
> From seasons such as these? (3.4.28–33)

There is a direct allusion to descriptions of suffering in Job which structure the play's plot and are not just incidental references to Biblical verses and episodes. Job also rails against the wickedness of social injustice when his wealth, health, and happiness are removed by Satan acting with God's permission:

> They cause the naked to lodge without garment, and without covering in the cold.
>
> They are wet with the showers of the mountains, and they embrace the rock for want of covering.
>
> They pluck the fatherless from the breast, and take the pledge of the poor.
>
> They cause him to go naked without clothing, and take the gleaning from the hungry. (Job 24:7–10)[45]

Job is eventually redeemed and reconciled to God, whereas Lear is not, unless one accepts A. C. Bradley's reading of his death as a moment of "unbearable joy."[46] But the use of the Book of Job to narrate a tragic story of suffering and redemption in post-Reformation England should not surprise us and it clearly indicates that the Bible had a significant impact on Shakespeare's imaginative world without providing obvious clues of religious belief.

What these references reveal is that Shakespeare, whatever his confessional allegiance, was clearly a close and careful reader of the Bible. Jonathan Bate has persuasively argued that Shakespeare probably read relatively few books, certainly compared to more obviously learned contemporaries such as Nashe and Jonson. What he did read – Holinshed's *Chronicles*, *A Mirror for Magistrates*, Montaigne's *Essays*, Plutarch's *Lives* – he read with scrupulous attention and used to form the substance of his diverse plays. One of the books he surely would have had access to was a Geneva Bible.[47] The Geneva Bible was an English translation produced by a group of prominent Protestant exiles during the reign of Mary (1553–8), which not only provided a distinctly Protestant text, but glosses to direct the reader. The translation placed great emphasis on particular words, so that "love" appears as often as possible to stress the extensive nature of God's mercy: the Geneva Bible translates 1 Corinthians 13:1 as "Though I speak with the tongues of men and Angels, and have not love, I am as sounding brass, or a tinkling cymbal," whereas the more conservative King James translation of 1611 changes "love" to "charity" (even going against the text of the Bishops' Bible, which also had "love," and that was supposed to be the base text for the King James translation); and the gathering of Christians to worship is translated as "congregation" as often as possible rather than "church," signifying the importance of the people not the hierarchy of the institution. (The Geneva Bible translates Acts 7:38 as "This is he that was in the Congregation, in the wilderness with the Angel, which spake to him in mount Sina, and with our fathers, who received the lively oracles to give unto us," while the King James has "church in the wilderness.") The extensive annotation to the Book of Revelation – expanded in the 1599 revisions to the annotations by Franciscus Junius – provides a clear anti-papal message detailing the progress of the world towards the imminent Last Judgement: for example, the gloss to "the woman ... arrayed in purple and scarlet" (18:4) reads, "This woman is the Antichrist, that is, the Pope, with the whole body of his filthy creatures, as is expounded ... whose beauty only standeth in outward pomp, and impudency, and craft like a strumpet," which leaves the reader in no doubt of God's message to mankind.

If Shakespeare had access to the Bible – and his plays indicate that he read it closely – then the Geneva version was surely the text he would have used, as it was the only easily available and affordable English translation. He would have heard the Bishops' Bible (1568, 1572), designed to replace Henry VIII's Great Bible (1540) read aloud in church but probably made use of the more readily available Geneva Bible, as Naseeb Shaheen argues.[48] The point that needs to be made is the same as that regarding the Catholic connections within his family and circle of friends and acquaintances. One did not have to be a committed evangelical Protestant to read the Geneva Bible. Nor, it should be added, did access to that text necessarily convert the reader to such a position.[49] It was surely a common experience in Elizabethan England for educated people to have families with significant Catholic elements and to be exposed to Protestantism through reading the relatively newly translated Bible, as well as attending church services.

Shakespeare has, accordingly, often been classified as a "church papist," or a "Parish Anglican," someone who attended church services out of duty, who probably believed in the importance of the national Church and the need for it to remain relatively intact and united as an institution, but who did not necessarily share all its beliefs.[50] He may well have looked back to the late Medieval Church and its ritual practices and communitarian values with nostalgia, or been glad, on balance, that some sort of change had broken the shackles of excessive priestly power. Or, perhaps, a combination of both, which was surely common at a time when many people in Europe were "Nicodemites," concerned not to cause trouble by making their belief public. And, if a Nicodemite was a person who did not honestly declare their confessional identity for fear of the consequences (they were named after Nicodemus, the Pharisee who visits Jesus in John 3:1–21, and becomes convinced that he is the Son of God but refuses to take any action), and Nicodemism can be characterized as an "attitude rather than a movement," then it is likely that Nicodemites could have been the largest category of religious believers in early modern Europe.[51] Certainly if defined this way then the number of Nicodemites would have dwarfed the number of convinced Protestants and probably Catholics too.[52] Furthermore, as Dairmaid MacCulloch has pointed out, the Church of England was actually designed and planned by Nicodemites, Protestants who had survived the reign of the Catholic queen, Mary, such as William Cecil Lord Burghley.[53] Nicodemites, hard to discover and just as hard to define, probably dominated European religious practices in the post-Reformation period.

It is hardly surprising that we can find little evidence of Shakespeare's religious convictions in his work or in his life, nor that his works should contain significant passages that employ Christian imagery. Everyone had a relationship to religion, but very few deliberately declared their allegiance unless they had to or were exceptionally brave, virtuous, or foolhardy. Indeed, we need to be careful about what we think we know, as a number of works that look like one declaration are really another, designed to cover the author's tracks, such as Lewis Lewkenor's *A Discourse of the Usage of the English Fugitives, by the Spaniard* (1595), which employs a familiar Protestant language to attack Spanish Catholicism, but was written by a prominent Catholic eager to declare his allegiance to the crown and allay suspicion of his loyalty.[54] If such texts are complicated, slippery, and evasive, we should expect drama to be far more recondite, because of its generic nature and because works on the public stage were hardly likely to be declarations of confessional allegiance.

In May 1606, Shakespeare's daughter, Susanna, was summoned before the ecclesiastical court in Stratford to answer the charge that she was one of twenty-one defendants reported by the churchwarden who had failed to take the Sacraments in the service immediately before Easter (April 20).[55] That year was a particularly bad time to transgress religious ordinances, coming less than six months after the Gunpowder Plot and just before the Oath of Allegiance was established, requiring subjects to declare their loyalty to James and renounce any claims of the Pope. The oath was disseminated widely in various proclamations as various anti-recusancy laws were passed in order to force the hand of subjects wavering in their loyalty.[56] Fines were severe, starting at £20, about the annual salary of a clergyman, rising to £60 for a third offense. Many of Susanna's co-defendants were known Catholics, including Margaret Reynolds whose family had sheltered a Jesuit priest and who regularly paid fines for non-attendance. Also included in the list were Hamnet and Judith Sadler, well known to the Shakespeare family, perhaps close enough friends to have had William name his twins after them.[57] Susanna missed the first summons to the vicar's court, although personally directed to do so by the apparitor (the civil servant who assisted the magistrates), but, in the end, her case was dismissed, as she clearly did eventually appear and explained her reasons for non-attendance to the satisfaction of the authorities. As Samuel Schoenbaum points out, she probably consented to take the Eucharist from then on as ten of her co-defendants are noted as having agreed to do so.[58]

What are we to make of this information? Perhaps Susanna was rebellious, careless, or had a very good reason for her actions, which the court accepted. But those would seem to be odd explanations of such behavior at a particularly sensitive and dangerous time. Perhaps this is really the best biographical evidence we have of the Shakespeare family's religious stance, demonstrating that they had Catholic allegiances. Or, rather, that Shakespeare's eldest child, posthumously famous for being "Witty above her sex," may have been a Catholic before her marriage to the physician, Dr. John Hall, on June 5, 1607. Hall appears to have had Puritan inclinations, which further complicates the picture of allegiances and suggests that, if Susanna was a Catholic, differences in religion were not insurmountable obstacles to unions and could be overcome.[59] Shakespeare seems to have been close to his son-in-law so a case can be made that he approved of the match, especially as he left a number of clues that he was rather less than pleased about the marriage of his other daughter, Judith, to Thomas Quiney (February 10, 1616).[60] Yet again, we are left with tantalizing information that points in different directions. Is this a sign that the Shakespeare family really was Catholic, but it was only Susanna who dared to make her faith public? Or is there some other reason why she failed to take communion? However we read the biographical evidence, what does seem clear is that religion was never simply an isolated aspect of early modern life but was firmly rooted in the society to which it belonged.

Notes

1 Alex Ryrie, *Being Protestant in Reformation Britain* (Oxford: Oxford University Press, 2013).

2 Arnold Hunt, "Licensing and Religious Censorship in Early Modern England," in *Literature and Censorship in Renaissance England*, ed. Andrew Hadfield (Basingstoke, UK: Palgrave, 2001), 127–46.

3 Ian Donaldson, *Ben Jonson: A Life* (Oxford: Oxford University Press, 2011), 138–44, 228–9, 256–9, *passim*.

4 Joseph L. Black (ed.), *The Martin Marprelate Tracts: A Modernized and Annotated Edition* (Cambridge: Cambridge University Press, 2008), lxxi–lxii.

5 Andrew Hadfield, *Edmund Spenser: A Life* (Oxford: Oxford University Press, 2012), 207.

6 For one rather eccentric attempt that tries to link Donne to the "Family of Love," see David Wootton, "John Donne's Religion of Love," in *Heterodoxy in*

Early Modern Science and Religion, ed. John Brooke and Ian MacLean (Oxford: Oxford University Press, 2005), 31–80.

7 On the authorship of *Henry VI Part 1*, see Brian Vickers, "Incomplete Shakespeare: Or, Denying Coauthorship in *1 Henry VI*," *Shakespeare Quarterly* 58 (2007): 311–52.

8 Brian Vickers, "Thomas Kyd, Secret Sharer," *Times Literary Supplement* 18 (Apr. 2008): 13–15; John V. Nance, "'We, John Cade': Shakespeare, Marlowe, and the Authorship of 4.2.33–189 2 *Henry VI*," *Shakespeare* 13 (2017): 30–51. On Wilkins and Fletcher see their ODNB entries.

9 N. W. Bawcutt, "Was Thomas Middleton a Puritan Dramatist?" *Modern Language Review* 94 (1999): 925–39.

10 See in particular Richard Wilson, *Secret Shakespeare: Studies in Theatre, Religion and Resistance* (Manchester: Manchester University Press, 2004) and the dubious book by Clare Asquith, *Shadowplay: The Hidden Beliefs and Coded Politics of William Shakespeare* (New York: Public Affairs, 2005).

11 James G. McManaway, "Shakespeare's 'Spiritual Testament,'" *Shakespeare Quarterly* 18 (1967): 197–205, 200. I am much indebted to McManaway's article: he concludes that the lost document discovered by Malone must have been genuine.

12 Wilson, *Secret Shakespeare*, 117.

13 David Scott Kastan, *A Will to Believe: Shakespeare and Religion* (Oxford: Oxford University Press, 2014), 25.

14 David Fallow, "His Father John Shakespeare," in *The Shakespeare Circle: An Alternative Biography*, ed. Paul Edmondson and Stanley Wells (Cambridge: Cambridge University Press, 2015), 26–40, at 36.

15 Kastan, *Will to Believe*, 21; Samuel Schoenbaum, *William Shakespeare: A Compact Documentary Life* (Oxford: Oxford University Press, 1977), 42.

16 Robert Bearman, *Shakespeare's Money: How Much Did He Make and What Did This Mean?* (Oxford: Oxford University Press, 2016), 22–3.

17 Cited in Bearman, *Shakespeare's Money*, 18.

18 Jeanne Jones, *Family Life in Shakespeare's England: Stratford-Upon-Avon, 1570–1630* (Stroud, UK: Sutton, 1996), 111.

19 Mark Eccles, *Shakespeare in Warwickshire* (Madison: University of Wisconsin Press, 1961), 123, 60–1; E. A. J. Honigmann, *Shakespeare, the Lost Years*, 2nd edn. (Manchester: Manchester University Press, 1998), 115–6.

20 Eccles, *Shakespeare in Warwickshire*, 79; Mark Nicholls, *Investigating Gunpowder Plot* (Manchester: Manchester University Press, 1991), 20–1.

21 See the ODNB entries on Sommerville and Arden; Wilson, *Secret Shakespeare*, 104–15.

22 Eccles, *Shakespeare in Warwickshire*, 56–7. See also Peter Milward, S. J., "Shakespeare's Jesuit Schoolmasters," in *Theatre and Religion: Lancastrian Shakespeare*, ed. Richard Dutton, Alison Findlay, and Richard Wilson (Manchester: Manchester University Press, 2003), 58–70.

23 Cited in Honigmann, *The Lost Years*, 3.

24 Honigmann, *The Lost Years*, 2–3, 126–7; John Aubrey, *Brief Lives*, ed. Oliver Lawson Dick (Harmondsworth, UK: Penguin, 1958, rpt. of 1949), 355.

25 David Bevington, *Shakespeare and Biography* (Oxford: Oxford University Press, 2010), 82–3, for an overview of biographers' positions.

26 On Whitgift see Powel Mills Dawley, *John Whitgift and the Reformation* (London: A. & C. Black, 1955) and V. J. K. Brook, *Whitgift and the English Church* (London: English Universities Press, 1957).
27 Jean-Christoph Mayer, *Shakespeare's Hybrid Faith: History, Religion and the Stage* (Basingstoke, UK: Palgrave, 2006), 131.
28 Alison Shell, *Catholicism, Controversy and the English Literary Imagination, 1558–1660* (Cambridge: Cambridge University Press, 1999).
29 Martin Butler, "Ben Jonson's Catholicism," *The Ben Jonson Journal* 19 (2012): 190–216, 192.
30 Ibid., 192–3. See also Richard Dutton, *Ben Jonson, Volpone and The Gunpowder Plot* (Cambridge: Cambridge University Press, 2008).
31 Butler, "Jonson's Catholicism," 199.
32 Ibid., 213.
33 James P. Bednarz, *Shakespeare & The Poets' War* (New York: Columbia University Press, 2001).
34 Donaldson, *Ben Jonson*, 111–22.
35 Paul J. Hammer, "Shakespeare's *Richard II*, the Play of 7 February 1601, and the Essex Rising," *Shakespeare Quarterly* 59 (2008): 1–35.
36 "Afterword: One of Those Days in England," in *This England, That Shakespeare: New Angles on Englishness and the Bard*, ed. Margaret Tudeau-Clayton and Willy Maley (Aldershot, UK: Ashgate, 2010), 221–4.
37 Mark A. Kishlansky, *Parliamentary Selection: Social and Political Choice in Early Modern England* (Cambridge: Cambridge University Press), 3–9.
38 Andrew Hadfield, *Shakespeare and Renaissance Politics* (London: Arden Shakespeare, 2004), 143–9, 97–110.
39 See Andrew Hadfield, "Shakespeare's Ecumenical Britain," in *Shakespeare, Spenser and The Matter of Britain* (Basingstoke, UK: Palgrave, 2003), 151–68.
40 Gayle Edward Wilson makes a case, not entirely successfully, that Jonson's poetry relies on biblical allusions in "Jonson's Use of the Bible and the Great Chain of Being in 'To Penshurst,'" *Studies in English Literature, 1500–1900* 8 (1968): 77–89.
41 Steven Marx, *Shakespeare and the Bible* (Oxford: Oxford University Press, 2000), 99–100.
42 In addition to Marx, *Shakespeare and the Bible*, see Charles Wordsworth, *Shakespeare's Knowledge and Use of the Bible* (London: Smith, Elder, 1880) and David Daniell, "Reading the Bible," in *A Companion to Shakespeare*, ed. David Scott Kastan (Oxford: Blackwell, 1999), 158–71.
43 Daniell, "Reading the Bible," 158.
44 The notion derives from Luther: see Martin Luther, *Selections from His Writings*, ed. John Dillenberger (New York: Anchor Books, 1961), 407–8. For its possible relevance to *Measure for Measure* see Roland Mushat Frye, *Shakespeare and Christian Doctrine* (Princeton, NJ: Princeton University Press, 1963), 291–2.
45 Marx, *Shakespeare and the Bible*, 75.
46 A. C. Bradley, *Shakespearean Tragedy: Lectures on* Hamlet, Othello, King Lear, Macbeth (London: Macmillan, 1918, rpt. of 1904), 291.
47 Jonathan Bate, "Shakespeare's Small Library," in *Soul of the Age: The Life, Mind and World of William Shakespeare* (London: Penguin, 2008), 141–57.

48 Naseeb Shaheen, *Biblical References in Shakespeare's Plays* (Newark: University of Delaware Press, 1999), 38–48.
49 Kastan, *Will to Believe*, 33–5.
50 Beatrice Groves, *Texts and Traditions: Religion in Shakespeare 1592–1604* (Oxford: Oxford University Press, 2007), 28; Kastan, *Will to Believe*, 37. See also David Bevington, "The Debate About Shakespeare and Religion," in *Shakespeare and Early Modern Religion*, ed. David Loewenstein and Michael Witmore (Cambridge: Cambridge University Press, 2015), 23–39.
51 Carlos M. N. Eire, *War Against the Idols: The Reformation of Worship from Erasmus to Calvin* (Cambridge: Cambridge University Press, 1986), 253.
52 Andrew Pettegree, *Marian Protestantism: Six Studies* (Aldershot, UK: Scolar Press, 1996), 89; Karl Gunther, *Reformation Unbound: Protestant Visions of Reform in England, 1525–1590* (Cambridge: Cambridge University Press, 2014), chap. 2.
53 Cited in Lady Anne Bacon, *An Apology or Answer in Defence of the Church of England*, ed. Patricia Demers (London: MHRA, 2015), 9. See also Norman Jones, *Governing by Virtue: Lord Burghley and the Management of Elizabethan England* (Oxford: Oxford University Press, 2015), 46.
54 For analysis of the significance of Lewkenor's text in terms of Elizabethan politics see Peter Lake, *Bad Queen Bess? Libels, Secret Histories, and the Politics of Publicity in the Reign of Queen Elizabeth I* (Oxford: Oxford University Press, 2016), 434–48.
55 Schoenbaum, *Compact Documentary Life*, 286.
56 James F. Larkin and Paul L. Hughes (eds.), *Stuart Royal Proclamations: Volume I: Royal Proclamations of King James I, 1603–1625* (Oxford: Oxford University Press, 1973), 84, 96, 111, 118.
57 Eccles, *Shakespeare in Warwickshire*, 125–6.
58 Schoenbaum, *Compact Documentary Life*, 287.
59 Park Honan, *Shakespeare: A Life* (Oxford: Oxford University Press, 1998), 357.
60 Katherine Duncan-Jones, *Ungentle Shakespeare: Scenes from His Life* (London: Thomson, 2001), 268.

3

HANNIBAL HAMLIN

The Renaissance Bible

"The Bible, the Bible, I say, the Bible only is the religion of Protestants."[1] In 1638, when William Chillingworth famously proclaimed this, it was hardly an original idea. At the launch of what became known as the Reformation, Martin Luther had preached the principal of *sola scriptura* (only the Scriptures), meaning that the Bible is the sole basis and authority for Christian faith and practice. Yet this idea predated even Luther, the Franciscan friar William of Ockham having said much the same thing a century earlier, even if this was a minority view in the Catholic tradition.[2] In fact, Catholics and Protestants shared the same Bible, as they do now, even if they read it in different languages and sometimes interpreted it differently. Despite Ockham's position, Catholic doctrine included numerous ideas that were nowhere to be found in the Bible, like the five sacraments rejected by Protestants but authorized by the Catholic Church: confirmation, marriage, penance, holy orders, and extreme unction. By Chillingworth's day, there was even an English Catholic translation of the Bible, published in 1582 (New Testament) and 1609–10 (Old and New together) from the press at the seminary for exiled English Catholics in France. Some English Catholics might well have read earlier Protestant English translations, and any who attended worship services in order to avoid fines or imprisonment would have heard such translations read aloud.[3] But then some Protestants, at least those learned enough to know Latin, continued to read the Vulgate Bible authorized by the Church of Rome. Whatever the precise (or imprecise) nature of his own beliefs (see Chapter 2), William Shakespeare knew the Bible well, since there are allusions to it in almost everything he wrote.

What exactly is the "Bible," or, as some Shakespeare characters call it, Scripture or Holy Writ?[4] The Bible is a book made up of many books (originally scrolls) written and assembled over a number of centuries, divided into two parts by all Christians: the Old Testament, consisting of the sacred writings of the ancient Jews (significantly reordered); and the New Testament, consisting of the four gospel accounts of Jesus's life and teachings, the Acts of the Apostles, the letters of Paul and other early Christians, and Revelation, which prophesies the end of time. There is also a collection of disputed texts that Protestants call the Apocrypha, which was included in the Septuagint, the third century BCE Greek translation of Hebrew Scriptures, but not in the Hebrew tradition itself. Most Protestant Bibles included these in a separate section between the two testaments, but Catholics placed them throughout the Old Testament, describing them as deuterocanonical (the "second canon") but not distinguishing them rigidly from the rest of the canon. Protestant attitudes to these writings varied; Luther, for instance, considered them valuable for moral instruction but not for theological truth. Other Protestants rejected them outright, and they were eventually dropped from many English Protestant Bibles in the later seventeenth century. During Shakespeare's lifetime, however, the principle English Bibles all included the Apocrypha, and readings from many apocryphal books were included in the liturgy of the Book of Common Prayer. The lively stories of Judith, Tobit, and the additions to Daniel, Susanna and the Elders, and Bel and the Dragon, were especially popular, and the wisdom writings of Ecclesiasticus and Wisdom were read alongside those of Ecclesiastes and Proverbs.

Shakespeare knew the Bible primarily in English translation, but then the Christian Bible has always been a translated book. Early members of the Christian movement like Paul read the Jewish Scriptures not in Hebrew but in the Greek of the Septuagint. This caused some consternation to Bible scholars like John Calvin, who had to come to terms with the realization that Paul was sometimes mistaken in his comments on Hebrew texts. In the New Testament, Jesus's words must have been translated into Greek by the gospel writers, since he would have spoken in Aramaic (as in fact he does briefly on the cross in Matthew and Mark: "*Eli, Eli, lama sabacthani*"). The Bible sanctioned by the Catholic Church was Jerome's Latin translation, and the Bible heard and read by Shakespeare was in English – mainly the Bishops' Bible of 1568 and the Geneva Bible of 1560 and after, as well as the Coverdale Psalms in the Book of Common Prayer – but this simply added further layers of translation to what was already there.[5] Jesus's own words had not been available, at least not in writing, to anyone after his death. Many post-Reformation Bible readers, like many modern ones, however, were untroubled by potential issues in translation. For instance, despite the variety of English Bibles in circulation in Shakespeare's day, most readers seemed to think of them as simply a series of drafts of the "English Bible," and Shakespeare alludes to several translations, perhaps because particular word choices appealed to him, or because he happened to have a particular version in his ear or on his desk.[6] Matthew Parker, the Archbishop who oversaw the translation of the Bishops' Bible, used in most English churches during Shakespeare's lifetime, nevertheless did not seem especially wedded to one English version over another, and it is telling that the preface to the King James Bible of 1611 actually quotes the Bible in the Geneva translation.

Given the centrality of the Bible to Christianity, it might seem odd to ask about the relationship between the Bible and religion, but the question is a legitimate one. Does a chapter on the Bible belong in a book on Shakespeare and Religion? No one would dispute that the Bible is a religious text, but there are in fact books or passages in the Bible that, taken on their own, do not seem especially religious, if by "religious" we mean having to do with God, his laws and teachings, the rituals of the church, prayer, how to live a good and godly life, and matters of sin, damnation, forgiveness, and salvation.[7] The book of Esther, as is often noted, makes no mention of God or anything most would call religious, though it does tell a story about the Jews in Persia. Esther is the most unusual case, but many of the historical books (Samuel, Kings, Chronicles) include material that seems similarly nonreligious. Parts of the story of Samson in Judges, for instance, do seem to involve religious beliefs and behaviors, as when his mother dedicates him to God, and Samson, as a Nazarite, vows never to cut his hair. We are told that as Samson grew, "the Lord blessed him," and that "the Spirit of the Lord began to strengthen him" (Judg. 13:24–5). When Samson slaughters "heapes upon heapes" of Philistines with the jawbone of an ass, we must read this as a religious act, however violent, since as he enters battle "the Spirit of the Lord came upon him" once again (Judg. 15:14–16). In *Love's Labour's Lost*, however, when Don Adriano de Armado and his page Moth discuss Samson, the conference seems to have nothing to do with religion:

> DON ADRIANO: Comfort me, boy:
> what great men have been in love?
> MOTH: Hercules, master.
> DON ADRIANO: Most sweet Hercules! More authority, dear boy, name more; and, sweet my child, let them be men of good repute and carriage.
> MOTH: Samson, master: he was a man of good carriage, great carriage, for he carried the town-gates on his back like a porter: and he was in love.
> (1.2.53–60)

Samson serves as well as Hercules for a powerful man who was a lover as well as fighter. Don Armado goes on to ask Moth about the woman Samson loved, and the conversation drifts off into half-witty remarks on complexion, but Samson's most famous lover, Delilah, is never mentioned, nor are any acts of Samson that might be labeled religious. He is just a legendary hero who happens to originate in the Bible.

Another of Samson's tales revolves around a riddle about a lion's carcass in which a hive of bees has made a home. Having seen this phenomenon, Samson turns it into a puzzle which he asks his companions to explain to him: "Out of the eater came meat, and out of the strong came sweetness" (Judg. 14:14). They cannot solve the riddle, so they threaten Samson's Philistine wife with burning if she does not find out the answer for them. She does, they tell Samson, he realizes what has happened, kills thirty men in order to give their clothes to his companions as the prize, and gives his wife "to his companion" (Judg. 14:15–20). Nothing about this episode is appropriate for a Sunday sermon, and when Shakespeare, in *Henry IV Part 2*, has the king say, "'Tis seldom when the bee doth leave her comb / In the dead carrion," he doesn't necessarily have anything overtly religious in mind either (4.2.79–80). Henry is expressing concern about his son, Hal, who, even after seeming to prove himself in the battle of Shrewsbury, is still wasting his life with his whores and highwaymen in the taverns of Eastcheap. Samson's riddle has been converted into a metaphor for something good being found in an unexpectedly nasty context. Hal is the honeycomb, and Eastcheap, or perhaps the company Hal keeps there, the dead lion. (Recalling *Henry IV Part 1*, Falstaff is several times compared to a lion, both by himself and Hal.) Or do both parts of the metaphor refer to Hal? In this case his father might be asking whether his son has yet some nobility within him, despite his apparently sordid condition. In either case, though the source of the king's metaphor is biblical, its application in the play is not religious.

The Bible was omnipresent in Elizabeth and Jacobean culture, so references to it emerge in all sorts of inappropriate contexts. In *Twelfth Night*, for example, the besotted Toby Belch sings a song about Babylon, "There dwelt a man in Babylon, lady, lady" (2.3.69). Actually, the song is a real one and not primarily about a man but a woman, Susanna. *An Excellent Ballad Entitled, the Constancy of Susanna* tells the story of Susanna and the Elders, from the Apocrypha, which was so popular it was painted on wall hangings as well as set to music.[8] While bathing, Susanna is spied on by two old men who tell her that unless she has sexual relations with them they will tell everyone they caught her *in flagrante delicto* with some young man. Susanna refuses; they follow through on their promise and she is brought to trial, whereupon the prophet Daniel cleverly exposes the elders, who are put to death, and restores Susanna's chaste reputation. That this story was so popular surely had as much to do with its titillating content as its moral lesson, and one wonders what exactly was depicted on the cloths hanging on tavern and parlor walls; none survives. Sir Toby's rendition of the song, in any case, never progresses to the virtuous Susanna, and his bellowing of it during his midnight revels seems entirely irreligious. Another song about Babylon is sung by Parson Evans in *The Merry Wives of Windsor*. In his melancholy, he sings verses (in his Welsh accent) from a setting of Christopher Marlowe's popular poem, "The Passionate Shepherd to His Love":

> To shallow rivers, to whose falls
> Melodious birds sings madrigals.
> There will we make our peds of roses
> And a thousand fragrant posies. (3.1.12–15)

Evans then forgets how it goes, and mixes in a line from Psalm 137 in its metrical version from the Sternhold and Hopkins psalter:

> Melodious birds sing madrigals –
> Whenas I sat in Pabylon –
> And a thousand vagrom posies.
> To shallow, etc. (3.1.18–21)

The "etc." may indicate that the actor continued in this muddled vein. The joke is obviously on Evans, so ignorant a parson that he cannot distinguish a pastoral seduction poem from a psalm. The content of Psalm 137, the Psalm of Exile, seems largely irrelevant, though it is a song partly about singing; the point is simply that, like Marlowe's poem, the psalm includes a river, which is how Evans's memory gets from one to other.

Indeed, some parts of the Bible itself seem to move from the non-religious to the irreligious. The Song of Solomon seems weirdly out of place in Holy Scripture, since, despite its beauty, it looks very much like a highly erotic love poem, which it may originally have been. Ancient tradition interpreted the poem allegorically, however, as figuring the love of God for Israel, his Church or (in the Catholic tradition) for the Virgin Mary. English Bibles tried to alert readers to this wholesome interpretation with introductory summaries, marginal notes, and running heads across the top of the page, like "Spiritual love," "The Church's beauty," and "Her desire to Christ." Despite these advisories, readers might not always have gotten the spiritual message. In the conversation between Don Armado and Moth about women's complexions, for instance, Armado states that his love "is most immaculate white and red" (1.2.75). That this is an allusion to the Song of Solomon – "As for my love, he is white and red coloured" (5:10, Bishops') – is indicated by the adjective "immaculate," which resonates in several directions. When the lover (whether interpreted as the man, Solomon, or Christ) says, "Open unto me, my sister, my love, my dove, my undefiled" (Song of Sol. 5:2), the word used for "undefiled" in the Latin Vulgate is "immacula," and the English "immaculate," literally "without spot," means also "virgin," and, as the OED notes, is used frequently to refer to the Virgin Mary. The Protestant interpretation of the Song of Solomon reads the beloved as the Church, and the headnote in the Geneva Bible makes clear that the Church "is inflamed with the love of Christ desiring to be more and more joined to him in love, and not to be forsaken for any spot or blemish that is in her." Meanwhile, for the Catholic tradition, the beloved is Mary, who is spotless, immaculate. Thomas More refers to the "immaculate mother of Christ" in his answer to a "poisoned book" entitled *The Supper of Our Lord*,[9] and the same description appears even in John Foxe's Protestant *Book of Martyrs*, albeit quoted from a Catholic source: "This matter I take in hand for truth sake that my brethren (whose salvation I seek) may the more obsequiously obey me, and better understand, how that I trusting upon your defence (next to Christ and his mother the immaculate virgin) resist the wicked, and am ready to help the faithful."[10] Even though Protestants believed that only Christ was immaculate, they could easily be aware that Catholics attributed the adjective to his mother as well. The point in *Love's Labour's Lost* may be that the Spanish Don Armado is, unsurprisingly, Catholic, yet since he is describing not the Virgin Mary but his love, the country maid Jaquenetta, the biblical reference seems mildly blasphemous from any Christian perspective. But then perhaps Shakespeare's joke is that Armado is misreading the Song of Solomon, taking it as a model for earthly romantic love rather the spiritual one the Church insists on. Is this biblical allusion religious? Not in any proper, orthodox sense, but then heresy and blasphemy can only exist within a religious context, so perhaps to be irreligious is still to be religious, even if wrongly so.

The same could be said for Macbeth's startlingly nihilistic speech:

> Tomorrow, and tomorrow, and tomorrow
> Creeps in this petty pace from day to day
> To the last syllable of recorded time;
> And all our yesterdays have lighted fools
> The way to dusty death. Out, out, brief candle,
> Life's but a walking shadow, a poor player
> That struts and frets his hour upon the stage
> And then is heard no more. It is a tale
> Told by an idiot, full of sound and fury
> Signifying nothing. (5.5.18–27)

The speech is essentially a pastiche of biblical verses from Job, wisdom Psalms, and Ecclesiasticus: "thou hast brought me into the dust of death" (Ps. 22:15); "How oft shall the candle of the wicked be put out? and their destruction come upon them?" (Job 21:17); "Doubtless man walketh in a shadow" (Ps. 36:6); "thou hast made my days as an hand breadth, and mine age as nothing" (Ps. 36:5); "A man without grace is as a foolish tale which is oft told by the mouth of the ignorant" (Ecclus. 20:18), for example. Even if audience members had not been able to cite chapter and verse for every biblical source, they would have recognized the language as strongly biblical. That Macbeth is expressing a pessimistic, starkly un-Christian view of life is not especially surprising, since many passages in the Old Testament and Apocryphal Wisdom books are bound to strike a Christian reader the same way. The weary skepticism of Ecclesiastes sometimes borders on atheism, as when the preacher writes, "it is better to be a living dog than a dead lion" (Eccles. 9:4). Earlier the preacher cannot say whether men go to heaven and animals do not, admitting that they may both "go to one place," which is presumably "vanity" or oblivion (Eccles. 3:19–21). Job says that God "destroyeth the perfect and the wicked" (Job 9:22), striking at the root of traditional beliefs in Providence and divine justice. Yet the shock of such statements depends on an orthodox Christian perspective, and to question God's justice or even the afterlife may be heretical, but it is still religious in the broadest sense. And, of course, Shakespeare's speech is delivered by Macbeth, who has murdered men, women, and children, his king and his friend; that his utterances are un-Christian is hardly surprising.

Then again, some biblical-seeming language in Shakespeare may actually not be alluding to the Bible directly. The English Bible was so deeply familiar in Shakespeare's England, and had been for a generation, so that inevitably biblical proverbs and idioms had become lodged in ordinary language, sometimes without their biblical origin being recollected. The reference to Samson's riddle may be an example, though it may also be that Shakespeare was aware of its source but wasn't interested in its original context. In *Richard III*, though, when, just before the climactic battle of Bosworth, Richard claims that "the King's name is a tower of strength" (5.3.12) Shakespeare might have taken the metaphor from Proverbs: "The Name of the Lord is a strong tower" (Prov. 18:10). But "tower of strength" was also a common figure in non-biblical contexts, and Shakespeare may have especially liked the irony of Richard using a metaphor that recalled his worst crime, the murder of the princes in the Tower. Beatrice, in *Much Ado About Nothing*, snaps back at her uncle, who has expressed a hope that she might be married:

> Not till God make men of some other metal than earth: would it not grieve a woman to be overmastered with a piece of valiant dust? to make an account of her life to a clod of wayward marl? No, uncle, I'll none: Adam's sons are my brethren, and truly I hold it a sin to match in my kindred. (2.1.43–7)

The overt reference to Adam makes clear that Beatrice is aware that her reference to man as "dust" derives from Genesis, where God creates Adam out of the "dust of the ground" (Gen. 2:7), and in order to appreciate the wit of her allusion, one must also remember that, unlike Adam, Eve was made out of flesh and bone, not dirt, new and improved, a Human 2.0. In *Cymbeline*, however, the beautiful lament Guiderius and Arviragus sing in mourning for Innogen (disguised as Fidele), who they believe to be dead, also refers to humans as dust, or at least returning to dust: "Golden lads and girls all must, / As chimney-sweepers, come to dust" (4.2.1–2). Is this an allusion to Genesis? Since the young brothers are not Christian (or Jewish), they are of course unaware of the Bible. Shakespeare certainly knew the Genesis story, but the idea of man as dust was also a commonplace, especially from its use in the Burial Service in the Book of Common Prayer. When the priest commits the body to the ground, "earth to earth, ashes to ashes, dust to dust," Genesis 2 (or really Genesis 3:19's curse on mankind, "because thou art dust, and to dust shalt thou return") is in the background, but the reference in *Cymbeline* is likely more generalized.

Many of Shakespeare's biblical allusions are clearly deliberate and meaningful, however. In *King John*, for instance, the Lady Constance wails in despair over the capture of her son Arthur by the forces of the English king:

> And father cardinal, I have heard you say
> That we shall see and know our friends in heaven.
> If that be true, I shall see my boy again;
> For since the birth of Cain, the first male child,
> To him that did but yesterday suspire,
> There was not such a gracious creature born. (3.4.76–81)

Constance's point is that since the very first child born to the present time, none has been better than her son, but the reference to Cain is obviously loaded, since he was not just the first child but the first murderer, and the murderer of his brother Abel. She is no doubt fully aware of this, since the allusion is appropriate, given that Arthur has been captured (and ordered killed) by his uncle – not a brother, but still a blood relative. The Cain and Abel story is also referenced in *Hamlet*, once obliquely and once directly. When we first meet Prince Hamlet mourning his father's death, his uncle Claudius, now king and stepfather, tries to console him, arguing that excessive grief is

> a fault to heaven,
> A fault against the dead, a fault to nature,
> To reason most absurd, whose common theme

> Is death of fathers, and who still hath cried,
> From the first corse till he that died today,
> "This must be so." (1.2.101–6)

Here Claudius's allusion is surely unconscious on his part, but the "first corse" in biblical history is Abel, murdered by his brother Cain. Since we later discover that Hamlet's father has been murdered by his brother, this same Claudius, the biblical allusion turns out to be grimly and ironically appropriate. Then, toward the end of the play, Hamlet and Horatio encounter two gravediggers preparing a new grave for Ophelia, though the young men do not know this. When a skull is tossed up on the ground, Hamlet meditates on whose it might have been:

> That skull had a tongue in it, and could sing once. How the knave jowls it to th' ground, as if 'twere Cain's jawbone, that did the first murder. This might be the pate of a politician, which this ass now o'erreaches, one that would circumvent God, might it not? (5.1.64–7)

The audience is already thinking about Genesis, since the gravedigger joked earlier about his working in "Adam's profession," given that "Scripture says Adam digg'd" (5.1.31). Scripture doesn't quite say this, but a radical rhyme popular since the Peasants' Revolt does:

> When Adam delved and Eve span,
> Who was then the gentleman?[11]

Hamlet's reference to Cain is also not entirely biblical, since no weapon is mentioned when Cain kills Abel. The jawbone comes from the Samson story in Judges, in which he slays a thousand men with a "jawbone of an ass" (Judg. 15:15). This mixing of biblical episodes derives from medieval biblical drama, as well as Bible illustrations, but the critical point is that Hamlet's reference to Cain underscores that play's focus on fratricide, as well as perhaps the sense that this sin is an inheritance from the Fall, a reminder of the generally corrupt human condition.[12]

Shakespeare's references to the Bible take a variety of forms. Some, as already mentioned, like those to Cain, Abel, and Samson, point to prominent characters: others include Adam and Eve, Jesus and Mary, Saul and David, as well as Dives and Lazarus, Noah, Goliath, Jonah, Jezebel, Daniel, and the Prodigal Son. Other references may evoke an entire story. The most important of these are the Fall of Adam and Eve that ruins Creation and humanity and brings sin into the world, and the Passion of Christ whose sacrifice redeems humanity from its sin resulting from the Fall. The main players in these tales come to represent the behaviors for which they are best known, whether good or bad. Thus, Pilate stands for authority evading responsibility for its actions, Judas for betrayal, especially of someone close, Peter for betrayal too, though due to weakness rather than malice, Eve for the sins of women (as the patriarchal tradition has it), the serpent, always understood to be Satan, for temptation, and so forth. Jesus Christ represents innocence, love, self-sacrifice, and suffering, though he also represents, in his Second Coming described in Revelation, judgment and retribution.

But these references to biblical characters or episodes are complicated by the traditional typological interpretation of the Bible, by which the meanings of characters and events or even words and ideas from the Old Testament are understood to be fulfilled only by their antitypes in the New. Thus, Adam, Moses, Isaac, David, Job, and Jonah are all seen as types of Christ, Eve as a type of Mary, the Flood as a type of the sacrament of Baptism instituted by John the Baptist and Jesus, the Exodus out of Egypt as a type for Christ's salvation of humanity. This means that allusions to one of these characters or events easily evokes others. So, when King Lear cries, "I will be the pattern of all patience," the audience should consider not only Job – "Ye have heard of the patience of Job" (James 5:11) – but also Christ, whom Job prefigures, and whose "passion" is in Christian theology the most perfect example of all "patience," both words deriving from the Latin root for suffering, "*passio*."[13]

The typological way of thinking may also explain Shakespeare's common practice of using biblical allusions to compare, whether favorably or unfavorably, dramatic characters to biblical models. The allusions linking Claudius to Cain are an example of this. The critical hunting for "Christ-figures" has sometimes been criticized,[14] but the truth is that Christ is the central figure in the Christian religion, and Shakespeare *does* in fact compare many characters with Christ (both positively and negatively) throughout his works. Cordelia in *King Lear* is a good example, and a positive one. She says to Lear, "O dear father / It is thy business I go about" (4.4.3–4), alluding to Jesus's words in Luke 2:49, "I must go about my father's business," and a Gentleman tells Lear,

> Thou hast a daughter
> Who redeems nature from the general curse
> Which twain have brought her to. (4.5.196–8)

The Gentleman, like everyone else in the play, lives in pagan Britain before the birth of Christ, so from his perspective he is presumably contrasting Cordelia with her two wicked sisters, but from a Christian perspective, redeeming nature from the general curse of the Fall is what Christ does on the cross, and the twain responsible for the curse are Adam and Eve. Cordelia is not Christ, of course, nor is the play a Christian allegory, as some have claimed. She dies once and for all, fully mortal, to no particular purpose, and because the other characters forgot about her, not because of her own willing self-sacrifice. The point is not about redemption in a cosmic sense, but about the redeeming of the general character of humanity by one good woman, and Cordelia is not like Christ in being divine, but simply in being innocent and suffering. In his final moments, Lear believes his beloved daughter has come to back to life, but it is not so; this is a pagan tragedy not a Christian comedy or romance.

By contrast, some other characters fare worse in being compared to Christ. Richard II explicitly compares himself to Christ, for instance, calling his courtiers Bushy, Bagot, and Green "Three Judases, each one thrice worse than Judas!" (3.2.132), when he thinks that they have betrayed him. It turns out they haven't, though, so his allusion is not only wrong but itself a kind of betrayal of their loyalty to him. Richard comes back to Judas later, however, with more accuracy, applying the name to those who demand and witness his abdication, despite their oaths of allegiance to him. "Did they not sometime cry 'All hail!' to me?" he asks. "So Judas did to Christ" (4.1.169–70). Yet even here, though he has been betrayed, Richard makes a very poor Christ figure. Even if one believes that kings have some share in divinity by divine right, Richard is not an innocent victim, let alone a willing sacrifice like Christ, but a corrupt and self-serving instrument of his own downfall. Shakespeare may have found the idea for Richard's allusions in a French history of Richard's deposition, but as a writer who delighted in puns he might have noticed that "deposition" can refer to both the dethroning of a king (as it is in Edward Hall's *Chronicle*) and the lowering of Christ's body from the cross.[15]

Shakespeare develops a similar critical contrast between a central character and Christ in several plays. Julius Caesar, for example, does not overtly compare himself to Christ, and could not, since Caesar was assassinated before Jesus was born, yet Shakespeare uses biblical allusions to encourage the audience to compare him to the Christian savior. For instance, Decius, one of the conspirators who is shortly to murder him, greets Caesar with "all hail!," the same phrase attributed above to Judas by Richard II, a phrase derived from the popular mystery plays (2.2.58). Similarly, earlier in the play, Caesar, processing through the crowds of Rome stops to listen to the soothsayer, asking, "Who is it in the press that calls on me?" (1.2.15). This echoes Jesus's question when, walking through a crowd, he is touched by a woman: "He turned him about in the press and said, Who hath touched my clothes?" (Mark 5:30). The questions are different, but the gospel account twice describes the crowd as a "press," as Caesar does, and this a rare word for Shakespeare, used in this sense, as a noun, only here and in two other works (*The Rape of Lucrece* and *Henry VIII*). Shakespeare's emphasis on Caesar's blood also contributes to his association with Christ. Christ's blood, viscerally present in the account of his scourging, crowning with thorns, crucifixion, and piercing, spiritually redeems humanity. Caesar's wife Calpurnia dreams that his statue spouts blood in which the smiling Romans bathe, and Decius interprets this (or pretends he does) as a positive sign that Rome from Caesar "shall suck / Reviving blood" (2.2.87–8). After the murder, Brutus seems to fulfill the prophetic dream in a different sense, saying,

> Stoop, Romans, stoop,
> And let us bathe our hands in Caesar's blood
> Up to the elbows, and besmear our swords.
> Then walk we forth, even to the marketplace,
> And waving our red weapons o'er our heads,
> Let's all cry, "Peace, freedom, and liberty!" (3.1.105–10)

Brutus may feel that the blood-letting has revived Roman liberty, but many Romans do not agree with him, and the assassination results in a brutal civil war, leading not to the re-establishment of the Republic but to the reign of the Emperor Augustus. Caesar's sacrifice, or rather the sacrifice (murder) of Caesar by the conspirators, saves no one, and there is no resurrection.

Are these biblical allusions religious? Shakespeare is certainly not writing mystery plays in the medieval mode, retelling Bible stories for the spiritual edification of the common people. He is telling stories that seem entirely secular, drawn from English and Roman history and other literary sources. Yet the "secular" was not perhaps a category that was even recognizable in Shakespeare's England. The Church was considered truly universal, whether one was Protestant (a member of the Church of England that included every good citizen and was headed by the king or queen) or Catholic (a member of the one true Catholic Church, transcending national borders, and ruled by the pope in Rome). No one was really outside the Church, unless they were damned, and even damnation is a religious category, not a secular one.[16] The religion of early modern Christians was not something they left behind in their parish churches; it pervaded every aspect of their lives, such that the term "religion" in the modern sense, as one aspect of a person or community among many others (like politics, profession, or family), would probably have been incomprehensible. Shakespeare was interested in the comparison of Cordelia, Richard II, and Julius Caesar to Christ for various reasons. Cordelia, a relative innocent, suffered and died trying to save her father; but thinking about innocent suffering for the sake of others without thinking of Christ was probably impossible for early modern Christians. Richard and Caesar are far from innocent, but Richard thought he was, at least relative to those who betrayed him, and his betrayal, like Caesar's, by those close to him may have been what suggested the comparison to Christ, betrayed by the archetype of all betrayers, Judas. Scholars disagree about whether Shakespeare knew Dante, but it is perhaps telling that both Judas and Brutus are in the mouth of Satan at the bottom of Dante's *Inferno*. Shakespeare's representation of Brutus is more ambivalent than Dante's, but then so is his representation of Caesar.

Not all of Shakespeare's biblical allusions are to characters and stories, however. Sometimes he incorporates or alludes to biblical verses that address theological ideas or Christian ethical teachings. *Measure for Measure*, for instance, alludes to a number of biblical passages on law and justice, the most obvious being the title's paraphrase of a verse from Matthew and Mark: "With what measure ye meet, it shall be measured to you" (Matt. 7:2, Mark 4:24). This sounds like retributive justice, the Old Testament "eye for an eye" (Exod. 21:24, repeated at Matt. 5:38), which the Duke pretends to demand at the end of the play: "An Angelo for Claudio, death for death" (5.1.402). But in the biblical passage, Jesus is actually advocating the golden rule, doing unto others as you would have them do unto you. Earlier in the play, Isabella urges Angelo to be merciful based on his share in the universal sinfulness of humanity:

> Why all the souls that were, were forfeit once,
> And he that might the vantage best have took
> Found out the remedy. (2.2.75–7)

Paul expresses this basic Christian theology in Romans, writing, "All have sinned, and are deprived of the glory of God, and are justified freely by his grace, through the redemption that is in Christ Jesus, Whom God hath set forth to be a reconciliation ... through the patience of God" (Rom. 3:23–5). Hamlet has a similar thought when asking Polonius to treat the players well. Polonius says he will "use them according to their desert," but Hamlet replies, "Use every man after his desert, and who shall scape whipping?" (2.2.485–6). Shakespeare likely has the Psalms in mind here rather than Romans, however: "If thou, O Lord, straitly markest iniquities, O Lord, who shall stand?" (Ps. 130:3); or "Enter not into judgement with thy servant: for in thy sight shall none that liveth be justified" (Ps. 143:2). That Hamlet is thinking in religious rather than simply ethical terms is reinforced by his subsequent statement that "the less they deserve, the more merit is in your bounty" (2.2.487–8). The point is intriguingly hard to categorize as either Protestant or Catholic. The emphasis on the lack of deserving leans towards a Protestant notion of unmerited Grace, and yet Luther and Calvin would have bristled at the suggestion that humans can achieve "merit" on account of any personal action, however bounteous. It sounds at first as if Hamlet is urging Polonius to imitate God in bestowing bounty even if undeserved (as it must be from the Protestant perspective), yet God gains no "merit" from his acts of Grace, since his perfection is beyond addition. Portia urges on Shylock the same action that Hamlet urges on Polonius, based on the same Psalm texts:

> Though justice be thy plea, consider this:
> That in the course of justice, none of us
> Should see salvation. (4.1.194–6)

Portia's famous speech on mercy strings together multiple biblical lessons. That the "quality of mercy ... / droppeth as the gentle rain from heaven" (4.1.180–1) is evident from biblical passages that describe mercy as "a cloud of rain, that cometh in the time of a drought" (Ecclus. 35:19) or the Song of Moses, which tells Israel, "My doctrine shall drop as the rain, and my speech shall [di]stil as the dewe, as the shower upon the herbs, and as the great rain upon the grass" (Deut. 32:2). Portia continues, "We do pray for mercy / And that same prayer doth teach us all to render / The deeds of mercy" (4.1.196–8), paraphrasing the passage in Matthew that includes the Lord's Prayer:

> And forgive us our debts, as we also forgive our debtors ... For if ye do forgive men their trespasses, your heavenly Father will also forgive you. But if ye do not forgive men their trespasses, no more will your Father forgive you your trespasses. (Matt. 6:12, 14–15)

We may question whether the motives of Portia's Venetian Christians derive from Christian teaching or profit-seeking; we may ask whether they practice what they preach, but the preaching is certainly biblical.

Falstaff in his mock-Puritan mode regularly refers to Paul and his teachings, though always twisting them in secular and even blasphemous directions. He is not as Machiavellian as Richard III, but he might say with him,

> I clothe my naked villainy
> With odd old ends stol'n forth of holy writ;
> And seem a saint when most I play the devil. (1.3.336–8)

For example, Falstaff defends his thieving to Hal on the basis of Paul's statement, "Let every man abide in the same vocation wherein he was called" (1 Cor. 7:20). Thieving is Falstaff's vocation and, as he says, "'tis no sin for a man to labour in his vocation" (*1 Henry IV*, 1.2.84–5). In *Henry IV Part 2*, the Hostess muddles Paul's instructions from Romans in her attempt to stop Falstaff and Doll Tearsheet from continual squabbling. "You cannot one bear with another's confirmities," she says. "One must bear, and that must be you [Doll], you are the weaker vessel" (2.4.48–9). Paul writes that "We that are strong, ought to bear the infirmities of the weak, and not to please ourselves" (Rom. 15:1). Infirmities are not "confirmities," a word cited in the OED only in this instance, perhaps suggesting confirmed infirmities, or conformity to certain "infirmities," which can mean not just illnesses and disabilities but moral weaknesses. That Doll should "bear" gets Paul entirely wrong, since the enormous Falstaff is presumably at least physically stronger than Doll; but the Hostess's mistake derives from confusing the senses of "bear" – "give birth" as opposed to "carry" – along with a reference to Peter's description of woman as "the weaker vessel" (1 Pet. 3:7). Some other characters are just as self-conscious as Falstaff in their misappropriations of Christian teaching, like the Clown in *All's Well That Ends Well*, who sets out to argue that one should befriend those who cuckold you, based on verses from Ephesians that were part of the Marriage Service in the Book of Common Prayer: "So ought men to love their wives, as their own bodies: he that loveth his wife, loveth himself. For no man ever yet hated his own flesh, but nourisheth and cherisheth it" (Ephes. 5:28–9). The Clown turns this upside down or inside out:

> He that comforts my wife is the cherisher of my flesh and blood; he that cherishes my flesh and blood loves my flesh and blood; he that loves my flesh and blood is my friend. (1.3.36–8)

The joke also depends on the understanding of husband and wife as "one flesh" (Ephes. 5:31, based on Gen. 2:23).

This chapter began by questioning whether allusions to the Bible could always be described as religious, or having to do with religion, and the best answer may be, almost. In a few instances characters, phrases, or ideas may seem to have become entirely detached from their original biblical contexts, but, even so, an audience may reattach them. Even if Don Armado thinks of Samson simply as a generic strongman, it is impossible to forget that he is a biblical one, even if that may not be especially significant to the play. The joking of characters like Falstaff is irreligious, yet the humor depends upon understanding the traditional religious context. Nevertheless, Falstaff is finally rejected by Prince Hall when he becomes Henry V, and while the young king never achieves his father's desired pilgrimage to the Holy Land, he does achieve a conquest of France, afterward calling for the singing of *Non nobis* (Ps. 115). The *Non nobis* – "Not unto us, O Lord, not unto us, but unto thy Name give the glorie" – attributes the English victory to divine Providence. One might suspect King Henry's sincerity, wondering whether his use of Scripture isn't much like Richard III's who can "clothe [his] naked villainy / With odd old ends stol'n forth of holy writ" (1.3.336–7), but he wouldn't be the first national leader to really believe that God was on his side. Yet other characters reference the Bible sincerely and without irony, as when old Adam offers his life savings to Orlando in *As You Like It*, expressing faith that God will still look after him:

> Take that, and He that doth the ravens feed,
> Yea providently caters for the sparrow,
> Be comfort to my age. (2.3.43–5)

Jesus says that "God feedeth the sparrows" and that no sparrow "is forgotten before God" (Luke 12:24, 12:6).

In sum, it may be said that the majority of Shakespeare's biblical allusions invoke – whether seriously, playfully, or even parodically – language, ideas, characters, and actions that conveyed religious meaning. The simplest explanation for the plethora of biblical allusions in Shakespeare (and other poets and playwrights as well) is that post-Reformation English culture was pervasively biblical. An Englishman couldn't enter a pub or inn without seeing Bible stories represented on the wall cloths or walk around moderately prosperous homes without finding the Bible pictured everywhere: on plates, spoons, and candlesticks, embroidered cushions, on mantelpieces, and bedsteads. State-mandated regular churchgoing involved a deep immersion in the Bible, from sermons and sung psalms, to the verses embedded in the liturgy, to stained glass and architectural sculpture (when they hadn't been smashed by radical iconoclasts). Yet the Bible was everywhere because religion was everywhere, and not just confined to particular days, hours, places, or activities. For Shakespeare and his audience, thinking with the Bible was natural and inevitable, reflecting a worldview in which religion encompassed everything – culture, history, politics, and all human behavior.

Notes

1 William Chillingworth, *The Religion of Protestants a Safe Way to Salvation* (London: L. Lichfield 1638), 375.

2 Brian Cummings, *The Literary Culture of the Reformation: Grammar and Grace* (Oxford: Oxford University Press, 2002), 19, referencing Roland Bainton, *The Bible in the Reformation*, Cambridge History of the Bible, ed. P. F. Ackroyd, et al. (Cambridge: Cambridge University Press, 1963–70), vol. 3, 2.

3 Alexandra Walsham described such crypto-Catholics as Church Papists. *Church Papists: Catholicism, Conformity, and Confessional Polemic in Early Modern England* (Woodbridge, UK: Boydell Press, 1993).

4 Shakespeare never uses the word "Bible."

5 There were two major revisions of the Geneva Bible, the Geneva-Tomson of 1576 (revised New Testament) and the Geneva-Tomson-Junius of 1599 (with revised notes for Revelation). It was available in many editions and a variety

of sizes and formats. Smaller formats of the Bishops' were also available, but it was printed far less often. The Coverdale Psalms come from the Great Bible (1539), Coverdale's revision of the Matthew Bible (1537), a combination of earlier translations by Coverdale and William Tyndale, revised by John Rogers. These Psalms were not included in the Book of Common Prayer but were regularly bound with it and printed for that purpose. See David Daniell, *The Bible in English: Its History and Influence* (New Haven, CT: Yale University Press, 2003).

6 For the argument about drafts, see David Norton, *The King James Bible: A Short History from Tyndale to Today* (Cambridge and New York: Cambridge University Press, 2011).

7 Defining "religion" continues to be a challenge for religious studies as well as other disciplines, especially when applied to earlier eras. For one introduction to the problem, see Jonathan Z. Smith, "Religion, Religions, Religious," in *Critical Terms for Religious Studies*, ed. Mark C. Taylor (Chicago: University of Chicago Press, 1998), 269–84.

8 See Tessa Watt, *Cheap Print and Popular Piety, 1550–1640* (Cambridge: Cambridge University Press, 1991).

9 Thomas More, *The Answer to the First Part of the Poisoned Book* (London: [1533]), fol. 256[r].

10 "The Copy of the Second Excommunication of Hildebrand against the Emperor," in John Foxe, *Acts and Monuments of Matters Most Special and Memorable, Happening in the Church* (London: John Day, 1583), 180.

11 Mark O'Brien, *When Adam Delved and Eve Span: A History of the Peasant's Revolt of 1381* (Cheltenham, UK: New Clarion, 2004).

12 Naseeb Shaheen, *Biblical References in Shakespeare's Plays* (Newark: University of Delaware Press; London and Cranbury, NJ: Associated University Presses, 1993), 559, notes that Cain kills Abel with a "cheke bon" in the Wakefield *Killing of Abel*. Many of the biblical allusions cited in this chapter are included in Shaheen's thorough catalog.

13 For an extensive discussion of allusions to Job in *King Lear*, see Hamlin, *Bible in Shakespeare*, chap. 8.

14 See Richard Levin, "On Fluellen's Figures, Christ Figures, and James Figures," *PMLA* 89, vol. 2 (1974): 302–11; Roland Mushat Frye, *Shakespeare and Christian Doctrine* (Princeton, NJ: Princeton University Press, 1963), 34–9.

15 *The Chronicque de la Traïson et Mort de Richart Deux Roy Dengleterre*, where Richard says to his followers, "for God's sake have patience, and call to mind our Saviour, who was undeservedly sold and given into the hands of his enemies," cited by Shaheen, *Biblical References*, 380–1. Edward Hall, *The Union of the Two Noble and Illustrious Families of Lancaster and York* (London, 1548), fol. viii[r]. Hall was one of Shakespeare's principal historical sources.

16 There has been much debate about whether there were atheists, in the modern sense of the term, in the early modern period. Some have argued this was simply not possible for early moderns, for whom the existence of God was unquestionable, whatever one believed about him or one's relationship to him. Others have disagreed, but even if there were some people who genuinely did not believe in God, there cannot have been many, and since the expression of this disbelief would have been a capital crime as well as heresy, we will likely never know

about them. See David Wooton, "Lucien Febvre and the Problem of Unbelief in the Early Modern Period," *Journal of Modern History* 60, no. 4 (1988): 695–730, and Tiffany Jo Werth, "Atheist, Adulterer, Sodomite, Thief, Murderer, Lyer, Perjurer, Witch, Conjuror, or Brute Beast? Discovering the Ungodly in Shakespeare's England," *Literature Compass* 10, no. 2 (2013): 175–88.

4

DANIEL SWIFT

The Drama of the Liturgy

"That same prayer doth teach us all to render / The deeds of mercy," Portia instructs Shylock on trial in Venice (4.1.197–8). This is at best condescension, for his prayers are precisely not the same as hers; at worst, it is cruelty, for she will soon force Shylock to convert to Christianity. She will, that is, impose her own community of prayer upon him, and in doing so will punish him until the point of ruin.

Shakespeare knew well the limits of confessional groups and set forms of prayer. "For charitable prayers, / Shards, flints, and pebbles should be thrown on her" (5.1.197–8) declares the priest before the funeral of Ophelia in *Hamlet*, and despite her brother's pleas – "What ceremony else?" (5.1.192) – denies her the full burial rite. He explains:

> We should profane the service of the dead
> To sing sage requiem and such rest to her
> As to peace-parted souls. (5.1.203–5)

There is a set and proper form of burial, but this is restricted to those who have died a Christian death and is therefore denied to her as a suicide and therefore one judged to fall outside the proper Christian community. The refusal of full burial rites can also be a punishment. In *Henry V*, the English king curses his French rival with the most terrifying vow he can: that he will "lay these bones in an unworthy urn, / Tombless, with no remembrance over them" (1.2.228–9). Rites can be granted or denied; sometimes piety can be faked using those same set forms of prayer. In *Richard III*, Buckingham stage-manages the rise of the scheming Richard by giving him a prop. "See, a book of prayer in his hand," he tells the crowds looking upon the villain who is about to be their king: "True ornaments to know a holy man" (3.7.97–8). Now this handling of a book of prayer makes a rhetorical claim: this unusual man who will be king is also common, the same as all.

In early modern England, for the hundred years between the issue of its first edition on March 7, 1549 and the government decree of January 4,

1645 that made its use illegal, the commonest literary work was the Book of Common Prayer. It was literary in the sense that its language was deliberately styled and formal, filled with tropes and figures, of rhyme, assonance, and particularly parallelism; and it was literary, too, in that the prayers included here were taken by many writers in the period as the prompts for new poems and creations. To modern eyes it looks oddly like both a play text and an anthology of poems. This was, as is often and sentimentally claimed, a golden age for English literature: it was also an age deeply marked by the struggles of the Reformation. The Book of Common Prayer was the definitive devotional text of this age. It established the correct form of Church services, the sacraments of Communion and baptism, and the rites of marriage, burial, churching, and confirmation; it set the cycles of morning and evening prayer, and the schedule of daily scriptural readings. It gave holy order to human time and a punctuation to worldly existence, particularly extreme moments of grief and joy, and those threshold moments of transition between stages of life that anthropologists call rites of passage. Its rituals welcomed newborns into the community of the living and bade farewell to the dead; confirmation marks adolescence while the marriage rite transforms two single individuals into a bonded pair. When anyone in Shakespeare's England invoked a book of prayer, or asked whether devotion had a set and proper form, they had this specific book in mind. This book sets out the proper form of burial, which is denied to Ophelia; it establishes the full cycle of proper English Christian devotion to which Shylock is condemned. Richard II was a fourteenth-century king, but in Shakespeare's late sixteenth-century play the particular book of prayers he handles would have been immediately apparent to the audience: not a medieval devotional book of hours but the early modern Book of Common Prayer.

The prayer book was common in three senses: or rather, it invoked three styles of commonness. First, it was widely diffused through sixteenth- and early seventeenth-century English culture and society. The most frequently reprinted books of Shakespeare's age were a version of the Psalms by Thomas Sternhold and John Hopkins, first published in 1562; a catechism called *The ABC*; and the Book of Common Prayer, and these last two are really one, for *The ABC* is heavily based upon the prayer book. The Book of Common Prayer went through approximately 525 editions between 1549 and 1729 in English alone; it was also published in French, Latin, and Welsh. Perhaps a million copies were published in this period, and the population of England in 1600 was roughly four million. When it was first issued in 1549, a royal proclamation set its price at 2 shillings and 2 pence unbound. By the end of the century, this price had plummeted to about 10d, due to the mass diffusion of copies.

"This same prayer doth teach us all," says Portia. Judith Maltby has traced the spread of what she calls "Prayer-Book protestantism" through England in the Elizabethan period while the print historian Ian Green documents the circulation of its prayers and set forms throughout the great flood of devotional material that dominated early modern publishing. He notes: "No other vision of prayer came near to having the same degree of penetration in the country at large, and among Protestants of all levels." While there was of course resistance to its order and its forms, the prayer book was the motor and heartbeat of Elizabethan faith, and this attachment only increased under James. "By the Jacobean era," writes Sharon Arnoult, "the Prayer Book had come to be seen, at least by some, as a bond in the timeless communion of English saints, linking the generations by embodying and expressing a distinctly *English* Reformed Christianity."[1]

The Anglican Church follows the Protestant conception of saints, which is more general than that of the Catholic Church: the "English saints" are simply those past worshippers who have worshipped properly and devoutly before us and inspire us with their past example. The prayer book was sanctified by time and repetition, and began to assume under King James I the quality it has retained until the present day – as a set text of Englishness.

There is, however, little that is distinctively English about the prayer book. It is written in English, but it is perhaps best seen as a translation of a foreign original rather than a new book, and its curious, contradictory genealogy is its second distinctive style of commonness. The prayer book was first issued in March 1549, and it was heavily based upon previous texts: upon Latin liturgy and medieval manuals of prayer. Thomas Cranmer was the main author of the prayer book – although the modern conception of authorship is highly anachronistic for this collage-like, co-authored text – and the most immediate source of the first 1549 edition was his own 1538 Latin breviary, which prescribed the daily round of prayer and readings from the Bible. This 1538 breviary in turn took as a major source a 1535 breviary written by the Spanish cardinal Francisco de Quiñones, which had been commissioned by Pope Paul III, a bitter enemy of Henry VIII. This great document of English Protestantism was built upon a text designed to bolster the European Catholic Church. "Rather than a newly coined book," writes Brian Cummings, "the 1549 text can be seen as a kind of sacred parody or even travesty (in the strict sense) of old ritual."[2]

This is simply pragmatic, for Cranmer wished to devise a new liturgy that would find popular support. "A ritual which has never been performed before may seem to those present not so much a ritual as a charade," notes the sociologist Roy Rappaport, and, as a consequence, new rituals that seek public support "are likely to be largely composed of elements taken from older rituals."[3] The prayer book faced two antagonistic problems: it was found to be both dangerously new and troublingly old. It lacked, for example, almost all that had defined popular Eucharistic piety – the parish procession, the elevation at the consecration of the Host, the peace, and the sharing of holy bread – so that the experience of churchgoing and prayer was transformed in both content and meaning. When the prayer book was first issued, it was met with fury across England. Rebels besieged Exeter, while in East Anglia rioters demanded the restoration of the traditional service. Four thousand people were killed in the southwest as government troops put down the rebellion.

The prayer book feels inevitable to us now; it has, as Sharon Arnoult notes, been worn into familiarity by the passage of time. Yet its early history is one of passionate contestation and frequent revision. The first prayer book of March 1549 was followed later in the same month by a new pontifical – the form for consecrating archbishops and bishops, which the English Church had adapted from Rome – and then in 1550 by *The Book of Common Prayer Noted*, which set the liturgy to music by John Merbecke. On November 1, 1552 a second prayer book was issued and became the official text. This version presented a liturgy more clearly marked by the Protestant tastes of the Edwardian Church, with less ceremony or suggestion of holy transformation, and was accompanied by an Act of Uniformity that warned that "a great number of people in divers parts of this realm [were] following their own sensuality."[4] Those local liturgies as had been used throughout the previous centuries – the most famous and widespread of them was the Sarum Rite, established by the eleventh-century Bishop of Salisbury – were no longer acceptable, and the Act enforced obedience to this new book on pain of imprisonment. It did not, however, last. In July 1553, King Edward died, and in the autumn his half-sister and successor repealed all the new liturgies. She sought to return the English Church to Rome, and publication of the prayer book therefore ceased during her reign. Following her death and the accession of Elizabeth to the throne in November 1558, the prayer book returned to the English Church. Her new edition of 1559 diluted the more extreme Protestant elements of the 1552 version, including most importantly the moment of the administration of Communion, and presented itself as a liturgical compromise that might – it was hoped – welcome many worshippers into the newly reformed English Church.

Each of these editions followed the same broad shape. After some occasionally defensive prefatory matter, the book begins, like the day, with the forms of morning prayer. These are followed by evening prayer and the calendar for the psalms, lessons, and readings proper throughout the year. The prayers for special occasions – in times of sickness or war, or directed to the monarch – are given in the Litany, and then the text of the scriptural readings for the celebration of Communion. The majority of the book is therefore an anthology of passages drawn from the Bible, and these in turn are followed by perhaps the most famous and contested section of the book, which is the order for the Church rites drawn from the traditional Catholic sacraments. These follow the arc of the human life as understood from the perspective of the Christian community. This begins with Communion, which marks and confirms the membership of the community of the Church, and is followed by the rite for baptism, which is the entry of newborns into that community. Baptism is followed and reinforced by the rite of Confirmation; and then in turn, in a vision of the ideal Christian life, matrimony. The later rites address the decline and death of man: the visitation of the sick, and a special Communion for them, followed by the burial of the dead. There is then a rite for the cleaning of women after childbirth, known also as churching, and a set of curses aimed at sinners called "A Commination." Many editions then included the text of the Psalms.

This general summary is perhaps, however, deceptive, for the prayer book was from its beginning a book in flux, and it never lost this fluid state. We might see it not as a single, authoritative text but instead a family of slightly different books, issued and revised, translated and rewritten, according to the devotional tastes of monarchs and the theological fashions of the day. The details of the rites and their specific words and phrases changed in subsequent editions: to take only the most controversial example of the period, the words spoken at administration of Communion are radically different in the 1549 and 1552 editions, and the 1559 edition perhaps most oddly combines these two previous versions into a single ambiguous text. It was never a perfect or original book, and this was plain to the worshippers of early modern England, for they saw its passing revisions and changing versions. When James acceded to the English throne in 1603 he too sought to mark the prayer book and, following the Hampton Court Conference of early 1604, issued yet another new version. This edition remained in use throughout the reign of his son Charles and yet, through all its editions, its troublesome genealogy and mongrel status were always remembered by its opponents. They condemned it for being insufficiently new, or too beholden to traditional Catholic practice. In 1640 the Root and Branch Petition, signed by 15,000 Londoners and presented to parliament by Oliver Cromwell, insisted that the prayer book's "Liturgy for the most part is framed out of the Romish Breviary, Rituals and Mass-Book" (BCP, xl). Radicals objected, too, that such set forms of prayer stifled spontaneity and therefore disrupted the individual's access to the divine. In 1644 the Westminster Assembly authorized the use of an alternate form, the *Directory of Public Worship of*

God, and public use of the Book of Common Prayer was made illegal on January 4, 1645.

Beyond its popularity and its multiplicity, the prayer book's third type of commonness is its participation in a surprising community: of liturgical drama. Liturgical drama had been played in the British isles since at least the middle of the tenth century and reached a peak in the thirteenth and fourteenth centuries with the Corpus Christi cycles, which placed the sacraments onstage. "To play the whole story," writes V. A. Kolve in his study *The Play Called Corpus Christi*, "is in the deepest sense to *celebrate* the Corpus Christi sacrament, to explain its necessity and power" (italics original).[5] The East Anglian Croxton *Play of the Sacrament*, in which the transformation of the Mass is enacted onstage, is the most famous example of this mode of drama, and this is precisely the style of playing that the Book of Common Prayer aimed to end. The first prayer book of 1549 was accompanied by an Act for the Uniformity of Service and Administration of the Sacraments, which made it a criminal offense to "in any interludes, plays, songs, rhymes, or by other open words, declare or speak anything in the derogation, depraving, or despising of the same book or anything therein contained or any part thereof." When in April 1559 the Elizabethan Church issued the new edition of the prayer book, this injunction was printed at the front of the volume, and punishment was set at a fine of one hundred marks for the first offense; four hundred marks for the second; and for the third, forfeit of all goods and possessions and life imprisonment. The strict rulings against liturgical drama continued. Following a proclamation "By the Queen" of 16 May 1559 the Crown would "permit none to be played wherein either matters of religion or of the governance of the estate of the Common weal shall be handled or treated." During the 1570s, a series of statutes issued by the Diocesan Court of High Commission in the North forbade that "the administration of the sacraments of Baptism or the Lord's Supper be counterfeited or represented," and when in 1604 the new Jacobean Church reauthorized the prayer book, it again included the preface, which specifically banned the dramatic performance or parody of Church rites.[6]

It has been tempting, for literary historians, to read this narrative of bans and interdictions and to follow them in assuming their success – in assuming, that is, that under such intense legal and governmental pressure the liturgical drama did die out in England, to be replaced by the English commercial theater of the 1580s and 1590s. The age of Shakespeare, that is, succeeds from – by evolution, successful separation – liturgical drama, just as the early modern age succeeds from the medieval. This has been most famously and influentially argued by Louis Montrose in his classic study *The Purpose of Playing*. "By 1580, the Corpus Christi play was no longer a vital cultural practice in Elizabethan England," he declares, and goes on to argue that the Elizabethan state appropriated the vibrant energies of traditional sacramental drama into its specifically Protestant and monarchic royal pageants, progresses, and Accession Day festivals. Alongside these state rituals, and working in concert, the commercial theater occupied the medieval Church's role as a space where the trials of daily existence could be addressed. One form replaced another. As Montrose explains, "the secure establishment and royal licensing of a fully professional, secular, and commercial theater in later Elizabethan London was contemporaneous with the effective suppression of the religious drama."[7] In this narrative, the Elizabethan Church suppresses religious drama; and there follows a neat division between Church rites and commercial plays; between the Book of Common Prayer and the works of William Shakespeare.

And yet: the prayer book looks, simply, like a play text. Here is an extract from the rite for the solemnization of Matrimony – the marriage service – from the 1559 Book of Common Prayer.

> Then shall the curate say unto the man:
>
> [Name] Wilt thou have this woman to thy wedded wife, to live together after God's ordinance in the holy estate of matrimony? Wilt thou love her, comfort her, honour and keep her, in sickness, and in health? And forsaking all other, keep thee only to her, so long as you both shall live?
>
> The man shall answer:
>
> I will.
>
> Then shall the Priest say to the woman:
>
> [Name] Wilt thou have this man to thy wedded husband, to live together after God's ordinance, in the holy estate of matrimony? Wilt thou obey him, and serve him, love, honour, and keep him, in sickness and in health? And forsaking all other, keep thee only to him so long as ye both shall live?
>
> The woman shall answer:
>
> I will.
>
> Then shall the Minister say:
>
> Who giveth this woman to be married unto this man?
>
> And the Minister receiving the woman at her father or friend's hands, shall cause the man to take the woman by the right hand, and so either to give their troth to other, the man first saying:
>
> I [name] take thee [name] to my wedded wife, to have and to hold, from this day forward, for better, for worse, for richer, for poorer, in sickness, and in health, to love and cherish, till death us depart, according to God's holy ordinance: and thereto I plight thee my troth. (BCP, 158–9)

There are three speakers – for the priest is given several titles, yet is one figure, which is an idiosyncrasy common in the prayer book – and four actors, each playing their roles, saying the set lines and moving at the set times. There is an audience, in silence, watching on. All play their roles; together, all combine to form the rite, and it is a powerful moment that reveals so much. A family is being formed here, although not wholly fairly, for the vows sworn by man and woman are unequal, as she promises to "obey" where he does not; in the short set forms the couple both transform their lives and imagine their deaths; the words are both copied from another and sincerely meant, and in all this the scene is powerfully dramatic.

Play and prayer book are troublingly similar, perhaps in competition. According to the great stage historian E. K. Chambers: "During the earlier part of Elizabeth's reign, Sunday was the usual day for plays. The trumpets blew for the performances just as the bells were tolling for afternoon prayer; and writer after writer bears testimony to the fact that too often the yards and galleries were filled with an appreciative crowd, while the preacher's sermon was unfrequented."[8] This analogy between theater and church was apparent to contemporaries, and became a clichéd term of abuse. When English Protestant reformers came to condemn traditional Catholic worship, they turned to a theatrical vocabulary. Calvin, in his exegesis of Job, mocked "the fine masquing knacks that are in the papacy"; Thomas Cranmer insisted that Latin service "is more like a play than a godly prayer"; Thomas Becon, one of Cranmer's chaplains, mocked the traditional Mass as "scenical and stage-like." There are countless examples of this rhetorical strategy, in the huge mass of religious controversy that dominated early modern publishing, and that strategy depended upon the proximity between play and liturgy.[9]

Prayer book and plays were supposed to be opposites, but for early modern audiences and worshippers the two forms did not look so far apart. What follows are two examples of Shakespearean liturgical drama. In the first, drawn from a single scene in the comedy *As You Like It*, the language of the prayer book is known to the characters speaking onstage, and is a source of both humor and gravity to them. The prayer book, that is, is on their side, and common between them. In the second, a brief reading of the play *Macbeth* as a complete liturgical drama, the prayer book rites are crucially in tension with the intentions and expectations of the characters onstage. The prayer book, that is, is apparently unknown to the speaking characters, and now the prayer book is therefore against them. In both, our own familiarity with the prayer book deepens our appreciation of what takes place onstage.

Out in the forest, where Shakespeare's characters retreat to find justice and to reassure themselves, Rosalind and Celia meet Orlando and decide to play a flirtatious game. This is a scene beloved by critics and audiences for its comical inversions – cross-dressing; a powerful woman deciding upon who she loves – and is perhaps an emblem of much that Shakespeare believed was essential to comedy. It is also, curiously, a scene of great severity: a parody that intends no disrespect but instead sets out a grand fidelity. Rosalind begins with an instruction:

ROSALIND [*TO CELIA*]: Come, sister, you shall be the priest and marry us. – Give me your hand, Orlando. – What do you say, sister?
ORLANDO [*TO CELIA*]: Pray thee, marry us.
CELIA: I cannot say the words.
ROSALIND: You must begin, "Will you, Orlando – "
CELIA: Go to. Will you, Orlando, have to wife this Rosalind?
ORLANDO: I will.
ROSALIND: Aye, but when?
ORLANDO: Why, now, as fast as she can marry us.
ROSALIND: Then you must say, "I take thee, Rosalind, for wife."
ORLANDO: I take thee, Rosalind, for wife.
ROSALIND: I might ask you for your commission; but I do take thee, Orlando, for my husband. (4.1.99–111)

The language is formal, and has a rule of its own. "I cannot say the words," says Celia, but Rosalind insists: "you must."

Several things are happening here, in this brief and apparently light scene. The words spoken by Orlando – which were added by Shakespeare, for they do not appear in his narrative source, Thomas Lodge's romance *Rosalynde* (1590) – have a double function. First, they bind Orlando and Rosalind to a spousal pre-contract. As Anne Barton has shown in a groundbreaking article, the centerpiece of early modern marriage custom was the dramatic performance of consent.[10] A handfast and an exchange of rings was sufficient to bind a couple. Consent expressed in the present tense formed an indissoluble bond; if the contract was conditional, sexual consummation made it binding; a church service, and the marriage rite, was required only to solemnize the union, and this is why the rite for matrimony in the Book of Common Prayer is called not "the marriage rite" but "the form of solemnization of matrimony."

Although Barton does not mention this scene, it is a spousal pre-contract. What these lovers say in this moment is sufficient to marry them, and Rosalind is very aware of the legalities. Orlando first swears to a *de futuro* (of the future) contract – "I will" – which is conditional upon future renewal. A *de futuro* spousal is not, on its own, legally binding, so Rosalind pushes Orlando further: "Ay, but when?" As he utters the words "I take thee" he enters into a *de praesenti* (of the present) contract, which is legally binding as soon as it is reciprocated. In the next line, Rosalind confirms: "I do take thee, Orlando, for my husband." They are now, according to the widely accepted laws of spousals, married. All that is further required is a church solemnization and sexual consummation.

The church solemnization, as set out by the prayer book, could not – of course – be played upon the Elizabethan stage; and yet, in this play, it appears. By an act of stage magic, it has already taken place, for these lines are a palimpsest of the expression of spousal consent and also, simultaneously, the marriage rite that follows this. According to the liturgy as set out in Book of Common Prayer, the solemnization has two movements. The priest demands of the man: "Wilt thou have this woman to thy wedded wife?" Rosalind's insistence, which Celia completes – "Will you, Orlando, have to wife this Rosalind?" – is therefore a direct quotation from the prayer book. The man must reply as Orlando does: "I will." Rosalind continues, "Then you must say, 'I take thee, Rosalind, for wife,'" and again she is quoting the liturgy, which instructs the man to begin, "I take thee to my wedded wife." Rosalind walks Orlando through the set phrases of liturgy, and even as the scene is so explicit it is also hidden, the Church rite cloaked under the popular spousal. "I cannot say the words," says Celia: she is not allowed to, by laws that forbade the stage parody of Church rites; she should not, for she is a woman and not a priest; and yet she does, and here the drama is working with the liturgy.

We might go one step further. The scene, as directed by Rosalind, improves upon the prayer book: it presents the moment of matrimony as a fantasy of equality, of fairness, love, and laughter. That which was strict in the liturgy is here playful; the lovers swear to an equal promise. The priest is a woman, and the wife is in charge; each of these roles and innovations is carefully specific, for the joy of the scene – and our recognition of that joy – is wholly dependent upon familiarity with the precise words of the prayer book. Besides the joy there is at least the potential for scandal here, with a woman priest and a bride in drag. But we might see the scandal and the joy as sharing a common cause: the sense that these words of love uttered in this moment matter, and are fundamentally important for they are true.

In *As You Like It* the liturgy is borrowed knowingly by the characters, with a wink; but liturgy may also be turned against those onstage, and here we move from comedy to tragedy. As Macbeth considers the murder of Duncan, he looks down and pleads: "Thou sure and firm-set earth, / Hear not my steps, which way they walk" (2.1.56–7). His wish is apparently illogical – a voiced appeal to silence? – and yet it is liturgically precise, and its component words "way" and "walk" have a specific set of associations. The phrase is scriptural, and echoes through the Bible, from Jeremiah 7:23, when God orders "walk ye in all the ways I have commanded you," and from Ecclesiastes 11:9, which instructs, "walk in the ways of thine heart." The phrase is common in the Psalms. Psalm 1 begins, "Blessed is the man that doeth not walk in the counsel of the wicked, nor stand in the way of sinners," and Psalm 128 opens, "Blessed is every one that feareth the Lord and walketh in his ways." This first context leads on to a second. Psalm 128 is the first of the cycle of psalms in the Book of Common Prayer's rite for the solemnization of matrimony, and this liturgical connection to marriage provided the phrase's dominant association for worshippers in this time. Following the prayer book, it appears in the Elizabethan homily "Of the State of Matrimony" – which insists, "Blessed is the man which feareth God, and walketh in his ways" – and as a common text for wedding sermons. William Massie, preaching at a wedding in Lancashire in 1586, took as his text this psalm and explicates the first line: "The second quality of the husband," he preached, "is to walk in the ways of the Lord."[11] The phrase from the Psalms became, by repetition in this specific context, a cliché of wedding counsel.

And yet, in the play, it is a negative: "hear not ..." Macbeth instructs us, for he apparently does not know what wider resonance lies here in his words. The phrase was conventional and it anticipates our recognition; once we hear this arrangement of words, we ought to know their connotation. For these words "walk" and "ways" suggest a simple teaching: we must follow proper Christian behavior within marriage. *Macbeth* is a play built upon the tension within a marriage, and it is precisely because Macbeth is married that he now considers murder. Its most famous scenes are those between a husband and wife, which makes this – curiously, and perhaps along with another domestic tragedy, *Othello* – Shakespeare's most domestic play. Here Macbeth, encouraged by his wife, is contemplating murder, and the well-worn phrase therefore reminds the audience of an absence. Here are a married couple, the play once more suggests, who have forgotten – or perhaps never knew – the truths and commands of liturgy.

This pattern of misapprehending the liturgy repeats throughout the play, as scenes again and again turn into failed versions of prayer book rites and as characters misunderstand the rituals they find themselves stranded within. Returning from the murder of Duncan, Macbeth looks at his blood-stained hands. These are both the sign and the proof of his guilt. "Will all great Neptune's ocean wash this blood / Clean from my hand?" he asks, and immediately answers himself:

> No: this my hand will rather
> The multitudinous seas incarnadine
> Making the green one red. (2.2.63–6)

The rich, Latinate word "incarnadine" is here used for the first time in English, and it describes the process of making red, as Macbeth fears that his guilt is so extreme that this newly shed blood will not be washed away but instead turn the green seas to its own color. This double image – a promised washing away of sin, and a red sea – is drawn from the prayer book. The rite for baptism, which welcomes a newborn child into the Christian community by cleansing him or her of sin, opens with a prayer. "Almighty and everlasting God," begins the priest, "which of thy great mercy didst save Noah and his family in the Ark, from perishing by water, and also didst safely lead the children of Israel, thy people, through the Red Sea, figuring thereby thy holy Baptism." The Red Sea in the holy land returns as Macbeth's nightmarish reddened waters, but where the play fears that this color will never be cleaned, the prayer offers the opposite, for it continues: "the Baptism of thy well-beloved son Jesus Christ didst sanctify the flood Jordan, and all other waters, to the mystical washing away of sin" (BCP, 142). Sin shall be washed away.

The play's fear is the opposite of the prayer book's promise; but behind these lines in the liturgy there is a further controversy, for the apparent efficacy of this prayer offended Puritan opponents of the Elizabethan Church. In 1572, a Puritan petition called the *Admonition to the Parliament* condemned this specific prayer. "The public baptism, that also is full of childish & superstitious toys," it declared, for "they say that God by the baptism of his son Jesus Christ, did sanctify the flood Jordan, and all other waters, to the mystical washing away of sin, attributing that to the sign which is proper to the work of God in the blood of Christ, as though virtue were in water, to wash away sins."[12] To suggest that water might wash away sin is in turn to imply that prayer is efficacious, and that liturgy might direct God's hand; this was, for Puritans, the remnant of a traditional Catholic superstition that should be cleansed from the reformed liturgy. Macbeth's doubt about the inefficacy of his perverted prayer echoes reformed doubt about the mechanics of salvation; he can find no virtue – or power – in the water for all such virtue resides only with the God he does not know how to reach.

The baptism rite continues immediately with a perfect image of an appeal to God. Over the child, the priest instructs: "Receive them (O Lord) as thou hast promised by thy well-beloved Son, saying, Ask and you shall have; seek and you shall find; knock and it shall be opened to you. So give now unto us that ask. Let us that seek find. Open the gate unto us that knock" (BCP, 142). The one who knocks is one who appeals to God, in the correct form, and such a proper appeal will in turn lead the worshipper back to God. This passage of the baptismal liturgy underpins the play, but it does not bestow its promise of forgiveness upon the murderer Macbeth.

Just as he is speaking his travesty of the Red Sea prayer, a sound from off-stage interrupts the scene. "Whence is that knocking?" demands Macbeth, and as his wife enters, the knocking continues. "I hear a knocking," she announces, and again "More knocking" (2.2.60, 68, 72). They can hear the knocking, but are not the ones who are knocking. They can hear, that is, the muffled sound of the prayer book's promises and phrases, but cannot understand them.

"I could not say 'Amen,'" confesses the wretched Macbeth, reflecting once more upon the murder (2.2.31). Throughout this short play he is surrounded by the ghosts and echoes of set forms of prayer, but none are available to him. Again and again, he misreads, mishears, misapprehends. The plot is driven by his almost willful failure to register liturgical echo. The witches promise that he may "laugh to scorn / The power of man, for none of woman born / Shall harm Macbeth" (4.1.78–80) and he quotes this like a prayer. "What's the boy Malcolm?" he asks:

> Was he not born of woman? The spirits that know
> All mortal consequences have pronounced me thus:
> "Fear not, Macbeth, no man that's born of woman
> Shall e'er have power upon thee." (5.3.3–7)

He mocks all weapons "Brandished by man that's of a woman born," and insists: "I bear a charmed life which must not yield / To one of woman born" (5.7.14; 5.8.12–13). The phrase appears in all versions of the story and the sources of the play, but Shakespeare adds its repetition. In this repetition, the phrase takes on weight and, for the audience, anticipation.

What Macbeth understands as the promise of immortality is the sound of his own inevitable death, for this phrase has one very specific set of liturgical associations in early modern England. As the Bible promises, in the book of Job, "Man that is borne of woman, is of short continuance, and full of trouble" (Job 14:1), and here the keywords insist upon the commonness of all men's fate. Macbeth of course believes himself to be an exception, exempt from human and divine law, and even from natural cycles. But he announces his blasphemy in the very phrases designed to prove its opposite. He claims immortality in the language of mortality. This key phrase that echoes through *Macbeth*, repeated so often that we must become familiar with it, was the centerpiece of both reformed and traditional liturgies of burial. It is drawn from the book of Job, but its most frequent application in early modern devotion is to burial. The phrase appears in the Sarum primer in Latin – "*Homo nat de muliere: brevi vivens tempore*" – and often with woodcut illustrations of a woman holding a baby or a man on his deathbed, and surfaces in the opening lines of the order for the burial of the dead in the Book of Common Prayer as the priest promises: "Man that is born of woman hath but a short time to live, and is full of misery" (BCP, 171).

This specific phrase reveals much about the indebted literary state of the Book of Common Prayer. The words are borrowed from the book of Job in the Bible and appear across manuals of prayer and liturgies in Catholic and Protestant churches, so they do not have any theologically particular association; through the force of endless association with burial, they assume a specific set of meanings that would have been familiar to all early modern worshippers and therefore all of Shakespeare's original audiences. In this moment, the play is designed to be familiar, or to be common, and that Macbeth apparently does not know the echo is proof both of his distance from the Church and the play's deep involvement in the liturgical culture of its time. For we must know the phrase, and therefore both sympathize with and judge Macbeth.

There are many more liturgical echoes in *Macbeth*. The play, although short, alludes in careful sequence to the rites of communion and confirmation, and as a whole becomes something closer to a parasite of the prayer book than any secular, freestanding work of art. The play is, perhaps, "a kind of sacred parody ... of old ritual," as Brian Cummings describes the 1549 Book of Common Prayer, quoted above. The examples I have given here, from two plays by Shakespeare, are only a small sample of the playwright's much wider plundering from the prayer book, which was for him both a source of key words and phrases and a dramatic skeleton for patterns of human action in the extreme moments of love and grief. But they suggest both that liturgy was dramatic, and that early modern drama was at times powerfully, and transgressively, liturgical.

There is, perhaps, a contradiction here between the commonness of liturgy and the exceptionality of Shakespeare. For he alone among the playwrights of early modern England adopted liturgical phrases and patterns of action with this level of intensity. Shakespeare's liturgical drama once more sets him apart from his contemporaries and, by extension, from his wider culture. This is, perhaps, the paradox of Shakespearean exceptionality: he achieved his specialness precisely by being, at times, common.

Notes

1 Judith Maltby, *Prayer Book and People in Elizabethan and Early Stuart England* (Cambridge: Cambridge University Press, 1998), 14; Ian Green, *Print and Protestantism in Early Modern England* (Oxford: Oxford University Press, 2000), 277; Sharon Arnoult, "Prayer Book, Polemic, and Performance," in *Negotiating the Jacobean Printed Book*, ed. Pete Langman (Farnham, UK: Ashgate, 2011), 50. Emphasis in original.

2 Brian Cummings (ed.), *The Book of Common Prayer: The Texts of 1549, 1559, and 1662* (Oxford: Oxford University Press, 2013), xvi. Further references to this work will be cited parenthetically in the text.

3 Roy A. Rappaport, *Ritual and Religion in the Making of Humanity* (Cambridge: Cambridge University Press, 1999), 32.

4 Henry Gee and William John Hardy (eds.), *Documents Illustrative of English Church History* (London: Macmillan and Co., 1914), 369.

5 V. A. Kolve, *The Play Called Corpus Christi* (Stanford, CA: Stanford University Press, 1966), 48.

6 Glynne Wickham (ed.), *English Professional Theatre 1530–1660* (Cambridge: Cambridge University Press, 2000), 34, 50, 69–70.

7 Louis Montrose, *The Purpose of Playing: Shakespeare and the Cultural Politics of Elizabethan Theatre* (Chicago and London: Chicago University Press, 1996), 25, 28.

8 E. K. Chambers, *The Elizabethan Stage* (Oxford: Clarendon Press, 1924), 1: 255. Bryan Crockett discusses the productive relationship between plays and sermons in *The Play of Paradox: Stage and Sermon in Renaissance England* (Philadelphia: University of Pennsylvania Press, 1995).

9 John Calvin, *Sermons of Master John Calvin, upon the Book of Job* (London, 1574), sig. A.vi.[v]; Thomas Cranmer, "Answers to the Fifteen Articles of the Rebels, Devon, Anno 1549," in *The Works of Thomas Cranmer*, ed. John Edmund Cox (Cambridge: Cambridge University Press, 1846), 2: 180; Thomas Becon, "A Comparison Between the Lord's Supper and the Pope's Mass," in *Prayers and Other Pieces*, ed. John Ayre (Cambridge: Cambridge University Press, 1844), 356.

10 Anne Barton, "'Wrying But a Little': Marriage, Law, and Sexuality in the Plays of Shakespeare," in *Essays, Mainly Shakespearean* (Cambridge: Cambridge University Press, 1994).

11 *The Second Tome of Homilies, of Such Matters as Were Promised and Instituted in the Former Part of the Homilies, Set Out By the Authority of the Queen's Majesty* (London, 1563), vvvv.ii.[r]; Samuel Hieron, *The Bridegroom* (London, 1613), A8[r].

12 Walter Howard Frere and Charles Edward Douglas, *Puritan Manifestoes: a Study of the Origins of the Puritan Revolt* (London: S.P.C.K., 1907), 26.

5

PHEBE JENSEN

Popular Religion

The subject of "popular religion" in late medieval and early modern England, for over a century the exclusive terrain of folklorists, was profoundly redefined in the late twentieth century in response to several related developments: the emergence of revisionist narratives of the English Reformation, new scholarly interest in local history and social history from below, a rise in the study of popular culture, and folklore's own self-critique of its traditional methodologies and focus. Because of this complex history, the present chapter begins by defining the term, before discussing references to popular religious culture in Shakespeare's work, including religious songs and ballads, the traditional festive activities associated with the liturgical year, religious drama, and visual culture. In many ways, sixteenth- and early seventeenth-century popular religious practices conformed to a central goal of Protestant reformers: to make the Bible the center of personal piety. But popular religion also diverged from sanctioned forms to include, on one end of the religious spectrum, vestigial practices that were often labeled (and sometimes actually were) Catholic and, on the other end, activities by Protestants who expressed their godliness in unconventional ways, such as the Puritan who reportedly "sings psalms to hornpipes" in *The Winter's Tale* (4.3.42).

Adopting provisionally a definition of popular religious culture as "independent activities" pursued outside the context of the physical church or sanctioned worship ceremonies, it is clear that in pursuing the ramifications of *sola scriptura*, Protestant reformers worked to align popular religion with the biblical and liturgical culture described in this volume's previous two chapters.[1] By dismantling the religious guilds that were the focal point for piety outside the Church, demoting traditional saints to objects of respect rather than veneration, discouraging (or outlawing) church ales and other calendrical festivity, and destroying the imagery in church decorations, Protestant reformers worked to purge popular religious culture of its extra-biblical content. Though the speed of the suppression varied by region, ce of reform accelerated in the Edwardian period, halted in the ., then resumed with subdued but effective vigor in the 1560s; vas well advanced by the 1570s.

speaking, this effort to align popular religion with the Bible sful. While early Protestant reformers such as John Bale and :con used popular forms such as plays and ballads to promote the Protestant faith, that initiative had been mostly abandoned by the 1590s. Meanwhile traditional religious practices, focused on the worship of the saints and festive activities associated with the religious year, declined. Fueled in part by religious zeal and in part by the profit motive, Protestantism increasingly permeated popular culture through printed material, including sermons, Bible study, catechisms, prayer books, treatises, and tracts.[2] The tremendous popularity of the metrical psalms, and more specifically of Sternhold and Hopkins's *The Whole Book of Psalms*, stands as a particularly powerful testament to the success of the Protestant reform of popular religion.[3] Decorative arts of the period similarly reflected a new emphasis on the word, both literally, in the text that replaced images on whitewashed church walls and the maxims that came to decorate godly households, and figuratively, in that most post-Reformation visual imagery represented scriptural stories from the Old and New Testaments, denuded of images of the Father or Son.[4]

But as scholarship in the past thirty years has shown, the process of Reformation was complex, multi-faceted, and incomplete. Despite the ascendancy of Protestantism, less officially sanctioned forms of worship, personal piety, and quasi-religious practices both endured and developed anew. In some cases, these were defiantly religiously conservative, even recusant. In others, conforming Protestants apparently saw no reason to give up traditional activities that they deemed doctrinally inoffensive, especially if they were separated from the Church or detached from their original devotional meaning. Indeed, Shakespeare's England was divided about whether some traditional activities – the popular festivity associated with the liturgical calendar, the acknowledgment (though not the veneration) of local and national saints, the use of prayers in healing rituals – could be purged of their popish associations, or whether they should be obliterated altogether. Extremists such as Philip Stubbes and William Prynne labeled all so-called superstitious practices as popish, when in fact, many Protestants participated in them. At the same time, and as the vitriolic catalogs in Stubbes, Prynne, and Barnabe Googe's *The Popish Kingdom* attest, vestiges of late medieval popular religion were legible in printed, theatrical, and material culture in almost every corner of the realm. Religious plays might have been repressed, stained glass smashed, and wall paintings whitewashed – though not, recent scholars have suggested, to quite the degree once thought – but memories of the saints and the popular religious culture they inspired endured, in almanacs, in wood and stone carvings, in domestic objects, in the flotsam and jetsam of phrases and sayings that constituted oral culture, and in literary forms.[5]

Meanwhile the evolving print industry infused popular religious culture with a growing body of devotional material, though only recently have scholars tended to consider print material as part and parcel of popular religious culture. Until historians began to concern themselves with questions about the popular beliefs of ordinary people, the study of the religious culture of the "folk" was the province almost exclusively of folklorists. Though the material gathered by these industrious and dedicated scholars can provide the modern scholar with fertile sources for primary material, the work of nineteenth-century folklorists should be handled with caution. By the Victorian period the field was guided by a "theory of survivals," whereby, as Ronald Hutton puts the case, "it was … postulated that many popular rituals were remnants of pre-Christian religious practice, which might be successfully reconstructed by a close comparative study of them."[6] Practically speaking, this meant that early folklorists replicated the more vituperative claims of the Protestant polemicists listed above, who claimed Catholicism was at heart a pagan religion, and conflated popular religion with both popery and superstition.[7] By focusing exclusively on oral tradition, folklorists tautologically proved the assumed identification of superstition and the old religion, as their work ignored the textual productions of Protestant print culture.[8]

It was folklorists themselves who in the 1960s rejected this "theory of survival" and the accompanying, romanticized view of a folk culture hermetically separated from elite, literate, or high culture. Around the same time, Peter Burke, Keith Thomas, and Hutton moved into the field, brandishing the archival tools of the historian and producing scholarship on popular religion, festivity, and popular culture that continues to be foundational for the study of popular religion in Shakespeare's world.[9] Burke's work, first published just before the complementary turn to cultural criticism in literary studies in the 1980s, initiated several decades of efforts by both historians and literary critics to define the term "popular culture," a project useful for conceptualizing the more narrow topic, popular religion. Recent work on popular culture avoids clear demarcations between highbrow and lowbrow, learned and ignorant, or literate and oral culture, to instead "emphasise," in words Burke himself wrote in 2010, "the 'intermingling' of elite and popular, the connections or the 'contamination' between them, the 'negotiations' between the two."[10] A key aspect of recent work in this area has nced sense of the relationship between orality and literacy – an ng that, as Adam Fox writes, in the early modern period "the of speech, script and print infused and interacted with each ıat "a song or a story, an expression or a piece of news, could miscuously between these three vehicles of transmission as it circulated around the country, throughout society and over time."[11]

Once print is added to the mix, the additional difficulty that arises in defining popular religious culture becomes its sheer ubiquity. Because religion was the bedrock set of beliefs that undergirded even apparently secular activities, cheap pamphlets on sensational murders or disasters that provoked providential intervention can be included in this category, as historians including Peter Lake, Michael Questier, and Alexandra Walsham have convincingly argued.[12] On the other hand, religion was often diluted when it appeared in popular forms, so that ballads on biblical subjects such as Susanna and the Elders, Job, or David and Bathsheba might, like their secular generic cousins, emphasize adventure, romance, and heroic derring-do over doctrine. A strong case can be made that popular culture in post-Reformation England was pervasively religious, even when not overtly so.[13]

Taking, of necessity, a narrower focus, this chapter focuses on the popular religious material that circulated through the culture in songs and ballads, festive celebrations, visual imagery, and Shakespeare's work for the London theater. Playing to literate and illiterate alike, that institution's artistic and rhetorical richness is arguably the product of the rich stew it made of the popular and elite, oral and literate, highbrow and lowbrow, old-fashioned and contemporary. Despite the prohibition against representing religion on the stage, popular religious culture was part of that powerful "gallimaufry of gambols" (*The Winter's Tale*, 4.4.309). In Shakespeare's works, references to contemporary religious culture appear throughout the canon, but they cluster in a few plays in which the playwright seems to embark on a more extended meditation on the relationship between popular religion, religious orthodoxy, and secular culture – exactly the points of controversy and contention sketched above.

"There Dwelt a Man in Babylon"

Among the drinking songs that Sir Toby, Sir Andrew, and Feste caterwaul in the middle of the night in the second act of *Twelfth Night*, making an "alehouse of my lady's house" (2.3.77), is a popular ballad of Susanna and the Elders with the first line, "There dwelt a man in Babylon" (2.3.69). In *The Merry Wives of Windsor*, Mistress Ford observes that Falstaff's language and intentions "no more adhere and keep place together than the

Hundredth Psalm to the tune of 'Greensleeves'" (2.1.48–50). In the same play, Evans the Parson appears to confuse the words of metrical Psalm 137 from Sternhold and Hopkins with Christopher Marlowe's poem, "Come live with me and be my love" (3.1.12–21). And the aforementioned "Puritan" at the sheepshearing festival in *The Winter's Tale* sings his psalms to hornpipes – an obscure wind instrument often associated in the period with revelry.

Each of these passages turns the juxtaposition of the religious and secular into the occasion for a joke, but they simultaneously point to the cultural intermingling of the pious and the profane in the popular music of early modern England. As Tessa Watt's *Cheap Print and Popular Piety* first showed, in the early years of the Elizabethan reign ballads on religious subjects were a high percentage of the total output – evidence that appears to reflect the early Protestant reformers' openness to using popular forms to promote their religious agenda. Though fewer ballads of a proselytizing nature were published after the 1570s, ballads with religious rather than secular subjects – to the extent the two can be clearly distinguished – continued to comprise a significant percentage of total ballad output into the seventeenth century. The most popular subjects for religious ballads included death and dying, attacks on popery, moral instruction on how to live a good life, general scourges against human sinfulness, descriptions of providential intervention, and stories from the Old and New Testaments and the Apocrypha (the latter singled out by Luther and his followers as especially appropriate for drama).[14] Particularly popular biblical subjects were stories of Susanna and the Elders, David and Bathsheba, Jonas, and Tobias, as well as the wisdom of Solomon, and Christmas-themed ballads and songs on the holy family. Arguably, this material has a certain doctrinal capaciousness not shared by more theologically precise popular religious material such as chapbooks, catechisms, and sermons, a lack of specificity that might have helped smooth the divisions of the Reformation, as it adapted material for widespread use by a population with varying religious tastes and beliefs.[15]

In *Twelfth Night*, the religious ballad "There dwelt a man in Babylon" is belted out with the same breath as "O'the tenth day of December" (2.3.73), a ballad on the Battle of Musselburgh Field in the reign of Edward VI; the popular drinking catch, "Hold thy peace" (2.3.60); and an art song from Robert Jones's *The First Booke of Songes and Ayres*, "Farewell, dear heart, since I must needs be gone" (2.3.86).[16] Though this juxtaposition is comic, it also reflects the actual mingling of religious and secular in popular music of the sixteenth and early seventeenth century. The ballads that traveled the country in pedlars' packs and in the voices of amateur or professional minstrels ran that gamut, as is suggested by the contents of a commonplace book associated with the early Elizabethan minstrel Richard Sheale of Tamworth, which included popular songs such as the "Ballad of Chevy Chase," as well as a penitential song apparently of Sheale's own devising, "Remember man thy frayle estate."[17] It appears that "even the most 'godly' of parishioners could see church and alehouse as compatible institutions," and extant ballads on drinking and good fellowship include moralized warnings about excess that could themselves be seen as part of popular religious culture.[18] Though Autolycus only sells secular ballads, he does also carry a "motion" (puppet show) of the Prodigal Son. The generic mixing evident in Sheale's repertoire and Autolycus's pack was also expressed in the practice of *contrafactum*, the juxtaposition of sacred words and popular melodies (or vice versa), widespread in the German Reformation and also evident in English psalms set to popular tunes (hence, perhaps, Mistress Ford's reference to the hundredth psalm to the tune of "Greensleeves").[19] The tune proposed for a ballad on the wisdom of Solomon, for example, was "The Spanish Pavin," a melody that also served "An Excellent New Medley" (*c.*1620), a ballad celebrating rustic misbehavior with a colorful cast of bawdy characters.

The dramatic action of the scene in *Twelfth Night* further emphasizes the interplay between the secular and the religious in popular culture. Feste offers Sir Toby and Sir Andrew "a love song or a song of good life" (2.3.30), a description that fits the moralized admonitions to live virtuous lives in slightly later ballads such as the "Hundred Godly Lessons," and "A Godly New Ballad."[20] Sir Toby of course chooses the love song, later proposing that they "rouse the night owl in a catch that will draw three souls out of one weaver" (2.3.51–2), summoning the common image of the religiously zealous weaver, a figure elsewhere in Shakespeare identified with psalm-singing, in Falstaff's insincere lament in *1 Henry IV* that he wishes he "were a weaver: I could sing psalms – or anything" (2.4.111–12).[21] There is no devotional timbre to the singing in *Twelfth Night*, and perhaps not much difference in the end between the "rousing catch" that might theoretically disturb the spiritual placidity of the weaver, and the popular ballad on Susanna and the Elders. Like many popular religious ballads, "There dwelt a man in Babylon" does not have a pointed theological message; as Watt has suggested, the appeal of the story may rest more with the romanticized central figure of a beautiful (and often naked) woman displayed as the object of male sexual attention.[22] Shakespeare does provide a brief glimpse of a more quietly pious use of religious songs in *A Midsummer Night's Dream* where, among the disruptions to natural and social order caused by her fight with Oberon, Hippolyta lists the lack of winter pastimes: "The human mortals want their winter cheer; / No night is now with hymn or carol blessed"

(2.1.101–2). Arguably, songs that accompany rituals in the plays – including Hymen's song at the end of *As You Like It*, and the dirge in *Cymbeline* – also use music to create a spiritualized atmosphere onstage. Primarily, however, in references to religious songs in the comedies, Shakespeare represents the amusing intermingling of the secular and the religious that seemed to characterize popular musical culture in early modern England.

Cakes and Ale

The musical revelry in *Twelfth Night* is also linked in that play to a second important category of popular religious material: the festivals and traditional pastimes that had once been tied to the seasonal celebrations of the late medieval Catholic liturgical year. The play's title, of course, alludes to one of the holy days that survived the English Reformation intact: the celebration of Epiphany that marked the end of the Christmas season. Those traditions are also recalled in Sir Toby's famous rejoinder to Malvolio, "Dost thou think because thou art virtuous there shall be no more cakes and ale?" – which Feste supports immediately with his line, "Yes, by St Anne, and ginger will be hot i'th' mouth too" (2.3.97–100). Cakes and ale spiced with ginger were the preferred refreshments at church ales. These annual festivals honoring a church's patron saint were devised both for communal merriment and to raise money for church repairs. The feast day for St. Anne (patron saint of many English parish churches) fell on July 26, a date conveniently located in the warm, secular half of the year, when there was the best chance of excellent weather for a convivial feast. Like other saints demoted at the Reformation, St. Anne lived on somewhat ambiguously in popular religious culture. A red-letter saint in the Sarum Rite, St. Anne was banished from the calendar (along with all other non-biblical saints) in the 1549 Protestant prayer book. She was restored as a black-letter saint in 1559, however, and inevitably appears in early modern almanac calendars, along with the medieval popes and bishops who crowd the pages of those ubiquitous pamphlets – traces of medieval popular religious culture lingering in post-Reformation England.

Feste's invocation of St. Anne recalls the central role saints performed as focal points for traditional festivity, but by the first production of *Twelfth Night*, church ales had been almost completely suppressed. As Hutton has shown, though such celebrations survived the first decade of the Elizabethan reign relatively intact, by the end of the century they continued as annual events only in scattered West Country and Thames Valley parishes.[23] Meanwhile the festival year was transformed, as David Cressy's work has shown, as new calendrical celebrations tied to national or political events replaced traditional religious celebrations such as Accession Day (November 17), the defeat of the Spanish Armada (August 8), and later, the thwarting of the Gunpowder Plot (November 5).[24] Yet, despite their transformation and repression, festive plays that recalled late medieval traditions continued. The Records of Early English Drama (REED) series has captured evidence of ongoing controversies over efforts to revive or continue festive celebrations that hotter Protestants deemed part and parcel of popery. In some cases, religious traditionalism motivated such activities; most of the time motives were decidedly mixed. These might include civic pride in a town's ancient traditions, an interest in creating good fellowship and neighborliness, the opposite wish to irk one's godly neighbors or an irritating local priest, or simply the desire to have a good time.[25]

The most virulent opponents of such pastimes were hotter Protestants, and Shakespeare clearly alludes to their objections to traditional festivity when Maria describes *Twelfth Night's* opponent of "cakes and ale," Malvolio, as "a kind of puritan" (2.3.119). Of course he is not, and Maria immediately corrects herself on this score – "the devil a puritan that he is" (2.3.124) – but the play clearly registers the cultural tensions over traditional pastimes and religious orthodoxy. Feste's very name invokes traditional festivity, and yet he also catechizes Olivia, claims to "live by the church" (3.1.2) while carrying the tabor and pipe associated with the Morris, and takes a final satirical turn dissembling as a priest in the dark house scene. Shakespeare's *Twelfth Night*, then, dramatizes the ways in which popular festivity still retained links to liturgical pastimes. Here again, as with popular songs, it is difficult to define, differentiate, and disentangle the secular from the religious.

Twelfth Night is the play that most directly refers to the religious controversies surrounding traditional pastimes in early modern England. Arguably, Shakespeare also alludes to those disputes more lightly in other plays, including *Henry IV Part 1*, *A Midsummer Night's Dream*, and *As You Like It*. For example, though in *As You Like It* the pastimes in the Forest of Arden are almost entirely secular – ballad singing, flytings of wit, mock combats, songs, and processions surrounding the hunt – they take place in a context that attaches moral weight to the camaraderie, community, and contemplative activities of the forest, where Duke Senior and his men find "Sermons in stones, and good in everything" (2.1.17). That the pastimes in the forest depict a version of "good life" (*Twelfth Night* 2.3.30) is particularly communicated at the moment Duke Senior welcomes Orlando to the company, repeating back the former's almost incantatory lines with language identifying the religious dimensions of hospitality as he acknowledges that he and his fellows have "seen better days, / And have with holy bell been knolled to church, / And sat at goodmen's feasts, and wiped our eyes / Of drops that sacred pity hath engendered" (2.7.120–3). Further, the assertion that Duke Senior lives in the Forest of Arden with his "many merry men ... like the old Robin Hood of England" (1.1.92–4) associates life in the forest with another key figure in late medieval pious festivity: Robin Hood, celebrated by parish guilds as the fervent worshipper of the Virgin Mary, and the focal point for the pious raising of funds for the Church.[26] In these ways, *As You Like It* associates festive play with neighborliness, hospitality, and a general sort of "right living" – exactly the virtues that some historians have seen as defining characteristics of popular piety and religious belief.[27]

Parish Plays

Parish drama is another category of popular religious activity that survived the Reformation in changed form. The cumulative work of the REED project, coupled with landmark scholarship by Paul Whitfield White, has revealed the extent to which these activities continued past the Reformation in the English provinces.[28] This drama included traditional saints' plays on one end of the religious spectrum, and Protestant polemical material on the other, but it was the cycle or mystery plays that had the greatest discernible influence on Shakespeare's work. Revised after the Reformation, the mystery plays were performed with official civic sanction – either as entire cycles or in series of selected pageants – into the reign of King James I. The mysteries did eventually end (though not as quickly as once believed), but individual cycle pageants, along with other plays on religious subjects performed by amateurs, continued to thrive in the provinces, especially at Christmas and Whitsuntide, times of the year traditionally associated with revelry.[29]

The exact nature of popular religious theatrical culture in Shakespeare's age is difficult to reconstruct, given fragmentary evidence. However, the mystery plays in particular clearly influenced Shakespeare, and it seems certain the playwright either saw these plays performed or came across them in printed form. They register in the canon most obviously in direct allusions, such as the huffing Herod in *Hamlet*, the daggers of lathe metaphorically wielded by Feste, and the stage-devils in *Henry VI Part 1*. But recent scholarship has also teased out more profound formal and dramaturgical debts. This work has shown that on the professional stage, popular religious drama sometimes undergirds visual and thematic motifs, shapes the physical use of space, and is recalled in snatches of old religious music and the handling of stage properties such as altars, tombs, crosses, and prayer books.[30] By revealing the continued irruption of the mystery plays in Shakespeare's work, this scholarship develops key early insights of Robert Weimann, expanding our understanding of Shakespeare's debt to popular religious drama with the new evidence the REED project is now bringing fully to light.[31]

Lazarus in the Painted Cloth

At once dramatic and visual, the surviving motifs of the late medieval stage overlap with another category of early modern popular religious culture: visual representations of religious themes, including painted cloths; wall paintings on churches, guildhalls, town halls, and private houses; stone and wood carvings; and domestic decoration on ordinary objects such as tables, plate, and cutlery. The rich visual idiom of religion in early modern England, recently emphasized in Tara Hamling's *Decorating the Godly Household* as well as Anthony Wells-Cole's study of the use of continental prints in Elizabethan house decoration, provides new possibilities for identifying links between Shakespeare's work and popular religious visual culture.[32] Although representations of God or Christ, images of miracles or saints, or any image likely to provoke worship in a viewer was destroyed early on in the Elizabethan reign, in fact there was a wide range of thinking on the acceptability of representing biblical scenes. Images in churches were considered especially hazardous because they appeared in a devotional context believed to increase the risk of idolatrous worship. But, as Hamling has argued, many Protestants – even so solidly reformist a divine as William Perkins – accepted the value of religious images for pedagogical purposes.[33] It now appears that some stained glass, wall-paintings, and carvings in churches, chapels, guild halls, and town halls survived longer than had previously been thought, the speed of destruction depending on the ideological orientation of the parish, the ability of the offending images to be destroyed without wrecking the church, and the specific iconography in question.

As is well known, Shakespeare's father John Shakespeare, in his capacity as Chamberlain of Stratford-upon-Avon, was directed to whitewash the wall-paintings and remove the rood screen in the Guild Hall in Stratford-upon-Avon the year before his son's birth, though it is unclear whether all the images in this chapel were destroyed at that time. In this context, Lady Macbeth's statement to Macbeth that "'tis the eye of childhood / That fears a painted devil" (2.2.57–8) takes on some historical poignancy: Shakespeare might himself have seen painted devils with his own eyes of childhood. And though most religious art had been removed from parish churches and cathedrals by the end of the sixteenth century, religious subjects were newly built into English domestic interiors, appearing in wall paintings, plasterwork, woodwork, and movables such as tapestries, cutlery, ceramics, and carved wood implements and furniture.

Shakespeare's work includes multiple references to paintings and painted cloths; a relatively small percentage of these allude to explicitly religious subjects. Perhaps not surprisingly, these references cluster around the figure of Falstaff, whose complex and irreverent relationship to religious culture has been well documented.[34] Falstaff asserts in his monologue at Shrewsbury in *Henry IV Part 1* that his impressed soldiers are "slaves as ragged as Lazarus in the painted cloth, where the glutton's dogs licked his sores" (4.2.21–3); his room at the Garter Inn, according to the Host in *Merry Wives*, is "painted about with the story of the Prodigal, fresh and new" (4.5.6–7), and in *Henry IV Part 2* he recommends that Mistress Quickly decorate her walls with "the story of the prodigal" (2.1.114). These stories were particularly popular for representation, not only on painted cloths and walls; the Prodigal Son saga was reproduced in many forms, including misericords, cushion covers, plates, and cutlery – even a Netherlandish shoehorn from the 1590s, now in the Victoria and Albert Museum.

As new work on material culture in early modern England expands our understanding of the post-Reformation religious visual idiom, it is spawning insightful interpretive work on this subject, such as John Astington's recent reading of *The Merchant of Venice* in terms of visual images of Jacob and Esau, and Hannibal Hamlin's analysis of *Macbeth* in the context of late medieval Doomsday rood screens.[35] Another example of a clear reference to visual religious imagery is Hamlet's description of the gravedigger – "How the knave jowls it to th' ground, as if 'twere Cain's jawbone that did the first murder" (5.1.64–6) – which refers not to the text in Genesis, but to a long-standing visual tradition that showed Cain killing his brother with an ass's jawbone; a representation of this episode survives today in the church of St. Edmund King and Martyr in West Kingsdown, Kent. When Simple in *The Merry Wives of Windsor* describes Master Slender to Mistress Quickly as having "but a little wee face, with a little yellow beard, a Cain-coloured beard" (1.4.19–20) he refers to yet another extra-biblical tradition about Cain. Though this line may recall the false beards worn in the Cain and Abel mystery-cycle pageant, it may also reflect church wall paintings of incidents from the book of Genesis.[36] In *As You Like It*, Orlando refers to one episode in the Prodigal Son parable that seems to have particularly piqued Shakespeare's interest, when he bitterly asks his brother, "Shall I keep your hogs and eat husks with them? What prodigal portion have I spent that I should come to such penury?" (1.1.29–30); Falstaff also refers to this moment in *Henry IV Part 1*, when he describes his soldiers "a hundred-and-fifty tattered prodigals lately come from swine-keeping, from eating draff and husks" (4.2.28–30). Shakespeare might have been especially struck by visual depictions of this scene, such as the much-copied Philip Galle print after a drawing by Maerten van Heemskerck, which captures the Prodigal's descent to the level of a beast, as he reaches, his eyes yearning, into the pig trough.[37] As these few examples suggest, Shakespeare's plays echo popular religious visual culture in ways we are only now fully beginning to appreciate.

Hermione's Statue

The Winter's Tale can conclude this brief survey of popular religion, first because that play reconsiders many of the issues raised here, but also because its critical history points to larger questions about the relationship between late medieval popular religion and the secularized rituals of the commercial London stage. Though the popular religious visual imagery described above mostly conforms to Protestant strictures about the danger of idolatry, the final scene of *The Winter's Tale* appears to provide an object lesson on the hazards of religiously tinged visual imagery. As Hamling explains, representational religious images were most dangerous when they appeared in a devotional context, such as a church or chapel; invoked worship in the viewer; involved free-standing sculptures, as in the words of the 1559 Injunctions, "men are not so ready to worship a picture on a wall, or in a window, as an embossed or gilt Image"; represented not a group, but an individual figure who could establish a focal point for personal worship; was sumptuously adorned; and depicted an especially important religious figure.[38] Hermione's "royal" statue (5.3.38) – free-standing, sculptural, vividly painted, preternaturally realistic, and depicting a "Lady" (5.3.44) who recalls to mind that most worshipped of late medieval English Saints, "Our Lady" – violates each of these criteria in turn. For an early modern audience, the scene's dramatic force would have invoked a strong sense of transgression, precisely noted by the characters' own worries about "magic" (5.3.110), "superstition" (5.3.43), and "wicked powers" (5.3.91). The scene dramatizes exactly what was prohibited from popular religious culture. Of course, Hermione is not a painted saint, and those fears evaporate the moment the statue moves. But before that point, the scene registers the charge of Shakespeare's most radical Protestant co-religionists – replicated in the work of nineteenth-century folklorists – that linked Catholicism and popular belief to magic, superstition, and superficial tricks of legerdemain, associations more lightly handled elsewhere in the canon, for example with the asperging fairies of *A Midsummer Night's Dream*.[39]

The depth and complexity of *The Winter's Tale's* engagement with religion precludes any simple identification of this work with Catholicism, but the dramatization of proscribed religious practices can serve here to remind us that popular religious culture was not monolithic in Shakespeare's time. Early modern Catholics were not all ignorant illiterates who confused hobgoblins with the devil and put faith in amulets and icons instead of the Christian savior. Operating under the radar of the authorities – increasingly so as the period progressed – Church papists and recusants participated in both older forms of communal festivity, and meditative, devotional traditions that had been reinvigorated with the principles of post-Tridentine Catholicism after the 1545–63 Council of Trent (*Concilium Tridentinum*) clarified and codified Catholic doctrine and liturgy. Supported by the admittedly intermittent presence of regular and Jesuit priests, improvising rosaries and other devotional material, and relying on illegally printed books (such as Henry Garnet's *The Societie of the Rosary*), early modern Catholics practiced lay piety that sometimes paralleled, but often diverged from, the activities of their conforming neighbors. For some members of the play's original audience, the fleeting moment of apparently idolatrous worship in the last scene of *The Winter's Tale* would have invoked devotional practices familiar through personal experience, memories of the recent past, or an awareness of the religious preferences of family, friends, or neighbors.[40]

The Winter's Tale also reiterates the difficulties of discriminating the secular from the religious in a culture that was fundamentally defined by Christian belief. The festival in Act 4 of *The Winter's Tale* is not a religious one, but rather a seasonal agricultural celebration in which pagan Bohemians revel, masquerade, flirt, dance, and sing. But it takes place in the context of a play with obviously religious overtones: a reverberating interest in the nature of grace, the deeply considered themes of sin, transgression, and forgiveness, the central role of the Delphic oracle. The sheepshearing scene recalls the religious origins of festival celebrations not only in Perdita's brief, anachronistic allusion to "Whitsun pastorals," but as its prepares for the final embrace of image-making and wonder – a necessary step in the communal process of repairing the effects of Leontes's deadly jealousy. That mania was indeed initially expressed in language invoking the pastimes, sport, music, and playing that radical reformers attacked as idolatrous, and it culminates in the king's iconoclastic desire to immolate Hermione, like a heretic "– say that she were gone, / Given to the fire, a moiety of my rest / Might come to me again" (2.3.7–9). As with early modern songs and ballads and the elements of medieval religious drama surviving in the dramaturgy of early modern stage, the secular and the religious are not easily differentiated in the festive and ritual world of *The Winter's Tale*.

Finally, the last scene of *The Winter's Tale* can help us reassess an important critical claim about the overarching relationship between popular religious culture and English Renaissance drama. Because the last scene of

The Winter's Tale temporarily equates the power of Shakespeare's theater with proscribed religious devotion, it has figured in the assertion, articulated in a line of scholars from E. K. Chambers to Stephen Greenblatt and Louis Montrose, that the suppressed artistic and cultural energies that fueled late medieval art and culture before the Reformation re-emerged, transformed, in the secular theater. Ritual repressed from popular culture and religious devotion, this narrative goes, flowered in a secular drama that simultaneously deployed and deplored those traditions, because (as Greenblatt has suggested about *King Lear*), "evacuated rituals, drained of their original meaning, are preferable to no rituals at all."[41] The recent reconsideration of religion on the Shakespearean stage – represented in part by the present volume – has offered important corrections to this admittedly powerful narrative. Our increased awareness of the ubiquity of religious motifs, language, imagery, and theological concepts in the early modern English drama, a growing understanding of the ways in which theatrical form emerged from late medieval drama, and the application of slightly revised definitions of what comprises religion in the period, make it possible now to think that especially important components of popular religious culture in Shakespeare's age were Shakespeare's plays themselves.

Notes

1 Robert Whiting, *The Blind Devotion of the People: Popular Religion and the English Reformation* (Cambridge: Cambridge University Press, 1989), 48.

2 Tessa Watt, *Cheap Print and Popular Piety, 1550–1640* (Cambridge: Cambridge University Press, 1991); Ian Green, *Print and Protestantism in Early Modern England* (Oxford: Oxford University Press, 2000).

3 Hannibal Hamlin, *Psalm Culture in Early Modern English Literature* (Cambridge: Cambridge University Press, 2004), 19–85; Green, *Print and Protestantism*, 503–52.

4 Tara Hamling, *Decorating the Godly Household: Religious Art in Post-Reformation Britain* (New Haven, CT: Yale University Press, 2010).

5 Alison Shell, *Oral Culture and Catholicism in Early Modern England* (Cambridge: Cambridge University Press, 2007), 1–22; Gillian Woods, *Shakespeare's Unreformed Fictions* (Oxford: Oxford University Press, 2013), 1–24.

6 Ronald Hutton, "The English Reformation and the Evidence of Folklore," *Past & Present* 148 (1995): 89–116, esp. 91; Peter Burke, "History and Folklore: A Historiographical Survey," *Folklore* 115 (2004): 133–9.

7 Alexandra Walsham, "Recording Superstition in Early Modern Britain: The Origins of Folklore," *Past and Present*, Suppl. 3 (2008): 178–206.

8 Adam Fox, *Oral and Literate Culture in England, 1500–1700* (Oxford: Oxford University Press, 2000), 6–10.

9 Keith Thomas, *Religion and the Decline of Magic* (Oxford: Oxford University Press, 1971); Ronald Hutton, *The Rise and Fall of Merry England: The Ritual*

Year, 1400–1700 (Oxford: Oxford University Press, 1994); Peter Burke, *Popular Culture in Early Modern Europe* (New York: Harper & Row, 1978).

10 Peter Burke, "Afterward," in *Literature and Popular Culture in Early Modern Europe,* ed. Andrew Hadfield and Peter Dimmock (London: Routledge, 2010), 209–25, esp. 209.

11 Fox, *Oral and Literate Culture*, 5.

12 Peter Lake, with Michael Questier, *The Antichrist's Lewd Hat: Protestants, Papists and Players in Post-Reformation England* (New Haven, CT: Yale University Press, 1999); Alexandra Walsham, *Providence in Early Modern England* (Oxford: Oxford University Press, 1999). On defining popular culture, see Andrew Hadfield, Matthew Dimmock, and Abigail Shinn (eds.), *The Ashgate Companion to Popular Culture in Early Modern England* (Farnham, UK: Ashgate, 2014).

13 Peter Lake, "Popular Religion," in *The Oxford History of Popular Print Culture, Volume 1: Cheap Print in Britain and Ireland to 1660*, ed. Joad Raymond (Oxford: Oxford University Press, 2011), 217–41.

14 James A. Parente, Jr., *Religious Drama and the Christian Tradition: Christian Theater in Germany and the Netherlands 1500–1680* (Leiden: Brill, 1987), 26–8 and 77–8.

15 Watt, *Cheap Print*, 119 and 125–7; Walsham, *Providence*, 1–6. For an alternative view, see Green, *Print and Protestantism*, 445–70.

16 Peter Seng, *The Vocal Songs in the Plays of Shakespeare* (Cambridge, MA: Harvard University Press, 1967), 101–8.

17 Andrew Taylor, *The Songs and Travels of a Tudor Minstrel: Richard Sheale of Tamworth* (Boydell & Brewer, 2012), 168.

18 Mark Hailwood, *Alehouses and Good Fellowship in Early Modern England* (Rochester: Boydell & Brewer, 2014), 106.

19 Katherine Steele Brokaw, *Staging Harmony: Music and Religious Change in Late Medieval and Early Modern English Drama* (Ithaca, NY: Cornell University Press, 2016), 132; Hamlin, *Psalm Culture*, 135.

20 Greene, *Print and Protestantism*, 453.

21 Hamlin, *Psalm Culture*, 38, though as Hamlin suggests in *The Bible in Shakespeare* (Oxford: Oxford University Press, 2013), the identification of psalm-singing and weavers was not perhaps as "proverbial" as has often been claimed, 249.

22 Watt, *Cheap Print*, 117–19.

23 On the medieval reform of popular culture, see Lawrence Clopper, *Drama, Play, and Game: English Festive Culture in the Medieval and Early Modern Period* (Chicago: University of Chicago Press, 2001).

24 David Cressy, *Bonfires and Bells: National Memory and the Protestant Calendar in Elizabethan and Jacobean England* (Berkeley: University of California Press, 1989); Muriel McLendon, "A Moveable Feast: Saint George Celebrations and Religious Change in Early Modern England," *Journal of British Studies* 76 (1999): 1–27.

25 Phebe Jensen, *Religion and Revelry in Shakespeare's Festive World* (Cambridge: Cambridge University Press, 2008), 1–22.

26 Paul Whitfield White, *Drama and Religion in English Provincial Society, 1485–1660* (Cambridge: Cambridge University Press, 2008), 43–65.

27 Martin Ingram, "From Reformation to Toleration: Popular Religious Culture in England, 1540–1690," in *Popular Culture in England c.1500–1850*, ed. Tim Harris (New York: St. Martins, 1995), 95–123, especially 109; Green, *Print and Protestantism*, 465.

28 White, *Drama and Religion, Theatre and Reformation: Protestantism, Patronage, and Playing in Tudor England* (Cambridge: Cambridge University Press, 1992).

29 Kurt A. Schreyer, *Shakespeare's Medieval Craft* (Ithaca, NY: Cornell University Press, 2014), 1–12; Helen Cooper, *Shakespeare and the Medieval World* (London: Methuen Drama, 2010), 59–60.

30 Brokaw, *Staging Harmony*, 188–231; Elizabeth Williamson, *The Materiality of Religion in Early Modern English Drama* (Farnham, UK: Ashgate, 2009); Schreyer, *Shakespeare's Medieval Craft*, 73–162; Rowland Wymer, "Shakespeare and the Mystery Cycles," *English Literary Renaissance* 34, no. 3 (2004): 265–85; Tom Bishop, "The Art of Playing," in *Medieval Shakespeare; Pasts and Presents*, ed. Helen Cooper, Ruth Morse, and Peter Holland (Cambridge: Cambridge University Press, 2013), 159–76; in the same volume, Janette Dillon, "From Scaffold to Discovery-space: Change and Continuity," 190–203.

31 White, *Drama and Religion*, 7; Robert Weimann, *Shakespeare and the Popular Tradition in the Theater: Studies in the Social Dimension of Dramatic Form and Function* (Baltimore, MD: Johns Hopkins University Press, 1978); Michael O'Connell, "Vital Cultural Practices: Shakespeare and the Mysteries," *Journal of Medieval and Early Modern Studies* 29 (1999): 149–68.

32 Anthony Wells-Cole, *Art and Decoration in Elizabethan and Jacobean England: The Influence of Continental Prints, 1558–1625* (New Haven, CT: Yale University Press, 1997).

33 Hamling, *Decorating the Godly Household*, 48–9.

34 Kristen Poole, *Radical Religion from Shakespeare to Milton: Figures of Nonconformity in Early Modern England* (Cambridge: Cambridge University Press, 2000), 16–44; Hamlin, *The Bible in Shakespeare*, 231–70.

35 John Astington, "Pastoral Imagery in *The Merchant of Venice*," *Word & Image* 31 (2015): 43–53; Hamlin, *The Bible in Shakespeare*, 271–304.

36 O'Connell, "Vital Cultural Practices," 157.

37 Reproduced, for example, in stained glass roundels at Strawberry Hill in Twickenham, St. Oswald's Church, Malpas, and St. Nicholas Chapel, Cholmondeley Castle.

38 Quoted in Hamling, *Decorating the Godly Household*, 49.

39 Jesse Lander, "Thinking with Fairies: *A Midsummer Night's Dream* and the Problem of Belief," *Shakespeare Survey* 65 (2012): 42–57; Alison Shell, "Delusion in *A Midsummer Night's Dream*," in *Shakespeare and Early Modern Religion*, ed., David Loewenstein and Michael Witmore (Cambridge: Cambridge University Press, 2014), 81–95.

40 Dillon, Anne, "Praying by Number: The Confraternity of the Rosary and the English Catholic Community, c.1580–1700," *History* 88 (2003): 451–71; Lisa McLain, *Lest We Be Damned: Practical Innovation and Lived Experience among Catholics in Protestant England, 1559–1642* (New York: Routledge, 2003).

41 E. K. Chambers, *The Mediaeval Stage*, 2 vols. (Oxford: Oxford University Press, 1903); Louis Montrose, *The Purpose of Playing: Shakespeare and the Cultural Politics of the Elizabethan Theatre* (Chicago: Chicago University Press, 1996), 19–40; Stephen Greenblatt, *Shakespearean Negotiations: The Circulation of Social Energy in Renaissance England* (Berkeley: University of California Press, 1988), 127.

6

HELEN SMITH

Grace and Conversion

Writing against the theater in 1633, William Prynne posed the question of whether actors and their delighted spectators might be close to conversion:

> Can Players, can Play-haunters then, *who spend their days in mirth, in carnal jollity*, in laughing, in rejoicing, in ribaldrous songs, in scurrilous jests, in amorous Poems, in wanton Comedies; in lewd discourses, in adulterous representations, wallowing in the very mire of sensuality, voluptuousness, and such like beastly sins, without the least remorse, be near to true repentance, or to the ways, the preparatives that lead and bring men to it? (Italics original)[1]

Unsurprisingly, the answer is no. Prynne's syntax is ambiguous: he seems to describe not dramatic audiences but plays themselves as briskly promiscuous. Poems are "amorous," comedies "wanton," discourses "lewd." Prynne does not just relate but revels in the allure of sensuous entertainment and the corresponding procrastination of the search for grace.

Conversion, whether within or between faiths, was a burning issue for theologians and an urgent question for many individuals in the late sixteenth and early seventeenth centuries. The schisms of the Reformation, and the visibility of the Catholic past made religious change central to English national identity, and an intimate part of family histories. A growing strand of English millenarianism looked forward to the Second Coming of Christ: an eschaton (end of days) that was supposed to be heralded by "the conversion of the Jews" invoked at the beginning of Marvell's poem "To His Coy Mistress." Proliferating sects offered Christians a dizzying variety of churches to which they might subscribe. And English Christians of all stripes were confronted not only by the magnificence and power of the Islamic Ottoman Empire, but also by diverse indigenous faiths, encountered in trade voyages, colonial projects, and missions, as well as at home in England, in gossip and news, or sometimes in the flesh.[2]

Writers across the spectrum of Christian belief offered models of how to convert, including the popular translation of the Spanish friar Luis de

Granada's *A Brief Treatise Exhorting Sinners to Repentance, Commonly Called, The Conversion of a Sinner* (1580, 1599, 1601), the blockbuster preacher Henry Smith's *The Sinners Conversion* (ten editions between 1593 and 1621), William Cowper's *A Mirror of Mercy or The Prodigal's Conversion* (1614 and 1615, with reprints in the *Works* of 1623 and 1626), an English translation of Niccolo Balbani's *The Italian Convert* (seven issues in 1635 and further editions in 1639, 1655, and 1668), and Thomas Shepard's *The Sincere Convert* (thirty-five editions between 1640 and 1742, including translations into Welsh and the Massachusetts language). A collection published in 1601 told its readers of *Eight Learned Personages Lately Converted (in the Realm of France) from Papistry, to the Church*; later in the same year, it had increased to *Ten Learned Personages*; by 1602 it had expanded to relate *The Confession and Public Recantation of Thirteen Learned Personages, Lately Converted in France*.

The dynamics of conversion were explored and reproduced onstage. Despite the declining popularity of dramas of conversion in the morality tradition, like William Wager's bluntly-titled *The Longer Thou Livest the More Fool Thou Art* (1569), at least forty-eight plays from this period feature converts and conversions.[3] The vogue for "Turk plays" that marked the 1590s and early years of the seventeenth century has been the subject of important recent scholarship. Staging the actual or potential conversion of Christian men to Islam, and of both men and women Muslims to Christianity, these plays raise unsettling questions of commercial and erotic identity.[4]

A closer reading of Prynne's antipathy to theater suggests that his concern was less the stage's distance from grace, and more its dangerous proximity to conversion of a kind. The shared ground of theology and theater is illuminated in the idea of "catastrophe," inherited from the Roman grammarian, Aelius Donatus, which refers to the final resolution, or "turn" of a play. The influential German reformer Philip Melanchthon wrote a commentary on Terence (a well-worn school text, and a source for Shakespeare's *The Comedy of Errors*). Melanchthon glossed "catastrophe" as "conversio," the "turn" of a comedy from danger towards well-being, a moment that is akin to spiritual regeneration both emotionally and in terms of plot.[5] Writing in 1624, an anonymous English religious controversialist used this dramatic concept to describe God's role in spiritual change, reflecting that "if repentance remorse, and compunction of spirit, cannot frame the master piece of Conversion, the *Catastrophe* shall be wrought by the violence of a stronger arm."[6] Though Shakespeare uses the term "catastrophe" mockingly – Edgar arrives "like the catastrophe of the old comedy" in *King Lear* (1.2.117), and in *Love's Labour's Lost* Don Armado's foolish letter promises "The s a nuptial" (4.1.70–1) – his is a theater to which dramatic al, and in which characters dwell repeatedly on the dangers

...in "convertěre" means variously "to turn about, turn in char- ...cter or nature, transform, or translate," a capaciousness of meaning that is retained in "conversion": a "turning in position, direction, destination."[7] Compare this to "peripeteia": "in classical tragedy (and hence in other forms of drama, fiction, etc.), a point in the plot at which a sudden reversal occurs." The term derives from post-classical Latin *peripetia*, "a turn right about, a sudden change (*a*1540), especially that on which the plot of a tragedy hinges (1579)."[8] Central to both conversion and drama is the turn; equally, both theater and theology hinge on the rhetorical device of *metanoia*: "the act or process of changing one's mind ...; *spec.* penitence, repentance; reorientation of one's way of life, spiritual conversion."[9]

Shakespeare's drama at first appears little concerned with conversion. King John's appearance as "a gentle convertite" (5.1.19) temporarily calms "this storm of war" (5.1.20) against France, but his pretended willingness to reconcile to Rome is soon revealed as a deception in a play whose concern with religious hypocrisy was self-evidently current in Elizabethan England. Jessica and Shylock convert from Judaism to Christianity; as we will see, both turns are figured in troubled terms. And, while the presence of a Moor – or rather an actor in black-face – on the English stage would have been likely to raise the specter of Islam for contemporary audiences, *Othello* is as silent on the subject of its hero's conversion as it is on the specifics of his racial and national origins.[10]

Yet conversion and its terms permeate Shakespeare's plays and poems, providing a narrative structure, and a supple and sometimes paradoxical language of racial and religious difference, personal transformation, inherited guilt, hypocrisy and revelation. Shakespeare's theater shared with theology a fascination with narrative, rhetorical, and imaginative turns; a concern for the permeability of the senses; an obsession with proof; and a deep-rooted curiosity as to the possibility and limits of personal transformation. This chapter explores the varieties of conversion, and the modalities of grace, experienced by Shakespeare's characters across a wide range of his plays, suggesting the subtle interrelationship of the structures of Shakespeare's drama, and his age's deep-rooted concern for the turns of the soul.

The true convert, concludes Prynne, will turn away from the stage: "A penitent heart, an humbled soul, a circumcised ear, an eye that weeps in truth for sin, *is altogether impatient of such objects*, such Enterludes, and delights." Prynne's attention to the paradoxical closure and openness of the convert's body (reflecting the "penitent" heart, open to God and closed to sin), chimes with his emphasis throughout the 1006 pages of *Histriomastix* upon the sensual pleasures of the theater. Spectators are vulnerable to seduction through eyes, ears, mouths, and noses. These were the sites at which corruption, but also grace, might enter. In a 1612 commentary on St. Paul's letter to Titus, clergyman Thomas Taylor asked the convert to inspect herself for evidence of grace, contrasting the bodily senses with the spiritual senses, belonging to the soul:

> hast thou thy spiritual *senses* restored thee? are thine eyes opened that thou canst say with the blind man; *One thing I know, that whereas I was blind, now I am sure I see?* hath he said *Ephata* ["be opened"] to thine ears, that now they are become the other sense of spiritual illumination, and understanding? dost thou savour the things of God? Is the word sweet to thy taste? dost thou feel the prickings of the Law, and the lenitives of the Gospel? (Italics original)[11]

The most famous example of the awakening of the spiritual senses came in the blinding of the persecuting Saul prior to his rebirth as the evangelist Paul.[12] The story of St. Paul was influential in the English Renaissance, so much so that in 1970 John S. Coolidge argued that seventeenth-century England experienced a "Pauline Renaissance." Paul's conversion was described in sermons and devotional texts, and depicted in drawings, paintings, and on decorative objects. Shakespeare's Richard III swears repeatedly by "Saint Paul" (1.1.145;[13] 1.2.36; 1.3.45; 3.4.75) in contexts that invoke the sensual force of Paul's conversion: "By holy Paul, they love his grace but lightly / That fill his ears with such dissentious rumours" (1.3.45–6). Unlike Paul, Richard refuses to convert, doggedly turning away from grace. When Richard attempts to blame the unfolding of history on "the doom of destiny," Queen Elizabeth bites back: "True, when avoided grace makes destiny" (4.4.219).

Central to the Christian understanding of conversion is the necessity of divine grace acting on the sinner. Grace is a complex word: a shorthand for benevolence as a property of God, bestowed freely and without regard to merit. The concept had a long Catholic heritage and was also central to reformed theology: Anne Locke's poem "expressing the passioned mind of the penitent sinner," for instance, appended to an English translation of Calvin's sermons on Isaiah 38 in 1560, asked readers to participate in its alliterative "confused cry, To crave the crumbs of all sufficing grace."[14] The word grace appears sixty times in *Richard III*, more than in any other of Shakespeare's plays. It weaves an uneasy alignment between the "grace" or lack thereof of the possessor of a noble title ("your grace"), the "grace and favour" of courtly life (3.4.90), and the revelation or lack of divine grace.[15] The irony of these competing meanings is encapsulated in Richard's apology

: "I do cry you mercy; / I did not see your grace" (2.2.104–5), a , in the context of his Pauline oaths, appears to audiences as the antithesis to Paul's healing blindness.

The transformations of vision are also Shakespeare's subject in *Much Ado About Nothing*. When Benedick quizzes himself about the possibility that he might, like Claudio, become a lover, he asks: "May I be so converted and see with these eyes?" (2.3.18). Later in the play, Margaret tells Beatrice: "And how you may be converted I know not, but methinks you look with your eyes as other women do" (3.4.67–8). In Act 1, Scene 1, Beatrice complains that "Courtesy itself must convert to Disdain if you come in her presence," prompting Benedick's quickfire response, "Then is Courtesy a turn-coat" – a renegade or apostate; in other words, a convert – (1.1.90–2). But Benedick and Beatrice are, in the end, converted not through their eyes, but through their ears. In a play that is centrally and self-consciously concerned with the arts of conversation, it turns out that simply hearing that the other is in love with them is enough to convert the pair's disdain into courtship.

As You Like It features conversions of various kinds: Duke Frederick abandoned his court and his murderous plots when he met "with an old religious man" and "After some question with him, was converted / Both from his enterprise and from the world" (5.4.144–6), a phrasing that suggests monastic seclusion. When Jaques learns of the existence of this sage relic, he declares, "Out of these convertites, / There is much matter to be heard and learned" (5.4.168–70). The play is haunted by the pre-Reformation past, set in a sacralized forest realm in which characters delight to hear "tongues in trees, books in the running brooks, sermons in stones, and good in everything" (2.1.16–17). Conversion is figured as conversation: a quasi-homonym that informed many writers' emphasis on the importance of godly speech in shaping the good Christian. At least until 1570, "conversation" and "conversion" existed as synonyms. Thus the 1535 Coverdale Bible celebrated "the conversation of the Heathen," and, in around 1570, Thomas Becon engaged in the knotty theological problem of "the conversation of the bread" during Mass.[16]

The word "convertite," placed here in the mouth of the learned melancholic Jaques, was first used as an English term in Bartholomew Young's 1587 translation of Boccaccio's *Amorous Fiammetta*. In Boccaccio, the beautiful and hypocritical Fiammetta uses the word to reflect upon the discrepancy of appearance and feeling, with a marginal note reminding the reader "How hard a thing is it to judge of another's holiness."[17] In around 1592, Christopher Marlowe's villainous Jew Barabas refused conversion to Christianity, spitting out, "No, governor, I will be no convertite"; two years later, Shakespeare, in *The Rape of Lucrece*, described the guilty Tarquin as "a heavy convertite."[18]

The Italian associations of "convertite" may have resonated for Shakespeare, as may its connection with women's sexuality: Italian *casa delle convertite* were religious foundations that housed former prostitutes. The poet and antiquary John Weever domesticated the term when he described "Horne-church" in London, which, he explained "was built by a female convertite ... and ... was called Hore-Church at the first."[19] Like the "harlots, bawds, and such like other pestilences" described by John Jewel as occupying "Monasteries of the Convertites," Tarquin is "taught how to bewail [his] unchaste life so sinfully passed over."[20] Tarquin's conversion haunts him, condemning him to tell and re-tell the story of his crimes, even as he slinks away from the view of the reader, and the poem.

In *As You Like It*, we get no further details of the religious old man. The fullest description of a conversion instead comes from Oliver, who, in contrast to Tarquin, establishes his "conversion" as a totalizing transformation:

> 'Twas I; but 'tis not I. I do not shame
> To tell you what I was, since my conversion
> So sweetly tastes, being the thing I am. (4.3.130–2)

Oliver's metamorphosis takes him out of himself. His murderous past self ("what I was") becomes the subject of his conversion narrative, distinct from his new being, which is identified entirely with his conversion: "the thing I am." Oliver's words both chime and contrast with Iago's declaration in *Othello*, "I am not what I am," a self-denying statement that Hannibal Hamlin identifies as an uneasy inversion of God's declaration of his self-sufficiency in Exodus 3:14: "I am what I am."[21]

Oliver's change of heart is exquisitely Pauline. It resonates with Sarah Beckwith's characterization of early modern "Calvinist discourses of the self, whose model of conversion is atemporal in that it insists on the complete death of the old self, and the complete and utter novelty of the new self."[22] In this, it stands in contrast to many early modern accounts, which describe conversion as a partial, faltering, and continuing process. His words also return us to the importance of the senses: Oliver "tastes" the sweetness of his conversion, experiencing it in bodily and all-consuming terms.

In its distinction between past and present, Oliver's conversion resonates with Thomas Taylor's instruction to: "Labour to find this change in thyself, and examine whether thou canst put difference between time past, and time present." If not, Taylor argues, "thou must set thy self down without comfort, as one that hath no sound proof of thy conversion. Enquire and make search whether thou canst find the *life* of grace in thy soul" (sig. Oo7^{v}). As

Taylor suggests, converts sought persuasive proof of their conversion. By the mid-seventeenth century, members of the English and American gathered churches collected together "proofs" as formal parts of their carefully staged conversion process, in processes akin to, but distinct from, the period's concern for the status and viability of legal proof.[23]

Still, Oliver's conversion is never quite described. As in numerous conversion narratives from the period, the fact of conversion is announced, but the experience remains obscure. Oliver's conversion is an example of what Lorna Hutson, writing of Shakespeare's fascination with legal structures, terms the art of the "unscene": that which is central to the drama yet never shown. *Othello* is the test case for the statement that conversion, in Shakespeare's plays, always takes place offstage. It stands in stark contrast with, for example, the elaborate dumb-show that presented audiences of Robert Daborne's *A Christian Turned Turk* (1612) with a vivid – and inaccurate – fantasy of conversion to Islam.

The movement of conversion is prefigured and announced throughout the History plays, structuring individual biographies and the larger cycle. In *Richard II*, Henry Bolingbroke (the future Henry IV) asks for news of his son, the "young wanton and effeminate boy" (5.3.10) and anticipates his reformation:

> As dissolute as desperate! Yet through both
> I see some sparks of better hope in him
> Which elder years may happily bring forth. (5.3.20–2)

Another father–son pairing appears: the Dukes of York and Aumerle. Exclaiming at the difference between "loyal father" and "treacherous son," Bolingbroke suggests the father's virtue is so strong:

> Thy overflow of good converts to bad,
> And thy abundant goodness shall excuse
> This deadly blot in thy digressing son. (5.3.63–5)[24]

Here, as elsewhere, Shakespeare associates the transformations of conversion with opposition: earlier in the same play, Richard II reflects, "the love of wicked men converts to fear" (5.1.66); in *Macbeth*, Malcolm exhorts Macduff, "let grief / Convert to anger" (4.3.231–2); and Tybalt, seeing Romeo at the Capulet ball, vows, "this intrusion shall, / Now seeming sweet, convert to bitt'rest gall" (1.5.90–1), a thoroughly bodily – though also thoroughly literary – metaphor. For Shakespeare, the violent contradictions of conversion threaten to dissolve into – or perhaps remain unresolved as – paradox. Hannah Crawforth describes paradox as lying "at the heart of Christianity; out of it grows true faith and through its distinctive form of logic the literary experience of this faith is generated."[25] Paradox structures the relationship between Tarquin and Lucrece after the rape, in a string of binaries in which the term "convert" speaks to ideas of sudden, and total, self-alienation:

> This forcèd league doth force a further strife;
> This momentary joy breeds months of pain;
> This hot desire converts to cold disdain:
> Pure Chastity is rifled of her store,
> And Lust the thief far poorer than before. (lines 689–93)

Like the story of Paul, the conversion of St. Augustine was profoundly influential during the early modern period. Arguing that the true convert has no place in the theater, Prynne invokes ancient as well as modern exemplars: pagan converts, he asserts, "immediately upon their baptism and sincere repentance did utterly renounce all Stage-plays as accursed Pleasures" (Eee1[r]). Augustine too, he tells us, turned away from worldly pleasures, as did Alipius, whose conversion Augustine describes. Augustine's conversion, which he had procrastinated for many years, came about when he heard a voice telling him "Tolle, lege" ("take up and read"), and chose a verse at random in the book he had been reading: Paul's epistle to the Romans. That verse, 13:13, reads, in the Geneva Bible, "So that we walk honestly, as in the day; not in gluttony, and drunkenness, neither in chambering and wantonness, nor in strife and envying." Marginal symbols at the word "gluttony" direct the reader to an alternative translation "Or, riot." Described by one commentator as "the *Fathers* conversion-Scripture" (italics original), this verse resonated for English readers, underpinning narratives of prodigality and reform that have been identified as central to the development of professional literary culture in this period.[26]

For audiences of *Henry IV Part 1*, then, Vernon's words describing Hal's anticipated reformation would have had an especial charge: "England did never owe so sweet a hope, / So much misconstrued in his wantonness" (5.2.67–8). Much earlier in the play, Hal's father, Henry IV, has expressed his disappointment at the contrast between Northumberland and the prince, lamenting that

> I by looking on the praise of him
> See riot and dishonour stain the brow
> Of my young Harry. (1.1.83–5)

The theme continues in *Henry IV Part 2*, as King Henry imagines the ruin to come "when [Hal's] headstrong riot hath no curb" (4.2.62) and demands of his son, "When that my care could not withhold thy riots / What wilt thou do when riot is thy care?" (4.2.263–4). In a striking image, he predicts "O, thou wilt be a wilderness again, / Peopled with wolves, thy old inhabitants!" (4.2.265–6). The desolation of this phrase has biblical overtones; the word "wilderness" appears 310 times in the Geneva Bible. In particular, it calls to mind not only the animal fury of Matthew 7:15, "Beware of false prophets, which come to you in sheep's clothing, but inwardly they are ravening wolves," but also the wilderness of Isaiah 34:13–15:

> And it shall bring forth thorns in the palaces thereof, nettles, and thistles in the strongholds thereof, and it shall be an habitation for dragons, and a court for ostriches …
>
> There shall the owl make her nest, and lay and hatch, and gather them under her shadow: there shall the vultures also be gathered, every one with her make.

Against this last verse, the Geneva editors inserted a marginal note: "Signifying, that Edom should be an horrible desolation and barren wilderness."

At the close of *Henry IV Part 2*, Henry V asks his followers to weep for his dead father, promising, "But Harry lives that shall convert those tears / By number into hours of happiness" (5.2.60–1). The word "convert" might, as we have seen, simply mean "turn." For an early modern audience, though, Harry's promise to "convert" his followers' tears, particularly in the context of personal transformation, would almost certainly have possessed religious connotations. His words come only eleven lines after he has assured his audience:

> This is the English, not the Turkish court:
> Not Amurath an Amurath succeeds,
> But Harry Harry. (5.2.47–9)

"Amurath" was Murad I (1362–89), the third Ottoman Sultan; Shakespeare may have known the name thanks to George Peele's play *The Battle of Alcazar*, published in 1594. King Henry's mention of the Turkish court as a counterpoint to English modesty would have lent an uneasy charge to Harry's promise to "convert" sorrow to joy.[27] The history plays return repeatedly to the memory of the Crusades: in *Richard II*, the Bishop of Carlisle remembers that:

> Many a time hath banished Norfolk fought
> For Jesu Christ in glorious Christian field,
> Streaming the ensign of the Christian cross
> Against black pagans, Turks and Saracens. (4.1.92–5)

Henry IV Part 1 opens with the king declaring his ambition to rekindle the crusades; at the end of *Part 2*, he dies not in Jerusalem, but in Westminster's

Jerusalem Chamber, fulfilling the prophecy of his death through a punning substitution.

Among all of Shakespeare's plays, *Othello* is the most centrally concerned with turning, as well as with the powerful Ottoman Empire. Encountering his drunken soldiers, Othello demands, "Are we turned Turks, and to ourselves do that / Which heaven hath forbid the Ottomites?" (2.3.151–2). "Turning" is used to most chilling effect, however, when Othello responds to Lodovico, saying of Desdemona,

> Ay, you did wish that I would make her turn.
> Sir, she can turn, and turn, and yet go on,
> And turn again. And she can weep, sir, weep. (4.1.243–5)

Compare this with Roger Williams's reflections upon England's church in a 1645 tract concerned with the conversion and baptism of the indigenous peoples of North America: "Yea what lamentable experience have we of the *Turnings* and *Turnings* of the *body* of this Land in point of Religion in few years?" (Italics original).[28] Aligning Desdemona's sexual fickleness with the "turns" of religious conversion, Othello's turns return upon themselves, turning Desdemona into a figure of constant motion.

Despite the recent critical interest in the trope of "turning Turk," it is only at the very end of the play that Othello imagines himself as both "a malignant and a turban'd Turk" (5.2.349) and, at the same time, as the noble Venetian who takes "by th'throat the circumcisèd dog," and stabs him (5.2.351). Prior to this moment, the language surrounding Othello, though ripe with references to race, has been concerned with his damnation or salvation within a Christian theology. As Cassio reflects in his drunken musings: "Well, God's above all; and there be souls must be saved, and there be souls must not be saved" (3.3.88–9). Towards the close of *Othello*, Gratiano reflects upon the tragedy, commenting that Brabantio,

> did he live now,
> This sight would make him do a desperate turn,
> Yea, curse his better angel from his side,
> And fall to reprobance. (5.2.205–8)

Brabantio's imagined "desperate turn" mirrors that of Othello, whose act of apostasy has been anticipated throughout the play: "Excellent wretch!," exclaims Othello in Act 3, "Perdition catch my soul / But I do love thee!" (3.3.90–1). And Iago insists that Othello is so smitten with Desdemona she could persuade him "to renounce his baptism, / All seals and symbols of redeemèd sin" (2.3.310–11), hinting perhaps at the adult baptism used to bring converts from Islam into the English Christian fold. Baptism is a figure to which Shakespeare returns: "Call me but love, and I'll be new baptised" Romeo promises Juliet (2.2.50), a playful pledge that nonetheless reminds audiences of his fickleness, and of the inconsistency of worldly loves and salvation.

The trope of turning Turk is not confined to *Othello*. In *Twelfth Night*, Maria delights at the success of her attempt to dupe Malvolio:

> Yond gull Malvolio is turned heathen, a very renegado; for there is no Christian that means to be saved by believing rightly can ever believe such impossible passages of grossness. He's in yellow stockings. (3.2.54–7)

A renegade was a convert to Islam, often taking advantage of opportunities for trade with, or advancement within, the Ottoman court:[29] elsewhere in Shakespeare, Iachimo, trying to seduce Imogen, calls Posthumus a "runagate to your bed" (*Cymbeline*, 1.6.137); King Richard lambasts Richmond as a "White-livered runagate!" (*Richard III*, 4.4.471); and Lady Capulet promises vengeance on the "banished runagate," Romeo (3.5.89). Maria's delighted mockery is one of several apparently lighthearted references to conversion to Islam in Shakespeare's plays: Hamlet jokes about joining a troupe of players "if the rest of my fortunes turn Turk with me" (3.2.250–1), while in *Much Ado About Nothing*, Margaret teasingly tells the new "convert" Beatrice, who has obligingly fallen in love with Benedick, "Well, and you be not turned Turk, there's no more sailing by the star" (3.4.42–3). And Henry V returns to the Turkish theme when he proposes to Katherine that the two of them will produce a son "half French, half English, that shall go to Constantinople and take the Turk by the beard" (5.2.181–91).

Mark Hutchings has identified fleeting references to Ottoman material in no less than thirteen of Shakespeare's plays from the 1590s.[30] Such mentions, Hutchings suggests, would have resonated across and between plays, especially as, for an attentive audience member, actors and props may have physically recalled other stage Turks.[31] These are puzzling moments, not of an urgent engagement with the threatening realities of English geopolitics, but of an often comic invocation of the transformations of conversion: a delight in the "perverse" alterations of which characters are capable.

Much Ado About Nothing stages another uneasy joke as Benedick declares he will love Beatrice: "If I do not take pity of her, I am a villain, if I do not love her, I am a Jew" (2.3.211–12), recalling for audiences Shakespeare's recent *The Merchant of Venice*. In that play, the clown Launcelot calls Jessica's paternity into doubt in the service of claiming her for the Christian faith: "Most beautiful pagan, most sweet Jew. If a Christian did not play the knave and get thee, I am much deceived" (2.3.10–12). Speaking of her own conversion, Jessica conflates religious and heterosexual desire, promising

"O Lorenzo, / ... I shall end this strife, / Become a Christian and thy loving wife" (2.3.19–20), and declaring "I shall be saved by my husband; he hath made me a Christian" (3.5.15). Jessica's conversion does not seem to be motivated by faith, but rather by an urge for sexual and social acceptance, substituting her gentile husband for Christ.[32]

Shylock's forced conversion is prefigured in Act 1, Scene 3. At the conclusion of a scene in which "the Jew" has consistently troubled the boundaries between Jewish usury and Christian ethics, Antonio reflects "The Hebrew will turn Christian: he grows kind" (l. 171). In the trial scene, Antonio urges mercy, while, ironically, insisting that he will have half of Shylock's fortune "in use" (a reference to Shylock's practice of usury). His second condition is that Shylock "presently become a Christian." The operations of grace raised knotty issues of compulsion and free will for Shakespeare's contemporaries. In 1598, William Perkins reflected, "When any man is converted this work of God is not done by compulsion, but he is converted willingly: and at the very time when he is converted, by God's grace he wills his co[n]version."[33] At the moment of conversion, divine compulsion is transformed into personal desire.

This paradoxical reflection circulated widely: Perkins liked it so much he reproduced it in another publication two years later, which was republished, confuted, and extended – always with these words preserved – by William Bishop in 1604, Anthony Wotton in 1606, and Robert Abbott in 1607. The Duke responds to Antonio's demands in terms that put in play his own religious conversion, or rather apostasy: "He shall do this, or else I do recant / The pardon that I late pronouncèd here" (4.1.387–8). Perhaps, then, an early modern audience might have accepted Shylock's words, "I am content," as having the potential at least to become, if not necessarily yet to be, sincere. But for twenty-first-century audiences, Shylock's consent, however performed, makes visible the queasy interrelation of religion, racial difference, and power.

In *Hamlet*, the terms of conversion undergo another transmutation. On the one hand, the "turn" of conversion appears conditional and digressive, oddly aligned with the notoriously procrastinatory and capacious plot. In Act 3, Scene 4, Hamlet pleads with the ghost against a conversion that is a dilution of purpose:

> Do not look upon me,
> Lest with this piteous action you convert
> My stern effects. Then what I have to do
> Will want true colour: tears perchance for blood. (3.4.126–9)

Later in the play, Claudius reflects that the populace love Hamlet so well that they, "dipping all his faults in their affection, / Work like the spring that turneth to stone, / Convert his gyves [fetters] to graces" (4.7.19–21). These ›act metaphors make the transformations of conversion intensely phys- Hamlet is imagined like wood dipped into a petrifying stream. A similar physicality haunts Lucrece's plea to Tarquin, as she prays that her tears will:

> like a troubled ocean,
> Beat at thy rocky and wreck-threat'ning heart,
> To soften it with their continual motion;
> For stones dissolved to water do convert. (lines 589–92)

In Lucrece's imagination, stones struck by waves do not simply dissolve, they change to water, becoming part of that which beats against them. This is a peculiar reversal of Hamlet's earlier cry in response to the ghost: "Look you, how pale he glares. / His form and cause conjoined, preaching to stones, / Would make them capable" (3.4.124–6). Where the OED glosses "capable" here as "susceptible," the term is surely also haunted by the idea that even stones might be made "able to perceive or comprehend" (def. 1b) or be possessed of "the needful capacity" for revenge (def. 5a). Delaying, the prince is less responsive than a stone.

Famously, Claudius attempts to convert and is unable to do so. He seems to follow the instructions set forth by Taylor, who tells his readers how to find proof of their own conversion: "Examine thy *motion* ... namely, whether thy cogitations, motions, speeches, actions public and private be changed, and have a new quality upon them; whether they are now holy, spiritual, heavenly, fruitful ... Canst thou *pray* in faith, and cry in assurance, Abba, Father?" (sig. Oo7v). As he struggles to intercede with God, Claudius instructs himself, "Make assay: / Bow stubborn knees, and heart with strings of steel / Be soft as sinews of the new-born babe!" (3.3.69–71). Recent scholarship has begun to investigate the degree to which stage effects were achieved by means of posture and gesture.[34] Where Hamlet (and *Hamlet*) worries about the connection between bodily deportment and sincerity, Taylor announces the two as inseparable: the experience of grace alters the quality of action and speech, in ways that can be scrutinized by the convert.[35] This is the change that Claudius struggles and fails to attain, as he kneels, but prays without faith.

The verb "assay" means "To put to the proof, try (a person or thing)," a definition that elides the human and the inanimate just as Claudius's words blur the distinction between his body and the material world, imagining a heart so hard it has turned to metal.[36] These imaginative conversions between inanimate and animate, object and subject, speak across Shakespeare's plays, and resonate with Leontes's plea to a statue in *The Winter's* Tale:

Chide me, dear stone, that I may say indeed
Thou art Hermione; or rather, thou art she
In thy not chiding, for she was as tender
As infancy and grace. (5.3.24–7)

Begging the stone to animate itself, Leontes quickly contradicts himself: paradoxically it is in its silence that the statue most closely imitates Hermione's tenderness.

The word "grace" is peppered throughout Shakespeare's works; according to the OED, he is the only writer to substitute the word for "God" in an oath. Thus, in *Macbeth* Malcolm swears "by the grace of Grace" (5.9.39), and, in *All's Well That Ends Well*, Helena pledges: "I will tell truth, by grace itself I swear" (1.3.192). Helena's words come as she promises to cure the mortally ill king. In this context, her emphasis on the "heedfull'st reservation" (1.3.197) with which her father commanded her to bestow his medical knowledge alerts us to the manifold temporalities of grace: it is an eternal property of God, an all-suffusing instant, and a period of merciful – perhaps even providential – delay. In *The Winter's Tale*, as Hermione departs for prison, she assures her women, "this action I now go on / Is for my better Grace" (2.1.121–2). Alongside its meaning as "Dramatic performance, acting," the term "action" had several connotations in this period. Perhaps the most pertinent here, given Hermione's use of the verb "to go," is "a devotional action": Hermione's new movement becomes a pilgrimage of sorts, though she cannot anticipate a "grace period" that will endure for sixteen years.[37]

Numerous critics have noticed the Christian resonances of Hermione's resurrection, a moment at which Paulina's words, "It is required / You do awake your faith" apply as much to the breathless audience as to the awe-struck Leontes (5.3.94–5).[38] Despite Hermione's appeal to the plural "gods" to "look down, / And from your sacred vials pour your graces / Upon my daughter's head!" (5.3.21–3), there is little doubt that the grace that Hermione imitates or embodies ("as tender ... as grace") resonates with the reading of this scene as both dramatic catastrophe and religious conversion (or vice versa).

Across Shakespeare's theater, ideas of religious change resonate, sometimes explicitly, sometimes with exquisite subtlety. His writings test the limits and range of both conversion and grace; in doing so, they tie together ideas of embodiment, physicality, the "unscene," noble character, and transformation. They form a way of thinking about the alterations of character, and offer a structure, centered around sudden and sometimes repeated turns, that allows for the revelations of stagecraft, as well as the revelation of grace. To Prynne's question, "Can Players, can Play-haunters be near to true repentance, or to the ways, the preparatives that lead and bring men to it?" the answer – fraught with the dangers as well as the promise of transformation – must surely be yes.

Notes

1 William Prynne, *Histrio-Mastix. The Players Scourge, Or, Actors Tragedy* (London: E[lizabeth] A[llde, Augustine Mathewes, Thomas Cotes] and W[illiam] J[ones], 1633), Eee1[r].

2 See especially Coll Thrush, *Indigenous London: Native Travellers at the Heart of Empire* (New Haven, CT: Yale University Press, 2017).

3 Lieke Stelling, "'Thy Very Essence Is Mutability'": Religious Conversion in Early Modern English Drama, 1558–1642)," in *The Turn of the Soul: Representations of Religious Conversion in Early Modern Art and Literature*, ed. Stelling, Harald Hendrix and Todd M. Richardson (Leiden: Brill, 2012), 59–83, 61.

4 See, in particular, Jonathan Burton, *Traffic and Turning: Islam and English Drama, 1579–1624* (Newark: University of Delaware Press, 2005); Jane Hwang Degenhardt, *Islamic Conversion and Christian Resistance on the Early Modern Stage* (Edinburgh: Edinburgh University Press, 2010); Matthew Dimmock, *New Turkes: Dramatizing Islam and the Ottomans in Early Modern England* (Aldershot, UK: Ashgate, 2005); Daniel J. Vitkus, *Turning Turk: English Theater and the Multicultural Mediterranean, 1570–1630* (Basingstoke, UK: Palgrave, 2003).

5 I thank Daniel Derrin for drawing the connections between "catastrophe" and "conversion" to my attention.

6 Anon, *A Gag for the Pope, and the Jesuits* (London: J[ohn] D[awson] for Edward Blackmore, 1624), A4[r–v].

7 OED, conversion, *n.* def. I.1.a.

8 OED, peripeteia, *n.* def. 1.

9 OED, metanoia, *n.*

10 On the play's vagueness about Othello's place of origin, see Emily C. Bartels, *Speaking of the Moor: from "Alcazar" to "Othello"* (Philadelphia: Pennsylvania University Press, 2008).

11 Thomas Taylor, *A Commentary Upon the Epistle of S. Paul Written to Titus* ([Cambridge]: Cantrell Legge for L. Greene, 1612), sig. Oo07[v].

12 John S. Coolidge, *The Pauline Renaissance in England: Puritanism and the Bible* (Oxford: Clarendon Press, 1970).

13 In most editions other than the New Cambridge Shakespeare.

14 Jean Calvin, *Sermons of John Calvin* (London: John Day, 1560), sig. A2[r].

15 Alistair Fox connects Richard's references to Paul to Sir Thomas More's *The History of King Richard III* and ideas of grace in "Richard III's Pauline Oath: Shakespeare's Response to Thomas More," *Moreana* 57 (1978), 13–24. Hannibal Hamlin offers a persuasive reading of the *Henry IV* plays as staging "an internal psychomachia between the forces of 'Grace,' represented by his Grace the King, and the 'flesh,' represented by Falstaff" in *The Bible in Shakespeare* (Oxford: Oxford University Press, 2013), 261.

16 OED conversation, *n.*, def. 11.

17 Giovanni de Boccaccio, *Amorous Fiammetta*, trans. Bartholomew Young (London: J[ohn] C[harlewood] for Thomas Gubbin and Thomas Newman, 1587), T1[v].

18 Christopher Marlowe, *The Famous Tragedy of the Rich Jew of Malta* (London: J[ohn] B[eale] for Nicholas Vavasour, 1633), C1[v]; William Shakespeare, *Lucrece* (London: Richard Field for John Harrison, 1594), F2[v].

19 John Weever, *Ancient Funeral Monuments* (London: Thomas Harper, 1631), Iii5[v].

20 John Jewel, *A Defence of the Apology of the Church of England* (London: Henry Wykes, 1567), Hh5[r]. A marginal header "Stews in Rome" drives home the association between the *casa de convertite* and the brothel; a link made by Hamlet, in the English context, when he commands Ophelia, "Get thee to a nunnery" (3.1.133).

21 Hamlin, *The Bible in Shakespeare*, 100–1 and 212–13.

22 Sarah Beckwith, *Shakespeare and the Grammar of Forgiveness* (Ithaca, NY: Cornell University Press), 159.

23 On the relationship between law and the literary arts, see especially Bradin Cormack, *A Power to Do Justice: Jurisdiction and the Rise of Common Law* (Chicago: University of Chicago Press, 2008); Lorna Hutson, *The Invention of Suspicion: Law and Mimesis in Shakespeare and Renaissance Drama* (Oxford: Oxford University Press, 2007); and Subha Mukherji, *Law and Representation in Early Modern Drama* (Cambridge: Cambridge University Press, 2006).

24 The word "blot" may also have had biblical overtones for audiences, especially coming after Bolingbroke's account of his own son's revels; compare 2 Peter 2:13, "Spots *they are* and blots, delighting themselves in their deceivings, in feasting with you."

25 Hannah Crawforth, "A Father to the Soul and a Son to the Body: Gender and Generation in Robert Southwell's *Epistle to his Father*," in *Conversions: Gender and Religious Change in Early Modern Europe*, ed. Simon Ditchfield and Helen Smith (Manchester: Manchester University Press, 2016), 61–80, at 69.

26 Samuel Crossman, *The Young Man's Monitor* (London: J. H. for S. Thompson and T. Parkhurst, 1664), K8[v]. On prodigality, see Richard Helgerson, *The Elizabethan Prodigals* (Oakland, CA: University of California Press, 1976) and Lorna Hutson, *The Usurer's Daughter: Male Friendship and Fictions of Women in Sixteenth Century England* (London: Routledge, 1994).

27 On Anglo–Ottoman relations, see especially Nabil Matar, *Islam in Britain, 1558–1685* (Cambridge: Cambridge University Press, 1998).

28 Roger Williams, *Christenings Make not Christians* (London: Jane Coe for I. H., 1645), A7[r].

29 See especially Matar, *Islam in Britain.*

30 Mark Hutchings, "The 'Turk Phenomenon' and the Repertory of the Late Elizabethan Playhouse," *Early Modern Literary Studies* Special Issue 16 (October 2007), 1–39, 5.

31 Hutchings, "The 'Turk Phenomenon,'" 4–5.

32 David Scott Kastan argues, "Marriage and apostasy (or is it marriage as apostasy) allow the daughter of 'a faithless Jew' (2.4.48) to 'become a Christian and [Lorenzo's] loving wife' (2.3.21), to become herself 'a gentle, and no Jew' (2.6.52), a salutary example of 'the unbelieving wife,' who, according to Paul, can be 'sanctified by the husband' (1 Cor. 7:14)," in *A Will to Believe: Shakespeare*

and Religion (Oxford: Oxford University Press, 2014), 97. See also Mary J. Metzger, "'Now By My Hood, a Gentle and No Jew': Jessica, the Merchant of Venice, and the Discourse of Early Modern English Identity," *PMLA* 113, no. 1 (1998), 52–63.

33 William Perkins, *A Reformed Catholic* (Cambridge: John Legat, 1598), A8r.

34 Farah Karim-Cooper, *The Hand on the Shakespearean Stage: Gesture, Touch and the Spectacle of Dismemberment* (London: Bloomsbury/Arden, 2016), esp. chaps. 3 and 4.

35 On the importance of gesture in preaching, see Arnold Hunt, *The Art of Hearing: English Preachers and Their Audiences, 1590–1640* (Cambridge: Cambridge University Press, 2010), esp. 84–90.

36 OED, assay, *v.* def. I.1.a.

37 OED, defs. 6, 17. See also def. 19.a. "Manner of acting; gesture, esp. in oratory or dramatic performance; (also) gesture or attitude depicted in a sculpture or painting."

38 See, for example, Julia Reinhardt Lupton, *Afterlives of the Saints: Hagiography, Typology and Renaissance Literature* (Stanford, CA: Stanford University Press, 1996), chap. 7.

7

CLAIRE MCEACHERN

Love

"Love is the *Character* and Badge of Christianity," declared the preacher Thomas Tuke in 1608, in his book the *Treasure of True Love*.[1] Or in our terms, love is the signature, calling card, or "brand identity" of Christianity, that which distinguishes it from other religions. The work of distinction is of course central to any religion, part of the effort to denominate believers from non-believers. So we find in the Judaeo-Christian tradition a succession of antonyms: monotheism vs. polytheism; Old Testament vs. New; works vs. grace. The first of these set Judaism apart from its rivals, as the first of the commandments declares: "Thou shalt have none other Gods before me." The second is among the means by which Christianity self-differentiates with respect to its predecessor and rival; the third, Protestantism with respect to *its* predecessor and rival, Catholicism. Foremost and fundamental to the identity of Christianity, however – especially the Christianities of Shakespeare's moment – is the contrast between "Law" and "Love."

Judaism and Christianity agree on the events of Genesis and their consequences for human ethical possibility, but Christianity from its inception had drawn the contrast with Judaism in terms of the best method of addressing those consequences – obedience to God's law, or mercy for those who inevitably failed in obedience? Love was a solution to the problem Law revealed (to Christian minds, at least), namely, the inability of incorrigibly errant human beings to obey it with any degree of competence or consistency. This love was twofold: first, it meant the love of his creatures that had moved God to sacrifice his only son in satisfaction of the penalty of Original Sin: "For God so loved the world, that he hath given his only begotten Son, that whosoever believeth in him, should not perish, but have everlasting life" (John 3:16). Second, it meant the "brotherly" love of Christ himself, who in dying for the sins of others demonstrated both obedience to God and the love of mankind enjoined upon us. Christ's example thus in effect supplies two addenda to the Decalogue: love God; and love not just your neighbor but your very enemy as yourself – "A new commandment give I unto you, that ye love one another: as I have loved you, that ye also love one another" (John 13:34). A vocabulary of love is not absent from the Old Testament, which teems with references to a "jealous god" unwilling to tolerate his worshippers' attraction to rival objects of worship. The Psalms resound with the languages of love, and Jesus's two "new" commandments are in fact found in the Old Testament (Deut. 6:4–5; Lev. 19:18). But what distinguished Christianity from its predecessor, and especially the various Christianities of Shakespeare's moment from their medieval predecessor, is the understanding that the human ability to even attempt compliance with law was utterly indebted to love. For with Protestantism's emphasis on salvation through grace alone rather than through human effort came an increased focus on the divine love that made salvation possible.

That said, the love that Reformation Christianity declared as its signature was of a very distinct kind. The desire for alliance is fundamental to human existence – hence the subject of much literature. It is what binds parents and children, spouses, siblings, kin and friends, tribe and nation – all "Nature's loves," in the term of the author of the 1587 *True Image of Christian Love*.[2] Such bonds are the stuff of classical ethics as well as Christian; they can inspire loyalty, devotion and tenderness, and self-sacrifice on behalf of one's loved ones. Early modern theologians viewed the feelings that attended these bonds as a potential means to approach the love Christ both preached and practiced. For instance, sixteenth-century writings on companionate marriage, including the Book of Common Prayer, urged marriage as a source of spiritual solace and strength. As John Donne wrote in his sonnet on his deceased wife, "Here the admiring her my mind did whet / To seek thee, God; so streams do show the head" (lines 5–6). Or, as Edmund Spenser coaxed, more slyly, in a courting sonnet to his future wife, "So Let us love, dear Love, like as we ought / Love is the lesson which the Lord us taught" (lines 13–14).[3]

Reformation thinkers understood that human loves thus could provide a rehearsal for divine love. Indeed, in Scripture, our earthly loves are foremost among the images that serve to describe the relationship of the soul or the Church to Christ. Testaments both Old and New describe a human being's relationship to the Church in terms of marital and erotic affiliation: "as a bridegroom is glad of the bride, so shall thy God rejoice over thee" (Isa. 62:5); "Husbands, love your wives, even as Christ loved the Church" (Eph. 5:25). In instances where metaphor or simile are not explicitly indicated by a "like" or an "as," such as in the frankly erotic language of the Song of Songs, commentators have, since the inception of Christianity, detected allegories of the relationship between Christ and his followers. So we find, in 1537, the Matthew Bible emphasizing the figurative meaning of the highly

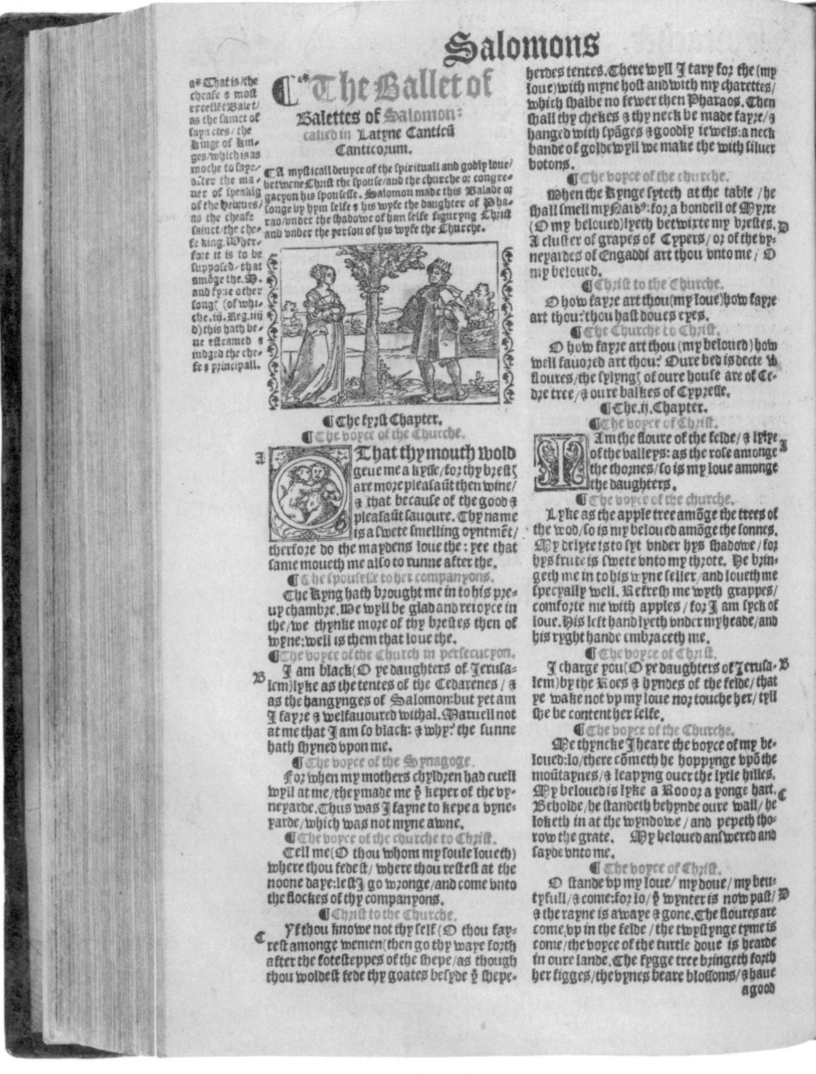

Salomons

a* That is/the cheafe & most excellẽt Balet/ as the sainct of saynctes/ the Kinge of kinges/which is as moche to saye/ after the maner of spekinge of the Hebrues/ as the cheafe sainct/the cheafe king. Wherfore it is to be supposed/ that amõge the. M. and fyue other songes (of whiche .iij. Reg. iiij d) this hath bene esteamed & iudged the cheafe & principall.

¶ a* The Ballet of Balettes of Salomon: called in Latyne Canticũ Canticorum.

¶ A mysticall deuyce of the spirituall and godly loue/ betwene Christ the spouse/and the churche or congregacyon his spousesse. Salomon made this Balade or songe by hym selfe & his wyfe the daughter of Pharao/vnder the shadowe of him selfe figuryng Christ and vnder the person of his wyfe the Churche.

¶ The fyrst Chapter.

¶ The voyce of the Churche.

A O That thy mouth wold
geue me a kysse/for thy brestes
are more pleasaũt then wine/
& that because of the good &
pleasaũt sauoure. Thy name
is a swete smelling oyntmẽt/
therfore do the maydens loue the: yee that
same moueth me also to runne after the.

¶ The spousesse to her companyons.

The Kyng hath brought me in to his preuy chambre. We wyll be glad and reioyce in the/we thynke more of thy brestes then of wyne: well is them that loue the.

¶ The voyce of the Church in persecucyon.

I am black (O ye daughters of Jerusa-
B lem) lyke as the tentes of the Cedarenes / &
as the hangynges of Salomon: but yet am
I fayre & welfauoured withal. Maruell not
at me that I am so black: & why? the sunne
hath shyned vpon me.

¶ The voyce of the Synagoge.

For when my mothers chyldren had euell wyll at me/they made me y keper of the vyneyarde. Thus was I fayne to kepe a vyneyarde/which was not myne awne.

¶ The voyce of the churche to Christ.

Tell me (O thou whom my soule loueth) where thou fedest/ where thou restest at the noone daye: lest I go wronge/and come vnto the flockes of thy companyons.

¶ Christ to the Churche.

Yf thou knowe not thy self (O thou fay-
C rest amonge wemen) then go thy waye forth
after the fotesteppes of the shepe/as though
thou woldest fede thy goates besyde y shepeherdes tentes. There wyll I tary for the (my loue) with myne host and with my charettes/ which shalbe no fewer then Pharaos. Then shall thy chekes & thy neck be made fayre/ & hanged with spãges & goodly iewels: a neck bande of golde wyll we make the with siluer botons.

¶ The voyce of the churche.

When the Kynge syteth at the table / he
shall smell my Nard⁹: for a bondell of Myrre
(O my beloued) lyeth betwixte my brestes. D
A cluster of grapes of Cypers / or of the vy-
neyardes of Engaddi art thou vnto me / O
my beloued.

¶ Christ to the Churche.

O how fayre art thou (my loue) how fayre art thou? thou hast doues eyes.

¶ The Churche to Christ.

O how fayre art thou (my beloued) how well fauored art thou? Oure bed is decte w floures/the sylynges of oure house are of Cedre tree/& oure balkes of Cypresse.

¶ The .ij. Chapter.

¶ The voyce of Christ.

I Am the floure of the felde/ & lylye A
of the valleys: as the rose amonge
the thornes/so is my loue amonge
the daughters.

¶ The voyce of the churche.

Lyke as the apple tree amõge the trees of the wod/so is my beloued amõge the sonnes. My delyte is to syt vnder hys shadowe / for hys frute is swete vnto my throte. He bringeth me in to his wyne seller/and loueth me specyally well. Refresh me wyth grappes/ comforte me with apples / for I am syck of loue. His left hand lyeth vnder my heade/and his ryght hande embraceth me.

¶ The voyce of Christ.

I charge you (O ye daughters of Jerusa- B
lem) by the Roes & hyndes of the felde/ that
ye wake not vp my loue nor touche her/ tyll
she be content her selfe.

¶ The voyce of the Churche.

Me thyncke I heare the voyce of my beloued: lo/there cõmeth he hoppynge vpõ the
moũtaynes/& leapyng ouer the lytle hilles.
My beloued is lyke a Roo or a yonge hart. C
Beholde/he standeth behynde oure wall/ he
loketh in at the wyndowe / and pepeth tho-
row the grate. My beloued answered and
sayde vnto me.

¶ The voyce of Christ.

O stande vp my loue/ my doue/ my beu-
tyfull/ & come: for lo/ y wynter is now past/ D
& the rayne is awaye & gone. The floures are
come vp in the felde / the twystynge tyme is
come/the voyce of the turtle doue is hearde
in oure lande. The fygge tree bringeth forth
her figges/the vynes beare blossoms/ & haue
a good

Figure 7.1 *The Bible, That Is to Say, All the Holy Scripture Contained in the Old and New Testament*. [The "Matthew" Bible] (London: John Day, [1537]), part 1, fol. 245v. Source: The Folger Shakespeare Library.

erotic Song of Songs by visually rendering the "Ballet of Balletes" [sic] as a duet between "the voice of Christ" and "the spousesse," or Church, with the individuated speech headings set off – uniquely in all the volume – in red-lettered "rubrics" (Figure 7.1).[4]

The difference of literal and figurative meanings of Scripture was in fact expressed by St. Paul as a difference marked by love: "written, not with ink, but with the spirit of the living God, not in tables of stone, but in fleshy tables of the heart … not of the letter but of the Spirit: for the letter killeth, but the Spirit giveth life" (2 Cor. 3:3; 6). This is the kind of contrast Portia, in the *Merchant of Venice*, draws in urging Shylock to be less literal about the pound of flesh owed him:

> Though justice be thy plea, consider this:
> That in the course of justice, none of us
> Should see salvation. We do pray for mercy,
> And that same prayer doth teach us all to render
> The deeds of mercy. (4.1.194–8)

Sometimes such metaphorical assignments could go the other way, such that spiritual language could serve as the language of erotic devotion. Petrarchan poetic conceits in early modern love poetry (such as imagining one's mistress as a goddess) often draw upon the language of religious worship. When Romeo and Juliet meet, they also compose a duet, building a sonnet together rich in religious terms:

> ROMEO: If I profane with my unworthiest hand
> This holy shrine, the gentle sin is this,
> My lips, two blushing pilgrims, ready stand
> To smooth that rough touch with a tender kiss. (1.5.92–5)

Yet thinkers also acknowledged that there were important differences between earthly loves and heavenly ones – between, as another homiletic writer in this moment put it, "that fond and lascivious Love, whereof the Poets are inventers" and "that holy and divine Love, whereof God himself is the only foundation."[5] As the typographical conversion of an explicit carnal meaning into an implicitly spiritual one suggests, human loves and divine ones do not always resemble each other. For one thing, human loves frequently engage bodies and their desires, both suspect quantities in Christian doctrine. Using human love to describe spiritual bonds sanctifies the former, whereas conscripting sacred language for carnal purposes can feel, as in Romeo's salvo, daringly transgressive (an effect perhaps intensified for Shakespeare's audience by the overtly Catholic species of Romeo's worship). For theologians, it was always important to remember that our loves of things of this world are only simulacra of the real thing – love of God – and as such not to be overprized in their own right. Or as Shakespeare's sonnet 105 has it, "Let not my love be called idolatry, Nor my beloved as an idol show" (lines 1–2). So too, sounding somewhat like a disapproving theologian, Othello believes in the last analysis that he has loved "not wisely, but too well" (5.2.340).

One interpretation of Adam's error in Paradise was that he loved his wife more than he loved his God. The marriage of the Macbeths has been called the most successful in Shakespeare's works, but also seen by some critics as an instance of a similarly uxorious man goaded on by a temptress. Frequently in Shakespeare's plays erotic devotion brings disappointment, and earthly doubts prompt metaphysical ones. For instance, Leontes, in *The Winter's Tale*, ties his faith in the universe to his conviction of his wife's infidelity: "If I mistake / In those foundations which I build upon, / The centre is not big enough to bear / A schoolboy's top" (2.1.100–3). We hear similar sentiments from Claudio in *Much Ado About Nothing*: "For thee I'll lock up all the gates of love ..." (4.1.98); Hamlet: "Get thee to a nunnery – why wouldst thou be a breeder of sinners?" (3.2.119–20); Othello: "when I love thee not, / Chaos is come again" (3.3.91–2); and Lear: "But to the girdle do the gods inherit; beneath is all the fiend's!" (4.5.122–3). Such despair is, it must be acknowledged, largely a male phenomenon; for the most part when it comes to erotic faith, Shakespearean men are the believers, women the believed-in.

The intensities and ecstasies of human loving could thus suggest to early modern thinkers the fervency with which we should also desire God. The pain often involved in loving another person could bring other kinds of suffering and martyrdom to mind. But in their tendencies to inspire partisan and ferocious allegiance human loves could also prove to be false images of, distractions from, or even obstacles to the love Christ exemplified. The latter was understood not only to surpass our loves of kin and kind, but in some sense to be categorically different from them, precisely on account of those very intensities. Christ's love required the lover to go above and beyond the near and the dear to embrace those persons who were not merely neighbors but maybe strangers, perhaps difficult to love, or downright unlovable.

Non-partisanal love could be especially difficult when it came to the love of someone not, strictly speaking, one's brother. The Friar in *Romeo and Juliet* hopes to use the lovers' bond to heal the civil breach between the Montagues and the Capulets: "For this alliance may so happy prove / To turn your households' rancor to pure love" (2.3.91–2). This is, however, the Friar's idea, not the lovers'; they just want to go to bed. When Romeo does try to speak terms of peace to his erstwhile "enemy" and new cousin, Tybalt, he is mocked by his friend Mercutio. Erotic love in this play, it seems, can only go so far to heal tribal enmities; the feud may not destroy the love between Romeo and Juliet, but it does destroy them. Similarly, in comedies such as *All's Well That Ends Well* or the *Merchant of Venice*, the fulfillments of the romantic plot fail to provide a solution to more trenchant problems of human hard-heartedness. In *Measure for Measure*, marriage is not the culminating coming together of soul mates but a lesser-evil practical management strategy for the intractable problem of human sexuality, as in St. Paul: "it is better to marry than to burn" (1 Cor. 7:9).

A common consequence of alliance is exclusion; of loyalty, breach. In some of Shakespeare's comedies, the bonds of community exact the cost of a scapegoat, a Malvolio or a Shylock, someone left out of the dance. With trust, devotion, and tenderness often comes violation, vengeance, and violence – for, as another devotional tract of the age put it, "all these [natural loves] being not governed by the divine spirit of direction, it is easy to know what harm cometh by them ... [they] maketh men blinder, perverteth the true order of Justice, and preferreth fools before wise men ... taketh away right judgment" (*True Image*, Sig. A2^{v}). Or as Bottom says, in *A Midsummer Night's Dream*, "to say the truth, reason and love keep little company together" (3.1.120–1).

The kind of love Christ exemplified, by contrast, was understood to be free from the fierce and sometimes damaging partisanship of human loves. As St. Paul expounds in Corinthians, that notoriously favorite reading of the most optimistic of human ceremonies, *true* love – i.e. love from and for God – "suffereth long: it is bountiful: ... doeth not boast itself: it is not puffed up: It disdaineth not: it seeketh not her own things: it is not provoked to anger: it thinketh not evil: it rejoiceth not in iniquity, ... It suffereth all things: it believeth all things: it hopeth all things: it endureth all things" (1 Cor. 13:4–7). So, while it might be possible to view Christ's urgings to love God and one's neighbor as just positive restatements of the commands to worship one god and not covet a neighbor's wife or goods, Christian love was different, as it were, in kind, from the "jealous" love that brooked no competitors and took no prisoners. It was a love that did not, as it were, come naturally.

Not surprisingly, Reformation thinkers, Shakespeare included, dedicated substantial effort to teasing out just what, precisely, was involved in the kind of love Christ enjoined, how it did and did not resemble our more familiar first-hand loves of kin and kind. "Who can sever love from charity?" asks Berowne in *Love's Labour's Lost* (4.3.334). Titles such as *An Introduction to the Love of God* (1574), the *True Image of Christian Love* (1587), or *Theophilus, or Love Divine* (1608) filled the London booksellers' shops. Questions about the various types of love were built into the very linguistic fabric of sixteenth-century English Christianity and aired in the inaugural controversies attending the earliest translations of Scripture into English. In 1528 William Tyndale was taken to task by Thomas More for his "heretical" translation of the New Testament into English, and chief among the sins More named was Tyndale's persistent rendering of the Vulgate's Latin word "caritas" as the English "love": "For though charity is always love, yet love is not, as you well know, always charity." Part of what More found objectionable was the substitution of what he considered to be the "broad and bawdy" word "love" for the more specific and less erotic charity: "since 'charity' signifies in Englishmen's ears not every common love, but a good, virtuous well-ordered love." More felt strongly that divine love required a special word of its own, not what we would call a "blanket" term, "common to the virtuous love that man bears to God and the lewd love there is between flekke and his make."[6]

What really riled More, however, was the suspicion that what lay behind Tyndale's choice of "love" over "charity" was an attempt to smuggle in through the choice of vocabulary the Reformed doctrinal emphasis on salvation by faith rather than through charitable good works:

> for since Luther and his cohorts have among their other condemnable heresies … that all our salvation depends on faith alone, and that … good works count for nothing, it therefore seems that [Tyndale] is purposely endeavoring to diminish the sacred sentiments that people associate with "charity," and is for that reason changing that name of holy, virtuous affection into the mere name of "love." (More, fol. lxxxv)

In other words, not only was human love itself liable to deceit and lewdness, the very *word* "love" could serve as a kind of feint.

Of course, this liability is not unique to this particular word, but, as words go, love is a rather important one, often with quite a bit riding on it. There is frequently a sense in Shakespeare's plays that characters' uses of the word "love" are less than honest, or at not as precise as we would wish, or perform multiple and sometimes contradictory functions. When King Lear asks his daughters "which of you shall we say doth love us most?" we get the feeling that "love" is doing a lot of different work in his request, some of it less than loving (1.1.46). Similarly, when Angelo, in *Measure for Measure*, tells Isabella her brother will live "if you give me love" (meaning her body), we can sense the elasticity of the term, even to the verge of misnomer (3.1.145). Such semantic uneasiness need not signify an attempt at euphemism or hypocrisy (let alone Reformation politics through other means). In the case of Angelo, for instance, he may be genuinely confused as to how to name the feelings Isabella prompts in him: "What's this, what's this? … What dost thou or what art thou, Angelo? / … What, do I love her / That I desire to hear her speak again?" (2.3.167–82). While Angelo ultimately classifies his attraction to Isabella as sexual and corrupt – "Most dangerous / Is that temptation that doth goad us on / To sin in loving virtue" (2.3.185–7) – it is arguable that Isabella's virtue *is* in fact appealing to his better nature – it's just that he isn't sure how else to name the attraction she stirs in him.

The slipperiness of the word "love" in Shakespeare's plays is often referred by its interpreters to the mysteries of the human heart. But we should not discount philological or grammatical factors for its elusiveness. The Greek of the New Testament uses at least six different words for love depending on the type and object thereof: *theleo* (inclined to; delight in); *agape* (to love, social or moral; affection or benevolence); *philadelphia* (brotherly love); *philarguria* (love of money); *philandros* (conjugal love); *philotheos* (lover of God).[7] So too, the Hebrew of the Pentateuch has least five roots, distinguishing among conjugal, compassionate, inordinate, delightful, and much-loved loves; even the Latin vulgate has both *caritas* and *diligere*. The humble Anglo-Saxon "love," on the other hand, is (as More complained) an all-purpose term, for in English we specify among types of love either by using an adjective – brotherly, filial, erotic, etc. – or sometimes, as Tyndale insisted, by scrutinizing the context alone. In *Othello*, for instance, "love" occurs sixty-six times, unadorned by any modifier. It describes a promiscuous array of affiliations, appearing in phrases as varied as Iago's question: "Whether I in any just term am affined / To love the Moor?" (1.1.39–40); Desdemona's declaration: "I did love the Moor to live with him" (1.3.244); Cassio's concern: "My general will forget my love and service" (3.3.18); and Othello's description of the Cypriots: "I have found great love amongst them" (2.1.197). In a play about the difficulty of knowing whether someone loves you, perhaps the trouble begins at the level of the sentence.

The need, at least in English, to decipher what is meant by "love" from the context of a statement is a point Tyndale had made in defending his translation: "the matter itself and the circumstances declare what love what hope and what faith is spoken of … though we say a man ought to love his neighbor's wife and his daughter a christen man doth not understand that he is commanded to desire his neighbor's wife nor his daughter." Peculiarities of English grammar and syntax were also involved: "verily charity is not known in English in the sense which *agape* requireth: we say not that this man hath a great charity to God but a great love … I say not charity God or charity your neighbor but love god and love your neighbor."[8] In other words, the English "love" is both noun and verb, but charity only the former.

Arguably Tyndale's claim that there is no verb form of charity is not wholly just: "to cherish" is at least a second cousin, etymologically speaking, to charity, deriving from the Old French *chérir* by way of the Middle English *cheriss*; charity from the Old French *chierté* and thence back to *caritas*. But as the Oxford English Dictionary also instructs us – in a point Tyndale might well have found useful – to "cherish" means to hold the loved object dear, to prize or to dote upon, perhaps even to an unseemly (idolatrous?) degree. It is no coincidence, perhaps, that the French word for the flesh – *la chair* – comes to mind). The sort of love Christ enjoined, by contrast, has the sense of an extension outward *beyond* the self, rather than of bringing something nearer to it – to give, rather than gather in.

There is of course something wonderfully axiomatic and essential about Tyndale's doughty Anglo-Saxon monosyllable; it conveys something of the fundamental quality of divine love with a simplicity redolent of Christ's own use of parable, features that continue to make his translation – well, beloved. But his reply to More did nothing to settle the question his work had raised, and throughout the sixteenth century we see translators of the Bible trying either to find or forge a vocabulary that could capture the nuances of love's several types. The Bishop's Bible of 1568/72 splits the difference, rendering Romans 13:9–10 as "Thou shalt love thy neighbor as thyself … charity worketh no ill to his neighbor." The 1611 King James version of Corinthians *does* sever love from charity: "charity suffereth long, and is kind; charity envieth not; charity vaunteth not itself, is not puffed up." Coverdale's 1535 English Bible coins the delightful "lovingkindness" to express divine love in two psalms: "Call to remembrance, O Lord, thy tender mercies and thy loving kindnesses" (25:6); "Nevertheless, my lovingkindess will I not utterly take from him" (89:33). English writers in this period were notoriously concerned with an alleged poverty of the English word-hoard relative to other classical and contemporary languages and worked to expand the lexicon by various neological methods (Shakespeare is recognized as a chief contributor to the effort). So, in addition to Coverdale's lovingkindness, we also find in this period such love-related coinages as love-affair (1598), love apple (1578), lovebird (1595), love-feast (1573), love-in-idleness (1578), love-juice (1593), lovelike (1621), loveling (1606), lovelock (1592), love-lorn (1637), lovemaking (1615), love-mate (1582), lovered (1609), loverlike (1552), loverly (1568), lovertine (1603), lovesickness (1592), loving cup (1584), loving knot (1596), and lovingness (1521).

None of these inventions are Shakespeare's, although he does use several of them. His plays similarly confront the ways in which love must be parsed and distinguished. And, as the list suggests, most of the inventive energy in this moment went into describing the nuances of erotic love; charity acquires few new forms in the period, and its compounds – charity ball, charity child – only begin to appear in the late eighteenth century. Interestingly enough, the one charity-related coinage of this moment – "self-charity" – does in fact belong to Shakespeare: Montano uses it in *Othello* to describe the actions taken in self-defense in a fight: "to defend ourselves … / When violence assails us" (2.3.184–5). The disproportionate dedication to increasing the vocabulary of erotic love could be due to the fact that divine love takes, in every sense of the term, no modifier. However, it could also be because it is inherently less interesting to us than our more familiar loves, which interest us precisely *because* of their frailties and vicissitudes. However magisterial the King James version of Corinthians, Tyndale's translation informs the versions that continue to be read aloud at weddings, precisely because it seems to apply more to the bond at hand. Shakespeare's Sonnet 116, that other nuptial favorite, comes closest to echoing the sense of Corinthians that love is eternal, unflappable, and unconditional: "Love is not love / Which alters when it alteration finds" (lines 2–3). However, the other 153 sonnets of the sequence (not to mention the thirty-some plays) tell quite a different story. An unfaltering, un-altering love may be enough to sustain a sonnet, but it is conspicuously lacking in drama.

The story of Christ's selfless death on the cross, of course, held the English stage throughout much of the medieval period, and in some parts of England well into the seventeenth century. But every play needs a problem, meaning that the faultiness and misfires of human loves make them exceedingly rich subjects for dramatic representation. Stories tend to seize on those times when, to cite *King Lear's* Gloucester, "Love cools, friendship falls off, brothers divide. In cities, mutinies; in countries, discord; in palaces, treason; and the bond cracked 'twixt son and father" (1.2.94–6). Who wants to go see a play about neighbors being kind to each other?

Of course, the rarity of divine love could be what makes it all the more remarkable in a fallen world, and spectacular in a play – somewhat like the fleeting balm of the few moments of loving-kindness in *King Lear*. Nor did divine love lack its conditions or austerities in this culture. God's grace may have been freely given in the sense that God didn't *have* to give it, but it did come with some strings attached, which depending on your brand of theology could range from the mild injunction that we should aspire to Christ-like behavior to the more severe enigma of predestination, which held that God had pre-selected an elect number of individuals for salvation and condemned the rest to eternal perdition. Jean Calvin may have defined brotherly love as "to do good to those from whom we expect the least recompense" (318),[9] but God's love for us was often described by theologians of the period as transactional, meaning that we ought to love God *because* of all his gifts. King Lear's shock that his elder daughters don't love him as they ought, considering "I gave you all!" can seem to us like the benighted thought of a king who thinks he can exchange land for love (2.4.243). However, the premise that children are indebted to their parents was not that different from the sentiments that we owe God thanks for the glories of the world or the gift of grace itself. Love in Shakespeare's plays is inevitably bound up with power relations. Conduct books of the period argued that parental love, being unalloyed by the needs of survival, was hence more purely love than the reciprocal. In fact, almost all loves in Shakespeare's plays must contend with the matter of inequality, a condition that is not just emotional (i.e. loving someone more than they love you) but social (between men and women, parents and children, and masters and servants).

Parental love is as complicated as any other kind of love in Shakespeare's plays, and not always what we think of as self-sacrificing or nurturing. Some scholars argue that due to a new emphasis in Shakespeare's moment on the psychic aspects of Christ's suffering on the cross, God the Father's more fearsome and awe-ful aspects come to the fore.[10] Fathers in Shakespeare's plays are often figures of censure. Prince Hal's father, Henry IV, is ashamed of his son's propensity for "riot and dishonor," wishing that the valiant Hotspur was his son instead: "O that it could be proved / That some night-tripping fairy had exchanged / In cradle-clothes our children where they lay" (1.1.85–7). Hermia's father in *A Midsummer Night's Dream* speaks of her as property: "As she is mine, I may dispose of her; / Which shall be either to this gentleman / Or to her death" (1.1.42–4). Portia's "will" is similarly curbed even though her father is dead. Leonato, in *Much Ado About Nothing*, threatens to kill his daughter for her alleged dishonor: "Thought I thy spirits were stronger than thy shames, / Myself would on the rearward of reproaches / Strike at thy life" (4.1.118–20). Juliet's father begins by considering her own choice of a husband – "She is the hopeful lady of my earth ... My will to her consent is but a part" (1.2.115–17) – but ends by threatening her with abandonment: "Graze where you will, you shall not house with me" (3.5.188). Desdemona's disappointed father is the first to voice the thought of her betrayal to Othello: "Look to her, Moor, if thou hast eyes to see: / She has deceived her father and may thee" (1.3.189–90). King Lear's rejection of Cordelia is the most extreme of these rejections: "Here I disclaim all my paternal care, / Propinquity, and property of blood, / And as a stranger to my heart and me / Hold thee from this forever" (1.1.107–10).

Such vindictiveness does not of course mean love is not present, but even when it is expressed affirmatively, the love of Shakespearean parents for their children (especially of fathers for daughters) can have a ferocious aspect. The stage image of King Lear cradling the body of Cordelia has been termed a "pieta," after the moment when Mary the mother of Jesus holds his crucified body in her arms. Shakespeare's swapping of genders is telling, for if fathers are forbidding figures, mother-love is comparatively absent from his works, and mothers rather scarce to begin with. Those who do exist seem to be cut from the same cloth as Lady Macbeth, who, though she knows "how tender 'tis to love the babe that milks me," tells her husband she would, "while it was smiling in my face, / Have plucked my nipple from his boneless gums / And dashed the brains out, had I so sworn / As you have done" (1.7.55–9). Lady Capulet seems less at ease with her daughter than the nurse, and even the latter – her fondness for her charge notwithstanding – urges bigamy upon Juliet as a means to cover up her own part in helping arrange the marriage to Romeo. Volumnia, mother of the warrior Coriolanus, proudly claims "when he was yet but tender-bodied and the only son of my womb ... To a cruel war I sent him" (1.3.4–11). Lear speaks of his "pelican daughters," referencing the legendary self-sacrificing pelican that feeds its children with the blood of its breast, but he speaks from the rather resentful parent pelican's point of view (3.4.72). Some of the tenderest moments of parent–child relations come in the reconciliations of Shakespeare's late plays, but often at great cost. Hermione, in *The Winter's Tale*, has kept herself alive for sixteen years in the hope of reunion with her lost child Perdita, but Perdita, abandoned by her father, has been kept alive by the kindness of strangers.

Probably the darkest aspect of divine love in this moment concerned the issue of predestination, the idea that salvation is determined by God – perhaps as long ago as prior to the creation of the world – meaning that human actions are not causes of our eternal deserts but merely effects of an eternal future already settled. This doctrine raises some disturbing questions: for instance, what kind of love requires pre-damning the majority of mankind prior to birth? Even more troubling may have been the question of how to know if one was among the saved: am I chosen? Even if one was so fortunate as to be among the elect and so confident as to be assured of it, there was always a disturbing sense that salvation was somewhat of a quota system, rather than a divine acknowledgment of a given person's virtues, since it was God's merits, not ours, that salvation instanced. Given such contexts, it is perhaps not surprising that Shakespeare's plays are populated by characters who find it difficult to believe they are loved. The leitmotif of cuckoldry is everywhere and haunting the purported humor of the situation of a man unwitting that his wife is unfaithful to him is the fear of being overlooked or going unrecognized, much as Leontes expresses to Hermione in *The Winter's Tale*: "You have mistook, my lady, / Polixenes for Leontes" (2.1.81–2).

In other words, in Shakespeare's works the analogy between human and divine loves may have been most resonant when it came to the difficulties of loving and being loved. Characters who have trouble believing that they are loved can call to mind the fears of the reprobate soul who either cannot believe he is chosen or fears he might be mistaken in his belief that he is. *Othello*, for instance, has been read by critics as an allegory of the problem Protestants faced in trying to ascertain signs of salvation in a world in which the desire for tangible and certain proof of God's presence was considered a kind of idolatry. Others have argued that the intensity of Othello's feelings for Desdemona recall the "jealous God" of the Old Testament; his focus on the handkerchief the Catholic investment in the supernatural power of things; and his doubts about Desdemona's fidelity a Protestant unable to trust in God's love of him (no wonder he's in trouble).[11]

Nor is the problem of keeping faith in love confined to erotic relationships; *King Lear* has not just one but two fathers who mistake the false devotions of children who don't love them at the expense of those who do. Shakespearean friendships are subject to the same fears and doubts as romantic relationships ("et tu, Brute?"). By some measures the most painful moment in Shakespeare's work comes in *Henry IV Part 2*, when Prince Hal, upon ascending to the throne, breaks his friend Falstaff's heart: "I know thee not, old man" (5.5.43).

Another source of dramatic conflict in Shakespeare's plays is the competition between different kinds of human love. Divine love was acknowledged to be the supreme form of love, but there was much rivalry among the more sublunary forms. For instance, a frequent movement of Shakespearean comedy is the assault on same-sex bonds in the pursuit of heterosexual union. In *A Midsummer Night's Dream*, Helena reproves Hermia when she believes she has forsaken their friendship: "will you rent our ancient love asunder, / To join with men in scorning your poor friend? / It is not friendly, 'tis not maidenly. / Our sex, as well as I, may chide you for it" (3.2.215–18). In *Much Ado About Nothing*, confirmed misogynist Benedict must break ranks with his male companions to become Beatrice's champion. Similar choices occur in *Love's Labour's Lost* and *Two Gentleman of Verona*.

Perhaps the fiercest competition between such ties comes in *The Merchant of Venice*. The seeming exorbitance of Antonio's language in describing his feelings for Bassanio tends to flummox modern critics. Whatever the nature of the feelings between the two men, there seems a disturbing asymmetry between Antonio's love for Bassanio and Bassanio's for him, although it is to the latter's credit (literally) that he hurries from his betrothed's company to try and rescue his friend from the consequences of the bond pledged on his behalf. However, Bassanio's gift of Portia's ring to the advocate who has saved Antonio suggests that homosocial and marital alliances are bound to conflict – as Antonio prompts Bassanio: "Let … my love withal / Be valued against your wife's commandment" (4.1.446–7). Portia's ultimate insistence that Antonio's claim upon her husband defer to hers is as ruthless in its own way as her treatment of Shylock. Characters named Antonio seem to share this fate. In *Twelfth Night*, the ship's captain Antonio believes himself abandoned by Viola's twin brother Sebastian when Viola, disguised as a boy, denies knowing him. His pain at the supposed rejection is, to our ears, extravagantly phrased:

> That most ungrateful boy...
> From the rude sea's enraged and foamy mouth
> Did I redeem ...
> His life I gave him, and did thereto add
> My love without retention, or restraint,
> All his in dedication. For his sake,
> Did I expose myself, pure for his love. (5.1.66–72)

In *Antony and Cleopatra*, the competition between erotic and political claims plays out on a world-historical stage with multiple casualties: Antony's none-too-subtly named page Eros kills himself rather than his master, and Antony's friend Enobarbus finds himself undone by his former general's generosity in the face of his own desertion.

Nevertheless, in this play as in all of Shakespeare's, there is always a lingering sense that, for all their failings – even, perhaps, because of them – human loves matter. They matter not merely as a simulacrum of divine love, or reminder of the superior value of the latter, but in and of themselves. Our loves for each other may be as flawed as we are, but they are uniquely our own, partly because, unlike divine love, they are customized – however destructively – to their objects. The conviction of specificity and the possessiveness that mark the love of another person – the sense that one's happiness is bound up in the love of a certain and unique person – are its saving graces as well its downfall. We are precious to each other in the particular. (God cannot love us as we love each other; for one thing, he is too far away. To him we appear like what Edgar relays of the sight from the top of Dover's cliff: "The crows and choughs that wing the midway air / Show scarce so gross as beetles ... one that gathers samphire ... seems no bigger than his head. / The fishermen that walk upon the beach / Appear like mice" [4.5.13–18].) Othello may pronounce against himself as one who loved not wisely but too well, as if love were a thing of which one could calculate the measure by degrees. But more often in these plays we feel, as in Antony's words to Cleopatra, "There's beggary in the love that can be reckoned" (1.1.15).

The conflicts between different sorts of human bonds are of course what plots are made of. More rare in Shakespeare's plays (as in life) are instances of characters enacting the kind of love described in Corinthians. It is not that there aren't plenty of Christ-like figures in the plays. Richard II, for instance, invokes the comparison on numerous occasions, as when describing his former courtiers as so many "Pilates" that "Have here delivered me to my sour cross / And water cannot wash away your sin" (4.1.240–1). Antonio, in *The Merchant of Venice*, seems bent on martyrdom at the hands of a vengeful Jew – "I am a tainted wether of the flock" – which in the context of the play's thematic concerns with law and mercy calls another sacrificial lamb to mind (4.1.114). Edgar in *King Lear* goes undercover as a Bedlam beggar, one of whom "who with roaring voices / Strike in their numbed and mortifièd arms, / Pins, wooden pricks, nails, sprigs of rosemary" (2.3.14–16). However, such claims can ring more of self-pity than compassion for another. Isabella, in *Measure for Measure*, can preach eloquently of charity to her predator Angelo: "Why all the souls that were, were forfeit once, / And he that might the vantage best have took / Found out the remedy" (2.2.75–7). But when told by Angelo that she can remedy her brother's plight with the forfeit of her chastity – "might there not be a charity in sin, / To save this brother's life?" – brotherly love can, quite literally, go hang: "More than our brother is our chastity" (3.1.186). Angelo's repugnant offer is a textbook instance of sexual harassment and the terms of her response may only mirror his coarseness but there is nonetheless something harsh and self-preening in Isabella's valuing of her body's sexual integrity over her brother's actual body.

Readers have identified other embodiments of Christian self-sacrifice in the plays. The more convincing tend to be female characters such as Cordelia or Desdemona. Cordelia's response to her father's conviction that she has reason not to love him – "No cause, no cause" (4.6.74) – is a paradigmatic instance of forgiveness. Desdemona dies claiming Othello's sins as her own. But even in these cases there is little sense of their suffering *achieving* anything, in the sense that Christ's suffering is alleged to have done; their deaths are simply instances of senseless waste. Perhaps only in Coriolanus does the hero's treating with his enemies and consequent death confer a benefit upon the community, although as in most tragedies, the hero's death doesn't save the world so much as bereave it of the one thing worth saving.

The ungainliness of such imitations betrays the Zeno's Paradox that haunts the mortal attempt to model Christ's example: always aspiring, never arriving. Reformation Christians were supposed to strive to imitate Christ, but always in the awareness of the presumption of actually fulfilling such an ambition. Perhaps the best instances of Christian loving in Shakespeare's plays are those that ruefully acknowledge the clumsiness of human effort to love like Christ, as well as the necessity for it. Acts of forgiveness are key to the resolutions of a number of Shakespeare's comedies (frequently, as in *Much Ado About Nothing*, *All's Well That Ends Well*, or *Measure for Measure*, this involves a woman forgiving a man). The closing movements of *The Tempest* also turn on the need for Prospero's forgiveness of his enemies, e epilogue begs our own: "As you from crimes would pardoned be, our indulgence set me free" (Epilogue, 19–20). (The forgiveness here lematic, however: Antonio has neither asked for nor accepts it.) The *Elizabethan Injunctions*, a list of religious recommendations, spoke of charity as "the knot of all Christian society" that could check "vain and contentious disputations" among Elizabeth I's subjects in matters of religion.[12] In displaying the universality of human folly and our providential preservation from the worst of its effects, Shakespeare's comedies could be said to urge a similar mutual generosity upon their audiences.

Similar cheek-turning motions are, not surprisingly, far harder to come by in the tragedies. For instance, among the number of Hamlet's myriad hesitations about fulfilling the ghost's charge, the idea of forgiving Claudius never appears. On the other hand, despite, or perhaps because of, *King Lear*'s setting in a pre-Christian universe in which all manner of barbarities have free reign, it is the play where we find characters come nearest to enacting the compassion (or "feeling-with") reminiscent of Christian charity. Many of these are instances of subordinates ministering to their alleged betters and abusers, at great risk to themselves. Kent defies banishment in order to serve his king; and Cornwall's servants rise up against him in order to defend and succor the blinded Gloucester. Gloucester himself is the agent of the play's most paradigmatic act of charity, when he acts to protect Lear from the storm despite having been forbidden to do so: "If I die for it – as no less is threatened me – the King my old master must be relieved" (3.3.17–18). It might of course be possible to describe Gloucester's charity to the king as a best-case instance of what we might call his signature move, the heedless act of affection that disregards the boundaries between licit and illicit objects of tenderness. But what makes his succor of the king so unlike the fathering of Edmund is that Gloucester recognizes and accepts the risk of damage rather than discounting it. He, like Lear, is an old man and as such particularly vulnerable to the elements and cruelty of one's children. No other character in the play knows what Lear suffers as he does. He indeed cares for Lear as he would care for himself, not so much hoping that consequences will not follow or that if they do he might be able to neutralize them, but because he *cannot not act* no matter what ensues. Gloucester may be guilty of loving in all the wrong places and at all the wrong times, but it is, at least, love, or an attempt at something like it.

In fact, the strongest charitable responses in Shakespeare's plays may lie less in the actions they represent than in the effects those representations have upon us as audience. Shakespeare repeatedly asks us to compass the difficult case – to extend our care and curiosity towards characters whose flaws challenge our sympathies and ethical standards. Sometimes, as in comedies, they display faults we may readily, even laughingly, acknowledge as our own. At other times there may be fewer grounds for self-recognition: most of us will never covet a crown, or kill a king, or divide a kingdom. The passions such projects inspire and require may seem far afield from our own, and perhaps easy from which to distance ourselves or to hold in censure. Some characters make us question the limits of empathy; *Macbeth* may persuade us to consider murderous usurpation from the point of view of the usurper, but does a Christ-like love really mean we should embrace an Iago or an Edmund? Yet time and again we are drawn towards difficult characters, cued by their charisma, our own curiosity, and of course the ingrained habits of literary response that ask us to see the world as a play's protagonist does, to feel with and for the figure before us. Is this love? Close enough.

Notes

1 *The Treasure of True Love, Or a Lively Description of the Love of Christ Unto His Spouse, Whom in Love He Hath Cleansed in His Blood from Sin* [...] (London, 1608), sig. C7^r^.
2 Adrian Savorine, *True Image of Christian Love*, trans. Richard Rikes (London, 1587), sig. A2^r^.
3 John Donne, "Holy Sonnet 17," in *The Norton Anthology of English Literature*, ed. Stephen Greenblatt, 9th edn. (New York: Norton, 2012), B:1414; Edmund Spenser, "Sonnet 68," in Savorine, *True Image*, 988.
4 *The Matthew Bible* (London, 1537), fol. lcxlvi^v^.
5 Ibid., sig. A1^r-v^.
6 See R. Chris Hassel, *Faith and Folly in Shakespeare's Comedies* (Atlanta: GA, 1984), 31. Sir Thomas More, *A Dialogue of Sir Thomas More, Knight ... Wherein Be Treated Divers Matters/ as of the Veneration & Worship of Images & Relics* (London, 1530), fol. lxxx^v^.
7 See C. S. Lewis, *The Four Loves* (n.p.: Harvest Books, 1971).
8 William Tyndale, *An Answer Unto Sir Thomas More's Dialogue Made by William Tyndale* (Antwerp, 1531), sig. B2^v^–B3^r^.
9 *A Commentary Upon the Epistle of Saint Paul to the Romans* (London, 1583), fol. 167^r^.
10 See, for instance, Debora Shuger, *The Renaissance Bible: Scholarship, Sacrifice and Subjectivity* (Berkeley and Los Angeles: University of California Press, 1998).
11 See, for instance, R. N. Watson, "Othello as Protestant Propaganda," in *Religion and Culture in Reformation England*, ed. Claire McEachern and Debora Shuger (Cambridge: Cambridge University Press, 1997), 234–57; and Lynda E. Boose, "Othello's Handkerchief: The Recognizance and Pledge of Love," *ELR* 5, no. 3 (1975): 360–74.
12 Gerald Bray (ed.), *Documents of the English Reformation* (Minneapolis, MN: Fortress Press, 1994), 345.

8

ADRIAN STREETE

Sin and Evil

Religious identity in Shakespeare's day is experienced in complex, multiple ways.[1] This is why scholars of early modern English religion often refer to religious belief as a spectrum.[2] During their lifetime a person could adopt a number of positions on that spectrum: John Donne started his life as a Roman Catholic and ended it as the Protestant minister of St. Paul's Cathedral; Ben Jonson was born a Protestant, converted to Roman Catholicism in prison, and then re-converted back to Protestantism some years later.

In Shakespeare's case, direct evidence for his own religious beliefs is patchy and partial. Whatever his personal faith might have been, Shakespeare wrote plays to entertain and to make money. Like all playwrights writing for the public theaters, he had to appeal to diverse audiences who held a variety of religious views.[3] This is another reason why his writings cover a wide range of religious identities and concepts.

Similar to his friend and rival Jonson, Shakespeare seems to have disliked extremes in religion. *King John* (*c.*1595) contains passages of anti-Catholic polemic criticizing the papal envoy Pandolf, and in plays like *Twelfth Night* (*c.*1600), *All's Well That Ends Well* (*c.*1602–4), and *Pericles* (*c.*1607–8), the Puritans come under fire. Shakespeare was also deeply interested in the two other major Abrahamic religions, Judaism and Islam, as we see in *The Merchant of Venice* (*c.*1596) and *Othello* (*c.*1604). Yet even when discussing Judaism and Islam, Christianity provides the major religious framework for Shakespeare's explorations of sin and evil. That many of these discussions are informed by Protestantism says less about what Shakespeare believed personally and more about the central place of that religion in early modern England.

Consequently, this chapter will look at how sin and evil are framed and debated in early modern Protestantism. It will argue that while Shakespeare's understanding of these topics is clearly informed by this Protestant framework, he uses sin and evil for a diverse array of dramatic ends.

The Theology of Sin and Evil

Early modern religious culture is steeped in the theology of sin and evil. Formal theological tracts, sermons, catechisms, books of popular piety, and literary works all draw upon biblical discussion of these topics, especially Genesis 1–3. In the Elizabethan Book of Common Prayer, the Minister performing the sacrament of baptism first reminds the congregation that "all men be conceived and borne in sin." He then asks those gathered to pray that God "will grant to these children, that thing which by nature they cannot have, that they may be baptised with water and the holy Ghost, and received into Christ's holy church, and be made lively members of the same" (141).[4] According to this theology, drawn from St. Augustine, sin is a kind of deficiency or privation of the good. This is a consequence of what Augustine calls Original Sin (*peccatum originale*) and the Fall. In the Garden of Eden God forbids Adam and Eve to eat of "the tree of knowledge of good and evil"; the penalty for doing so is death (Gen. 2:17). The Serpent tells Eve that God's warning is false, that if she eats the fruit of the tree she will not die, and that both she and Adam "shall be as gods, knowing good and evil" (3:5). Adam and Eve both eat the fruit of the forbidden tree, and this Original Sin causes God to punish them and to cast them out of the garden (3:9–24). In Reformed theology, the sacrament of baptism offers an external assurance that the divine grace made possible by Christ's sacrifice on the cross for humanity's sins will be made available to the individual.[5] Baptism is a promise that a person may in time "receive remission of their sins by spiritual regeneration" (BCP, 142), thus confirming their salvation. In the meantime, humans will continue to sin. Most of these will be everyday or actual sins (*peccatum actuale*) caused by an inherently sinful nature. Other sins may be more serious: acts such as blasphemy or apostasy are mortal sins (*peccatum mortalia*) that can be signs of damnation. Humans must therefore continue to ask God for forgiveness for sin in the hope that the "spiritual regeneration" promised by baptism will eventually be realized.

We can be reasonably sure that Shakespeare would have encountered this theology from hearing the Book of Common Prayer and the Homilies read in church.[6] A particular passage in the "Homily for the Nativity and Birth of Jesus" helps us to understand how sin and evil were commonly discussed. The passage in question discusses Adam before and after the Fall:

> Instead of the image of God, he was now become the image of the devil; instead of the citizen of heaven, he was become the bond-slave of hell, having in himself no one part of his former purity and cleanness, but being altogether spotted and defiled; insomuch that now he seemed to be nothing else but a

> lump of sin, and therefore by the just judgement of God was condemned to everlasting death.[7]

Similar imagery recurs throughout the plays. In Act 2, Scene 5 of *Twelfth Night*, Sir Toby and Sir Andrew joke with Maria about the letter she has delivered to gull Malvolio. Toby asks Maria, "Wilt thou set thy foot o'my neck?" (2.5.155) – much like St. Michael does to the defeated Devil[8] – and asks whether he will "become thy bondslave?" (2.5.157–8). Maria explains her plan to have Malvolio make a fool of himself before Olivia, saying it will "turn him into a notable contempt" (2.5.169), and the scene concludes with Toby saying that he will follow Maria "To the gates of Tartar [i.e. Hell], thou most excellent devil of wit" (2.5.170). This is a comic Fall with Maria as the "Devil" and Toby and Andrew as her fallen accomplices in "evil." More ominously in the first tetralogy of history plays, Richard, Duke of Gloucester, later Richard III, is variously referred to as a "heap of wrath, foul indigested lump" (2 *Henry VI*, 5.1.157), "an indigested and deformèd lump" (*3 Henry VI*, 5.6.51), and a "Foul devil" and "lump of foul deformity" (*Richard III*, 1.2.50; 1.2.57).[9] As we will see later, this sinful, devilish agency is actively embraced by Richard, as expressed in the language of the Homily. Shakespeare also returns to the notion of sin as an indelible spot. When Richard II learns of Bushy, Bagot, and Green's confederacy with Bolingbroke, he asks that "Terrible hell / Make war upon their spotted souls for this!" (3.2.133–4). When Hamlet confronts Gertrude about her relationship with Claudius, she says: "Thou turn'st mine eyes into my very soul, / And there I see such black and grainèd spots / As will not leave their tinct" (3.4.89–91). When Iago is trying to "prove" Desdemona's infidelity to Othello, he says that her handkerchief is "Spotted with strawberries" (3.3.436). Iago's choice of adjective is designed to evoke moral (and sexual) impurity.[10] Only a few lines later Othello is crying "Arise, black vengeance, from thy hollow cell" (3.3.448). Perhaps most memorably, Lady Macbeth's "damned spot" (5.1.30) marks her tainted flesh and conscience that cannot retain their original "purity and cleanness" (see 5.1.37). Throughout his writings, Shakespeare reshapes theological commonplaces about sin and evil that his audience would have known, weaving them into the fabric of scenes, dialogues, and dramatic identities.

Original Sin, the Fall, and Typology

Early modern Protestants were taught that the Old Testament prefigures the saving work of Christ in the New Testament. Whereas Genesis shows us the old, sinful Adam, Christ in the Gospels is the new, sinless Adam who redeems humanity through his sacrifice (see Rom. 5:8–21; Eph. 4:22–4). This kind of interpretation is known as typology.[11] The idea here is that Old Testament characters like Adam are figures or types who prefigure or anticipate the arrival of Christ, the fulfillment of all types. As the Apostle Paul explains in Romans 6:6, "our old man [Adam] is crucified with him [Christ], that the body of sin might be destroyed, that henceforth we should not serve sin." Shakespeare weaves the story of the old and new Adam into a number of his plays. He also manipulates the idea of typology for diverse dramatic ends.

A good example is found in *A Comedy of Errors* (*c*.1593). Possibly written for a learned legal audience at the Inns of Court, this comedy of mistaken identity, based on a play by the ancient Roman playwright Plautus, is set in Ephesus, an ancient city near the northeastern Mediterranean. Ephesus – and Corinth, another location mentioned in the play – is also associated with the Apostle Paul.[12] Like Shakespeare's other classical plays, *The Comedy of Errors* intertwines the pagan and the Christian to dramatic effect. At the start of Act 4, Scene 3, the servant Dromio of Syracuse meets his master Antipholus. Dromio mistakenly thinks that his master has been in prison and asks if he has been released by the sergeant: "What, have you got redemption from the picture of old Adam new apparelled?" (4.3.13–14).[13] The joke here works on a number of levels. After the Fall, Adam and Eve feel shame at their nakedness and they and God cover their bodies with clothing (Gen. 3:7, 21). Like the first parents, the sergeant's clothes are a reminder that, like the old Adam, he is also a sinful creature. The idea that Antipholus could receive "redemption" from such a figure is meant to be ridiculous. The sergeant might release him from prison, but only the new Adam, Christ, can offer redemption from sin. The sergeant is no type of Christ, no "figure of him that was to come" (Rom. 5:14), as Paul says. Typology is part of the verbal fun here because it fails dramatically. The audience know that it is actually Antipholus of Ephesus who has been arrested. (Much of the play's comedy arises because the Dromios are identical twins who are mistakenly identified as each other.) Dromio is speaking to the wrong man. Antipholus of Syracuse is understandably confused: "What Adam dost thou mean?" (4.3.14). Dromio's reply offers another comic riff on typological reading: "Not that Adam that kept the paradise, but that Adam that keeps the prison. He that goes in the calf's skin that was killed for the prodigal. He that came behind you, sir, like an evil angel, and bid you forsake your liberty" (4.3.15–18). The sergeant is not Adam but instead wears clothing made from the skin of the calf killed by the father of the Prodigal Son (Luke 15:11–32). The end of the line may also allude to Christ's rebuke to Peter, "Get thee behind me Satan" (Matt. 16:23). While both of these examples shift the audience's focus from the Old to the New Testament, they have nothing to do with the typological understanding of the old and new Adam. Antipholus's reply – "I understand thee not" (4.3.19) – perfectly captures the comic confusion of Dromio's attempt at theology. Partly the enjoyment of this exchange for Shakespeare's learned audience lies in watching two classical "pagans" who, historically speaking, know nothing of Christian theology, debating its terms and concepts to comedic ends.[14] Yet, as Patricia Parker has noted, the play's juxtaposition of classical and biblical modes may also have had far-reaching theological implications for that audience.[15]

Shakespeare also uses typology to consider gender. In *Much Ado About Nothing* (*c.*1598), dramatic and comic tension is produced because Beatrice challenges the cultural assumption that an unmarried woman must inevitably be, in the words of her uncle Leonato, "fitted with a husband" (2.1.42). Perhaps not surprisingly, she turns to Eden to reject this logic:

> Not till God make men of some other metal than earth: would it not grieve a woman to be overmastered with a piece of valiant dust? to make an account of her life to a clod of wayward marl? No, uncle, I'll none: Adam's sons are my brethren, and truly I hold it a sin to match in my kindred. (2.1.43–7)

Because God made man from the earth, for a woman to obey a man as the marriage rite enjoins is for her to agree to be mastered by nothing else than dust. In order to make marriage equitable, the entire Eden story would have to be other than it is. Beatrice does not mention the verse stating that Eve is made from a rib of Adam's side (Gen. 2:21–4). Rather she takes seriously the claim that men and women are of "one flesh" (Gen. 2:24). This being the case, women cannot be subjected to men because all humans must be "brethren." To marry a man is to marry one's brother, recasting marriage as a sinful act of incest. This is a comedic *reductio ad absurdum* of one of early modern Protestant culture's central narratives. It is also a slyly subversive speech. Beatrice attacks what we might call the typology of patriarchy. The claim that a single woman can only achieve her proper fulfillment in marriage is questioned both here and in the remainder of the play. Even when they "formally" reconcile to marriage at the end of play, Beatrice never verbally consents to the match. She continues to quibble and equivocate, saying that she only yields "upon great persuasion" (5.4.93–4). Benedick then "stop[s]" (5.4.96) her mouth with a kiss and she says no more. This is a decidedly ambivalent moment. Is this patriarchal victory absolute or temporary? Like his intended, Benedick has also spoken "against" (5.4.103) marriage throughout the play. How sincere is his conversion? Although the generic demands of comedy insist on the formal resolution of marriage, the end of *Much Ado About Nothing* hardly represents a ringing endorsement of the institution. The subject of Eden is likely to remain a point of contention for this particular couple long after the wedding music has stopped.

Prophecy and Evil

The Gardener's prophecy in *Richard II* is only one of many that litter the History plays.[16] Shakespeare uses prophetic language and imagery to explore the historical effects of sin and evil, especially as they relate to monarchical power. We might think here of the prophetic words of John of Gaunt in *Richard II* (see 2.1.31–68), the prophetically inspired insults of Queen Margaret to Richard, Duke of Gloucester in *Richard III* (see 1.3.110–303), or Joan la Pucelle's language of maleficent prophecy in *Henry VI Part 1* (see 5.3.1–29). In *Henry IV Part 2*, the king reflects on his inability to contain civil dissent in his kingdom. He recalls the words of the king that he deposed, Richard II, which have now "proved a prophecy":[17]

> "Northumberland, thou ladder by the which
> My cousin Bullingbrook ascends my throne?" –
> Though then, God knows, I had no such intent
> But that necessity so bowed the state
> That I and greatness were compelled to kiss. –
> "The time shall come," thus did he follow it,
> "The time will come that foul sin, gathering head,
> Shall break into corruption." So went on,
> Foretelling this same time's condition
> And the division of our amity. (3.1.68–78)

As he does elsewhere, Henry IV alternates between the effort to atone for the sin of deposing Richard and trying to justify what he has done. The king is haunted by the thought that civil discord is the price he must pay for his foundational sin. He attempts to justify his actions by using the word "necessity." While this can mean something unavoidable, in the late sixteenth century the word gained more specific political connotations.[18] Drawing on the writings of ancient historians like Tacitus and on modern theorists like Machiavelli, thinkers like the influential neo-Stoic Justus Lipsius argued that necessity is linked both to self-interest and self-preservation. A ruler has to do what is necessary, which may not always correspond to what is right. Necessity, in other words, may cover a multitude of sins. It is, as a character in another play puts it, "deceit, bred by necessity" (*3 Henry VI*, 3.3.68).

Warwick picks up on the king's use of the word necessity, arguing that "a man may prophecy, / With the near aim, of the main chance of things / As yet not come to life, who in their seeds / And weak beginnings lie intreasured" (3.1.77–80). Essentially Warwick claims that prophecy is advanced guesswork. Most states are unstable and so a prophecy predicting instability could be made at almost any time by anyone. He continues: "by the necessary form of this / King Richard might create a perfect guess" that Northumberland would turn on him and on Henry (3.1.82–3). Because prophecy deals in cause and effect that can be predicted by almost anyone, it can be used to justify action based on necessity. It can validate contingent actions that may not be virtuous but which are politically effective. Henry agrees: "Are these things then necessities? / Then let us meet them like necessities; / And that same word even now cries out on us" (3.1.87–9) and he resolves to oppose the rebellion led by Northumberland.[19]

The connection between prophecy, sin, and evil is discussed in other dramatic genres. Julius Caesar recounts the prophetic dream of his wife Calpurnia. She sees his statue bleeding and the citizens of Rome bathing their hands in the blood, "warnings and portents / And evils imminent" (2.2.80–1), as Caesar notes. It is the alternative interpretation of the dream offered by the conspirator Decius that persuades Caesar to go to the Senate and, of course, to his death. In *Hamlet* Gertrude expresses her fear for Ophelia's mental condition as follows: "To my sick soul, as sin's true nature is, / Each toy seems prologue to some great amiss" (4.5.16–17). It is the queen's awareness of her own sinful nature that validates the prophecy here, an unusual spin on the belief that prophets are inspired by God and are therefore godly individuals.

In *Measure for Measure* Angelo also uses prophecy to reject Isabella's argument that her brother should not die for breaking the law:

> The law hath not been dead, though it hath slept.
> Those many had not dared to do that evil
> If the first that did th'edict infringe
> Had answered for his deed. Now 'tis awake,
> Takes note of what is done, and like a prophet
> Looks in a glass that shows what future evils –
> Either now, or by remissness new conceived,
> And so in progress to be hatched and born –
> Are now to have no successive degrees,
> But here they live, to end. (2.2.93–102)

Angelo first says that if the law had been enacted harshly when the first crime against it was committed, no one would break the law again. But although the law has been laxly enforced, it now awakens and is personified as a prophet who is able to look into the future to see what sin and evil might ensue. With access to this privileged knowledge, the prophetic law is now able to prevent those sins from ever coming to light, killing them before they are able to be birthed.[20] Angelo depicts the prophetic law as committing infanticide, perhaps even abortion. That he sees this as a necessary sin in order to prevent, as he believes, the greater sin of sexual infidelity is shocking indeed. It is a cruel, perhaps even evil morality that Angelo enforces in Vienna.

Election and Damnation

Like much of the liturgy found in the Book of Common Prayer, the rite of baptism quoted earlier is colored by the theology of election and reprobation. This idea is found in many forms of Christianity. Yet the claim that God has predestined before their creation that some humans will be saved and others damned receives particular emphasis in early modern Protestantism. During Shakespeare's day there was considerable theological controversy over these points. Speaking generally, then, many forms of Roman Catholicism acknowledge that, through the exercise of free will, humans may contribute in some form towards their salvation. By contrast, many forms of Protestantism believe that free will is tainted by the Fall and that saving grace is a gift solely from God. The divine decree of election and damnation cannot be altered by human action. During Shakespeare's day, the question of whether a person might know definitively if they were elect or reprobate was a pressing pastoral concern. Taking their lead from theologians like Calvin, both Church and state were exercised by this subject: how far should ministers and preachers go in exploring predestination with their congregations?[21] Both Elizabeth and James passed legislation that attempted to curb discussion of these points. Too much pastoral exploration of election and reprobation could be seen as impious prying into God's mysteries. There was a related concern that too much emphasis on this subject could lead vulnerable souls to despair of their salvation. Yet despite these concerns, election and reprobation remained at the center of theological, pastoral, and literary debate.[22]

Shakespeare was very interested in the epistemological ambiguities presented by election and reprobation: signs may lead a person to think that they are saved or damned.[23] Signs are also uncertain things that can be imperfectly known or else lead a character and an audience astray.[24] Full knowledge of election or damnation is only ever confirmed after death. Shakespeare also evokes election and reprobation as a way of exploring the validity of an individual's spiritual reformation away from sinfulness. *Henry IV Part 1* dramatizes the young Prince Hal's relationship with Sir John Falstaff. In Act 1, Scene 2, Shakespeare returns repeatedly to the language of predestination. Falstaff starts by undercutting Hal's claims to kingly graces, quibbling on how Hal should be addressed: "majesty I should say, for grace thou wilt have none" (1.2.13–14). The possibility that Hal lacks kingly and godly grace is emphasized by his association with Falstaff and his crew of roaring boys and girls engaged in all manner of dubious activities. Can an "heir apparent" (1.2.46) who behaves in such a way dispense righteous justice once he is king? Falstaff tells Hal that he heard a Lord of the Council speaking about him in the street. Hal responds with a biblical allusion to Proverbs which Falstaff then mocks:

> O, thou hast damnable iteration, and art indeed able to corrupt a saint. Thou hast done much harm upon me, Hal, God forgive thee for it. Before I knew thee, Hal, I knew nothing, and now am I, if a man should speak truly, little better than one of the wicked. I must give over this life, and I will give it over. By the Lord, an I do not I am a villain. I'll be damned for never a king's son in Christendom. (1.2.72–7)

At the start of the speech, Falstaff uses language associated with predestinarian Puritanism. He says that Hal is quoting the Bible in a damnable way in order to corrupt him from his godly status as "a saint," that is to say, one who has assurance of their election. Falstaff mockingly adopts this Puritan persona and language. Yet the suggestion that the Bible is being used in such an ungodly way that it requires forgiveness from God also carries a frisson of unease. This is a deeply religious culture where the Bible is venerated as the word of God and a sacred book. Jesting with Scripture is always a double-edged activity.

Falstaff then shifts focus, saying that before he knew Hal he had no knowledge of his predestined status; now, having consorted with the prince, he believes himself marked for damnation. He plans to repent, to "give over" his life to God because, if he does not, this will confirm his damnation (see 1.2.74–8). He refuses to imperil his soul for Hal's sake. Of course, the audience are not meant to take Falstaff's expression of intent entirely seriously, as subsequent events prove. Nevertheless, it is worth noting how in this speech Falstaff offers in miniature the narrative of repentance undertaken by Hal over the course of this play, *Henry IV Part 2*, and *Henry V*. Hal explains what this will mean to the audience in his speech that concludes the scene:

> So when this loose behaviour I throw off,
> And pay the debt I never promisèd,
> By how much better than my word I am,
> By so much shall I falsify men's hopes.
> And like bright metal on a sullen ground,

My reformation, glitt'ring o'er my fault,
Shall show more goodly, and attract more eyes
Than that which hath no foil to set it off.
I'll so offend, to make offence a skill,
Redeeming time when men think least I will. (1.2.168–77)

It is Hal's turn to offer the audience a double-edged speech. He assures them that the bad behavior and dissolute company that he keeps is only temporary. Indeed, his later "reformed" self will seem all the more goodly/godly by comparison.[25] Yet the claim that Hal "make[s] offence a skill" is troubling. He is knowingly tricking those who watch him, manipulating vice in a way that casts doubt on his probity. Can sin be used in the service of virtue? Redemption has both theological and fiscal implications.[26] Indeed, we might notice the various metaphors of artifice used here. Hal claims to be better than his word, but he still uses those words to "falsify men's hopes." His "reformation" is likened to a "glitt'ring" metal applied to a "sullen" surface: the appearance may be shiny and attractive to the eyes but what lies underneath remains tainted by sin. There is even the hint of idolatry here: Hal will be praised for having the image of virtue, not the thing itself. Is his "reformation" truly godly or is it an expedient act of dissembling? These are problems that Shakespeare explores further in *Henry V*.

The Contingency of Sin

Once he becomes Henry V, Hal rejects Falstaff in summary fashion, telling him to repent, consider his state of grace, and reform himself (2 *Henry IV*, 5.5.43–68). Falstaff tells Shallow not to "grieve at this," that Hal "must seem thus to the world," and that what they heard was "but a colour," a pretence (5.5.72–80). Once more we are in a world where signs of spiritual reformation are decidedly ambiguous and not necessarily to be trusted. As Shallow says, this is "A colour I fear that you will die in, Sir John" (5.5.81), a prophecy that indeed comes to pass in *Henry V* (see 2.3.5–36). As we saw in the discussion of *Henry IV Part 2*, Shakespeare is interested in the political value of sin. Is it possible to sin well? Can sin ever be used contingently to achieve something good? The action opens with the Archbishop of Canterbury and Bishop of Ely worrying about a bill in parliament that would mean their losing lands to the state. They discuss Henry's "reformation," stating that he is now "full of grace" (1.1.22) and that spiritual contemplation "whipped th' offending Adam out of him, / Leaving his body as a paradise / T' envelop and contain celestial spirits" (1.1.29–31; see also 1.2.29–32). Yet this new paradise is a ground where "commonwealth affairs," "war," and "policy" (1.1.41–5) become the focus of attention. Like

Hal, the prelates see his former behavior as a "veil of wildness" (1.1.64) that obscured his true nature. Are they concerned with the king's spiritual health? Or do they see the king's reformed self as something that can be manipulated for their own ends? As Canterbury says, "miracles are ceased, / And therefore we must needs admit the means / How things are perfected" (1.1.67–9). Many early modern Protestants were skeptical of non-biblical miracles. Canterbury imagines a disenchanted, even Machiavellian world, one where contingent actions or "means" are the way to achieve "perfection." This may strike us as a somewhat dubious claim. The word "means" has a wide range of possible meanings in early modern English. While it may simply connote the methods used to achieve an end, it can also mean a mediator between God and man, an opportunity, or a midway position between two extremes. It can also refer to a tenant who acts as an intermediary between a Lord and another tenant in feudal law.[27] This throws new light on the Archbishop's intentions. By deflecting the king's attention away from ecclesiastical land and towards France, Henry will act as an inadvertent intermediary between the Church and Parliament, enabling the former to protect their feudal and political status. Canterbury's long and deliberately confusing speech about the Salic Law and Henry's claim to the French throne shows the prelate willing to risk much in persuading the king to act: "The sin upon my head, dread sovereign" (1.2.97). The Archbishop urges "blood and sword and fire, to win your right" (1.2.131). This claim may be sanctioned by just war theory, but it is also somewhat jarring coming from an individual who, in a post-Reformation context, is the most powerful primate in England, one responsible for the spiritual welfare of the state.[28] The last word spoken by Canterbury before Henry decides to go to war is "policy" (1.2.220). While this term may refer to civil order, it also implies Machiavellian means, relating to the cunning use of politics to achieve contingent ends. This is another kind of necessity. Canterbury teaches Henry how to sin expediently.

The king shows that he has learned his lesson in the terrifying speech before the gates of Harfleur. He conjures up a vision of hellish assault by his soldiers:

> What is it then to me if impious war,
> Arrayed in flames like to the prince of fiends,
> Do with his smirched complexion all fell feats
> Enlinked to waste and desolation? (3.4.16–18)

Henry implicitly likens himself to the Devil, the infernal commander of damned souls who, nonetheless, does not take responsibility for the evil done in his name. The culpability is not his but rather the Governor of Harfleur.

The king asks him: "What rein can hold licentious wickedness / When down the hill he holds his fierce career?" (3.4.22–3). As the out-of-control carriage careers downhill, the person who once held the reins can only watch as it causes carnage below. The audience is meant to be discomforted by the king's logic and by his refusal to take responsibility. This is indeed a devilish thing to do. Shakespeare is alluding here to some of the central paradoxes within the Christian theology of sin and evil. God is responsible for creating all things (see Isaiah 45:7), yet the Devil is the agent of evil.[29] The Devil is agent of evil, but humans are responsible for its commission. Henry is God's representative on earth who also behaves like the Devil. The king is an absolute monarch who refuses culpability for what his soldiers might do to the residents of Harfleur. The city submits and the threat passes. Yet Henry still refuses to observe conventional theological distinctions: "There is some soul of goodness in things evil / Would men observingly distil it out. / For our bad neighbour makes us early stirrers, / Which is both healthful and good husbandry" (4.1.4–7).[30] Seeing evil performed makes us more likely to do good. Henry may be right, but the idea that evil may be used to do good is a contentious one in early modern theology. As St. Augustine asks, "how can a bad will produce a good?"[31] Critics have argued that in a time of war Henry needs to do what works, not necessarily what is right. And yet the play returns insistently to the king's willingness to harness sinfulness for contingent ends: "if it be a sin to covet honour / I am the most offending soul alive" (4.3.28–9). A similar logic is used by another conflicted figure, the puritanical deputy Angelo in *Measure for Measure*. Attempting to persuade Isabella to sleep with him in exchange for her brother's life he asks her, "Might there not be a charity in sin / To save this brother's life?" (2.4.63–4). When she refuses, he echoes Henry before Harfleur, claiming that Claudio's ensuing death will be solely her fault: "thy unkindness shall his death draw out / To lingering sufferance" (2.4.167–8). Shakespeare shows us that authority is most culpable when it refuses to take responsibility for the sin and evil that it either permits or performs.

The Devil's Agency?

As we saw in the previous section, the question of who is ultimately responsible for sin – God, the Devil, or humans – is a vexed one in Christian theology. The problem is compounded by the fact that the Devil is an arch manipulator, a liar whose promises and language can never be trusted. As Lucifer, he was once as bright as a morning star.[32] As Satan in the popular imagination he continues to use all the tools available to him, even those properly belonging to God, to cause harm. When the devilish Richard

Gloucester, later Richard III, plots to get rid of those who stand in his way, he shows the audience how he will achieve his aims:

> But then I sigh, and with a piece of scripture
> Tell them that God bids us do good for evil.
> And thus I clothe my naked villainy
> With odd old ends, stol'n forth of holy writ,
> And seem a saint when most I play the devil. (1.3.334–8)

The possibility, as Antonio puts it in *The Merchant of Venice* (*c.*1596), that "The devil can cite Scripture for his purpose" (1.3.94) is given full expression by Richard. He can persuade others to do evil in the name of good, manipulating the spiritual and rhetorical power of Scripture, and appearing most saintly when he is in fact doing his worst. Part of Richard's dramatic appeal, especially in the first three acts of the play, is that he involves the audience. Theatrical pleasure is created in seeing how and when Richard enacts his plans. Does this make the audience complicit in his devilish activity? Perhaps. Evil can only have agency if humans facilitate its workings. Similarly, Richard cannot exist without the participation of the audience. He states that "like the formal Vice, Iniquity, / I moralise two meanings in one word" (3.1.82–3). He devilishly prods the audience, goading them into taking his side, encouraging them to pay attention to him above all others, feeding off their energy. Once he attains the crown in the final two acts, his addresses to the audience fall off, and the power of his devilish activities lessens.

More than his predecessor, James VI and I had a keen interest in supernatural forces. An account of his involvement in the trial of some witches in North Berwick called *Newes from Scotland* was published in 1592, followed by his better-known *Daemonologie* of 1597. James became king of England in 1603 and a few years later Shakespeare offered one of his most far-reaching dramatic explorations of demonic suggestion in *Macbeth* (1606). As in *Richard III*, the relationship between devilish agency and truth is to the fore. When Macbeth is named Thane of Cawdor, thus affirming the Witches' prophecy, Banquo says: "What, can the devil speak true?" (1.3.105). And in Act 5 when Birnam Wood advances in seeming defiance of nature, once more proving the Witches right, Macbeth begins "To doubt th' equivocation of the fiend, / That lies like truth" (5.5.42–3). Between these two dramatic poles, this is a play where truth and lies are dangerously unmoored. Devilish behavior is cloaked in human guise and "nothing is, / But what is not" (1.3.140–1). The closer we are to evil the harder it is to tell whether the fair is foul, or the foul is fair.

Macbeth fervently wishes that his assassination of Duncan "Could trammel up the consequence and catch / With his surcease success" (1.7.3–4).

This is like imagining that sin is a bee sting; painful for sure, but a one-off thing that, with the right treatment, can be localized and contained.[33] What Macbeth finds instead is that the sting spreads. Sin is restless, spreading through the body politic, goading him into further wickedness in the vain hope that the next act will be the defining one that will make everything stable once more. But there is no fixity to be found. He now sees things "Which might appal the devil" (3.4.50) and despises living in a twilight world where evil infects the waking and sleeping mind: "Better be with the dead / Whom we, to gain our peace, have sent to peace, / Than on the torture of the mind to lie / In restless ecstasy" (3.2.19–22). The irony is that no act of sin can attain peace for its actor. Sin is a kind of nullity that, paradoxically, can never be satisfied. This is why when Macduff says that "Not in the legions / Of horrid hell can come a devil more damned / In evils to top Macbeth," Malcolm replies with a checklist of all Macbeth's surfeits: he is "bloody, / Luxurious, avaricious, false, deceitful, / Sudden, malicious, smacking of every sin / That has a name" (4.3.55–60). He is sinfully excessive, insatiable even, like the evil he represents. His reign ends with him being served by Seyton (a homonym for Satan) and he is described as one whose evil exceeds even language: "The devil himself could not pronounce a title / More hateful to mine ear" (5.7.9–10); "I have no words; / My voice is in my sword, thou bloodier villain / Than terms can give thee out" (5.8.6–8). Macbeth is beyond words. Someone in this state is, quite literally, no-thing. As I noted at the start of this chapter, evil was understood in this period as privative. Evil is not a thing as such but an absence of the good. In this sense, evil is nothing. Macbeth concludes his most despairing speech by saying that life "is a tale / Told by an idiot, full of sound and fury / Signifying nothing" (5.5.25–7). For all the evil that he does, Macbeth ends with nothing, morally, politically, and metaphysically.[34] Through him, Shakespeare explores the paradox that the nothing of evil can, through sinful agents, quickly become a something that can topple minds and states alike.

Conclusion

Although Shakespeare was not a theologian, sin and evil were clearly central to his dramatic world. His theatrical imagination was sparked by the possibilities of sin, its moral implications for identity and state, and by the intriguing paradox that evil is a nothing that "creates." Shakespeare shows how sin and evil cause mayhem in a fallen world. He also shows how they may be used for reasons of expediency or necessity. In some cases, an inclination towards evil might even help to attain the greater good. Shakespeare works in a culture that tends to view good and evil in absolute terms. Sometimes, as with Iago or Edmund, he presents us with characters who may well be absolutely evil. But he is also interested in less absolute conceptions of good and evil, asking us to consider the moral and ethical utility of the choices that characters make at relative points between these theological poles.

Notes

1 I am grateful to Hannibal Hamlin for many helpful suggestions on this chapter.

2 See Peter Lake with Michael Questier, *The Antichrist's Lewd Hat: Protestants, Papists and Players in Post-Reformation England* (New Haven, CT and London: Yale University Press, 2002).

3 See Alison Shell, *Shakespeare and Religion* (London: Bloomsbury/Arden, 2010), 30–78.

4 Brian Cummings (ed.), *The Book of Common Prayer: The Texts of 1549, 1559, and 1662* (Oxford: Oxford University Press, 2011). See also Daniel Swift, *Shakespeare's Common Prayers: The Book of Common Prayer and the Elizabethan Age* (Oxford: Oxford University Press, 2013).

5 See Michael Allen, "Sacraments in the Reformed and Anglican Tradition," in *The Oxford Handbook of Sacramental Theology*, ed. Hans Boersma and Matthew Levering (Oxford: Oxford University Press, 2015), 287–90.

6 See Hannibal Hamlin, *The Bible in Shakespeare* (Oxford: Oxford University Press, 2013), 9–42.

7 "Homily or Sermon Concerning the Nativity and Birth of our Saviour Jesus Christ," *Renaissance English Texts*, ed. Ian Lancashire (Toronto, ON: University of Toronto, 1994), 426, The Anglican Library, www.anglicanlibrary.org/homilies/bk2hom12.htm. To modern eyes, passages like this can seem unrelenting, emphasizing the distance between a punitive God and a depraved humanity. But it is important not to forget that this kind of rhetoric has a pastoral and affective purpose. By stressing how far humans have fallen, the Homily also emphasizes God's love for "the children of wrath" (429), the magnitude of his "abundant grace" (435), and the need for repentance: "What greater love could we silly creatures desire or wish to have at God's hands?" (436).

8 See Revelation 12:7–9 where the archangel Michael defeats a "dragon" also referred to as the Devil and Satan. In traditional iconography, Michael is often shown with his sword drawn and his foot on the Devil's neck.

9 The word "lump" is often used in the New Testament (see Romans 11:16; 1 Corinthians 5:6–7; and Galatians 5:9) as a metaphor for spiritual regeneration, standing in ironic counterpoint to the wicked Richard.

10 To be spotted is often a mark of sin in the Bible, to be without spot a mark of salvation (see Jeremiah 13:23; 1 Peter 1:19). In this period, "spot" is also a euphemism for a woman's vulva.

11 On typology, see Jean Daniélou, *From Shadows to Reality: Studies in the Biblical Typology of the Fathers* (London: Burns & Oates, 1960).

12 See Patricia Parker, "The Bible and the Marketplace: *The Comedy of Errors*," in *Shakespeare from the Margins: Language, Culture, Context* (Chicago and London: University of Chicago Press, 1996), 56–82.

13 Quoted from *The Norton Shakespeare*, ed. Stephen Greenblatt et al. (New York and London: W. W. Norton, 1997). The New Cambridge edition has "What, have you got the picture of old Adam new-apparelled?" (*Comedy of Errors*, 4.2.12–13).
14 See also the Gravediggers' scene in *Hamlet* where the first asks the second: "What, art a heathen? How dost thou understand the Scripture? The Scripture says Adam digged. Could he dig without arms?" (5.1.33–5).
15 See Parker, "The Bible and the Marketplace," 56–82.
16 See Janette Dillon, *Shakespeare and the Staging of English History* (Oxford: Oxford University Press, 2012), 97–110.
17 For the speech in *Richard II* cited by Henry IV, see 5.1.55–68.
18 Definition 5c, OED.
19 See also Henry's prophetic rebuke to Hal at 4.3.220–65.
20 Compare Ulysses' argument that Achilles must either "be cropped / Or, shedding, breed a nursery of like evil / To overbulk us all" (1.3.312–14).
21 See John Calvin, *Institutes of the Christian Religion*, III.1, ed. John T. McNeill and trans. Ford Lewis Battles (London: Westminster Press, 1961), 922–3.
22 See John Stachniewski, *The Persecutory Imagination: English Puritanism and the Literature of Despair* (Oxford: Oxford University Press, 1991).
23 See the discussion between Cassio and Iago in Act 2, Scene 3, of *Othello*. The former states that "there be souls must be saved, and there be souls must not be saved" (2.3.89–90). This stark depiction of Calvinist predestination is underscored by Cassio's (drunken) insistence of spiritual hierarchy: "The lieutenant is to be saved before the ensign" (2.3.95–6). The concern in *Macbeth* with spiritual states, evil actions, and the ambiguity of signs (the Witches, the Dagger, Banquo's Ghost that only Macbeth can see) have also been read in relation to debates about predestination.
24 The pastoral scene between Corin and Touchstone in Act 3, Scene 2, offers a comic reflection on this problem.
25 See Michael Davies, "'Falstaff's Lateness': Calvinism and the Protestant Hero in *Henry IV*," *The Review of English Studies* 56, no. 225: 351–78.
26 See Hamlin, *The Bible*, 237–8 (drawing on Paul Jorgensen).
27 Definitions 2a, 4a, 7a, and 1a, from OED.
28 See Paula Pugliatti, *Shakespeare and the Just War Tradition* (London and New York: Routledge, 2016), 197–228.
29 As the sole embodiment of the good, God cannot also be responsible for evil. The problem is that this seemingly reserves an area of creation for which God is not responsible, meaning that he is not omnipotent, something that cannot be granted according to orthodox Christian theology. The effort to reconcile God's goodness in relation to the existence of evil is known as theodicy.
30 Compare this sentiment to the Bastard's speeches in *King John* at 1.1.259–76 and 2.1.594–9.
31 Saint Augustine, *The City of God*, vol. 1, trans. John Healey (London: J. M. Dent, 1947), 352.
32 See Isaiah 14:12. The Devil is named in Revelation 12:9.
33 See Luke Wilson, "*Macbeth* and the Contingency of Future Persons," *Shakespeare Studies* 40 (2012): 53–62.
34 Compare with Leontes's speech in *The Winter's Tale*, 1.2.285–98.

9

GARY KUCHAR

Compassion, Affliction, and Patience

More than a recurring theme, compassion in Shakespeare is a vital dramaturgical principle. Throughout his plays, Shakespeare encourages his audience to respond to characters much as Ariel, the spirit of compassion in *The Tempest*, inspires Prospero to respond to his nemeses with "a touch, a feeling / Of their afflictions," to "relish all as sharply / Passion as they" (5.1.21–4). Wondrously struck by Ariel's capacity to sympathize with those in affliction, Prospero insists that he should be more "kindlier moved" than his attendant Spirit towards the sufferings of his enemies (5.1.24). After all, he is a human who feels things just as intensely as other mortal beings while Ariel, a Spirit, presumably does not. Through this epiphany, Prospero models an ethically mature response to the events of *The Tempest* that broadly conforms to other works as well.

Crucially, Shakespeare's concern with compassion is often complexly mediated by biblical allusion, especially allusions to the sufferings of Christ. In many instances, patterns of biblical allusion engender a process of compassionate yet critical identification with characters. While demonstrating that Shakespeare was a subtle reader of Scripture, and that he recognized the theological weight borne by specific biblical passages in post-Reformation England, such allusions generally interrogate the period's hotly contested religious tensions for dramatic purposes more than they show him taking sides one way or another. Yet if Shakespeare exploited religious and political conflict for theatrical ends, he generally did so in ethically suggestive ways. One example of this lies in the way he participated in rethinking compassion within the shifting contexts of a Reformation culture in which religious and political change was often as much a matter of emotion as of doctrine. In Shakespeare's world, that is, religious and political contestations were not simply a matter of disembodied, intellectual debates about true authority. Instead, they were often expressions of the ideology of affect, the lived experience of emotion as an inherently social phenomenon inflected by the complications of competing belief systems. Hence the profound significance of drama in the period, particularly dramas partly structured by biblical allusion.

Richard II

In *Richard II*, for example, responses to the tragic hero are informed by the patterns of contrast and similarity between Richard and Christ that are developed over the course of the final three acts. Even before Bolingbroke has actually deposed Richard, the king majestically refashions himself as a persecuted, Christ-like monarch, whose absolute authority is rooted in a supreme sense of divine right. At his most extreme, he goes so far as to subsume Christ's passion into his own magnificent capacity for sovereign sorrow. On the verge of deposition, Richard laments that whereas Christ "in twelve / Found truth in all but one, I in twelve thousand none" (4.1.170–1). Only slightly more overstated than most of his identifications with Christ, such parallels repel even as they invite the audience's sympathy as Richard actively pursues suffering rather than passively undergoing it as Christ does. In drawing this distinction, Shakespeare significantly complicates the political and theological dimensions of compassion in the play, allowing for several distinct, even contrary, responses.

From a pro-Ricardian standpoint, Richard's overstated identifications with Christ do not negate his authority so much as they reaffirm the royal Christology on which it rests. If such allusions call his character into serious question, they nevertheless ultimately confirm the official view that John of Gaunt expresses when he rejects rebellion as a crime against God (1.2.37–41), thus echoing state sanctioned publications like *The Homily Against Disobedience* (1571) in which all rebellion against the monarch is prohibited. This type of response arises from the awareness that in losing his kingship Richard undergoes something that is far worse than death. As a divinely anointed sovereign, Richard inhabits the mystic body of the king, the immortal office that legally rests on the authority of the mystical body of Christ or *corpus mysticum*.[1] In this tradition of monarchy, the king is not only a mortal person but also a divinely sanctioned office consisting of a second, immortal body. Viewed in strongly absolutist terms, Richard's loss of the second body is not merely akin to Christ's passion but may be said to actually participate in it. Hence Bishop Carlisle's prophecy during the deposition scene that Richard's downfall will make "this land be called / The field of Golgotha and dead men's skulls" (4.1.143–4). If the play does not plainly endorse Carlisle's absolutism, it can nevertheless sustain the widely held Tudor view that Bolingbroke was a "foul traitor" responsible for the civil wars that Carlisle accurately foresees (4.1.135).

Not everyone shared this view in Elizabethan England, however. Some in Shakespeare's audience may have thought Richard's style of absolute kingship offensively foreign; perhaps even foreign enough to justify the king's deposition, if not his murder.[2] Unlike her successor King James I, Queen Elizabeth did not make strongly absolutist claims to divine right. Although she exploited the symbols of sacred monarchy to great effect, Elizabeth nevertheless opted for a slightly more constitutionalist form of monarchy than her successor. From this less absolutist perspective, Richard's suffering may look more like a maudlin parody of Christ's passion than a true incarnation of it.[3] Such a reading finds support in Richard's final seconds when the gap between his actions and Christ's becomes most acute. Just before his murderers enter the stage, Richard cries out as he attacks his keeper: "Patience is stale, and I am weary of it!" (5.5.103). Rejecting one of medieval Christianity's seven virtues, Richard ignores the fact that it is patience and not over-wrought emotion that defines Christ's virtue. From this anti-Ricardian perspective, whatever sympathy one may feel for Richard, it is not the sacred *compassio* that he and Carlisle seek to inspire. On the contrary, those who recognize the justice in Richard's deposition, but who nevertheless weep with Richard in the final scenes, necessarily separate Richard the man from Richard the divinely appointed king. Seen this way, the final scenes do not inspire sacred *compassio* so much as they evoke a complicated sense of fellow feeling for an exquisitely imaginative man who was born into a role for which he was ill-suited. Appropriately enough, it is Richard's exquisitely sensitive imagination that inspires our compassion, the very faculty we need to "feel with" Richard in his final moments.[4] Viewed this way, *Richard II* encourages a mode of compassion that remains divorced from unqualified absolutism and the royal Christology on which it rests, allowing viewers to weep with the man while rejecting the tyrant.

Admittedly, many of Shakespeare's original viewers may not have known how they felt about the justice of Richard's downfall, or his conception of divine right. As a result, they may have experienced a complicated blend of the varying kinds of compassion articulated within the play itself as they enjoyed watching both sides of the argument unfold. But whether they realized it or not, even non-committed viewers were implicated in the play's questioning of the politics of compassion. Rather than simply evoking the audience's emotions, Shakespeare's *Richard II* interrogates the various meanings of royalist affect within the variegated and shifting contexts of Tudor England.

In doing so, *Richard II* exploits a major crux in post-Reformation Christology, particularly as it played out in the traditions of *imitatio Christi*. In late medieval and post-Reformation Catholic Christianity, believers were encouraged to identify with Christ's passion as fully as possible. By suffering with Christ's agony, it was thought, one becomes sanctified through intimacy with God's pain.[5] Whatever his true motivation, this is precisely what Richard II seeks to do once Bolingbroke returns to reclaim his inheritance. In appropriating medieval forms of sacred *compassio*, however, Richard inadvertently exposes some of the reasons Protestant reformers set stricter limits on this style of devotion. Wary of any attempt to earn salvation or sanctification through acts of will, Protestant reformers stressed the absolute uniqueness of Christ's suffering. This led them to temper the idea that Christians could imitate Christ's grief through devotional practices of *compassio*. So while Protestants were taught to imitate Christ, the focus of their imitation was less on the sufferings of the Crucifixion than it was for late medieval and post-Reformation Catholics. This meant that when Protestants did focus on Christ's suffering in the passion, the devotional accent tended to be placed on the unique nature of his divine pain rather than on attempts to participate in it through imitation. As a result, sacred *compassio* became a highly contested affect in the period replete with devotional, aesthetic, and ecclesiastical consequences. By calling attention to some of the problems with the medieval *imitatio Christi* tradition that Protestants exposed in the period, *Richard II* theatrically exploits contestations over the limits of Christian *compassio* and *imitatio* in the period.

This is not to suggest that Shakespeare's play rejects Richard's medieval outlook in favor of a less idolatrous and thus more putatively Protestant conception of the state's sanctity. After all, Richard's style of absolutism is largely a post-Reformation development, one that was as easily adopted by Protestant monarchs such as James I as by Catholic monarchs in France and Spain. To this extent, the play cannot be mapped according to any straightforward Protestant/Catholic opposition. Instead, its dialectical use of biblical allusion shows the play engaging with the period's competing political-theologies and the various modes of compassion engendered by them.

King Lear

Similar kinds of dialectical patterning also occur in *King Lear*, Shakespeare's most complexly biblical exploration of compassion. If Richard ends his journey by rejecting patience, then King Lear effectively begins his by avowing that he will be its very pattern (3.2.35). The difference in plot is telling because the question of whether Lear's agony amounts to a belated journey into wisdom or a meaningless fall into despair lies at the very heart of the play. How we answer this question partly depends on how we respond to the play's dialectical patterning of biblical allusion. In particular, it depends on whether we see these allusions as demonstrating the broadly Christian view that in having compassion for people who are somehow responsible for their affliction we express virtue even as we further cultivate our capacity for it – or not.

Although set in pre-Christian Britain, Lear's Job-like experience in the play is framed by the "little apocalypse" that Jesus announces in Mark 13, his warnings about the terrors, wars, and false prophets to come. Shockingly, Christ's apocalyptic vision is first evoked in Edmund's deceitful warning to Edgar that their father's supposed plan shall "succeed unhappily, as of unnaturalness between the child and the parent, death, dearth ... divisions in state, menaces and maledictions" (1.2.144–6).[6] This ruse both parodies and exemplifies Jesus's warning to the disciples about false prophets. Evidently aware that some had been led to mistakenly believe that the end of the world was nigh, an issue that is also taken up in 2 Thessalonians 2, Jesus warns:

> Take heed lest any man deceive you ... when ye shall hear of wars
> and rumors of wars, be ye not troubled: for *such things* must needs be:
> but the end *shall* not *be* yet. For nation shall rise against nation, and kingdom
> against kingdom ... Yea, and the brother shall deliver the brother
> to death, and the father the son, and the children shall rise
> against their parents, and shall cause them to die ...
> but whosoever shall endure unto the end, he shall be saved
> ... Take heed: watch, and pray: for ye know not when the time is ...
> I say unto you, I say unto all men, Watch. (Mark 13:5, 7–8, 12–13, 33, 37)[7]

Edmund's allusion to this passage is as deliciously blasphemous as it is richly ironic. After all, Edmund's Machiavellian attempt to seize the occasion ironically summarizes the play's major events more closely than he could realize. This is partly because he unleashes Christ's idioms in inverted form, thereby putting into motion the conception of patience that Christ teaches, and that Cordelia, Kent, and Lear arguably demonstrate in the play, however imperfectly.

Edmund's deceitful warning to Edgar resonates across the whole of the play, including the final scene in which Lear bears the dead body of his daughter Cordelia. Partially framed by the biblical dialectic between hope and despair expressed in Mark 13, the final scene presents a reverse Pietà in which a grieving father holds his murdered daughter rather than Mary her son. The final scene leaves us asking with Kent, "Is this the promised end?" and with Edgar, "Or image of that horror?" (5.3.237–8). Not unimportantly, these are the questions that Christ's disciples had to ask during the Crucifixion. What is more, these questions resonate more darkly than the other three gospels in the Gospel of Mark with its perfunctory description of the Resurrection and its sharply critical portrayal of the disciples' lack of faith. In recalling the apocalyptic vision of Mark, the play ends by having us ask if Cordelia's compassionate grace has been fruitless, Lear's perseverance vain, and their reconciliation a fleeting cheat? If we answer yes to these questions then Edmund's prophetic vision subsumes Mark's, leaving us in a godless whirlwind somewhere beyond the very possibility of despair. But before we do so, we should bear in mind that in posing these questions we are addressing the very issues at stake in the Gospel of Mark, a gospel in which Jesus displays acute skepticism about the clarity of signs and in which he teaches the disciples that they should, as Patrick Grant notes, "suffer in a good cause, but [that] they ought not to be over-hasty in interpreting what exactly their suffering means."[8] Such questioning is the very stuff of *King Lear*.

Intriguingly, the question of perseverance that Edmund's allusion to Mark sets into motion was an unusually charged issue in 1605 to 1606. Only one year earlier King James had gathered some of England's finest minds at Hampton Court to discuss the future shape of the Church of England, including the theologically decisive question of perseverance. Following performances by Shakespeare's troupe during the 1603–4 Christmas revels, James pursued an agenda that included the question of whether the elect always persist in saving grace through faith or whether they could fall out of it in the course of their lives. By addressing the issue of election raised in Mark 13, the conference attendees were dredging up a conundrum that had riven late-Elizabethan Cambridge. So intense was the controversy at Cambridge that Church leaders felt obliged to draw up the Lambeth Articles (1595), a series of nine dogmatic propositions on the question of election. According to the official account of the Hampton Court Conference, James intervened in the debate over perseverance by warning against the dangers of presuming that the elect persist in saving grace while nonetheless insisting on God's omnipotence over matters of election. In doing so, he softened some of the sharper edges of Calvinist thought but without submitting to the more radical idea that the sins of the elect are of no consequence vis-à-vis salvation or what is known as antinomianism.[9] In the immediate wake of the Hampton Court conference phrases like "I will be the pattern of all patience" (3.2.35) would likely resonate for Shakespeare's patron King James I and others as "I shall persevere," or in the idioms that Mark 13 (one of the source-texts for debates about election) uses, "I will endure," which Lear later says in 3.4.18.

Indeed, by evoking the question of perseverance through patience Lear draws general attention to his spiritual condition. Most importantly, his theological idioms heighten his dramatic response to suffering and the compassion he now has for the "poor naked wretches" with whom he identifies (3.4.28). By raising the hotly charged issue of perseverance in Act 3 and by infusing it with apocalyptic exigency built up from Act 1, Shakespeare gives Lear's reaction to the storm an almost unbearable emotional intensity. Such intensity would not have been lost on King James who explicitly commented on both of the theological issues charging the storm scene in *King Lear*. Aside from the question of perseverance, which he addressed at the Hampton Court Conference, he published a commentary on chapter 20 of the Book of Revelation in 1588, which was reprinted in 1603. At the same time, however, the question of spiritual perseverance may have been on the minds of those who read the 1605 reissue of Robert Southwell's illegally printed *An Epistle of Comfort*. Likely reprinted due to an expected crackdown on Catholic recusants resulting from the Gunpowder Plot, Southwell's text encourages Catholics to be unwavering in support of their faith even at the cost of torture and death. Although written by a Jesuit who was executed as a traitor in 1595, Southwell's text is alluded to at least once in *Lear* (see below). Designed to spiritually nourish those who had been "restrained in Durance for the Catholic Faith," *An Epistle* draws heavily on Mark 13. Like Edmund, Southwell deploys Christ's apocalyptic vision as a means of inducing fear and terror in his auditor. But unlike Shakespeare's villain, Southwell was motivated by a genuine desire to help others avoid the punishments of hell rather than a self-serving and cynical desire to serve his own turn. Viewed in these contexts, it becomes clear that in writing about perseverance Shakespeare was addressing one of the most politically charged theological issues at stake in James I's early reign.

But rather than addressing questions of perseverance in any sort of polemical manner, Shakespeare takes his historical moment in 1605 as the occasion for exploring Lear's compassion and the discovery of love revealed through it, however fleeting it may be. Caught in a storm that could very well kill him, Lear cries out to others facing the same terrors now besieging him:

> Poor naked wretches, whereso'er you are
> That bide the pelting of this pitiless storm,
> How shall your houseless heads and unfed sides
> ... defend you
> From seasons such as these? O I have ta'en
> Too little care of this. Take physic, pomp,
> Expose thyself to feel what wretches feel,
> That thou mayst shake the superflux to them
> And show the heavens more just. (3.4.28–31, 32–6)

As Debora Shuger observes, the term "superflux" refers to the practice of giving a percentage of one's income (or superfluity) to the poor on the belief that a certain amount of wealth is owed to them out of the principles of Christian charity. Viewed in this context, Lear's prayer amounts to a painful epiphany in which "the pagan king for a moment grasps the nature of Christian *caritas*" or neighborly love.[10] As such, this scene is a classic example of how the experience of compassion bears within it an element of wonder, a connection stressed in Philip Sidney's discussion of how tragedy stirs "the affects of admiration and commiseration."[11] This concern with the wondrous shock of compassion is deepened later in the play when Edgar exclaims, after seeing the mad Lear enter, "O thou side-piercing sight!" (4.5.84), thus alluding to the Roman soldier's piercing of Christ's side in John 19:34. In both instances, we witness how what Edgar elsewhere calls the "art of known and feeling sorrows" widens one's sense of the horrors the world has to offer (4.5.213). But even more, we see how such expanded perception bears with it the possibility of renewed fellowship via "good pity" for the sufferings of others (4.6.214).

The power of Lear's epiphany lies in the way it emerges out of his affliction. Rather than retreating from suffering into self-pity as Richard II repeatedly does, Lear now accuses himself of not adequately siding with the downtrodden in the pursuit of justice. Placing himself as an ally of the divine, however that may be understood in the play, Lear expresses the compassionate solidarity with the poor and afflicted that is expressed in Isaiah 58:6–7: "Is not this the fasting, that I have chosen, to loose the bands of wickedness ... and that thou bring the poor that wander, unto thine house? when thou seest the naked, that thou cover him, and hide not thy self from thine own flesh?" While feeling himself to be one with the poor, Lear arrives at a view of divine justice that is modeled on human notions of fairness and reciprocity. Sadly, such notions rarely render human affliction intelligible in theological terms and they will certainly not make sense of subsequent events in Shakespeare's play. Lear's universe is one where God, should he exist, "maketh his sun to rise on the evil, and on the good, and sendeth rain on the just, and unjust" (Matt. 5:45). Ultimately, the play rejects the kind of divine justice that Lear seeks in Act 3, so seeking it in the final scene is as beside the point as refuting it. The question the play raises is whether there is an alternative vision of affliction available to Lear, one that permits an affirmation of life in the overwhelming absence of reciprocal justice shockingly suffered in the wake of Cordelia's death.

How we answer this question partly depends on the way we read the moment in the play where Lear expresses renewed feeling for God's presence, now uniquely expressed in the Christian singular rather than the pagan plural. As Lear and Cordelia are taken to prison after France's defeat, the king offers what consolation he can to the daughter he loves so dearly. In doing so, he further discloses the sense of vulnerability that he guarded against in the play's opening scene through hostile and exaggerated displays of authority:

> No, no, no, no! Come, let's away to prison.
> We two alone will sing like birds i'th'cage.
> When thou dost ask me blessing, I'll kneel down
> And ask of thee forgiveness: so we'll live,
> And pray, and sing, and tell old tales, and laugh
> At gilded butterflies, and hear poor rogues
> Talk of court news, and we'll talk with them too –
> Who loses and who wins; who's in, who's out –
> And take upon's the mystery of things
> As if we were God's spies; and we'll wear out
> In a walled prison packs and sects of great ones
> That ebb and flow by th'moon. (5.3.8–19)

This beguiling passage exquisitely captures the play's overall dialectic, the way it oscillates between a meaningful world that promises loving mercy and a nihilistic one that is emptied of value by vanity and death. From the pessimistic standpoint, Lear's speech before his imprisonment shows him retreating into the very fantasy world that he sought at the opening of the play, a carefree nursery world with his beloved daughter Cordelia. Viewed this way, Cordelia's selfless act of bravery appears to have been for naught. Not only has Cordelia failed to liberate Lear, but he has learned nothing of real value in the interim as he now retreats back into himself once again. Rather than a redemptive sacrifice, her death appears as a meaningless waste.

But from the more optimistic perspective, Lear's speech suggests a moving vision of what might have been and what yet may be. Rather than expressing a desire to escape from life, his speech shows him accepting and returning Cordelia's love, offering his own attempt at consolation, avowing his responsibility for her situation, bravely enduring prison, and, not least of all, confessing his faith in the divine, which is now expressed in the singular. Suggestively, Lear's confession of faith comes last in the speech, summing the whole thing up: "And take upon's the mystery of things / As if we were God's spies." No longer a presumptuous ally of God, Lear is now more modestly God's spy. The result is a non-ironic echo of Christ's call to "watch," which Edmund earlier travestied. In this respect, Lear casts Cordelia and himself in the role of spiritual watchman that the prophet Habakkuk assumes in the opening to his book's second chapter: "I will stand upon my watch ...

and see what [God] would say unto me, and what I shall answer to him that rebuketh me" (2:1).[12] Meditating on readiness and hope in a time of crisis, Habakkuk serves as God's watchman precisely insofar as he embodies a non-reciprocal understanding of the principle that the "just shall live by ... faith" (2:4). Crucially, Habakkuk's stark vision ends by rejecting the naive view that God rewards the virtuous and punishes the wicked in this world in a manner that conforms to human rationality. In Habakkuk we read:

> For the fig tree shall not flourish, neither *shall* fruit *be* in the vines: the labour of the olive shall fail, and the fields shall yield no meat: the sheep shall be cut off from the fold, and there shall be no bullocks in the stalls: But I will rejoice in the LORD: I will joy in the God of my salvation. (Hab. 3:17–18)

This vision conforms to St. Augustine's teaching that any faith grounded in fear of punishment or desire for reward is servile rather than filial, self-oriented rather than God-oriented. After the Reformation, this teaching was expressed more rigorously by Protestants who saw filial fear as a gift of election rather than a means of acquiring grace as it often was for Catholics such as Robert Bellarmine.[13] What was generally agreed on though, is that a mature disciple of Christ follows God's commandments out of love and reverence whatever the cost, much as Kent follows Lear, not out of self-serving policy, as Edmund follows Cornwall. In this respect, the claim that Christian *caritas* is a self-serving form of compassion may apply to perversions of the ideal but not to the ideal itself. To this extent, Lear's desire to be a spy of God provides some evidence for the feeling that he does not die in a state of meaningless despair. From such a perspective, Lear expires, as Gloucester does, because "his flawed heart – / Alack, too weak the conflict to support – / 'Twixt two extremes of passion, joy and grief, / Burst smilingly" (5.3.187–90). The pain that kills Gloucester does not arise out of pointless anguish but from an overabundance of love and shame, both highly meaningful affects. Seeing Edgar as though for the first time, Gloucester dies with a restored vision of his family's future while nevertheless acknowledging his role in jeopardizing it. His vision is belated and fatal but not nihilistic or meaningless. Similarly, when Lear deludes himself into thinking that Cordelia is still alive, what he is arguably protecting himself from is not absurdity and total loss but an overwhelming awareness that his grief is born out of an unbearable, imperfectly realized love. Thus, if the world of Lear does not offer justice or transcendent redemption, it nevertheless does offer, at least from this perspective, meaning and value, however transient both may appear within the play's broader flow of time.

As F. W. Brownlow has shown, Lear's attempt to console Cordelia draws part of its dramatic power and ethical complexity from its echoes of Southwell's

Epistle of Comfort.[14] Suggestively, Lear's speech recasts Southwell's argument that it is an honor to be imprisoned for the Catholic faith in the process of telling Cordelia that it is a gift to be imprisoned with her. According to Southwell, "prison is a school of divine and hidden mysteries, to God's friends."[15] What is more, Southwell encourages imprisoned Catholics to hone their devotion and virtue just as caged birds "not only sing their natural note, both sweetlier and oftener ... but learn also diverse other, far more pleasant and delightsome" (100^{v}). In turn, Lear's gilded butterflies parallel Southwell's "captives of the world" who "flatter themselves with the vain title of liberty" triumphing "in their chains of gold, in their jewels of pearl and precious stone" (108^{rv}). But what effects would such allusions have for those with ears to hear? How do they inform the dynamics of compassion in the play?

For auditors who saw Southwell as a martyr of the true faith, hearing his ostensibly treasonous words in the mouth of the king of Britain would surely have been astonishing. After gasping at the poignancy of the allusion, such auditors may have felt a deep sense of emotional identification with Lear and then, perhaps, confused, pause over what it all means. After all, Lear says nothing about the righteousness of his cause or Cordelia's claim to authority. Distancing himself from politics, the scene is domestic and devotional not dynastic or doctrinal. That said, Lear's attempt to console Cordelia shows him displaying some of the courage and all of the poetic sensibility that Southwell possessed in consoling Catholics such as the imprisoned earl of Arundel, Philip Howard. In doing so, Lear inspires not only pity but also compassion and commiseration, all the while leaving us wondering just how sound his advice, like that of Southwell's, really is.

But given that Southwell was a widely popular writer whose readership extended beyond the Catholic recusant community, how would those who saw Jesuits as part of a conspiratorial fifth column have responded to such parallels between Lear and Southwell? While we can only speculate, such audience members may have seen these parallels as confirming the view that Lear is deluded as he goes to prison. From this perspective, Lear's attempt to console Cordelia would be seen in the context of Southwell's effort to convince recusants that jail is to be embraced and celebrated along with torture and martyrdom. Viewed this way, Lear's poetry is more a matter of ongoing blindness than renewed insight and hence less worthy of compassion than critique.

Alternatively, those who did not have a polarized view of Southwell may have heard such allusions differently. For them, such allusions may have recast Lear's tender intensity in the light of Southwell's courage and, in turn, Southwell's poetic tenacity in the light of Lear's bravery and depth of feeling. From this standpoint, what emerges from Lear's speech is not the transcendent vision of suffering that Southwell promulgated but a renewed encounter with bare life, the Job-like reduction of human existence to the state of "Unaccommodated man" that Lear rediscovers through Edgar in the role of Poor Tom (3.4.96). At such moments, the ligatures binding relationships are broken so as to be remade as Lear and Cordelia further reconstitute their love for one another, just as Lear and Gloucester re-forged their ties earlier, as did Edgar and Gloucester before them. Fragile and imperfect though they are, these moments are nevertheless ones of promise and poignancy in the play. If nothing else, they open windows onto possible worlds, modes of sociality based in compassion and reconciliation rather than revenge and self-pity. This is not to say that *King Lear* is either a Catholic or a Protestant play. On the contrary, it is to simply observe that the play's dramatic power partly lies in its capacious ability to sustain competing views simultaneously, not entirely unlike the scriptural text on which it so liberally and critically draws.

At the end of *King Lear* Shakespeare includes his audience in this process of remaking social bonds when he offers us an opportunity to extend the circle of compassion all the way to Edmund, if not to Regan and Goneril whose deaths, at least according to Albany, touch "us not with pity" (5.3.206). Mortally wounded by the disguised Edgar, Edmund betrays his disavowed desire for love and recognition and then calls off the order to murder Cordelia out of a newly discovered desire to do some good despite his own ostensible nature (5.3.217–18). In another example of tragic belatedness, Edmund finally acts for the sake of others. This invitation to extend the circle of compassion to one of the play's key villains is a striking example of how compassion discloses the effects of social structures on people's lives. For Edmund's final moments invite us to consider the extent to which his actions were conditioned, if not caused, by sociological contingencies rather than the astrological or providential forces that he earlier mocked. In any event, Edmund's death scene suggests the importance of identification to Shakespeare's dramaturgy in *King Lear*. It is one thing to have compassion for Cordelia's selfless suffering, but it is quite another to feel sympathy for the self-inflicted tribulations of the sublimely egoistical Edmund. After all, Aristotle believed that compassion only occurs when we judge a person not responsible for his or her situation, while stoics generally saw it as a form of weakness that is to be avoided.[16] In *King Lear* we experience the possibility of a more generous form of compassion than Aristotle envisioned, one more akin to St. Augustine who saw compassion as a means of cultivating virtue.[17]

The Winter's Tale and *Henry VIII*

Shakespeare's investment in biblically inflected themes of affliction and patience, along with dramaturgical issues of compassion and identification bound up with them, are central to his last plays. This is especially true of the closely related characterizations of Hermione in *The Winter's Tale* and Queen Katherine of Aragon in *Henry VIII*, which was co-written with John Fletcher. As Gordon McMullan notes of these two characters: "Each is the daughter of foreign royalty; each defends herself passionately yet unsuccessfully in a public court-room; each rejects the ritual that sustains a patriarchal political realm; each believes in a version of the truth that her husband cannot understand; ... and each loses the struggle, at least in the material world."[18] Moreover, both characters were performed at Blackfriars Theatre, the very site in which Aragon's trial took place in 1529 when King Henry VIII sought to divorce her in order to marry Anne Boleyn.

Rather surprisingly, Hermione's self-defense in her trial scene evokes not only the memory of Queen Katherine but also that of Anne Boleyn.[19] Mirroring a decisive moment in English history, Hermione's trial scene calls indirect attention to the dangerous story that Shakespeare cannot tell in *Henry VIII* due to its still ongoing significance for Jacobean Britain. Like Hermione, Boleyn was indicted for infidelity and treason; but in Anne's case, four suspected lovers were charged and eventually executed along with her, including her own brother George, 2nd Viscount Rochford. Among other things, the parallels between Hermione and Boleyn put Henry VIII's tyranny into much sharper focus than Shakespeare's guardedly subtle depiction of him in the history play. To be sure, part of the power of Hermione's trial scene lies in the way she summons memories of two recent English queens who were enemies in life but who now become obliquely united in death through Hermione's eloquence and patience in the face of affliction. As a result, Hermione's trial scene furthers the exoneration of Katherine that arguably takes place in *Henry VIII* and in doing so further blurs the Catholic queen's memory with the memory of Anne Boleyn (Bullen in *Henry VIII*). The overall effect of Hermione's trial scene is to inspire an enormous degree of compassion on the part of the audience as recent British history is refracted in the light of romantic tragi-comedy.

The connection between Hermione and recent Tudor history in *The Winter's Tale* is established in her opening statement during the trial scene:

> [I]f powers divine
> Behold our human actions (as they do)
> I doubt not, then, but innocence shall make

False accusation blush, and tyranny
Tremble at patience. You, my lord, best know,
Whom least will seem to do so, my past life
Hath been as continent, as chaste, as true
As I am now unhappy – which is more
Than history can pattern, though devised
And played to take spectators. (3.2.26–35)

Hermione's distinction between real life and what "history can pattern" poignantly, if obliquely, evokes the events Shakespeare both included and excluded from *Henry VIII*. For instance, Hermione here recalls the stress Shakespeare puts on Katherine's avowal of patience, going so far as to give her an attendant with the very name so that otherwise innocuous lines such as "Nay, Patience, / You must not leave me yet" (4.2.165–6) resonate in both literal and metaphorical terms in Katherine's closing scene.

Katherine's capacity to inspire compassion in *Henry VIII* is rooted in her Roman Catholic faith, which is routinely established vis-à-vis biblical allusion, especially to the Psalms and Job. As Paul Stevens observes, Katherine presents herself as the "servant without blemish 'lost among ye, laughed at, scorned' (3.1.106)," eventually confirming with Job at her moment of truth that she knows her "Redeemer liveth" (Job 19:25).[20] The insistent presence of the Psalms in *Henry VIII*, Stevens concludes, "seems to suggest that history is only there to illustrate Scripture. And Scripture is there throughout the play."[21] If Stevens does not account for some of the play's key ironies, he nevertheless demonstrates how Katherine inspires our sympathy through biblical allusion, presenting a more convincing case for sanctity and religious authority than Richard II.

One of the basic parallels between Hermione and Katherine lies in their mildly strained rejection of vengeance along Christian lines. In appealing to her royal birth, Hermione summons the memory of her father the Emperor of Russia:

O, that he were alive, and here beholding
His daughter's trial! that he did but see
The flatness of my misery – yet with eyes
Of pity, not revenge. (3.2.118–21)

Katherine lashes out at Wolsey and Campeius in similar terms when she declares: "I will not wish ye half my miseries, / I have more charity. But say I warned ye; / Take heed, for heaven's sake take heed, lest at once / The burthen of my sorrows fall upon ye" (3.1.107–10). These strained rejections of vengeance demonstrate nobility and humanity at once, thereby earning our compassion. Even more, though, they show that for those oppressed by authoritarian power a certain level of double-speak is the cost of making one's mind known.

In speaking truth to power, Shakespeare's heroines also find themselves deploying the potentially subversive force of martyrological discourse. In a culture where the line between traitor and martyr was often hotly contested, such language had enormous dramatic and political force. Exploiting this energy, Shakespeare has Hermione respond to Leontes's threat of execution by fearlessly retorting, "The bug which you would fright me with, I seek. / To me can life be no commodity" (3.2.90–1). After news of her son Mamillius's sudden death over the apparent fate of his mother, Hermione swoons, perhaps echoing the popular iconographical tradition in which Mary's participation in her son's agony is figured by her fainting at the foot of the cross. From that point on, the scene is dominated by Paulina, who further wields the martyrological knife in order to make Leontes realize that what he has done cannot be undone by mere penance or fiat. Picking up Hermione's martyrological language, Paulina bravely cries:

> What studied torments, tyrant, hast for me?
> What wheels? racks? fires? What flaying? boiling?
> In leads or oils? What old or newer torture
> Must I receive. (3.2.172–5)

As such self-representation makes clear, royal suffering is never an individual or isolated affair. Hermione's agony is literally shared by her son who dies at the very thought of her grief as though he were still physically a part of her. Moreover, her agony is passionately participated in by her subjects, and very soon her remorseful husband as well. In Shakespeare, a monarch's suffering often bleeds across families, persons, and generations just as a martyr's does.

As much the loss of a living symbol of the state as that of an individual person, a queen's death establishes the perfect conditions for compassionate identification to metastasize into melancholia, the kind of loss one feels when one does not know what exactly one has lost. Yet just as a royal's death is over-determined in meaning and affective investment, so too is her resurrection. Through Hermione's apparently miraculous return to life, Shakespeare stages more than the reconciliation of a family; he imagines the regeneration of a kingdom and not simply that of Sicilia. By conflating Hermione with Aragon and Boleyn, Shakespeare obliquely links Catholicism and Protestantism in one beloved person. In doing so, he imaginatively heals the extended family that both rules and embodies the English state. Viewed in these oblique but unmistakable royalist and religious contexts, *The Winter's Tale* symbolically purges past traumas in order to open the way towards a less fractious, more conciliatory national future. This is drama as healing art.

Central to the late romances' art of political healing is a dramaturgy of compassion in which we rejoice with those who rejoice and weep with those who weep while still remaining cognizant of the characters' various vanities and faults. The idea that drama can play this kind of spiritually and socially regenerating role is a recurring, if sometimes muted, idea in Shakespearean drama. It gets articulated, for example, in Gower's prologue to *Pericles* when he tells us that the play ("a song that old was sung")

> hath been sung at festivals,
> On ember-eves and holy days,
> And lords and ladies in their lives
> Have read it for restoratives.
> The purchase is to make men glorious. (0.1, 5–9)

Socially binding nobles and commoners together, oral and written transmissions of Pericles's agonizing triumphs are figured here as morally exemplary in ways that are broadly consonant with the heroes of chivalric romance or even the saints of medieval legend. While the idea that Pericles's suffering amounts to a spiritually edifying *via dolorosa* is eventually qualified by the play's self-parodying irony, Gower's account of the play nevertheless gives expression to some of the higher ideals towards which Shakespearean drama sometimes aspired. If these ideals are often rooted in biblical and Christological traditions of compassion, they nevertheless often depart from them, sometimes testing their resources to the breaking point, sometimes reinventing them anew.

Notes

1 For this classic reading of *Richard II* see Ernst H. Kantorowicz, *The King's Two Bodies: A Study in Medieval Political Theology* (Princeton, NJ: Princeton University Press, 1998), 24–41.

2 For this approach to the play see, for example, David Womersley, *Divinity and State* (Oxford: Oxford University Press, 2010), 281–99.

3 For a fuller reading along these lines see Gary Kuchar, *The Poetry of Religious Sorrow in Early Modern England* (Cambridge: Cambridge University Press, 2008), 48–61.

4 Kuchar, *Poetry of Religious Sorrow*, 7.

5 See Jan Frans van Dijkuizen, *Pain and Compassion in Early Modern English Literature and Culture* (Cambridge: D. S. Brewer, 2012), 1–88.

6 These lines are included in 1.2 in the 1608 Quarto text, but not in the 1623 Folio. See Jay Halio's New Cambridge edition, Appendix, 293.

7 For related discussions of this allusion, which appears in the 1608 Quarto edition but not in the 1623 Folio, see John Reibetanz, *The Lear World: A Study*

of King Lear in Its Dramatic Context (Toronto, ON: University of Toronto Press, 1977), 26 and Joseph Wittreich, *"Image of That Horror": History, Prophecy, and Apocalypse in King Lear* (San Marino, CA: Huntington Library, 1984), 106.

8 Patrick Grant, *Reading the New Testament* (Grand Rapids, MI: William B. Eerdmans, 1989), 10.

9 For James's intervention see William Barlow *The Sum and Substance of the Conference ... at Hampton Court (1605)*, in *A History of Conferences and Other Proceedings Connected with the Revision of the Book of Common Prayer, 1558–1690*, ed. E. Cardwell, 3rd edn. (Oxford: Oxford University Press, 1849), 181.

10 Debora Shuger, "Subversive Fathers and Suffering Subjects: Shakespeare and Christianity," in *Religion, Literature, and Politics in Post-Reformation England, 1540–1688*, ed. Donna B. Hamilton and Richard Strier (Cambridge: Cambridge University Press, 1996), 53.

11 Cited in Robin A. Bowers, "The Merciful Construction of Good Women: Katherine of Aragon and Pity in Shakespeare's *King Henry VIII*," in *Christianity and Literature* 37, no. 3 (1988): 29–51, 33.

12 For a different reading of this allusion see Piero Boitani, *The Gospel According to Shakespeare,* trans. Vittorio Montemaggi and Rachel Jacoff (Notre Dame, IN: University of Notre Dame Press, 2013), 37–8.

13 Paul Cefalu, *Moral Identity in Early Modern English Literature* (Cambridge University Press, 2004), 117–20.

14 F. W. Brownlow, *Shakespeare, Harsnett, and the Devils of Denham* (Newark, NJ: University of Delaware Press, 1993), 129–31.

15 Robert Southwell, *An Epistle of Comfort*, ed. D. M. Rogers (Ilkey, UK: Scolar Press, 1974), 106[v].

16 See Martha Nussbaum, *Upheavals of Thought: The Intelligence of Emotions* (Chicago: University of Chicago Press, 2003), 306–10.

17 See St. Augustine, *The City of God*, trans. Henry Bettenson (London: Penguin, 1984), 9.5 and 14.9.

18 William Shakespeare and John Fletcher, *King Henry VIII (All Is True)*, ed. Gordon McMullan (London: Arden Bloomsbury, 2000), 119.

19 See McMullan, *Henry VIII*, 129–30 and William Shakespeare, *The Winter's Tale*, ed. Stephen Orgel (Oxford: Clarendon Press, 1996), 29–32.

20 Paul Stevens, "*Hamlet*, *Henry VIII*, and the Question of Religion: A Post-Secular Perspective," in *Shakespeare and Early Modern Religion*, ed. David Loewenstein and Michael Witmore (Cambridge: Cambridge University Press, 2015), 231–57, 245.

21 Stevens, "*Hamlet*, *Henry VIII*," 245.

10

JEAN-CHRISTOPHE MAYER

Providence and Divine Right in the English Histories

The plays containing the most allusions to religion in the whole of the Shakespearean corpus are the dramatist's English history plays – the ten or so plays that encompass the reigns of six medieval English monarchs, with the exception of *Henry VIII*, which partly covers that of the second Tudor king.[1] Moreover, as a genre, the history play, almost by essence, invites conjectures about time and destiny. This has been accentuated by the way critics have grouped some of the works together as tetralogies (that is, sets of four plays) – those dealing with the unstable events in England and France between 1399 and 1485. Thus, the term "First Tetralogy" has often been used to describe Shakespeare's first four English history plays written in or around the early 1590s – *Henry VI Part 1*, *Henry VI Part 2*, *Henry VI Part 3*, and *Richard III*. The "Second Tetralogy" includes *Richard II*, *Henry IV Parts 1 and 2*, and *Henry V*, plays composed in the second half of the 1590s.[2]

Viewing these works as tetralogies has been productive in the sense that it has emphasized clear cyclical or serial elements in them.[3] Yet the groupings can cause confusions. Though composed first, the "First Tetralogy" describes historical events that *followed* the "Second Tetralogy" (the latter would be a "prequel" in modern terms) and *Henry VI Part 1* was composed after *Henry VI Parts 2 and 3*. More to the point, "tetralogical thinking" can lead to teleological interpretations of Shakespeare's plays. Two works by E. M. W. Tillyard in particular, *The Elizabethan Picture* (1943) and *Shakespeare's History Plays* (1948), exerted a lasting influence over Shakespeare studies.[4] Tillyard argued that there was a teleological and providential Tudor myth of history running through the two tetralogies. According to him, Shakespeare had found this myth in the English chronicles. They allegedly demonstrated that the deposition and subsequent murder of Richard II, an anointed sovereign appointed by divine right, was the act that triggered divine retribution. It led to civil war and dynastic conflicts over generations until the nation was saved by the Tudors, or more precisely by God's providential agent, the future Henry VII (Henry Tudor, Earl of Richmond), who defeated Richard III at the battle of Bosworth in 1485.

It is true that Shakespeare probably used Edward Hall's providentialist and pro-Tudor *The Union of the Two Noble and Illustrious Families of Lancaster and York* (1548) in the original (his influence can be felt at times in the *Henry VI* plays), even if his main source for his historical drama remained the 1587 edition of Raphael Holinshed's *Chronicles of England, Scotland, and Ireland*. It is undeniable that the playwright imported providential ideas and themes into his works, but, as we shall see, even his *Henry VI* plays, supposedly influenced by Hall's tendentious *Union*, do not simply act out a divine plan.

What has to be borne in mind is that Shakespeare's principal source, the 1587 edition of Holinshed's *Chronicles*, reflected the work of a consortium of five men who did not all hold the same religious or political beliefs.[5] In their analyses of the *Chronicles* modern historians have pointed out that the language of providentialism is never totally consistent, as the causation of historical events is frequently attributed to a mix of chance, misfortune, fate, or Providence.[6] In effect, Shakespeare used a "polyvalent" text[7] and "a profoundly unstable and fractured one, mirroring the incomplete victories and defeats of various parties in the battles for the soul of the nation."[8]

Therefore, the chronicles offered dramatists like Shakespeare much miscellaneous material to be shaped and many shadowy figures to be turned into engaging characters. Their world, like that of Shakespeare's plays, was not a godless universe, even if the chroniclers never provide definitive or dependable answers to the workings of history. It was perhaps the silences inside the paradoxically rich narrative of the chronicles that Shakespeare wished to probe for the sake of his religiously disoriented audiences, who lived in a country that needed to rebuild and explore its links with its Catholic past in order to get to grips with its place in history and Christendom.

Shakespeare seems to have been specifically interested in the connection of Providence to sovereignty and politics. A number of medieval and Tudor historians and lawyers had equally explored those specific links in the recent past. When building the plots of his history plays it is easy to imagine that he needed to investigate the forces animating situations and characters alike. Not only was he interested in the unfolding of history, but also in how political power constructed itself dramatically (and often paradoxically) with the help of religious discourse. He anatomized rulers' so-called special relationship to Providence and to the divine. Shakespeare's potentates appeal differently to their "divine rights," and the staging of their verbal and political strategies was a way for the dramatist to instill a tragic and poetic dimension into his histories, for instance through monologues or soliloquies that struck spectators' memories powerfully. In what follows, we shall focus first on sovereignty, revelation, and the question of Providence, and then we shall move on to divine right, which, as suggested, is a closely connected notion. Building on what we establish in the first two parts, and beyond the chronicles and Tudor political theory, we shall explore what sacred kingship may have meant for Shakespeare and his audiences. In the course of this chapter, our main corpus will be the English history plays (the two tetralogies, *King John*, and *Henry VIII*), but also other works, such as *Hamlet*, which shed useful light on our central topic.

Sovereignty, Revelation, and the Question of Providence

Henry VI Parts 1 and 2 multiply allusions to the supernatural and repeatedly point to apparent signs of God's presence. Nonetheless, so-called expressions of divine Providence turn out to be misleading in most cases. Shakespeare in fact stages characters – sovereigns or top politicians – who are prone to interpret signs hastily, incompletely, or superficially. A prominent example of superficial misreading is the so-called miracle scene of *Henry VI Part 2*, when the king is hawking with Gloucester and Winchester at St. Albans and a citizen interrupts them to call them to witness a miracle. One blind man by the name of Simpcox, who was allegedly worshipping at the nearby shrine of St. Albans, has suddenly recovered his sight. The blind man, who is also apparently lame, is brought before the king and Gloucester. The latter suspects that he is lying about his sight and his lameness and calls the town beadle to have him whipped. When the beadle arrives and he faces the unsavory prospect of being whipped, Simpcox and his wife admit to having lied all the way. Interestingly, as Ronald Knowles remarks, "All three sources record that it is Gloucester who is overjoyed at the miracle ... Shakespeare transfers it to Henry's pious credulity and contrasts Gloucester's worldly astuteness here."[9] The dramatist thus consciously departed from his historical sources in this instance to underline Henry's blind faith, which makes him read the falsely blind as truly blind. Indeed, the nation's leader mistakenly attributes to God what is in fact mere trickery – he swiftly falls for the false miracle: "Poor soul, God's goodness hath been great to thee; / Let never day nor night unhallowed pass, / But still remember what the Lord hath done" (2 *Henry VI*, 2.1.84–6).

It is tempting to interpret Gloucester's ensuing exposure of the false blind man as a proto-Protestant gesture. The source for this story, however, is Thomas More's *Dialogue of the Veneration and Worship of Images* (1529).[10] Moreover, the Duke of Gloucester himself hardly has time to reap the fruits of his spectacular exposure of the false miracle. He too is blind to the political machinations around him; and these are revealed to us as Buckingham arrives, just after the Duke's triumph, to announce that the Duchess of Gloucester has been arrested and charged with sorcery and high treason. Thus, the man who set out to expose the false miracle is himself exposed because of his wife's occult practices, leaving the audience to wonder at the dramatic irony of an episode that has blurred reference points, shattered confessional certainties, and undermined rulers' insightfulness.

A passage in the same play that ties in with this one is the scene of the trial by combat (2.3) between an apprentice by the name of Peter Thump and an armorer called Thomas Horner, the former having brought a petition against his master "for saying that the Duke of York was rightful heir to the crown" (1.3.24). During this scene, which might be comical – were it not for the ensuing death of the accused – much drinking is done by the supporters of each contestant and by the contestants themselves before the fight. Peter, who kills his master in the fight, is relieved to be alive and certain that he "prevailed in right" (2.3.92). Henry is also convinced that the outcome of the duel reveals God's will and that divine justice has been done (2 *Henry VI*, 2.3.93–8).

The king thinks he has detected the finger of God in these events, and yet York – who is no innocent party in the play – offers the hint of a conflicting interpretation. Were it not for the effects of alcohol, the armorer would perhaps have prevailed over his apprentice: "Fellow, thank God, and the good wine in thy master's way" (2.3.89–90). The Duke thus questions in passing the reliability of the interpretation of signs in the play.[11] Yet the skepticism is not pervasive in *Henry VI Part 2*. There are scenes where Shakespeare seems to cast all ambiguity aside and plays rather with the possibility that signs can sometimes reveal a divine nemesis at work. This is the case when Sir William Vaux comes onstage to tell the king that Winchester is dying and that the Cardinal is delirious, tormented, and somewhat blasphemous. Henry interprets this in a moral light almost immediately: "Ah, what a sign it is of evil life / Where death's approach is seen so terrible" (2 *Henry VI*, 3.3.5–6). For once, what we have been shown of the character onstage does not conflict with the king's interpretation. At the Cardinal's bedside, Henry (ever hopeful) tries to find signs of repentance, and it does not come as much of a surprise when Winchester does not produce the sign that would indicate either his contrition or God's forgiveness (even if all signs remain open to interpretation of course): "He dies and makes no sign. O God, forgive him" (2 *Henry VI*, 3.3.29).

As these various passages suggest, Shakespeare is in fact sending conflicting signals. He seems more concerned about opening a debate on the possible interpretation of signs and on God's degree of involvement in human affairs than about giving tangible answers. Moreover, so-called holy sovereigns, their servants, and even their clergymen are not portrayed as active agents of some godly Providence. While the chronicles' often inconsistent or incomplete record of events was no doubt perplexing, the fluctuations of Elizabethan and Jacobean so-called religious orthodoxy may not have helped Shakespeare and his contemporaries either.

On the face of it, many Protestant writers considered that the Revelation had happened once and for all, that the spirit of God would no longer speak, aside from through the Scriptures, and that one should not seek to know God's intentions, or try to read the signs of any further Revelation of his divine will.[12] One is left to wonder what those writers would have made of Shakespeare's prophecies, those staged omens that – through the agency of drama – often turn out to be true, especially, but not solely, in *Henry VI Part 2*.[13]

In her study of Providence in early modern England, Alexandra Walsham shows that Protestant views on Providence were not clear-cut and that it was a subject of discord not only between Catholics and Protestants, but also among Protestants themselves.[14] The view that "miracles are ceased" may have been proverbial – so much so that the expression would appear in Shakespeare's own *Henry V* (1.1.67), placed somewhat anachronistically in the mouth of the Archbishop of Canterbury – it was nevertheless far from unanimously embraced by all Protestant writers. In fact, it seems that the argument was often used by Protestant controversialists as an expedient way of disarming their Catholic opponents, at the snap of a finger as it were. Protestants were aware that the idea of God's miraculous intervention in human affairs was, after all, part of the Christian heritage they shared with Catholics – even if, of course, most clergymen insisted that real miracles were extremely rare.

For Protestant theologians, then, miracles had not quite ceased, although the Protestant concept of miracle was "hedged about with a number of significant qualifications." The very popular *Acts and Monuments* (first published 1563) by English Protestant martyrologist John Foxe included, for example, stories of "incombustible organs and spectral tokens." Yet "'Special providences' and miracles were not spontaneous or impromptu interventions; they were events for which God had foreseen the need and built into His plan for humanity before the beginning of time."[15] Still, the notion of "special Providence" enabled Protestants to get themselves out of a tight corner and combat their opponents on an almost equal polemical footing, especially when they sought to win over those who wavered most in their convictions.[16] Many were indeed hesitant and remained so, like Shakespeare's Lord Lafew, who in a much later play – *All's Well That*

Ends Well (first performed in 1603) – would seem to put his faith in "special providences," or indeed miracles: "They say miracles are past, and we have our philosophical persons, to make modern and familiar, things supernatural and causeless. Hence is it that we make trifles of terrors, ensconcing ourselves into seeming knowledge, when we should submit ourselves to an unknown fear" (2.3.1–5). Lafew's ambiguous phrasing indicates that the Shakespearean stage was conscious of these issues.

The use and abuse of "special providences" by Elizabethan controversialists led polemicists onto dire doctrinal ground and did little to restore people's faith in God's Providence, as the Almighty appeared strangely factionalized. The exploitation of Providence ultimately went against the evangelical wish to spiritualize human experience by raising it above the level of the supposed harm and charms of witchcraft.[17]

Might standing over right, or one faction purporting to embody not only the wishes of the commonwealth, but also the will of God, is Shakespeare's skeptical vision of the medieval English civil wars. Richard Plantagenet, Duke of York, does not live in the fear of his "holy" sovereign, Henry VI. York considers Henry VI an ineffective king, one who is not endowed like himself with the conquering might of a heroic figure, in the (partly pagan) tradition of a Greek mythical hero, or of Christopher Marlowe's all-mighty and wrathful Tamburlaine:

> That head of thine doth not become a crown;
> Thy hand is made to grasp a palmer's staff
> And not to grace an awful princely sceptre.
> That gold must round engirt these brows of mine,
> Whose smile and frown, like to Achilles' spear,
> Is able with the change to kill and cure.
> Here is a hand to hold a sceptre up
> And with the same to act controlling laws.
> Give place! By heaven, thou shalt rule no more
> O'er him whom heaven created for thy ruler. (2 *Henry VI*, 5.1.96–105)

If we believe York, the sacred power of kingship is not so much conferred to the king by religion, but by might, by the magic of York's heroic arms. For him, heroism is sacralized to the point of standing in place of God's Providence ("like to Achilles' spear"). References to the hand (the hero's instrument) largely outnumber those to the crown in the passage. For York, sacred kingship has a concrete and palpable meaning: the sovereign is sacred because it is his own will (although he still outwardly claims divine favor) and because he has all the means at his disposal to be persuasive. The would-be conqueror king turns the contemplative king into a disoriented pilgrim holding indeed "a palmer's staff" rather than a royal scepter.

A later member of the House of York, Richard, Duke of Gloucester (the future Richard III) pictures himself in similar terms. Is he not, after all, "determinèd to prove a villain" (*Richard III*, 1.1.30) – that is, both a voluntary agent of evil and potentially an instrument of a higher purpose?[18] Moreover, from the outset of another play, *King John*, a disconcerting ambivalence seems to be at work as far as Providence is concerned. In the opening scene, our dramatic interest is immediately aroused when Queen Eleanor in an intriguing aside tells John that God is witness that he is an unlawful king:

> KING JOHN: Our strong possession and our right for us.
> ELEANOR: Your strong possession much more than your right,
> Or else it must go wrong with you and me;
> So much my conscience whispers in your ear,
> Which none but heaven and you and I shall hear. (1.1.39–43)

Does this mean that God is not on the king's side? Or does it mean that it is God's will that an illegitimate king should reign? These differences were touchy issues when Shakespeare wrote his play. They pose the question of agency and to what extent actions are self-willed in a Christian context.

To go back to *Richard III*, it could be argued that if the Earl of Richmond (the future Tudor king, Henry VII) finally gains the upper hand over Richard, it is not so much because of his right to the crown, or divine Providence, but because Richard's criminal reign has paved the way for him. Richmond does not really hold more rights to the crown than Richard, who, it may be worth noting, is the only elected king in Shakespeare's two tetralogies, even if he is elected by popular but enforced acclamation. Is not Richmond also usurping (as tyrants would) God's prerogative when using his warlike rhetoric: "All for our vantage. Then in God's name, march! / True hope is swift and flies with swallow's wings; / Kings it makes gods, and meaner creatures kings" (5.2.22–4). Richmond's "true hope" and his next line may be construed as hubristic too from a Christian standpoint.

By the same token, one could claim that Richard, because he is seen by many as the embodiment of supreme evil, exorcises the evils of the English civil wars and allows the houses of Lancaster and York to be united. To some extent, Richmond could be construed as the one who reaps the providential fruits of a dramatic process that has unraveled without him: "Richmond is something new, something from outside the play's system as we have seen it so far. Yet not altogether so, for in a deeper sense Richard has generated Richmond."[19] Richmond may claim to be waging a holy war (5.3.241–3; 5.3.254–5), but Shakespeare makes sure that the scapegoated tyrant too has a voice. Indeed, Richard throws Richmond's arguments back at him, for to him they are imbued with simplistic providentialism. Heaven, and God's Providence, belong to no one: "Not shine today? Why, what is that to me / More than to Richmond? For the self-same heaven / That frowns on me looks sadly upon him" (5.3.287–9).[20]

As we have seen, there are fragments of providentialism in Shakespeare and a constant (and frequently ironic) attentiveness to the interpretation and processes of legitimization of human action. Predictively, this dramatic inquisitiveness extends also to potentates' supposed special relationship with divine authority. Prior to investigating Shakespeare's treatment of divine right, it is essential to bear a few contextual elements in mind.

Divine Right: Legal and Constitutional Contexts

The divine right of kings was never a consensual constitutional theory, even during the late medieval ages. It was more akin to a set of various propositions, which evolved through troubled ages and whose aim was to provide some sort of stability from a legal and political point of view. In what is still the best account of the "theory," *The Divine Right of Kings* (1896, 2nd ed. 1914), John Neville Figgis offers a useful summary of the main characteristics of what never formed a unified concept:

1. Monarchy is a divinely ordained institution.
2. Hereditary right is indefeasible.
3. Kings are accountable to God alone.
4. Non-resistance and passive obedience are enjoined by God.[21]

Each point in Figgis's list was the source of numerous debates among medieval and early Tudor legal theorists (the charter agreed to by King John in 1215 and known as "Magna Carta" remained an important thorn in the side of royalty, as it sought to limit kings' rights). The divine right of kings was certainly not a fixed theory, but rather a shifting body of texts riddled with legal difficulties. Be that as it may, times of political turmoil such as the War of the Roses (the series of civil wars in England fought for possession of the crown from 1455 to 1487) prompted legal specialists to try to redefine and consolidate the much-abused notion of royal sovereignty. John Fortescue, Chief Justice of the King's Bench, published *De Laudibus Legum Angliæ* (1471), which was translated in 1567 by Robert Mulcaster and became the main legal reference work for the Elizabethan and Jacobean periods. Fortescue insisted that the king's person was dual but unified. What medieval historian Ernst Kantorowicz famously called "the curious legal fiction of the 'King's Two Bodies' " – the king embodying both a mortal person and an eternal office – stemmed from a series of articulated theological, legal, and philosophical discourses that created the illusion that, by analogy, every ruler was an image of Christ – a mortal but eternal being.[22]

For Fortescue, and depending on the situation, a ruler could be both above and subject to the kingdom's laws. The authority of the sovereign can be "royal" in the sense that it is the expression of the "prince's pleasure": "And such is the dominion that the civil laws purport when they say: The prince's pleasure hath the force of a law."[23] Nonetheless, the king's powers are "political" too, as the monarch must enforce laws that are independent from him: "But from this much differeth the power of a king, whose government over his people is politique. For he can neither change laws without the consent of his subjects, nor yet charge them with strange impositions against their wills" (f. 26^r). Despite the potential incompatibility of the two powers entrusted to the king, Fortescue asserted that "royal" and "political" powers were indissoluble: "he governeth his people by power not only royal but also politique" (f. 25^v). In other words, a king is subject to the common law, but sovereigns also have exceptional powers, which place them above the law. One can see how unsustainable Fortescue's arguments could be, especially in the late Elizabethan and Jacobean periods when the king's prerogatives were such a controversial subject.

Early modern monarchy would have been an institutional miracle if the union of these two almost incompatible powers (royal and political) were perfectly embodied in a mortal and fallible human being. It is no wonder that ultimately, as will be seen later in this chapter, the person of the mortal sovereign tried to efface his mortal body and to hide it behind his immortal one. In so doing, he progressively disappeared behind the sacredness of the institution. Ultimately, and in the course of at least two centuries, the disappearance of the sovereign's mortal body behind the institution led to the birth of the modern state.

Divine Right in Shakespeare

According to Figgis and, well before him, to medieval and Tudor theorists, hereditary right was supposed to be an emanation of divine right, all laws being of divine origin. Nonetheless, Shakespeare's stage exposed bigoted and manipulative uses of divine Providence. The dramatist's exploration of divine right is circumspect, occasionally biting, and conscious of how political discourse can feed on religion to create its mystique or mysticism.

Genealogy and hereditary rights are bywords for political wrangles. Shakespeare's drama suggests that any notion of an "heir apparent" is visibly a sham or an argument constructed after the fact, just like Falstaff's comical justification in *Henry IV Part 1*: "was it for me to kill the heir apparent? Should I turn upon the true prince? ... The lion will not touch the true prince. Instinct is a great matter. I was now a coward on instinct" (2.4.222–5). The truth is that Falstaff really mistook Prince Hal – the heir apparent – for a menacing thief to whom he did not oppose any resistance.

In fact, there are few direct references to the divine right of kings in Shakespeare's history plays. This was not only because the alleged "theory" was an amalgamation of frequently contradictory and partly impenetrable texts, but also because Shakespeare was aware that the subject was touchy and that it could only be treated obliquely. Queen Elizabeth had produced no heir (nor had Edward or Mary before her) and the question of her succession continued to be open and the cause of much anxiety. Direct mentions are usually found in the margins of the main dramatic action of the play. In *Richard II* "Old John of Gaunt" (1.1.1) vehemently denounces the kingdom's decadence, but refuses to take part in the action by avenging his brother Woodstock:

God's is the quarrel, for God's substitute,
His deputy anointed in His sight,
Hath caused his death, the which if wrongfully
Let heaven revenge, for I may never lift
An angry arm against His minister. (1.2.37–41)

In the same play, the Bishop of Carlisle holds on to some kind of divine right, but his words, which go counter to the political reality around him, only stress the powerlessness of Richard II – the news of his abdication having reached us a few lines before (4.1.107–10):

And shall the figure of God's majesty,
His captain, steward, deputy, elect,
Anointed, crownèd, planted many years,
Be judged by subject and inferior breath. (4.1.125–8)

They also cause him to be arrested on the spot by Northumberland for capital treason (4.1.150–1). Dramatic irony is at its height here, with Carlisle bent on defending the divine rights of a monarch who has just renounced a sanctified kingship.

In *King John* references to the divine right of kings are less specific and appear to be just one argument among others to counter the papacy and defend national sovereignty. Responding to Cardinal Pandulf, the Pope's legate, John answers emphatically:

What earthy name to interrogatories
Can task the free breath of a sacred king?
Thou canst not, cardinal, devise a name

So slight, unworthy, and ridiculous
To charge me to an answer, as the Pope. (3.1.147–51)

Of course, members of Shakespeare's audience were no doubt well aware of King Henry VIII's break with Rome (and some might even have recalled the sacking of Rome in 1527 by Charles V, which weakened the powers of the papacy quite considerably). Thus, the above passage might have had an additional ring to the ears of many.

Richard II: From Royal Mystique to Spiritual Lyricism

But what of *Richard II*? Was this not the play where the notions of Providence and sacred kingship were debated most? Moreover, even if the divine right of kings remains mostly backstage, *Richard II* is akin at times to a tragic lyric on the destiny of kings and their sacred aura. Arguably, and well beyond considerations of religious doctrine or legal theory, Shakespeare saw in the history of Richard of Bordeaux material that he could use to stage the tragic but spectacular demise of a sovereign in sacred office.

In some regards, Richard II can be compared to Henry VI for his idealism. Yet, in the case of Richard, it is important to distinguish between elements of royal mystique, with which he consciously surrounds himself to create a personal mythology during his fall, and a humble sort of lyricism that lends a genuinely tragic dimension to the character.

On his return from Ireland, Richard is no longer the reckless character he was at the beginning of the play. From Act 3 onwards, the king is more and more dependent on the mystique of his sovereign role. He makes few, if any, political decisions and prefers to focus on the elaboration of his myth of sacred kingship, which he sees as a source of power. He wraps himself in the idealistic belief of a divinely sanctioned and untouchable sovereignty. Likewise, Henry VI had almost completely cut himself off from the temporal world. Nevertheless, contrary to Richard, Shakespeare's contemplative and saint-like king had little faith in the power of his ideals on the political real. In *Richard II*, the sovereign lives an impossible fantasy dream, and as his political power wanes, his fantasy life increases drastically. Using an implicitly providential argument, the Bishop of Carlisle encourages Richard in his beliefs and goes so far as to equate sanctified kingship with political might: "Fear not, my lord. That power that made you king / Hath power to keep you king in spite of all" (3.2.27–8). Comforted by such arguments and despite the warnings of some of his followers, the king continues to perfect his myth in a passage that has become famous:

Not all the water in the rough rude sea
Can wash the balm off from an anointed king.

> The breath of worldly men cannot depose
> The deputy elected by the Lord.
> For every man that Bullingbrook hath pressed
> To lift shrewd steel against our golden crown
> God for His Richard hath in heavenly pay
> A glorious angel. Then if angels fight
> Weak men must fall, for heaven still guards the right. (3.2.54–62)

This passage has long been interpreted as proof of Shakespeare's belief in the divine right of kings, regardless of the fact that it is a personal statement made by a fictional character, who, at this point in the play, has very few cards left to play. Neither is Richard the embodiment of the traditional medieval sovereign here. He pieces together legal and Christian elements, which, as we have shown, never formed an orthodox and consensual whole. Richard's Providence is indeed "special," but only in the sense that it is self-serving ("God for His Richard"). What is expressed is closer to an absolutist conception of monarchy, according to which there is no difference whatsoever between the private person of the king and his body politic, that is, the mystical body of the state.

Richard's allegedly sanctified personal myth will of course suffer a severe blow as he is ultimately defeated on the political field. Yet he is far from vanquished on the linguistic terrain. It could be claimed that there is a potent spiritual side to his tragic lyricism, especially when he becomes aware that royal mystique is fundamentally hollow and that the king is but a man who should be humbled by existence.[24] Alongside Richard's histrionics, there are glimpses in him of intense lucidity and of more genuine belief. When Richard asks his queen to go to France and retire to a religious convent, his words come close to recalling the allegorical and redemptive spiritual journey of Everyman, in the late fifteenth-century morality play of the same name: "Our holy lives must win a new world's crown / Which our profane hours here have stricken down" (5.1.24–5).

These fleeting moments should not be confused with others where Richard stage-manages his own deposition and overemphasizes the supposed sacrilegious nature of the act. At no point do his words have an impact on the action of the play. His self-interested "theory" of the divine right of kings has more of an effect on consciences – the audience's, but also his successor's, the future Henry IV.

More broadly, *Richard II* is a work that explores the idealism attached to kingship. It shows its political utility, but points to its untenable, or at least frailer, aspects. It was not fortuitous that none of the editions printed during Elizabeth I's reign (1558–1603) contained the scene at the heart of Act 4, Scene 1 in which King Richard is deposed by his own Parliament.[25] The passage appeared in the fourth quarto edition of the play published in 1608. With the queen's succession still remaining unresolved in the 1590s, the story of Richard II served as a way for polemicists of all denominations to debate issues like the rights of succession to the throne of various candidates and questions such as who had the authority to appoint monarchs.[26]

On August 4, 1601, as she perused some of the historical archives of the Tower of London, presented to her by her Antiquarian, William Lambard, documents pertaining to Richard II's distant reign are said to have carried for her an immediate contemporary resonance: "so her Majesty fell upon the reign of King Richard II saying, 'I am Richard II. know ye not that?' " adding, "He that will forget God, will also forget his benefactors; this tragedy was played 40 times in open streets and houses."[27] The Earl of Essex's supporters had commissioned Shakespeare's *Richard II* to be performed at the Globe Theatre in London a few months before on February 7, 1601, on the eve of their ill-fated coup against Elizabeth. There is good reason to believe that the memory was still fresh in the queen's mind as she perused the documents.[28]

The Mysteries of State

If Providence proved to be impenetrable (who could claim to know God's will after all?) and too easily appropriated to serve different agendas, and if divine right turned out to be a series of texts that could expose the inevitable frailties of the natural body of the sovereign, how could the early modern state maintain its legitimacy and find stability?

At the turn of the seventeenth century, some legal theorists developed the idea that to hide the king behind his official mask, or sacred office, would give sovereignty more leeway and authority. In this view, the ruler is no Machiavellian figure in disguise, but like God, his will is inscrutable and his works happen, while he remains concealed. In other words, the sovereign becomes a *deus absconditus*, a distant God. What would be known as the "Mysteries of State," was a rational effort to endow rulers with their own sphere of action, one that remained mostly out of view. In a society still deeply imbued with religion, a theory that eventually led to the constitution of the modern state apparatus still had to be based on religious discourse. In a 1606 treatise entitled *A Comparative Discourse of the Bodies Natural and Politique*, the lawyer Edward Forset introduced these new ideas through the traditional biblical theme of the Fall of Adam, the latter having usurped God's prerogative by seeking to taste the forbidden apple of knowledge. Forset states that

> it is easy to offend in the curiosity of inquiring into State-secrets; there is even in that kind also a forbidden Apple. And it hath ever been reckoned an

> audaciousness not to be digested, to intrude with temerity, where restraint hath placed a cross barre. If every body must know all, counsel were no counsel. The body politique as the natural, is whole and close chested.[29]

Hence is the mortal body of the monarch theoretically entitled to be protected and legitimized by his sacred office. *Hamlet*'s King Claudius is one who dreams of such a protective veil, or "hedge," between him and those who would pry into his guilty secrets: "There's such divinity doth hedge a king / That treason can but peep to what it would, / Acts little of his will" (4.5.124–6). The only sovereign in the whole of Shakespeare's history plays who appears to have achieved the union of the king's two bodies is Henry V. However, Shakespeare's Henry is someone who has become a prisoner of his own office, or body politic. The king's human side disappears behind his role as charismatic ruler, which he is forced to play. For a moment, before the battle of Agincourt, he tries to lay aside his office to plead his case before the most skeptical of his soldiers. Still in disguise though, he speaks of the king's personal self. Nevertheless, his use of the third person is strangely dehumanizing and shows that it is difficult for him to speak directly of his humanity: "All his senses have but human conditions. His ceremonies laid by, in his nakedness he appears but a man" (*Henry V*, 4.1.99–100). These lines have trouble hiding the fact that as a king he has cut himself off from the rest of mankind and that his inhumanity is the price he has to pay for self-preservation, that is, for disappearing behind his body politic.[30]

Shakespeare's only play on the reign of a Tudor monarch, *Henry VIII* (first performed in 1613 under the reign of the Stuart King James I) is equally circumspect. On the face of it, the work appears to be a fable on absolutism with a king who is remote, almost visibly absent, and who constantly hides his real intentions. On closer scrutiny, Henry is no *deus absconditus*, nor is he a prime mover onstage. In fact, dramatic language partly escapes him, and numerous scenes are rife with rumours about him. The king is not aloof because he is dealing with mysteries of state. On the contrary, what we witness is the journey of a ruler attempting to regain power after severely neglecting his duties. According to some, the kingdom is led by a man who has lost all vision: "Heaven will one day open / The king's eyes, that so long have slept, upon / This bold bad man" (2.2.40–2, alluding to Cardinal Wolsey).

By the end of the play, and despite his persistently limited control over dramatic language, the king has sought to master the visible world. He has been self-consciously on show as a sovereign during several ceremonies – the coronation of Anne Boleyn and the baptism of the future Elizabeth I (4.1.35–118 and 5.4.1–76). Wearing a more official and public mask, he needs to see, as well as be seen. With almost divine eyes he spies on his ministers and his courtiers. He is not behind the veil of majesty, but "*at a window above*" (5.2.18), in order to come at last to Thomas Cranmer's rescue, like a *deus ex machina*, when the reformist archbishop is accused of heresy (5.2.156–214).

Conclusion

A legal theorist like Edward Forset might argue that it is possible and advisable to hide the mortal body of rulers behind the sacredness of their office. Shakespeare's stages of history show us that the establishment of kingship on any type of sacred authority (Providence, divine right, or "mysteries of state") is a potential source of conflict. His history plays not only thrive dramatically on contention, but also make the contradictions and silences of his chronicle sources resound meaningfully and problematically. His drama does not transgress or adhere to an orthodox divine theory of sovereignty. It seeks to establish a dialogue between an ideologically conflicted past and a religiously and politically troubled present. It stages characters shaping their earthly and spiritual journeys with shreds of shifting religious, theological, and legal discourse. No metaphysical certainty is ever expressed, but as Shakespeare's sovereigns reflect on their journeys, a spiritual sense of destiny often emerges from their dilemmas, especially when they reach out to us with distinguishable fragments of religious discourse in their last moments.

Notes

1 I have compiled these statistics with the help of M. Spevack's *Harvard Concordance to Shakespeare* (Cambridge, MA: Harvard University Press, 1973). The play that contains the most allusions is ... *Richard III*! The key words in my search avoided all oaths and focused on words such as "religion," "Bible," "belief," "faith," "God," "divine," etc.

2 "Tetralogy thinking" was deeply influenced by the work of E. M. W. Tillyard, *Shakespeare's Elizabethan History Plays* (1944), "which remains the exemplary exegesis of tetralogy thinking," and by the Polish critic Jan Kott in *Shakespeare our Contemporary* (1965). See Stuart Hampton Reeves, "Theatrical Afterlives," in *Shakespeare's History Plays*, ed. Michael Hattaway (Cambridge: Cambridge University Press), 231 and 234–5.

3 See, for instance, Nicholas Grene, *Shakespeare's Serial History Plays* (Cambridge: Cambridge University Press, 2002).

4 E. M. W. Tillyard, *The Elizabethan Picture* (London: Chatto & Windus, 1943) and *Shakespeare's History Plays* (London: Chatto & Windus, 1948). See also Lily B. Campbell, *Shakespeare's "Histories": Mirrors of Elizabethan Policy* (San Marino, CA: The Huntington Library, 1947) for more teleological interpretations.

5 Ian W. Archer, Felicity Heal, and Paulina Kewes, "Prologue," in *The Oxford Handbook of Holinshed's Chronicles*, ed. Paulina Kewes, Ian W. Archer, and Felicity Heal (Oxford: Oxford University Press, 2013), xxix.

6 Alexandra Walsham, "Providentialism," in *The Oxford Handbook of Holinshed's Chronicles*, 432–3.

7 Ibid., 442.

8 Peter Marshall, "Religious Ideology," in *The Oxford Handbook of Holinshed's Chronicles*, 416. In this light, Annabel Patterson's argument that Holinshed's *Chronicles* conveyed proto-democratic middle-class values appears overstated. See her *Reading Holinshed's Chronicles* (Chicago: University of Chicago Press, 1994) and her much-cited article "Rethinking Tudor Historiography," *The South Atlantic Quarterly* 92 (1993): esp. 205–6.

9 William Shakespeare, *King Henry VI Part 2*, Arden 3, ed. R. Knowles (London: Thomson Learning, 2001 [1999]), 201 (note to line 65).

10 See Geoffrey Bullough (ed.), *Narrative and Dramatic Sources of Shakespeare*, vol. 3 (London: Routledge; New York: Columbia University Press, 1960), 90.

11 As Knowles remarks, "If this is Providence, it is of a kind difficult to credit, except in the simple mind of this king": Ronald Knowles, "The Farce of History: Miracle, Combat, and Rebellion in 2 *Henry VI*," *Yearbook of English Studies* 21 (1991): 169.

12 See D. P. Walker, *Unclean Spirits, Possession and Exorcism in France and England in the Late Sixteenth and Early Seventeenth Centuries* (London: Scolar Press, 1981), 17.

13 See Bullough, *Narrative and Dramatic Sources*, 93.

14 Alexandra Walsham, *Providence in Early Modern England* (Oxford and New York: Oxford University Press, 1999), 228–9.

15 Ibid., 229–31. For Foxe, see 231.

16 Ibid., 280.

17 Ibid., 241.

18 Anthony Hammond has indeed remarked that "the verb can be read in the passive voice, implying that Richard's role has been determined by providence": William Shakespeare, *King Richard III*, Arden 2, ed. A. Hammond (London: Methuen, 1981), 127 n.

19 Alexander Leggatt, *Shakespeare's Political Drama: The History Plays and the Roman Plays* (London: Routledge, 1988), 49.

20 Richard is here mocking the biblical commonplace: "he sendeth rain on the just and on the unjust" (Matt. 5:45).

21 John Neville Figgis, *The Divine Right of Kings* (Cambridge: Cambridge University Press, 1914 [1896]).

22 Ernst H. Kantorowicz, *The King's Two Bodies, A Study in Mediaeval Political Theology* (Princeton, NJ: Princeton University Press, 1957), vii, 336–83. See also Marie Axton, *The Queen's Two Bodies, Drama and the Elizabethan Succession* (London: Royal Historical Society, 1977), esp. 14.

23 John Fortescue, *A Learned Commendation of the Politic Laws of England*, trans. Robert Mulcaster (London: Rychard Tottill, 1567), fol. 26^{r}. STC: 11194. Further references to this work will be cited parenthetically in the text.

24 See *Richard II*, 3.2.160–2 and 164–8.

25 These were: Q1 (1597), Q2 (1598), Q3 (1598).

26 See, among the more audacious, the English Jesuit Robert Persons's *A Conference About the Next Succession to the Crowne of England* ([Antwerp], 1594). STC: 19398. The work was printed in 1594 (under the pseudonym of R. Doleman); it began to appear in England in 1595, despite the government's efforts to stem its circulation.

27 Cited in J. Nichols, *Bibliotheca Topographica Britannica*, vol. 1 (New York: AMS Press, 1968 [facsimile reprint of 1780–1790 ed.]), appendix 7, 525.

28 Paul E. J. Hammer, "Shakespeare's *Richard II*, the Play of 7 February 1601, and the Essex Rising," *Shakespeare Quarterly* 59, no. 1 (2008): 1–35.

29 Edward Forset, *A Comparative Discourse of the Bodies Natural and Politic* (London: John Bill, 1606), 98. STC: 11188.

30 See Anne Barton, "The King Disguised: Shakespeare's *Henry V* and the Comical History," in *The Triple Bond: Plays, Mainly Shakespearean, in Performance*, ed. Joseph G. Price (University Park and London: Pennsylvania State University Press, 1975), 102–3.

11

M. LINDSAY KAPLAN

The Merchant of Venice, Jews, and Christians

Both Christian and Jewish characters in *The Merchant of Venice* see themselves as distinct from, and even antithetical to, each other. The Duke distinguishes between Christians and Jews, explaining that Shylock shall "see the difference of our spirit" (4.1.364) in the stark contrast between the Duke's proffered pardon and Shylock's merciless attempt to extract a pound of flesh from Antonio.[1] Shylock also insists on the divergence between Jews and Christians in a number of instances, presenting them as enemies with fundamental differences: he hates Antonio because "he is a Christian" and counters that Antonio "hates our sacred nation" (1.3.34; 1.3.40). However, elsewhere in the play, this distinction appears to dissolve, notably in Portia's request that the litigants before her be identified: "Which is the merchant here, and which the Jew?" (4.1.170). Furthermore, characters of both faiths even insist on the similarity between Christians and Jews. Although he views Christians as disparate from Jews, Shylock also asserts their physical and emotional similarities (3.1.46–53). How do we understand the play's mixed representation of Jews and Christians? Does it simply offer a range of conflicting views, or can we find a more coherent argument emerging from this diversity?

In order to answer this question, we should first consider what the term "Jew" signified in early modern England. Since the Jewish community had been expelled from England at the end of the thirteenth century, few early modern English men and women would have had contact with openly practicing Jews. Yet a small number of observant Jews, secretly observing converts from Judaism, and full converts did reside in England during the time Shakespeare wrote.[2] Furthermore, English travelers encountered Jews abroad and a number of texts circulated in the period describing European Jewish communities.[3] In addition to possible exposure to living Jews and eyewitness accounts of their customs, the English would also have inherited a voluminous and complex literature produced for more than a millennium by Christian theologians about Jews. Although some of these authors had direct contact with Jews and Judaism, they often employed representations of Jews in order to prove arguments about Christian truth; they thus frequently developed ideas that served rhetorical purposes rather than depicting an accurate or sympathetic view of Jews. Jeremy Cohen has named this invention the "'hermeneutical Jew' – that is, the Jew as constructed by the discourse of Christian theology."[4]

Christian theologians focus intensively on defining Jewish identity in part because it helps delineate the shape of Christian identity. Christianity grew out of Judaism; not only did the new religion need to define itself both against and in relation to the older one, but early Christians also justified themselves through recourse to Jewish texts and practices in arguments with other contemporary religions. Additionally, ideas about Jews and Judaism serve as an important means of constructing and stabilizing Christian identity during periods of stressful internal changes and external threats. They register in Christian Scriptures at the advent of Christianity in debates about the requirements of membership in the Jesus movement. They appear in the writings of the Church Fathers who deploy ideas about Jews, Jewish Scripture, and observance in controversies within Christian communities and with other faith groups, including Jews, heretics, and pagans. Medieval Christians facing a split between Eastern and Western Churches, continuing calls for church reform, the multivalent threat of Islam, fears of the mounting popularity of heretical movements, not to mention new questions about the proper place of Jews in Christendom, often utilize ideas about Judaism in attempts to define and defend Christian identity. Given the tradition of Christianity using Judaism as a means of defining itself, we should not be surprised to find Jews frequently implicated in various debates about English religious identity in the tumultuous decades of the sixteenth century that follow the Protestant split from the Catholic Church.

Early modern English definitions associated with the word "Jew" signify in complex and contradictory ways. The term could denote the historical children of Israel, often viewed positively as God's chosen people, as well as the contemporary people who observe Jewish law, often reviled as enemies of the Christian faith for rejecting Jesus and his teachings. Constructions of Jewish identity could also connote Christian identities: English Protestants style themselves as God's newly chosen people of Israel, suffering at the hands of their Catholic enemies just as pagan enemies persecuted the Hebrews; paradoxically, members of the Church of England disparage Catholics as well as non-conforming Christians for "Judaizing," that is, behaving like Jews. As in previous eras, in the early modern period the use of the term "Jew" does not establish a binary contrast in which Christian identity can be defined and stabilized, but a word containing multiple significances that often raises further questions about what it means to be Christian or Jewish.[5]

The complex and even contradictory representations of Shylock and Jessica in *The Merchant of Venice* operate like the early modern construction of Christian identity itself, which simultaneously validates Jews as a model to be emulated, challenges Jews by contesting and appropriating their chosen or elect status, seeks the integration of Jews through conversion, and degrades Jews as enemies to be destroyed. The overdetermined meaning attached to the word "Jew" troubles our ability to understand Shylock and Jessica as either psychologically or theologically consistent characters. We might better grasp their significance by viewing them as "hermeneutical Jews" who embody paradoxical fantasies about Jewish, and thus Christian, identity. If Jessica represents, in part, the idea of Jew as proto-Christian, Shylock, for all of his complexity, is reduced to the menacing Jewish enemy who justifies Christian aggression. Although both of these characters, by virtue of their respective conversions, are in fact Christians at the play's conclusion, aspects of their "Jewish" identity nevertheless persist. This speaks less to the question of the efficacy of conversion and more to the continued usefulness of the "Jewish" ideas Shylock and Jessica represent for the shaping of Christian identity.

Early Modern English Views of Jews and Christians

The numerous texts produced in the wake of the establishment of the Church of England often employ a range of views about Jews to support a point of Church doctrine and/or to disparage Christian opponents. I focus here on five argumentative stances these discourses advance by means of the "hermeneutical Jew" to show how they range from representations of stark contrast to complete identification of Christians with Jews. The notion that the Jews constitute the enemies of Christians poses the most extreme juxtaposition of the two faiths. In his treatise on Church governance, *Of the Laws of Ecclesiastical Polity* (1593), the prominent Anglican theologian Richard Hooker accurately rehearses, without endorsing, this traditional claim that presents the Jews as antithetical to Christians:

> [T]he *Jews* were the deadliest and spitefullest enemies of Christianity that were in the world, and in this respect their orders so far forth to be shunned ... For no enemies being so venomous against Christ as *Jews*, they were of all other most odious, and by that mean least to be used as fit Church-patterns for imitation ... there be small cause wherefore the Church should frame itself to the Jew's example, in respect of their persons which are most hateful. (Italics original)[6]

Hooker articulates this point in debating the extent to which the observances of the Jews could serve as authority for ceremonies of the Church of England. Although he argues in favor of these rites, his presentation of an opposing argument paints the Jews in the strongest adverse terms. They are the most deadly, spiteful, venomous, odious, hateful enemies of Christ and Christians, not only because of their religion, but even "in respect of their persons."[7]

However, while the Jews might epitomize the enemy of the faith, in the sixteenth-century conflicts between Catholic and Protestants as well as within intra-Protestant debates, a Christian opponent poses the more immediate and formidable threat. In these arguments, authors often use this antithetical construction of Judaism to disparage Christian antagonists. For example, Hooker situates his discussion of Jewish antipathy to Christians in defending himself against charges from other Protestants that disparage as too "Jewish" the ceremonies he supports.[8] One means by which Protestants sought to delegitimize the Catholic Church was to demonstrate its anti-Christian similarity to Judaism.[9] Andrew Willet, another influential Anglican theologian, employs this strategy in his *Tetrastylon Papisticum* (1593), a critique of Catholicism:

> In most of their chief questions, [Catholics] are fain to beg some help of the Jews and run to their beggarly ceremonies, as St. Paul called them, for succour ... To prove their traditions beside scripture, they allege the unwritten traditions of the Jews. And yet we read of no such authentical traditions which they had, but those which were unlawful and superstitious, condemned by our Saviour Christ.[10]

Claiming that Catholics have no scriptural warrant to authorize their ceremonies, Willet asserts that they turn to inauthentic, unlawful, and superstitious traditions of the Jews. Here Jewish precedent serves to undermine Catholic customs. But Willet takes his argument further to argue that Catholics exceed Jewish error:

> And yet never did the Jews use half of those ceremonies ... as papists do ... The Jews themselves would blush to behold such things ... Nay they do not content themselves with an apish imitation of Jewish ceremonies, but they also belie them, and father upon them such things as they never used ... They cumber religion with their burdensome inventions: so that the Jews' case was more tolerable (than theirs that live under Popery) who were subject only to legal ceremonies, not to the inventions of men.[11]

The Catholic Church not only adopts Jewish observance but invents and ascribes practices to Jews that the latter never actually followed. Here, Catholics, in passing off their innovations as derived from Judaism, behave in a manner even worse than the Jews. Catholic defenders also use the idea of the Jewish enemy to attack Protestant opponents. In his *Demands to be Proponed of Catholics to the Heretics* (1576), the English Catholic priest Richard Bristow challenged his Protestant opponents by naming them "Heretics," traditional foes to the true Christian faith: "Christ and his Christians have, besides schismatics and heretics, two other kinds of enemies, to wit, Paynims and Jews: and ... ancient writers have made many goodly books against those enemies ... [L]et [Protestants] be ... demanded, whether they dare take part also with the very Jews and Paynims against the Christians, yea and against the Godhead of Christ himself."[12] Bristow derides Protestants as schismatic and heretical by including them among pagan and Jewish enemies of "Christ and his Christians." However, the primary status of Jew as enemy informs his attack on Protestants, insofar as he refers to authoritative theologians of the latter as "their Rabbis" and their church as "their synagogue."[13] The identification with the Jews serves to degrade further the status of the Protestants.

However, as God's chosen people and recipients of divine revelation that is Hebrew Scripture, Jews could also serve as a positive example and source of authority for Christian self-legitimation. Protestants could situate the structure and practices of their church and government within the traditions of Judaism to counter Catholic charges of innovation and schism. English Protestants advancing opposing doctrines also drew on Jewish sources to justify their differing positions.[14] In his treatise, *The True Difference Between Christian Subjection and Unchristian Rebellion* (1585), Thomas Bilson defends the authority of the English state over the Anglican Church against contrary Catholic claims of papal superiority over secular rulers. Bilson brings as evidence the example of the supreme authority of rulers of the people of Israel, arguing that even though "[t]here was an high Priest over the twelve Tribes with surer and better authority than your holy father [the pope] can show for him-self ... & yet this notwithstanding the kings of Judah commanded both Pri[e]st and people for matters of religion."[15] Thus, secular kings rightly exercise authority in spiritual matters. Bilson affirms that "The best Christian Princes have followed the steppes of the kings of Judah," citing that for eight centuries Christian emperors ruled over bishops and the pope himself. He concludes: "It is no doubtful question, but a manifest truth that the best Princes before Christ, and after Christ for many years, meddled with the reformation of the Church, and prescribed laws both Ecclesiastical and Temporal."[16] The example of the Jews provides divine sanction to the Protestant position that kings have the power not only to rule over but also to reform the Church.

The positive example of the Jews served not only to justify theological and political arguments, but also as an object of identification.[17] A founding theologian of the Protestant movement, John Calvin, boldly claims an equal status for Jews and Christians in his *Institutes of the Christian Religion* (first published in English in 1561). In a discussion of the similarity of Hebrew and Christian Scriptures, he announces:

> [A]ll those persons, from the beginning of the world, whom God has adopted into the society of his people, have been federally connected with him by the same law and same doctrine which are in force among us ... The covenant of all the fathers is so far from differing substantially from ours, that it is the very same; it only varies in the administration ... Moreover the apostle [Paul in 1 Cor. 10:1–11] makes the Israelites equal to us, not only in the grace of the covenant, but also in the significance of the sacraments ... we have no reason to arrogate any preeminence to ourselves ... since the Lord not only favoured them with the same benefits, but illustrated his grace among them by the same symbols ... know ye, that the Jews also were not destitute of such symbols ... They were baptized in their passage through the sea, and in the cloud by which they were protected from the fervour of the sun.[18]

Calvin traces an unbroken continuity from God's original people, the Jews, to contemporary Christians, understanding them as sharing the same law and doctrine. The contract that God made with the fathers, that is the Jews, is identical to that which binds Him to Christians. Here the special relationship of the Jews with God serves to authorize that of Christians as well. However, Calvin also contends that the special status enjoyed by Christians, including the grace of baptism and the Eucharist, was similarly accorded to the Jews when they passed through the Red Sea and were protected by divine clouds in the Exodus from Egypt (Exod. 13:18–22, 14:19–31). Thus, his equating of Jews and Christians creates a mutual validation of each to the other.

However, in identifying with Jews, Christians also effectively imagine their replacement. In a discussion of God's visible Church, Hooker, like Calvin, places Protestants in an unbroken line from the original "people of God," the Jews, similarly equating the two groups and legitimizing the former:

> God hath had ever, and ever shall have, some church visible upon earth ... [T]he people of God ... had forsaken the living God, and of him were likewise forsaken ... Howbeit retaining the law of God, and the holy seal of his covenant, the sheep of his visible flock they continued even in the depth of their disobedience and rebellion ...
>
> [Catholics] ask us where our Church did lurk, in what cave of the earth it slept, for so many hundreds of years together before the birth of Martin Luther. As if we were of opinion that Luther did erect a new Church of Christ. No the Church of Christ which was from the beginning, is, and continueth unto the end.[19]

He argues that even though the people of Israel sinned, they nevertheless maintained their connection to God and comprised His congregation which extends even to the present day. This argument for the legitimacy and continuity of the congregation of Israel creates a history in which Hooker can locate the Protestant movement, thus deflecting charges that Luther created a new Church. However, even while he draws on their example for authenticity, he also erases Jews from their own history. The original covenant between God and Israel does not represent Judaism, which extends even to the current moment, but "the Church of Christ which was from the beginning." Ancient Israel constitutes an already Christian Church fully revealed at the coming of Jesus. Contemporary Jews "are excluded out of the bounds of the church," viewed "as aliens and strangers."[20] Thus Hooker's "continuity" essentially reads Christianity back into Jewish Scripture and history, ultimately replacing Judaism with Christianity.

Merging and Maintaining Christian and Jewish Identities in *The Merchant of Venice*

Many readings of the play seek to stabilize its meaning either as ultimately philo- or antisemitic or by arguing that it presents a unified representation of Jews. While we can locate moments where the play contrasts a distinct, evil Jewish identity to a positive Christian one, or the reverse, it elsewhere counterbalances these binaries by blurring differences between Christians and Jews to the point that they threaten to transform into each other. For example, Shylock's caustic rejection of Bassanio's dinner invitation strikingly dissolves the stark contrast between Christian and Jew, even while appearing to insist on it. Although Bassanio's offer suggests an inclusive and generous impulse that should characterize the behavior of a good Christian, in fact Shylock's refusal follows Church doctrine more closely. He insists: "I will not eat with you, drink with you, nor pray with you" (1.3.30). Medieval canon law prohibited Christians from sharing meals with Jews: "All clerics and laymen shall henceforth avoid the banquets of Jews, nor shall anyone receive them to a banquet."[21] Hooker's *Laws of Ecclesiastical Polity* attests to an early modern awareness of this proscription in a discussion of early Church council rulings, in which he explains that they "forbid co[m]munion with *Jews*."[22] Communion would of course include prayer, as well as eating and drinking.

Shylock appears to reference Jewish dietary laws prohibiting consumption of pork as a reason for declining Bassanio's invitation. Yet, rather than citing verses from the Hebrew Bible as proof-texts, "the swine ... is unclean unto you" (Lev. 11:7, Deut. 14:8), he offers as justification an episode from

Christian Scripture (Matt. 8:28–32, Mark 5:1–13, Luke 8:26–33):[23] "Yes, to smell pork, to eat of the habitation which your prophet the Nazarite conjured the devil into" (1.3.27–8). The Gospels' accounts describe Jesus driving devils from a possessed man (or men) into a herd of swine; since the demons request that they be allowed to inhabit the bodies of the pigs rather than be cast into "the deep," his action can be read as merciful (Luke 8:31–2).[24] Shylock's implication that pork should not be eaten because Jesus viewed the animals as worthy of demon possession seems tendentious, since the devils, and not Jesus, chose the pigs as their new abode. However, closer consideration of the relevant scriptural texts, both Hebrew and Christian, reveal a link between the dietary prohibition and devils inhabiting the pigs. The verses in Leviticus and Deuteronomy describe pork as "unclean" in prohibiting its consumption. Two of the Gospel accounts describe as "unclean" the devils that are driven into the swine (Mark 5:8, 13; Luke 8:29) and all three accounts explain that the possessed person(s) has been dwelling among tombs, a place of ritual pollution. Presumably, by entering into the bodies of swine, these spirits render the animals unclean. Thus, Shylock adduces this event from Christian Scripture as evidence in support of the Jewish rationale – uncleanness – for avoiding pork.

Shylock similarly works to obscure the boundaries between the two faith groups by employing Christian texts to support Jewish practice in his description of Jesus as "your prophet the Nazarite." The term appears in Matthew 2:23: "And [Jesus] went and dwelt in a city called Nazareth, that it might be fulfilled which was spoken by the Prophets, *which was*, That he shall be called a Nazarite."[25] The King James Bible follows the New Testament Greek Ναζωραῖος (Nazoraios) or "Nazarene," reflecting the sense suggested by the text that this word marks Jesus as an inhabitant of Nazareth.[26] Matthew explains that this appellation fulfils a prophecy: "he shall be called a Nazarene." Although Hebrew Scripture never refers to anyone as a "Nazarene," Matthew likely has Judges 13:5 in mind, in which an angel of the Lord appears to Samson's mother to announce that she will conceive a son. The angel warns her to avoid wine and unclean things and cautions her not to cut Samson's hair: "for the child shall be a Nazarite unto God."[27] The term "Nazarite" derives from the Hebrew root, נזר (nezer), to separate or dedicate oneself. One becomes a *nazir* by vowing for a specified period of time to refrain from eating grapes and grape products, from cutting one's hair and from coming into contact with a dead body. By taking on these restrictions, the *nazir* acquires a status of increased ritual purity, holiness, and consecration to God similar to that of the high priest. In addition to this voluntary category, the Bible includes those who are *nazirim* from conception, such as Samson and Samuel; in this respect they are similar to prophets.[28] These original meanings would have been available to any careful Bible reader in the audience.[29] Thus Shylock's use of "Nazarite" as *nazir* accords Jesus the roles of prophet (as the play text affirms) and priest honored in the Jewish tradition.[30] Furthermore, the ascription to Jesus of a ceremonial practice abrogated by Christianity, and one that even in Hebrew Scripture involves the unnecessary adoption of ritual stringency, has the uncanny effect of emphasizing Jesus's status as a Jew. It also creates strong resonances with the other themes of eating, drinking, and bodily pollution evoked in the Gospel narrative, applying Jewish meanings to the Christian event.

Shylock again applies his Jewish hermeneutic in the aside he makes upon Antonio's entrance on the stage: "How like a fawning publican he looks!" (1.3.33). This much-debated line gains clarity when we turn again to the Gospels and consider the episode from which it is drawn. Luke explains that Jesus related this parable "unto certain which trusted in themselves that they were just, and despised others" (18:9). He tells of two Jews who go the Temple to pray: a Pharisee who asserts his sanctity by enumerating his good deeds and a humble tax-collector, or publican, who confesses his sin and begs for God's mercy. The Pharisee's self-satisfaction extends so far that he thanks God for not making him as other men: "extortioners, unjust, adulterers, or even as this Publican" (18:11). Jesus concludes by stating the publican was "justified," not the Pharisee: "for every man that exalteth himself shall be brought low, and he that humbleth himself shall be exalted" (18:14). Shylock appears to occupy the position of the Pharisee in disdaining Antonio and impugning his feigned humility. He does exalt himself over Antonio only to be abased later in the play. However, the Pharisee's attitude also duplicates Antonio's attitude and fate. The merchant "hates [Shylock's] sacred nation," publicly denounces his money-lending, insults him as a devil, evil soul, villain, misbeliever, and dog, spits on and kicks him (1.3.40–3, 90–2, 103–21). In response, Shylock suffers these outrages patiently (1.3.98–121). Antonio is ultimately redeemed from Shylock's murderous bond, but not before he is humiliated and abased. Which is the Pharisee and which the publican? Insofar as the merchant and the Jew can represent either party, both of whom are Jewish in the parable, the stark distinctions between the two begin to soften.

On the one hand, these examples could support the traditional Christian claim that Jews fail to interpret Scripture correctly. Yet Christian typology, which reinterprets Hebrew Scriptures not according to their literal meaning but as evidence of the advent of Jesus as Messiah and God, also constitutes a type of misreading. In construing Christian Scripture to support Jewish Law,

Shylock employs a "Christian" interpretive strategy in bestowing/imposing a new meaning to the text.

Conversion provides another site where the distinction between Jews and Christians appears to dissolve as Jewish identity transforms into a Christian one. When he agrees to lend Antonio money, Shylock does so as a friend, that is, he offers a Christian loan, interest-free:

> I would be friends with you, and have your love, ...
> Supply your present wants, and take no doit
> Of usance for my monies ...
> This is kind I offer. (1.3.131, 133–5)

In making a "kind" offer, Shylock suggests that affection motivates his action, but "kind" also connotes "kin"; Shylock lends interest-free as one would to a relation. The Biblical laws governing lending prohibit charging interest of a "brother."[31] Antonio understands both meanings of Shylock's "kindness" as "friendly" and "familial" and takes his behavior as evidence of the Jew's transformation:

> Hie thee, gentle Jew.
> The Hebrew will turn Christian, he grows kind. (1.3.170–1)

In Antonio's description, Shylock inhabits a liminal or double identity here as a Jew who is "gentle": a conflated term of "gentile" and "gentle," that is, one who has improved his status by converting to Christianity.[32] By understanding Shylock as growing "kind," the merchant suggests the Jew will become his kin by converting or "turn[ing]" to Christianity.[33]

Jessica similarly traverses the boundaries between Jew and Christian, though more successfully than her father. Launcelot identifies her as a "most beautiful pagan, most sweet Jew," yet she plans to "Become a Christian" and marry Lorenzo (2.3.10–11; 2.3.20). The play leaves open the moment of her conversion, which calls into question her status at the play's end, but also suggests that she is already Christian. In describing "gentle" Jessica's skin as "fair" and "white," Lorenzo classifies her with other Christians in the play; the term "fair" also describes the appearance of Portia and Antonio. If Gratiano and Launcelot challenge the legitimacy of Jessica's conversion (3.2.217, 3.5.1–14), she insists on her status as a Christian: "I shall be saved by my husband; he hath made me a Christian." Others also perceive her as Christian in contrasting her to her Jewish father, either explicitly or implicitly (Salerio in 3.1.31–3; Lorenzo in 2.4.33–7). Additionally, in extracting her father's wealth from him and in her attentive response to sweet music, her actions in the play align her with the behavior of other Christians (5.1.69–88).[34]

The direct equation of Jew and Christian, absent any discussion of conversion, also appears in the play. While Shylock and Portia oppose each other in ways that seem to reinforce their respective identities as Jew and Christian, they both offer visions of a single identity that encompasses both faith groups. Shylock famously challenges Antonio's antagonism based on religious difference:

> what's his reason? I am a Jew. Hath not a Jew eyes ... hands, organs, dimensions, senses, affections, passions? Fed with the same food ... warmed and cooled by the same winter and summer as a Christian is? (3.1.46–50)

Although he concludes ominously that Jews resemble Christians in taking revenge, even here Shylock effectively questions the basis and validity of their difference. Revenge does not constitute a motive particular to Jews, in contrast to "Christian" mercy; both groups alike seek vengeance, again attesting to their shared identity. In her speech praising mercy, Portia initially seems to contrast it to Shylock's call for strict enforcement of the law:

> Therefore, Jew,
> Though justice be thy plea, consider this:
> That in the course of justice, none of us
> Should see salvation. We do pray for mercy,
> And that same prayer doth teach us all to render
> The deeds of mercy. (4.1.193–8)

However, her discussion of mercy includes everyone; neither Christians nor Jews can be saved by the law alone. Both rely on God's mercy for salvation and should imitate God in showing compassion to others. While some Christian theologians argue that Jews seek to be justified by law alone, in fact mercy plays a central role in both Judaism and Christianity; Portia's inclusive speech seems to reflect this knowledge.[35]

The unstable dividing line between Christians and Jews also includes moments in which the former face the threat of transforming into the latter.[36] Launcelot's protracted and incoherently humorous rationale for leaving Shylock's service offers many justifications, but he closes on one with ominous implications: "for I am a Jew if I serve the Jew any longer" (2.2.91–2). The statement "I am a Jew" appears elsewhere in Shakespeare's plays as a proverbial phrase suggesting a counterfactual situation in which the speaker would be behaving badly (*1 Henry IV* 2.4 and *Much Ado About Nothing* 2.3); however, in this context it can also carry the sense that Launcelot runs the risk of being converted to Judaism by remaining in service to Shylock.[37] Proximity to Shylock's family seems to have a similar effect. Although he speaks in jest, Lorenzo refers to Shylock as "my father Jew" (2.6.26). Even if ultimately Jessica, not Lorenzo, converts to a new faith, his speech registers another possibility, that he will become a Jewish son. If Jessica's husband can make her a Christian, Lorenzo's wife could make him a Jew.

Similarly, Portia's actions as Balthazar, the young doctor of law, counter-intuitively align her more closely with a Jewish rather than a Christian identity. In rejecting Bassanio's request that s/he pervert the law to save Antonio, Portia earns Shylock's praise as "a Daniel, / [a] wise young judge" (4.1.219–20). The complexity of her position here appears in the two names ascribed to her: Balthazar could refer to one of the three wise men who worships the infant Jesus, or the Babylonian king who oppresses the Jews; Daniel, a Jewish prophet, opposes the latter and prophecies his death.[38] Portia thus represents a pagan king who was an early devotee of Jesus, and a pagan king whose oppression of the Jews is punished by death. This mixed status emerges in Portia/Balthazar's actions. When s/he urges Shylock to show mercy, he rejects her plea by insisting on a strict reading of the agreement: "Is it so nominated in the bond?" (4.1.255). However, she mirrors, rather than opposes Shylock's strategy, in her reading of the bond:

> This bond doth give thee here no jot of blood.
> The words expressly are "a pound of flesh."
> Take then thy bond, take thou thy pound of flesh,
> But in the cutting of it, if thou does shed
> One drop of Christian blood, thy lands and goods
> Are by the laws of Venice confiscate. (4.1.302–7)

Portia, who has just characterized herself as "an unlessoned girl, unschooled, unpractised" (3.2.159) here proves a better literal reader of the law than Shylock. Paul establishes the distinction that "the letter killeth, but the Spirit giveth life" (2 Cor. 3:6); Christian theology develops the notion that the Jews read Scripture according to the letter, and therefore misunderstand its true meaning.[39] Portia/Balthazar thus reads like a Jew in this scene. Furthermore, the distinction s/he makes between flesh and blood has particular resonance in Hebrew Scripture, which equates blood with life and enjoins non-Jews as well as Jews to separate blood from the flesh before eating the latter (Gen. 9:4).[40] Portia/Balthazar wins her case against Shylock not through employing "Christian" mercy, but through her superior interpretation and deployment of legal texts.

And yet, the concluding scenes of the play provide a strong counterbalance to these moments in which the boundaries of Christian and Jewish identities seem to dissolve. While Portia deploys a "Jewish" literal and legalistic reading of the bond, she does so to serve the interest of Christian Venetians. Shylock's action against Antonio reveals not simply a vengeful moneylender, but a Jewish enemy of the faith. She does not forbid Shylock from spilling human blood, but rather warns that if he "dost shed / One drop of Christian blood" (4.1.305–6) he will forfeit his lands and goods to the state of Venice. Rather than relying on a simple prohibition of murder shared by Jews and Christians alike, Portia distinguishes and privileges Christian life, revealing it to be co-extensive with the interests of the Venetian state. While Jews living in early modern Venice in fact enjoyed the status of citizens under civil law,[41] Portia/Balthazar identifies Shylock as a foreigner:

> If it be proved against an alien
> That by direct or indirect attempts
> He seek the life of any citizen
> The party 'gainst the which he doth contrive
> Shall seize on half his goods, the other half
> Comes to the privy coffer of the state,
> And the offender's life lies in the mercy
> Of the Duke only, 'gainst all other voice.
> In which predicament I say thou stand'st. (4.1.345–3)

However, the source of this alien status which puts Shylock's life and property at the mercy of the state derives not from secular law but theology. As Hooker explains, the Christian Church "holdeth for aliens and strangers ... Jews [who] ... are excluded out of the bounds of the church."[42] Ultimately, the trial scene reaffirms the distinctions between Christians and Jews and privileges the interests of the former over the latter.

Even the prospect of Shylock's conversion, which should signal the triumph of Christianity in successfully transforming Jews into Christians, ultimately serves to reinforce rather than erase boundaries dividing the two faiths. Antonio's request that as a condition of his pardon Shylock "presently become a Christian" (4.1.383) raises the prospect of eroding entirely the distinction between the play's strongest Christian and Jewish antagonists. Rather than merging two equal identities, this process subsumes and erases the Jew by turning him into a Christian. Shylock appears to submit to this condition, although his departure in an indisposed state reinforces the fact that his acceptance is coerced, not voluntary. While he does not reappear on the stage, he is mentioned in the final scene when Portia gives to Lorenzo and Jessica "From the rich Jew, a special deed of gift, / After his death, of all he dies possessed of" (5.1.292–3). Shylock's status as "the rich Jew" even after his conversion has presumably taken place would seem to challenge the efficacy of this transformation. The inability to transform Jews into Christians would seem to threaten a core doctrine of Christian belief. However, the value of the persistent (and resistant) idea of the "rich Jew" lies not in his wealth that nourishes Christians like the manna with which God fed Israel, but in the very concept of "Jew" that remains distinct and thus available for use in shaping Christian identity.

If early modern English attitudes offer more positive evaluations of Jews, especially when compared to more palpable and urgent Christian antagonists in the wake of the Reformation, nevertheless these ameliorated attitudes towards Jews remain instrumental to the interests of Christianity, rather than represent an acceptance of contemporary Jews and Judaism. While the play offers a nuanced and complex representation of a range of Jewish and Christian identities, ultimately ideas about Jews serve the interests of the dominant Christian culture that creates them. The apparent contradiction of Jessica's voluntary conversion versus Shylock's coerced and possibly unsuccessful one resolves with the realization that the Jewish identity of both characters endures to the play's end. Their status as Jews, albeit constructed diversely and to different ends, remains necessary for the process by which Christians form, distinguish, and authorize their own identity.

Notes

1 William Shakespeare, *The Merchant of Venice*, ed. M. M. Mahood (Cambridge: Cambridge University Press, 2003).

2 James Shapiro, *Shakespeare and the Jews* (New York: Columbia University Press, 1996).

3 Yaacov Deutsch, *Judaism in Christian Eyes: Ethnographic Descriptions of Jews and Judaism in Early Modern Europe* (Oxford: Oxford University Press, 2012).

4 Jeremy Cohen, *Living Letters of the Law: Ideas of the Jew in Medieval Christianity* (Berkeley: University of California Press, 1999), 2–3.

5 Achsah Guibbory, *Christian Identity, Jews, and Israel in Seventeenth-Century England* (Oxford: Oxford University Press, 2010).

6 Richard Hooker, *Of the Lawes of Ecclesiastical Polity* (1593), bk. 4, chap. 11, 189–90.

7 See also Guibbory's discussion in *Christian Identity*, 4, 64.

8 The chapter heading to this discussion reads: "Their exception against such Ceremonies as we have received fro[m] the Church of Rome, that church having taken them from the Jews." Hooker, *Of the Lawes*, 189.

9 Guibbory, *Christian Identity*, 57–8.

10 Quoted in M. Lindsay Kaplan (ed.), *"The Merchant of Venice": Texts and Contexts* (Boston: Bedford/St. Martin's, 2002), 270.

11 Kaplan, *"The Merchant of Venice,"* 272–3.

12 Ibid., 274–5.

13 Ibid., 276.

14 Guibbory, *Christian Identity*, 21–4; 62.

15 Thomas Bilson, *The True Difference Between Christian Subjection and Unchristian Rebellion* (Oxford: Joseph Barnes, 1585), 199.

16 Ibid.

17 Guibbory, *Christian Identity*, 21–88 *passim*.

18 John Calvin, *Institutes of the Christian Religion*, trans. and ed. by John Allen (Philadelphia: Presbyterian Board of Publication, 1844), bk. 2, chap. 10, secs. 1–2, 5: 385–7.

19 Hooker, *Of the Lawes*, 3.1: 128–9.

20 Ibid., 3.1: 127.

21 Amnon Linder (ed.), *The Jews in the Legal Sources of the Early Middle Ages* (Detroit, MI: Wayne State University Press; Jerusalem: Israel Academy of Sciences and Humanities, 1997), 673.

22 Hooker, *Of the Lawes*, 4.11: 194.

23 While she does not analyze this phenomenon, Emma Smith notes Shylock's tendency to quote Christian, rather than Jewish, Scripture: "Was Shylock Jewish?" *Shakespeare Quarterly* 64, no. 2 (Summer 2013): 188–219, 209–10.

24 Although the herd of pigs immediately charges into a body of water and drowns, so the kindness of this action is left in question.

25 The Geneva Bible (1560). In Anne Barton's commentary on *The Merchant of Venice*, she explains that both the Bishop's Bible and the Geneva Bible employ the term "Nazarite," which she glosses as "Nazarene." *The Riverside Shakespeare*, ed. G. Blakemore Evans (Boston: Houghton Mifflin, 1974), 258, note to 1.3.34.

26 King James Bible (1611), Matt. 2:23.

27 While Samson does not appear to be an apposite precursor of Jesus, Christian exegesis does understand the former as a type of the latter, insofar as angels announce the birth of each. See M. R. James, "Pictor in Carmine," *Archaeologia* 94 (1951): 141–66, 151.

28 Jacob Milgrom and Aaron Rothkoff, "Nazirite," in *Encyclopaedia Judaica*, 2nd edn., vol. 15, ed. Michael Berenbaum and Fred Skolnik (Detroit, MI: Macmillan Reference USA, 2007), 45–7.

29 For example, Willet makes mention of the *nazir* in his criticism of Catholic attempts to justify their practices with recourse to Jewish law: "Vows and Monkery proved by the example of the Nazirites and Rechabites, amongst the Israelites." Quoted in Kaplan, "*Merchant of Venice*," 271.

30 While not published until after the composition of the play, Thomas Coryate offers a fascinatingly resonant account of a conversation with a Venetian rabbi: "I casually met with a certain learned Jewish Rabbi that spoke good Latin. I … asked him his opinion of Christ … he made me the … answer … that Christ forsooth was a great prophet, and in that respect as highly to be esteemed as any prophet amongst the Jews that ever lived before him; but derogated altogether from his divinity. [In response to Coryate's attempt to convert him,] He again replied that we Christians do misinterpret the Prophets, and very perversely wrest them to our own sense, and for his own part he had confidently resolved to live and die in his Jewish faith." Quoted in Kaplan, "*Merchant of Venice*," 142–3.

31 The Hebrew Bible permits charging interest for loans to strangers, but not to brothers (Exod. 22:25, Lev. 25:35–7, and Deut. 23: 19–20). In refusing to practice usury with Antonio, Shylock actually follows both Jewish and Christian interpretations of these laws. Kaplan, "*Merchant of Venice*," 188–92.

32 M. Lindsay Kaplan, "Jessica's Mother: Medieval Constructions of Jewish Race and Gender in *The Merchant of Venice*," *Shakespeare Quarterly* 58 (2007): 1–30, 21–2.
33 Although Bassanio doubts Shylock's sincerity here, Antonio rightly predicts that Shylock will convert; the merchant stipulates conversion as one of the provisions of the "merciful" pardon the Jew receives in Act 4.
34 For a fuller argument for the play's representation of Jessica as a Christian, in contrast to her father, see Kaplan, "Jessica's Mother."
35 Martin Yaffe makes a similar point in *Shylock and the Jewish Question* (Baltimore, MD: Johns Hopkins University Press, 1997), 9.
36 For a discussion of this phenomenon in the play, see Janet Adelman, *Blood Relations: Christian and Jew in the Merchant of Venice* (Chicago: University of Chicago Press, 2008).
37 Canon law prohibited Jews from holding Christian slaves and domestic servants, in part out of fear that the masters would influence their dependents to convert to Judaism. See Walter Pakter, *Medieval Canon Law and the Jews* (Ebelsbach: R. Gremer, 1988), 132.
38 See Daniel 5:17–30 and David Lyle Jeffrey (ed.), *A Dictionary of Biblical Tradition in English Literature* (Grand Rapids, MI: W. B. Eerdmans, 1992), 73, 83, 472.
39 Cohen, *Living Letters*, 51, 59.
40 While Jewish law requires that Jews remove blood from meat before eating it, it also includes this restriction in the seven principles given to Noah, derived from Genesis 9, that are thought to apply to non-Jews as well. Steven S. Schwarzschild et al., "Noachide Laws," in *Encyclopaedia Judaica*, vol. 15, 284–7. Hooker lists the seven precepts delivered by God to the sons of Noah, which includes: "not to eat of any living creature whereof the blood was not first let out." Hooker, *Of the Lawes*, 4.11:191.
41 Kenneth Stow, *Catholic Thought and Papal Jewry Policy, 1555–1593* (New York: Jewish Theological Seminary of America, 1977).
42 Hooker, *Of the Lawes*, 3.1: 127.

12

JENNIFER R. RUST

Religious and Political Impasses in *Measure for Measure*

Measure for Measure (1604) is widely recognized as one of Shakespeare's most religiously allusive plays: critics have noted that it includes over thirty biblical allusions, beginning with the title of the play itself, which is derived from the Sermon on the Mount (Luke 6:36–8).[1] The title is embedded in the play at a climactic point that exemplifies the vexed relations between politics and theology that run throughout the drama. The allusion occurs in the final act, at the hinge of tragic judgment and comic mercy, in the speech of the sovereign figure of Vienna, the Duke Vincentio, who has spent most of the play disguised as a holy friar. No other personage in the play confounds political and religious authority so thoroughly, and the dissonant notes in this speech reflect the perplexity of the relationship between these two forms of authority in the play overall. As the full scope of his deputy Angelo's transgressions is revealed, the Duke appears to pronounce a final verdict:

> The very mercy of the law cries out
> Most audible, even from his proper tongue:
> An Angelo for Claudio, death for death;
> Haste still pays haste, and leisure answers leisure;
> Like doth quit like, and measure still for measure.
> Then, Angelo, thy fault's thus manifested
> Which, though thou wouldst deny, denies thee vantage.
> We do condemn thee to the very block
> Where Claudio stooped to death, and with like haste.
> Away with him. (5.1.400–9)

The Duke's scriptural allusions are strikingly mixed. The most obvious biblical echo is of Christ's Sermon on the Mount, where the audience is enjoined to adopt a merciful spirit in judgment, always bearing in mind the failings of the judge as well as the transgressor:

> Be ye therefore merciful, as your Father also is merciful. Judge not, and ye shall not be judged: condemn not, and ye shall not be condemned: forgive,

> and ye shall be forgiven. Give, and it shall be given unto you: a good measure, pressed down, shaken together and running over shall men give into your bosom: for with what measure ye mete, with the same shall men mete to you again. (Luke 6:36–8)

While the Duke clearly plays upon Christ's language in the passage, in many ways the speech seems to recall more strongly the Old Testament law that Christ seeks to modify, echoing such phrases from the Mosaic law as "if death follow, then thou shalt pay life for life, eye for eye, tooth for tooth, hand for hand, foot for foot" (Exod. 21:23–4). The context of the speech reinforces the idea of retaliation: Angelo, who is supposed to have unjustly taken the life of Claudio, is being sentenced to undergo the same fate as the man he wronged. Rather than following the supersessionary pattern familiar to early modern Christians (in which the old law is overcome and fulfilled by the new dispensation of Christ), the Duke's speech contaminates the New Testament moment with the Old Testament in a way that obscures rather than clarifies the order he seeks to execute. Where the audience might expect the Duke to speak of the justice of the law, he instead speaks of its "mercy," which he then conflates with the retaliatory "death for death," evocative of Exodus. While the Duke claims to speak in the very voice of the law – its "proper tongue" – this tongue seems tied, knotted around conflicting scriptural precedents.

The Duke's struggle to find the right biblical precedent to express his authority at this moment is consistent with the adventures of a ruler who strains to inhabit the role of a "power divine" (5.1.362). Some critics have read the dissonant allusiveness of the Duke's speech as a signal to Isabella that she should follow the example of Christ and seek mercy for Angelo, despite the wrongs he has committed against her, as indeed she does moments later when she kneels beside Mariana: "Most bounteous sir, / Look if it please you on this man condemned / As if my brother lived" (5.1.437–9).[2] At the least, these incongruities might be harbingers of the Duke's ultimate leniency toward Angelo when Claudio is resurrected as a result of the Duke's own earlier machinations. However, considering that the title of the play as a whole is derived from this passage (to which the Folio draws attention by printing both instances of "measure" in italics), the dissonances in the Duke's language may be related to larger tensions between pastoral and political authority: the encouragement toward mercy reflects a pastoral concern for the improvement of souls, while the demand for judgment reflects a political imperative to instill social order by stern example.

This contradictory dynamic influences the overall interpretation of the play. While clearly *Measure for Measure* is deeply involved with religious questions, its precise religious orientation remains controversial among scholars. On one hand, some critics have discerned a strong "anti-Puritan" strain running throughout the play, associated most strongly with the portrayal of Isabella's antagonist, the "precise" Angelo (1.3.51), who reflects the stern traits of godly Protestants in Shakespeare's London, but who is ultimately revealed to be hypocritical and corrupt.[3] Furthermore, the play's heroine, Isabella (a novice of the Order of Saint Clare), is the most prominent Shakespearean character to aspire to life in a Catholic religious order. On the other hand, the most striking example of an early reader response to the play occurs in a 1632 Second Folio owned by an English Jesuit seminary in Valladolid, Spain: *Measure for Measure* is the only play completely excised from that volume.[4] Whatever the anti-Puritan slant of the play, it was evidently not considered fit reading for Jesuit missionaries in training, despite their avowed goal to reclaim England from Protestant heresy. *Measure* is at once deeply engaged with religious concerns, yet potentially offensive to several divergent major religious movements in Shakespeare's time. The absence of a clear partisan preference in such a religiously charged era suggests the play may be concerned with developments in religious and political government that transcend the confessional differences inspired by the Reformation.

The divided reception of the play may be linked to the predicament that establishes its plot. Although the play seems to foreground sexual vice as the problem most overtly plaguing Vienna, there are hints of an underlying crisis, an emergent and escalating pressure exerted from a strident, religiously motivated asceticism, which is embodied variously by Puritan and Counter-Reformation figures. The pressure of such forces on the Duke's government may be discerned in the Duke's withdrawal from the body politic, his adoption of the guise of the Friar, and his simulation of pastoral activities that seek to restrain not only lax sexual morals but also extreme asceticism. These efforts, however, appear only partially successful, as the Duke proves to be an awkward or inept pastor in several instances. Throughout these episodes, religion appears more as an impasse than a resource for the political order, fragmenting rather than unifying the commonwealth. The Duke's feigned pastoral persona succeeds in addressing these fractures in only a limited, provisional manner.

Scholars so frequently associate *Measure*'s Duke with the newly minted English monarch of 1604, King James I, that they sometimes dryly evoke a "King James Version" of the play.[5] James aspired to be recognized as ruling by "divine right;" this aspiration extended to the Scriptures themselves as the king authorized the standard English translation of the Bible that still bears his name and that was intended to supplant the exhaustively glossed,

Calvinist-oriented Geneva Bible that deeply influenced early modern English religious culture (and that Shakespeare himself drew upon extensively).[6] The Duke's aspirations to rule by divine right are both more furtive and more flagrant: he not only echoes scriptural rhetoric when he acts as a secular sovereign but he also actually adopts the costume of cleric, posing as Friar Lodowick, to observe the "passes" (5.1.363) of his subjects and to dissimulate sacramental rites. The Duke's heresy, however, is only a somewhat more exaggerated version of the Royal Supremacy of the monarch over the English Church, inaugurated by Henry VIII in 1534. In a world in which myriad aspects of social life had been governed by a church that was usually distinct from the authority of the sovereign, the expansion of political sovereignty to include the spiritual authority of the church introduced a new range of challenges for English rulers, who increasingly became involved in social and theological questions that had not been their traditional domain. Perhaps, as some critics have more recently suggested, the more apt royal analogue to *Measure*'s Duke is Henry rather than James.[7]

Both Henry and James styled themselves as absolute monarchs, and critics have frequently discerned a similar aspiration to absolute rule in *Measure*'s Duke. Their evaluations of the character and ultimate success of the Duke's absolutist tendencies, however, differ according to their inclinations to read the play in terms of either secular power or sacred virtue. Some critics take a dark view of this theme, in which the Duke as Friar achieves omniscience over his subjects; he is able to scrutinize their most private transgressions and ultimately to manipulate them to conform to his ideal of state order. In this interpretation, religious elements in the play (such as the Friar's habit and practices like marriage and confession) are "mere politic devises," emptied of their spiritual significance and turned into instruments to serve secular power.[8] On the other hand, critics who wish to affirm the vitality of religion in the play have a more positive assessment of the Duke's double role as ruler and religious authority: in this reading, the Duke's disguise signifies his sacred sovereignty and underscores his providential role as an agent of Christian grace, mercy, and reconciliation at the end of the play.[9]

Both of these lines of argument are too quick to stabilize a dramatic world and religious climate that are actually far more volatile and inchoate. When the instability of the play's religious milieu is taken into full consideration, the Duke's strategies look less absolutely triumphant in either secular or religious terms. In its fractured religious environment, *Measure*'s Vienna is not unlike Shakespeare's London, a milieu that mingled godly Calvinists, Catholic recusants, church papists, and lukewarm conformists to the established Church, all of whom were almost certainly represented in the play's original audiences. Whether or not the Duke is an avatar of James or any other English ruler, the divergent religious tendencies of the supporting cast plausibly reflect conflicting strains in the English populace at large.

The pressure of a religiously divided commonwealth may be discerned in the Duke's explanation of his decision to go undercover, in which his concerns vacillate between a preoccupation with vice and an anxiety about overzealous virtue. In a penitential speech early in the play, the Duke confesses his sins of omission as a governor. He has failed to uproot the "headstrong weeds" (1.3.21) choking his commonwealth, an image that evokes the exuberant overgrowth of a fallen world, a promiscuous overrunning of order. However, as the scene unfolds, the Duke reveals that he is more preoccupied with the austerity and zeal of his substitute Angelo, the deputy to whom he has entrusted "mortality and mercy in Vienna" (1.1.44). Although it initially seems that the Duke wants Angelo to re-establish order in the city, a secondary, but perhaps more urgent, agenda underlies the Duke's actions:

> Lord Angelo is precise,
> Stands at a guard with envy, scarce confesses
> That his blood flows, or that his appetite
> Is more to bread than stone. Hence shall we see,
> If power change purpose, what our seemers be. (1.3.51–5)

In referring to Angelo as "precise," the Duke uses a term that was also applied to ascetic "Puritan" Protestants in early modern England. The Duke casts Angelo's "precision" in negative, even inhuman terms; it is associated with the deadly sin of "envy" and a denial of the body. The Duke jarringly adapts the biblical script of the temptation of Christ to characterize his agenda toward Angelo: he is skeptical that Angelo is actually capable of upholding the role of the abstemious Christ he seeks to imitate when he "scarce confesses ... that his appetite is more to bread than stone." The Duke allusively compares himself to the devil in the gospel of Matthew, the "tempter" who implores Christ to prove his divinity by issuing a "command that these stones be made bread" (Matt. 4:3). As he articulates his plan to test his deputy, the Duke implies that he perceives Angelo's model of ascetic, Puritanical government to be a greater threat than the unruly "weeds" that supposedly overrun his state. His adoption of a pastoral role as Friar is driven as much by the challenge posed by Angelo's stern, but possibly hypocritical, mode of governance as any sense of general lawlessness in the city.

Although the lax respect for law in the city is seemingly opposed to Angelo's strident legalism, on a deeper level these problems are inextricably linked: both are symptoms of an impasse between a fragmented religious discourse and a desire for social and political stability in Vienna. The impasse reflected in the dissonances of the Duke's confessional discourse also inflects the prior scene, which opens with a series of bawdy exchanges among a set of dissolute gentlemen that is also curiously charged with references to theological controversy. Ironically, it is Lucio, perhaps the most dissipated of the lot, who insists on a theological frame of reference:

> 1 GENTLEMAN: Heaven grant us its peace, but not the King of Hungary's.
> 2 GENTLEMAN: Amen.
> LUCIO: Thou conclud'st like the sanctimonious pirate that went to sea with the ten commandments but scraped one out of the table.
> 2 GENTLEMAN: Thou shalt not steal?
> LUCIO: Ay, that he razed.
> 1 GENTLEMAN: Why, 'twas a commandment to command the captain and all the rest from their functions: they put forth to steal. There's not a soldier of us all that, in the thanksgiving before meat, do relish the petition well that prays for peace.
> 2 GENTLEMAN: I never heard any soldier dislike it.
> LUCIO: I believe thee, for I think thou never wast where grace was said.
> 2 GENTLEMAN: No? A dozen times at least.
> 1 GENTLEMAN: What? In metre?
> LUCIO: In any proportion, or in any language.
> 1 GENTLEMAN: I think, or in any religion.
> LUCIO: Ay? Why not? Grace is grace, despite of all controversy: as, for example, thou thyself art a wicked villain, despite of all grace. (1.2.4–22).

Despite its comic tone, this dialogue establishes several substantial theological questions about the status of biblical law (the "ten commandments") and the nature of "grace" (divine mercy and love) that foreshadow serious debates among the main protagonists later in the play. The passage illustrates that even among the city's dissipated gentlemen, religious questions are matters of lively debate. Lucio's reference to the "sanctimonious pirate" who defaces biblical commandments foreshadows Angelo's transgressions, particularly insofar as Angelo initially appears as the type of godly magistrate who favors a strict Old Testament legalism, but then falls far below that standard. The pirate is an emblem of hypocrisy: he demands the empty appearance of a body of divinely ordained laws, but he readily disfigures God's word when it inconveniently contradicts his illicit earthly business.

Lucio portrays divergence in religious doctrines as an impasse that may be mocked but not finally resolved. His jesting assertion that "grace is grace, despite of all controversy" implies a critique of Puritanism, insofar as the same godly types who advocated that secular law should adhere to Old Testament models tended also to favor a predestinarian theology of grace: God's grace, they said, will be bestowed only on an elect few, mysteriously determined at the beginning of history. From a predestinarian perspective, works of penance or charity can never attain this grace; all who lack election are reprobate and irredeemably damned. Although he clearly does not offer an elaborate theological argument, Lucio's assertion that "grace is grace" loosely alludes to a contested verse in Paul's Letter to the Romans: "if [election] be of grace, it is no more of works: or else were grace no more grace" (Rom. 11:6). Thomas Fulton claims that Lucio's "dismissive allusion" to Romans subverts Calvinist claims "to make grace dependent on only one biblical reading, or on only one salvific model."[10] Whatever the merits of Lucio's theological critique, it is nonetheless difficult to see him or his companions as spokesmen for a positive religious alternative to strict godly Puritanism, particularly since, in the next breath, they start "figuring diseases" (1.2.42) of a sexual nature in each other. While religious discourse permeates the scene, it is also portrayed as a source of division or "controversy" that is unable to sustain a healthy social order.

These socio-religious dissonances extend to the ritual of marriage, as exemplified by Claudio's plight. Claudio enters the scene under arrest, the first example of Angelo's severe new regime. Ironically, while his more offensive compatriots remain free, Claudio is sent to prison for far more mild misconduct: impregnating his betrothed before they have exchanged formal, public vows of matrimony. Claudio and Juliet's dilemma was also a common circumstance in early modern England, as ecclesiastical court records show. In Vienna under Angelo's rule, however, the transgression is handled not as a penitential matter in an ecclesiastical court (as it would have been in England, even after the Reformation), but by the secular criminal legal system, as a capital offense. This legal response would have seemed as outrageous to most of Shakespeare's audience as it does to modern audiences, but some radical Protestants of Shakespeare's time did argue that civil authorities should use the death penalty to address the problem of "fornication," citing biblical precedents, including Mosaic law.[11] In his willingness to execute such penalties, circumventing the normal ecclesiastical and communal means for addressing the issue, Angelo is again affiliated with this faction. In the play, Claudio is prosecuted under an old law, a "drowsy and neglected Act" (1.2.151), which again may reference the Old Testament orientation of Puritans. However, nearly every other character in the play is horrified by this official response – including Claudio's pious and ascetic sister Isabella, who exclaims, on learning the news, "O, let him marry her." (1.4.49).

Although Angelo's criminal prosecution may seem too severe, the couple's circumstances do highlight some contradictions in the social and religious understanding of marriage in Vienna, demonstrating that incoherent traditions also contribute to the larger religious impasse in the play. Claudio's explanation illustrates these tensions:

> Thus it stands with me. Upon a true contract
> I got possession of Julietta's bed –
> You know the lady, she is fast my wife,
> Save that we do the denunciation lack
> Of outward order. This we came not to
> Only for propagation of a dower
> Remaining in the coffer of her friends,
> From whom we thought it meet to hide our love
> Till time had made them for us. But it chances
> The stealth of our most mutual entertainment
> With character too gross is writ on Juliet. (1.2.126–36)

Claudio's description of Juliet as "fast my wife" evokes the traditional practice of the "handfast," which remained current into the seventeenth century. In this statement, Claudio establishes that he and Juliet are betrothed: they have publicly exchanged a promise to marry before witnesses, but they have not officially sealed the marriage with a "denunciation … of outward order," presumably a wedding in church. Despite this lack of "outward" ceremony, they have proceeded to engage in sexual relations, resulting in a visible pregnancy. This common practice may be linked to the pre-Reformation theology of sacramental marriage. According to medieval canon law, a legitimate sacramental marriage could be confirmed by sexual relations between two baptized partners without the involvement of a priest or a public ceremony in church. This understanding began to erode in the early modern period, particularly after the Reformation rejection of the sacramental status of marriage and Counter-Reformation revisions to the marriage rite that made the ecclesiastical role more prominent.[12] Nonetheless, the lingering influence of the older sacramental tradition, as well as continuing ambiguities in English ecclesiastical law, meant that arrangements such as Claudio and Juliet's were far from extraordinary in early seventeenth-century England.[13]

This confusion in English nuptial traditions reinforces the sense that the institution of marriage is an emblem of a larger religious impasse in the play. Although Claudio and Juliet's "most mutual entertainment" recalls an older ideal of sacramental marriage, the stated reason for deferring the formal ceremony casts their relationship in a more materialistic light: the wedding is delayed to encourage "the propagation of a dower" – to increase the amount of money Juliet's family ("her friends") would pay Claudio at their marriage. In seeking to make a monetary profit from their union, the couple engages in a kind of erotic usury that deforms the sacramental bond and renders their relationship comparable to the exchanges of Vienna's thriving sex trade. Ironically, this bid to "propagate" money from the marriage is thwarted by the natural "propagation" represented by Juliet's pregnancy.

Thus, while Claudio and Juliet signify in part the vitality of a traditional religious conception of marriage, this significance is muddled by economic motives that delay the formalization of their marriage. The sacramental is mingled with the contractual in this relationship, which becomes another emblem of religious disarray.

Against the imperfect and sometimes confused religious habits and beliefs of the citizens depicted in this scene, the play positions two apparently stalwart ascetics with distinctly opposed confessional associations who hold themselves apart from the disorder of the larger city. As already noted, the "precise" Angelo is imaginatively affiliated with a strain of hot Protestantism characterized by ascetic personal conduct, a predestinarian theology of grace, and a desire to promote a biblically inspired strict legalism. The Puritan ascetic Angelo is countered by the Catholic ascetic novice Isabella, who challenges not only his stern legal code as she pleads for the life of her brother Claudio, but also, insofar as she unwittingly provokes him into sexual desire, his sense of himself as an individual endowed with divine grace. (Angelo later laments on this loss: "Alack, when once our grace we have forgot, / Nothing goes right: we would, and we would not" [4.5.31–2]).[14]

Although Isabella's position is ultimately more sympathetic, the play does potentially invite audiences to view her strident assertions of purity skeptically, and critics continue to debate how to evaluate her. To some critics, such as J. W. Lever, she has seemed nearly as monstrous as Angelo, particularly when she appears to place her personal sanctity above her brother's life in the wake of Angelo's sexual coercion: "Then Isabel live chaste, and brother die: / More than our brother is our chastity" (2.4.185–6).[15] Lines such as these have been received as either symptomatic of an overly rigid and literalistic Catholic religiosity in need of charitable correction or as an admirable defense of a woman's right to physical and spiritual self-determination.[16] Whether we view Isabella in a critical or idealized light, she represents a religious force that must be taken seriously in the greater scheme of the play. Both the Duke and Angelo, in their own distinct and disturbing ways, acknowledge Isabella's force in their various efforts to contain her.

As Angelo and Isabella embody two distinct strains of asceticism that represent convergent pressures on the Duke's government, they also enact an allegorical debate between legal justice and mercy that exposes enduring tensions at the heart of any Christian commonwealth. This debate culminates in a reversal of positions that reveals the fragility of both ideals of law and mercy, their vulnerability to corruption in a state of fallen humanity. At the outset of this debate, both Angelo and Isabella assert their positions in intense formulations that are antagonistic but also legitimately derive from various sources within the Christian tradition. Their arguments reveal again how religious difference becomes an impasse for social and political order in the world of the play.

During his initial interview with Isabella, Angelo defends the ideal of the law that inspires his prosecution of Claudio with an argument that merges the civil law with the figure of biblical prophecy. He rebuffs Isabella's claim that Claudio's offense is so common that it does not warrant such a harsh penalty:

> The law hath not been dead, though it hath slept.
> Those many had not dared to do that evil
> If the first that did th'edict infringe
> Had answered for his deed. Now 'tis awake,
> Takes note of what is done, and like a prophet
> Looks in a glass, that shows what future evils –
> Either now, or by remissness new conceived
> And so in progress to be hatched and born –
> Are now to have no successive degrees,
> But here they live to end. (2.2.93–102)

Angelo personifies the law as a "prophet" who acts autonomously to purify the human world of "evil," mimicking the agenda of biblical prophets who sought to cleanse their communities of sin through the preaching of jeremiads that envision the fruits of "future evils." The law transcends the cycles of fallen nature by cutting off the life process of crimes: the punishment of evils will allow them "no successive degrees." The law must sacrifice Claudio "now" as an example to prevent more widespread degradation in the future. Angelo's concept of the law evokes an abstract and impersonal form of justice figuratively associated with the moralistic rhetoric of Old Testament prophecy.

Isabella pursues an equally idealistic and biblically sanctioned set of arguments for mercy, drawing instead on the incarnational logic of the New Testament. Isabella confronts Angelo's insistence on the strict letter of the law with an appeal to the medieval doctrine of the Atonement:[17]

> ANGELO: Your brother is a forfeit of the law,
> And you but waste your words.
> ISABELLA: Alas, alas!
> Why all the souls that were, were forfeit once,
> And he that might the vantage best have took
> Found out the remedy. How would you be
> If he, which is the top of judgement, should
> But judge you as you are? Oh, think on that,
> And mercy then will breathe within your lips
> Like man new made. (2.2.73–81)

Isabella counters Angelo's claim that Claudio is "forfeit" to the law by broadening the frame of reference to include all humanity ("all the souls"). All "souls" were "forfeit" to God's law as a result of Original Sin, but instead of demanding the profit (the "vantage"), divine justice provides a "remedy": Christ's sacrifice, which redeems the debt of original sin that humans themselves could never repay, restores and renews the community between God and humanity. Isabella reminds Angelo of the fundamentally imperfect nature of any human law when measured against the universal scope of salvation history. Isabella casts the scheme of salvation in economic rather than legalistic terms; God is more a creditor who forgives debtors than a judge who condemns sinners. Isabella evokes this economy of grace to short-circuit Angelo's legalistic absolutism. It allows her to position Angelo's authority as contrasting rather than continuous with God's own authority, a point she emphasizes when she places this creditor God at the "top of judgement." Isabella assumes that if Angelo reflects on his own sinfulness, he will experience a spiritual rebirth and emerge as the Pauline "man new made," dwelling in the life of "mercy" rather than the death of the law: "For the Law of the Spirit of life *which is* in Christ Jesus, hath freed me from the law of sin and of death" (Rom. 8:2, italics original).

Angelo, however, remains impervious to the theology of grace that underlies Isabella's argument, extending his affiliation with a hyperbolic variant of a Reformation worldview. The reformers rejected the doctrine of the Atonement to which Isabella appeals. While Christ is still understood as the redeemer of humanity, the action of salvation is conceived in juridical rather than economic or transactional terms; God's decisions are not comprehensible in human terms, and thus appear arbitrary and impersonal.[18] Angelo channels this sense of arbitrary impersonality when he tells Isabella, "It is the law, not I, condemn your brother" (2.2.82). Angelo's lack of a transactional understanding of justice and mercy may also account for the apparent arbitrariness of his fall into "sense" or sensuality. He conceives his desire for Isabella precisely in response to her reiteration of the request that he examine his own flaws before judging her brother's: "Go to your bosom, / Knock there, and ask your heart what it doth know / That's like my brother's fault" (2.2.140–2). When Angelo complies, he experiences an abrupt lapse into a sexual desire far more corrupt than Claudio's: "She speaks, and 'tis such sense / That my sense breeds with it" (2.2.146–7). The rational or moral "sense" that Isabella speaks immediately dissolves into a new "sense" of lust. Angelo suddenly moves from one extreme to another, skipping over the relational moment of identification that Isabella has invited. Angelo cannot mediate the recognition of his own sinfulness by acknowledging that he holds this in common with others. This personal failing reenacts the larger impasse created by religious divisions in Vienna.

The ascetic extremes represented by Angelo and Isabella collide and collapse midway through the play, creating an opening for the Duke to assert his own government, a hybrid of pastoral and political governance. In contrast to the ascetics, the Duke is preoccupied with government as a matter of ordering worldly existence; his relative lack of concern with salvation or other transcendent ends is ironically most manifest when he is disguised as a friar. Indeed, the Duke's habit as a friar paradoxically serves to heighten the differences between his approach to government and that of a true pastor. However, it is premature to see the Duke's efforts as a form of successful secularization in the modern sense. While he may attempt to appropriate pastoral modes of government, these attempts fail in various ways: as sacramental acts, but also even as more mundane efforts at spiritual consolation. Particularly in the later acts, the Duke engages in increasingly harried efforts at governance, some ethically dubious despite the pastoral cover he attempts to provide (such as the infamous "bed trick" plot and subsequent "head trick" scheme). More government, but not necessarily more effective government, becomes the hallmark of the Duke's rule. If we can discern the outline of a potential secular state in these machinations, it is not as a positive eventuality, but rather a dim, negative capability.

The Duke's deficiencies as a pastor are most evident when he attempts to assume the role of a confessor. One of the most vivid instances of this is his attempt to console the imprisoned Claudio as he contemplates his impending execution: "Be absolute for death: either death or life / Shall thereby be the sweeter" (3.1.5–6). The opening of this consolation sets the tone for the whole: the Friar-Duke posits "death" and "life" as "absolutes" – the possibility of an afterlife is not admitted. The possibilities for consolation are contained entirely within the worldly realm, even when the Friar-Duke appears to make reference to celestial horizons. He counsels Claudio to remember: "a breath thou art, / Servile to all the skyey influences / That dost this habitation where thou keepst / Hourly afflict" (3.1.8–11). While the "skyey influences" seems to allude to a heavenly realm, the frame of reference is astrological. The "influences" are the stars and planets – material bodies to which human life remains "servile" – not a truly transcendent horizon of salvation. The Duke's materialistic discourse appears more indebted to pagan philosophy than Christian *ars morendi*. Scriptural allusions or even glancing references to the divine are conspicuously missing from this speech. This absence is underscored by the fact that Claudio himself – the soul supposedly being consoled – must supply the missing biblical reference. After the Duke's exhortation, Claudio responds: "To sue to live,

I find I seek to die, / And seeking death, find life" (3.1.42–3), paraphrasing the gospel of Matthew: "For whosoever will save his life, shall lose it: and whosoever shall lose his life for my sake, shall find it" (16:25). Claudio himself, rather than his pastor, introduces a faint note of grace into the dialogue; his allusive lines work as a reminder that these characters act within a Christian universe, but they also underscore the lack of spiritual guidance in the Duke's preceding speech. While the Duke-as-Friar assumes the semblance of a spiritual guide, his words of comfort reveal that his orientation remains entirely worldly.

The Friar-Duke's most dramatic failure as a pastor occurs in his attempt to prepare Barnadine for execution; this failure illustrates the fundamental weakness of the Duke's government. The Duke seeks Barnadine's head to substitute for Claudio's in a plan to thwart Angelo's unjust decision to proceed with the execution. Barnadine, a murderer, is characterized as "careless, reckless, and fearless of what's past, present, or to come: insensible of mortality, and desperately mortal" (4.2.126–8), a perverse mix of asceticism and dissolution. Yet, despite Barnadine's "careless" posture, he rejects the Friar-Duke's efforts to prepare him to face death: "Friar not I. I have been drinking hard all night, and I will have more time to prepare me, or they shall beat out my brains with billets. I will not consent to die this day, that's certain" (4.3.45–8). His rationale for resistance is a curious combination of carnal (hard drinking) and spiritual (desire for more time to prepare properly for the afterlife). His explicit refusal of "consent" lends a political edge to his resistance; from this perspective, pastoral and political government appear necessarily contingent on the acquiescence of the flock or citizenry. In the face of this refusal, the Duke resigns his authority: "to transport him, in the mind he is, were damnable" (4.3.58–9). Barnadine marks a limit the Duke cannot cross, despite his assumed habit. The Duke's expressed concern about "damnation" signals not simply his failure to govern Barnadine, but also his distance from becoming a truly secular ruler. Although he was incapable of evoking spiritual comfort with Claudio, here he appears sensitive to the spiritual consequences of disregarding the integrity of the sacraments.

The breakdown in the Friar-Duke's authority in Act 4 shadows the resolution of the play in the next act, where Barnadine's resistance is potentially echoed in the silence of the figure who is otherwise most unlike him: Isabella. In the long concluding scene, the Duke wavers between his identities as Friar and sovereign, appearing as one and then the other before he is revealed as both before the eyes of his citizens. Insofar as the fully disclosed Duke enforces marriage as a remedy for transgressions, a pastoral concern and a sacramental institution appear to become instruments for reinforcing the order desired by a secular government. However, several further elements of this final scene complicate reading the conclusion as an exercise in secularization. The first is the return of Barnadine and the Duke's effort to cover over the failing that this prisoner has exposed. While he expresses a quasi-pastoral concern for Barnadine's "earthly faults" (5.1.476) in pardoning him, the Duke delegates his spiritual guidance to a true Friar: "Friar, advise him; I leave him to your hand" (5.1.478–9). While we might see the Friar here as an adjunct to the Duke's secular government, the Duke's referral also clearly delineates a boundary between sovereign and sacred powers: the care that Barnadine requires lies outside the compass of the sovereign.

More significantly, the Duke's attempt to include himself and Isabella in the final marriage scheme confounds an understanding of marriage as a pure instrument of secular power. The meaning of his approach toward marriage in the final moments of the play is itself ambiguous: is it a sign of his strength (obtaining the woman he denied to Angelo) or his weakness (he requires deeper affiliation with the moral and spiritual authority Isabella maintains)? If we understand it in religious terms, the potential marriage evokes both the Reformation (recalling the marriage of the former monk Luther to a nun) and older tropes of the Church as the bride of Christ (from this perspective, the prospective marriage is mystical or allegorical).[19]

Given Isabella's status as a novice and the Duke's playing at pastor, it is more apt to see the marriage prospect as a sign of an ongoing negotiation between the idea of the commonwealth as a mystical, sacramental body, and a civic, contractually ordered body politic. The tentative status of the marriage is marked by the contrast between the Duke's two efforts at making the proposal: the first cast as a hierarchical imperative ("Give me your hand, and say you will be mine" [5.1.485]) and the second, more egalitarian and communitarian in tone ("if you'll a willing ear incline, / What's mine is yours, and what is yours is mine" [5.1.528–9]).[20] The Duke would seem to require affiliation with Isabella's sanctity, but he cannot demand it. The need to reiterate the proposition suggests uncertainty about its acceptance, an uncertainty that the play itself does not dispel, as the text does not give us Isabella's reply. Isabella's silence has been interpreted variously as acquiescence or as resistance; its final meaning is always deferred, open to varying interpretations in performance. In the context of a reading of the relationship between theology and politics in the play, this silence, coupled with Isabella's religious identification, represents an element of theology that remains immune to full assimilation to the sphere of political power – persisting as both a potential threat to and a potential resource for that power.

Notes

1 Thomas Fulton cites both the "over thirty" figure for biblical allusions in the play and the eponymous allusion to the Sermon on the Mount in his article, "Shakespeare's *Everyman: Measure for Measure* and English Fundamentalism," *Journal of Medieval and Early Modern Studies* 40, no. 1 (2010): 119, 121. These biblical sources are suggested by Brian Gibbons in the New Cambridge Shakespeare edition of *Measure for Measure* (Cambridge: Cambridge University Press, 1983), "Introduction," 1; and Barbara Mowat and Paul Werstine in the New Folger Library edition of *Measure for Measure* (New York: Washington Square Press, 1997), 235–8. Also see Fulton, "Shakespeare's *Everyman*"; and see Andrew Barnaby and Joan Wry, "Authorized Versions: *Measure for Measure* and the Politics of Biblical Translation," *Renaissance Quarterly* 51, no. 4 (1989): 1225–54.

2 For the idea that the Duke's speech drops hints that remind Isabella of her "Christian obligation to mercy," see Mowat and Werstine, *Measure for Measure*, 237. Louise Schleiner suggests that the Duke stages this sequence as a "playlet" designed, in part, to provoke Isabella to "true forgiveness," in "Providential Improvisation in *Measure for Measure*," *PMLA* 97, no. 2 (1982): 234.

3 Peter Lake with Michael Questier, *The Antichrist's Lewd Hat: Protestants, Papists and Players in Post-Reformation England* (New Haven, CT: Yale University Press, 2003): 675–6.

4 David Scott Kastan, *A Will to Believe: Shakespeare and Religion* (Oxford: Oxford University Press, 2014): 61–76.

5 Richard Levin, "The King James Version of *Measure for Measure*," *Clio* 3, no. 2 (1974): 129–63. More sophisticated variants include Debora Shuger, *Political Theologies in Shakespeare's England: The Sacred and the State in* Measure for Measure (London: Palgrave, 2001); and Jonathan Goldberg, *James I and the Politics of the Literature* (Baltimore, MD: Johns Hopkins University Press, 1983).

6 Barnaby and Wry explore the possible relevance of this translation project to *Measure for Measure* in "Authorized Versions."

7 Sarah Beckwith, *Shakespeare and the Grammar of Forgiveness* (Ithaca, NY: Cornell University Press, 2011): 76; and Alison Shell, *Shakespeare and Religion* (London, New Delhi, New York, Sydney: Bloomsbury, 2010): 170.

8 Goldberg, *James I*; and Jonathan Dollimore, "Transgression and Surveillance in *Measure for Measure*," in *Political Shakespeare: New Essays in Cultural Materialism*, ed. Jonathan Dollimore and Alan Sinfield (Ithaca, NY: Cornell University Press, 1985): 72–87.

9 Shuger, *Political Theologies*; and Roy Battenhouse, "*Measure for Measure* and Christian Doctrine of the Atonement," *PMLA* 61, no. 4 (1946): 1029–59.

10 Fulton, "Shakespeare's *Everyman*," 123–33.

11 For these debates, see Victoria Hayne, "Performing Social Practice: The Example of *Measure for Measure*," *Shakespeare Quarterly* 44, no. 1 (1993): 15–16.

12 For historical background on the evolution of marriage in Western Europe, see John Bossy, *Christianity in the West: 1400–1700* (Oxford: Oxford University Press, 1985), 19–26. Bossy attributes the trend toward requiring a public ecclesiastical or civil wedding ceremony to growing demands to make marriage a more orderly "social institution," 23.

13 On the fluid, and sometimes ambiguous, process of betrothal and marriage in early modern England, see Hayne, " Performing Social Practice," 3–8.

14 Musa Gurnis addresses the epistemological difficulty of these lines in "'Most Ignorant of What He's Most Assured': The Hermeneutics of Predestination in *Measure for Measure*," *Shakespeare Studies* 42 (2014): 157–8.

15 Lever argues that Isabella's choice must be judged critically: for her, "chastity is an aspect of physical self-regard," introduction to the Arden edition of *Measure for Measure* (London: Methuen, 1965), lxxix.

16 For a skeptical view of Isabella's valuation of her chastity and spiritual vocation as a nun, see Darryl J. Gless, *"Measure for Measure," the Law and the Convent* (Princeton, NJ: Princeton University Press, 1979); for a more sympathetic appraisal of Isabella's aspirations, see Jessica Slights and Michael Morgan Holmes, "Isabella's Order: Religious Acts and Personal Desires in 'Measure for Measure,'" *Studies in Philology* 95, no. 3 (1998): 263–92. Barbara J. Baines argues that Isabella's insistence on chastity is best understood in social and secular terms as a primary source of authority in early modern culture, "Assaying the Power of Chastity in *Measure for Measure*," *Studies in English Literature, 1500–1900* 30, no. 2 (1990): 283–301.

17 On the Christian narrative of the Atonement as an overarching pattern in the play, see Battenhouse, "*Measure for Measure*"; on Isabella's speech specifically, see 1036–7.

18 On this shift in the interpretation of the Atonement in the Reformation, see Bossy, *Christianity*, 91–4.

19 Marc Shell, *The End of Kinship:* Measure for Measure, *Incest, and the Ideal of Universal Siblinghood* (Palo Alto, CA: Stanford University Press, 1988), 167–8.

20 On this shift, see Julia Lupton, *Citizen-Saints: Shakespeare and Political Theology* (Chicago: University of Chicago Press, 2005), 152–3.

13

BRIAN CUMMINGS

Remembering the Dead in *Hamlet*

GHOST: But howsomever thou pursues this act
Taint not thy mind, nor let thy soul contrive
Against thy mother aught. Leave her to heaven
And to those thorns that in her bosom lodge
To prick and sting her. Fare thee well at once.
The glow-worm shows the matin to be near,
And gins to pale his uneffectual fire.
Adieu, adieu, adieu. Remember me. (1.5.84–91)[1]

Remembering, as much as revenge, is the key action of *Hamlet, Prince of Denmark*. Old Hamlet commands his son to revenge him, but only in so much as fully to recollect him. The verb, "to remember," is a strange word: does it mean *to keep in mind* something that is already there, or *to bring back* something that has gone? Nothing, not even killing his murderer, can bring old Hamlet back. The command, "Remember me," contains a more forlorn suggestion: *do not forget* me, do not allow me to disappear altogether into thin air. Somehow, anyhow, memory is required to retain him, or recall him, or to revive him in the minds of those who remain.

So young Hamlet declares in answer, redoubling his response:

HAMLET: And shall I couple hell? Oh fie! Hold, hold, my heart,
And you my sinews grow not instant old
But bear me stiffly up. Remember thee?
Ay thou poor ghost, whiles memory holds a seat
In this distracted globe. (1.5.93–7)

But does he protest too much? Young Hamlet repeats the words of old Hamlet, but in the process, he reverses the speech act and perhaps hedges his bets. Fatherly command gives way to a haunting filial question. In the transposition between the two utterances, the two Hamlets reveal something of the ambiguity of the call to recall. "Remember" was one of the most familiar injunctions of the pre-modern scribal world, as the formula for making a legacy in a will. The dead wanted to be remembered via the prayer of the living. Old Hamlet makes his last testament, and in a familiar gesture of inheritance, asks for his memory to be maintained in death. Yet the question mark in the tone of the son who is left behind testifies to the inherent doubt of misrecall that is embodied in any act of remembrance. The call to remember is hemmed in by a sense in which any external stimulus to memory is thought to be weak or unfulfilled. Memory claims to forestall loss, but always also reinforces it.

The Reformation in *Hamlet*

In the twentieth century, it was commonplace to concur with A. C. Bradley, in outline if not in method, that "[t]he Elizabethan drama was almost wholly secular; and while Shakespeare was writing he practically confined his view to the world of non-theological observation and thought."[2] This *ex cathedra* pronouncement, first published in 1904, comes early on in *Shakespearean Tragedy*, the book that founded Shakespeareanism as a modern academic discipline. With a few exceptions, it acted as an epitaph for modern Shakespeare studies, or even as something like a secular anathema, banishing religious reflection on Shakespeare to the outskirts of the subject, the preserve of theological colleges or the critically insane. An example of the consensus is A. D. Nuttall's British Academy Shakespeare Lecture of 1988. Barnardo's strange, uncanny demand in the opening line of the play, "Who's there?" (1.1.1), becomes for Nuttall a metaphysical question. "Who is there," Nuttall asks, "in the darkness, among the dead?"[3] Nuttal claims that Shakespeare for this purpose invented a new philosophical language of "agnosticism." There is an obvious problem of anachronism here, of conjuring into being a philosophical exceptionalism for Shakespeare to suit the modern age, attributing to him beliefs possessed by no one else in his century.

In the twenty-first century, by contrast, a remarkable transformation has taken place. It can be epitomized by Stephen Greenblatt's statement, published appropriately enough in 2001, that *Hamlet* shows how "a young man from Wittenberg, with a distinctly Protestant temperament, is haunted by a distinctly Catholic ghost."[4] The insight is confirmed when we consider Scandinavia, and especially Denmark, was the most fertile ground for Lutheranism.[5] Greenblatt's book, *Hamlet in Purgatory*, placed "the religious turn" in literary studies in plain view. He saw the play as possessed by different ways of remembering the recent past, resonating deeply with the divided experience of sixteenth-century England. Claudius refers to his nephew's intention in "going back to school in Wittenberg"

(1.2.113). All Europe knew Wittenberg as the university of that prince of German Protestants, Martin Luther, who posted his 95 Theses to the door of the university church there on October 31, 1517. That action began the Reformation, tearing apart not only Germany and England but also most of Europe for the next 150 years. What did Shakespeare mean by this? Did he give young Hamlet (as Greenblatt suggests) a "Protestant temperament"? Claudius, too, struggles with a new religion, as he tries (and fails) to find a language of personal penitence through prayer:

> Pray can I not
> Though inclination be as sharp as will.
> My stronger guilt defeats my strong intent,
> And like a man to double business bound,
> I stand in pause where I shall first begin,
> And both neglect. (3.3.38–43)

As well as reflecting at an individual level Claudius's struggle with his conscience, and Hamlet's reluctance to take revenge, the scene also tests the process of liturgical process. The sacrament of penance gives way to an enactment, whether true or false, of personal repentance.[6]

Most famously, as Hamlet himself comes nearer and nearer to his own death, his words are transfixed by what it means to encounter the divine:

> There's a divinity that shapes our ends,
> Rough-hew them how we will. (5.2.10–11)

Behind Hamlet's anxiety about how to understand the shape of his life lies the counterfactual tradition of interpreting divine Providence, a tradition newly contested by English Calvinist theology.[7] The question is therefore at the same time about *where* to locate religion in a new world of divided confessions and consciences, and also about how confessional context is felt to affect *who* Hamlet imagines himself to be.

As for Old Hamlet, he appears to show the opposite confessional colors by telling his son that he comes direct from purgatory:

> GHOST: I am thy father's spirit,
> Doom'd for a certain term to walk the night,
> And for the day confin'd to fast in fires,
> Till the foul crimes done in my days of nature
> Are burnt and purg'd away. (1.5.9–13)

His "doom" is his fate or destiny, but the word also puns with the Last Judgment, or "doom," an image of which was often depicted in wall-paintings at the west end of the church although sometimes at the entrance to the choir above the rood loft. Both idea and image were clearly associated with the doctrine of purgatory. The dead and the living in some sense "walk the night" together, since the parish could see the fires of purgatory in front of them either during Mass or else as they left the church with the west wall in view.

The doctrine of purgatory was among the earliest of Catholic ideas to be rejected by the English Reformers. In 1563 this was confirmed in the 22nd Article of Religion: "The Romish Doctrine concerning Purgatory, Pardons, Worshipping and Adoration as well of Images, as of Relics, and also Invocation of Saints, is a fond thing, vainly invented, and grounded upon no warranty of Scripture, but rather repugnant to the word of God."[8] Purgatory was thereby declared a fiction, a cognitive invention, something that cannot be brought to mental apprehension but exists only in the fantasy of the imagination. In Stratford-upon-Avon, the town corporation ordered the removal of images in the Church of the Holy Cross in 1564, but the rood loft, with its doom above, was only taken down four years later. The Dance of Death, on the North Wall, was allowed to remain in place. Whether this was due to equivocation or to forgetfulness, it is impossible to say.

Shakespeare's play, Greenblatt argues, is haunted by Reformation ambiguity between old and new. Since 2001, it has become commonplace to see *Hamlet* as a Catholic play, or else a play of residual Catholic feeling. Much of this depends on unsatisfied (and perhaps unsatisfactory) biographical adventure into Shakespeare's beliefs; or if that is impossible, at least those of his father, John. So John Shakespeare's spiritual testament ("I, John Shakespeare, have made this present writing of protestation, confession, and charter, in presence of the blessed Virgin Mary") can here be played off against the text of William Shakespeare's Last Will and Testament ("I Commend my Soule into the hands of god my Creator, hoping & assuredly believing through the only merits of Jesus Christ my Saviour").[9] The conventional Catholic language of the one can be paired *ad nauseam* against the conventional Reformed language of the other, but neither absolves us of a responsibility to work through the intractable and multiple forms of religion in the sixteenth century.

Yet perhaps the critical dichotomy between old and new *Hamlets*, as between old and young Hamlets, is not quite what it seems. Even Bradley acknowledged that the religion of *Hamlet* was distinctive: "While Hamlet certainly cannot be called in the specific sense a 'religious drama,' there is in it nevertheless both a freer use of popular religious ideas, and a more decided, though always imaginative, intimation of a supreme power concerned in human evil and good, than can be found in any other of Shakespeare's tragedies."[10] Hamlet is disturbed, Bradley says, by the appearance of his father as "the messenger of divine justice." The figure of the ghost is thus a "reminder" – or perhaps, a "symbol" – of the failure of ordinary experience to match up to the horizon of eternity. It is a similar story when Hamlet tries to replace this with an alternative religious worldview of divine Providence. For all his difference from Bradley, Greenblatt, too, sees the play as confronted by a sense of religious failure. *Hamlet* shows "a deliberate forcing together of radically incompatible accounts."[11] It is caught between a corporeal Catholic culture of death and a Protestant belief in the immanence of spirit. *Hamlet* at once expresses disgust towards a materially endowed physicality, and yet simultaneously longs for it, hence the impossible appearance of the ghost as simultaneously ethereally spectral and clumsily, shamblingly, real.

Indeed, Greenblatt sets up a radical dichotomy between purgatory and its subsequent decline. From the fullness of medieval material experience we pass into the Protestant sphere of the spiritual, the doctrinal, the symbolic. Catholic England provided a "powerful method of negotiating with the dead"; this was replaced by what Greenblatt calls a failure of adequacy in Protestant ceremonies of death. Into this realm of the imaginary, or locus of emotional loss, the theater steps. The space of the stage substitutes for the space of Purgatory. The ghost of Hamlet's father turns Shakespeare's theater into what Greenblatt describes as a secularized "cult of the dead." This is a historical scenario Greenblatt has repeated over and over again. Shakespeare's theater is the desacralized ritual shell of dramatic illusion left over once a kernel of belief is removed, after the Reformation.

Hamlet and Remembering the Dead

One way of reading this is to reflect on the practice of remembrance of the dead, which was written in to medieval religion: "The dead, whose names were recited week by week in the bede-roll at the parish Mass, remained part of the communities they had once lived in, and the objects they left for use in the worship of that community preserved their names and evoked the gratitude of the living towards them."[12] A material witness to this practice is the commonplace habit by which an obit (a service for the dead) of the departed will be added to a book of ritual such as a missal or a Book of Hours. The day of death is recorded in the Kalendar, adding a member of the family, a beloved father or daughter, to the catalog of saints. In the Broughton Missal, recently acquired by Lambeth Palace Library as MS 5066, such details are added to by an accretion of records of physical artefacts furnished or refurbished for the local church. These records cover 150 years in the life of the parish of All Hallows in Broughton, a small village near Preston in Lancashire, up to the Reformation. In the Kalendar for November an annotation is added in the bottom margin to mark that "the new stone cross in our Kirkyard of All Hallows of Broghton" was finished on November 13, 1512, in the presence of the priest, Edward Bale, in the 32nd year of his benefice. In the same year, it is said, the images of "Our Lady Saint Cathryn Saint Margret Saint Nicholas Saint James" were repaired and repainted.[13]

The Reformation put paid to such memories, obliterating them with the stroke of a pen. The new, vernacular, and reformed Book of Common Prayer opened up a gulf not only between Protestant England and the world of the medieval church, but between the living and the dead. In the first edition of 1549, some room for relationship still existed. At the moment of the committal of the body to the earth, the priest "*casting earth upon the Corpse*," was to say: "I commend thy soul to God the father almighty, and thy body to the ground, earth to earth, ashes to ashes, dust to dust."[14] But this allowance was removed in the revised edition of 1552. As Eamon Duffy comments: "The dead could still be spoken to directly, even in 1549, because in some sense they still belonged within the human community. But in the world of the 1552 book the dead were no longer with us. They could neither be spoken to nor even about, in any way that affected their well-being."[15] At first sight, the exchange between the generations in *Hamlet* speaks to this gulf that opened up between the living and the dead. The office of the dead in the medieval church bound the departed and the mourners together, in affection and in duty as well as in kinship. The ghost of Hamlet's father refers to himself as a soul in purgatory. The medieval liturgy of the Dirige explicitly engages the surviving relatives in assisting the souls of the departed beyond death, making good, by acts of penance, in order to reduce the term in purgatory their loved ones might endure. The ghost makes a direct reference to liturgy by referring to "the matin to be near" (1.5.89). Matins marked not only the coming of morning, but also a basic part of the Dirige in the Office of the Dead in the Salisbury rite used in Stratford until 1548. In post-Reformation liturgy this exchange was divested of meaning, and the Office abandoned. The dead "could no longer be spoken to." Indeed, in the 1552 Order of Burial, the corpse is strangely absent, a cipher. The living are in mourning but the departed is long gone.

Nonetheless, the Book of Common Prayer contained ambiguous attitudes to memory. On the one hand, there is the striking fact that the verb, "to remember," one of the keywords of the medieval culture of death, not once appears in the Order for the Burial of the Dead, whether in the 1549 or 1552 or any subsequent versions. However, it is not as if remembering is forgotten altogether. If we look at the 1559 version, which was used in the churches familiar to Shakespeare both in Stratford and in London, the arts of memory are key to the action of penitence in the Litany: "Remember not Lord our offences, nor the offences of our forefathers, neither take thou vengeance of our sins: spare us good Lord, spare thy people whom thou haste redeemed with thy most precious blood, and be not angry with us for ever."[16] In the General Confession, memory is similarly key to the performance of penitence: "we do earnestly repent, and be heartily sorry for these our misdoings, the remembrance of them is grievous unto us" (134). Remembering is also a key to the subjective inculturation of faith. "In the Baptism of infants," it is said, "every man present may be put in remembrance of his own profession made to God in his Baptism" (141). This urge to remember is also prominent in the Visitation of the Sick: "O most merciful God, which according to the multitude of thy mercies, dost so put away the sins of those which truly repent, that thou rememberest them no more" (167). In the service of Commination for Ash Wednesday, the exhortation, "let us remembering the dreadful judgement hanging over our heads, and being always at hand, return unto our Lord God" (178), is once again the prelude to proper repentance.

The liturgical reformation of memory finds its epicenter, of course, in the translation of the Roman Mass into the English Holy Communion. The background here is the gospel narrative in which Christ says to his disciples at the Last Supper (in the Latin of the Vulgate) *facite in meam commemorationem*. The text of Luke 19: 11 is then repeated by St. Paul in 1 Corinthians 11:24, so that every time the action of eating and drinking the bread and wine is repeated, the death of Christ is proclaimed to the world. In the pre-Reformation Mass, the physical action of remembering is embodied in the complex sequence of bodily actions of the priest in the Canon of the Mass. He kisses the altar, joins his hands before his breast, and makes the sign of the cross three times over the host and the chalice, before opening his arms, keeping his hands before his breast, neither higher nor wider than his shoulders, with fingers joined and the palms facing each other.

In the English Reformation this elaborate embodiment of memory culture in the actions of the liturgy was dismantled. However, remembrance does not disappear, but is instead reconstituted. Christ's words were newly rendered in the 1559 Communion: "Take ye and eat, take and drink ye all of this, do this in remembrance of me" (131). The Book of Common Prayer recasts not only the nature of the sacrament but also the nature of memory, indeed the one is central to the meaning of the other: "he hath instituted and ordained holy mysteries, as pledges of his love, and continual remembrance of his death, to our great and endless comfort" (131). Remembering is not a way of reenacting, in the now, the sacrifice of Christ but instead a way of retaining in the mind the promises, covenants, and prophecies of God. *A Declaration of the Sacraments* of 1548 gives a particularly clear English rendition of the theory of sacraments that developed in Swiss Protestantism: they are "Signs and ceremonies, giving them names that could not but keep his covenants in mind."[17] The *Declaration* goes on to provide a theory of memory in line with this doctrine of the sacraments: "And hereof ye see that our sacraments are books of stories only and that there is none other virtue in them than to testify the covenants and promises made in Christ's blood. And here of ye perceive that where nought is understood by the sacrament or ceremonies / there they be clean unprofitable" (sig. B4v). Early English Protestants held such ceremonies in suspicion. The ritual actions of the priest in the Mass, holding the host aloft, kissing the book, smacked to them of superstition, and suggested that the Mass involved the changing of substances in the bread and wine, as if by magic. *A Declaration of the Sacraments* forms part of the controversial groundwork in which the Book of Common Prayer attempted to put this idea of memory into action. Yet in the midst of the doctrinal questions lurked a different problem of human memory. Individual lives stretched back before the changes or lingered on into a new religious era. A priest ordained in the medieval church might not die until late in the reign of Elizabeth, by which time he would have seen four or five doctrinal régimes. Meanwhile his parishioners could recall one form of liturgy even as they experienced another.

Interpretations of *Hamlet* in recent years have tended to repeat the trajectory proposed by Duffy, in which the Reformation is a simple model of replacement, the doom disappearing into whitewash. This lies behind Greenblatt's theory of desacralization in the theater. However, Duffy's own work has revealed a different kind of memory story. In *Marking the Hours*, he describes a Book of Hours produced in Bruges for the English market.[18] The manuscript circulated in Suffolk and Norfolk for much of the fifteenth century and into the sixteenth century; at this point it passed into the hands of the Roberts family of Middlesex, a prosperous family in Willesden and Neasden since the thirteenth century. An extensive set of annotations by the family includes prayers and the signature of Edmund Roberts (1521–85).[19] We might be tempted to think of Roberts as a recusant, but he was firmly conformist to whatever religious orders prevailed at the time. In 1553 he happily returned to the Catholic faith, but he died a Reformed Elizabethan. He uses the book whatever the season, as an object of family devotion in the widest sense, recording the dates of children's births into the 1570s.

Such a phenomenon is sometimes described as a continuity of Catholicism.[20] This is a simplification: the Reformation worked very differently in 1590 from 1530 or even from 1560. In the process, different generations kept up with these changes in different ways. In the late sixteenth century people lived alongside each other who could still recall pre-Reformation practices; or who (like Roberts) had changed sides under Edward, Mary, and Elizabeth; or who (like Shakespeare) were born into a distinctively post-Reformation culture, still riven with division. Within such a culture, human beings readily remember what they have half forgotten; or equally, they reinvent, repress, or diverge into denial. The mixed messages of *Hamlet* borrow constantly from this mingled inheritance of belief, practice, and memory.

Ghosts and Religious Memory

The ghost is the thing everybody remembers about *Hamlet*.[21] The encounter between old and young Hamlet is uncanny in all kinds of ways, not least in the context of medieval and later forms of liturgy. In the Dirige the living speak to the dead, for sure: but the dead *do not usually speak back*. This obvious fact has sometimes been missing from attempts to assimilate *Hamlet* within a world of Catholic sensibility, or Shakespeare with his own father's Catholic past. Speaking to the dead is not the same as being spoken to. Ghost stories do attach themselves to tales of purgatory, but they do so without official theological sanction, and when they occur, they suggest some failure or obstruction in the traffic of souls from one life to the other. A fifteenth-century chronicle recounts a Weymouth shipman going on pilgrimage to Santiago de Compostela to have Masses said there for his parents. On his return he is haunted by the ghost of his uncle. The uncle has tried but failed to communicate with him for nine years and demands that he return as a beggar to Compostela to have Mass said and to distribute alms for him, that I "be delivered of the pain that I suffer."[22]

The ghost's worry here, as later in *Hamlet*, is that no one is listening. Such a worry is accentuated after the Reformation, but it is not an altogether newly minted Reformed concern. The ambiguity is registered in Salisbury in July and August 1538. Trouble was in the air due to the destruction of the monastic shrines. An angel was said to have appeared to Henry VIII, ordering him go on pilgrimage to St. Michael's Mount in Cornwall. The ghost of the queen, Jane Seymour, was also said to be abroad with a similar message, "God save the King, I trust we shall go a pilgrimage again."[23] Queen Jane would remember pilgrimages and shrines from her childhood and early adulthood, but her soul, influenced by Reformed piety, may not have been so ready to pray for their renewal. The people of Salisbury nonetheless invoked her memory in the interests of their own desire for the proper performance of religious memory. The ghost story acts as a compensatory tale in which the specter gives voice to what we can only call fabricated memory reclaimed as prophecy.

Thomas More in his *Supplication of Souls* (1529) confessed that there was no country in Christendom immune to ghost stories, in which a man "shall not hear credibly reported of such apparitions diverse times there seen and appearing."[24] A monk of Byland in North Yorkshire in the fifteenth century provided a copious treasure trove, as described by a master of the twentieth-century genre, M. R. James.[25] However, as Peter Marshall has wittily argued, ghosts were always "theologically incorrect."[26] The idea that the appearance of a ghost concurs with conventional reflections on the doctrine of penance or purgatory is a misnomer. On the contrary, the ghosts of Byland Abbey wrestled bodily with the living, and could only be bid good riddance via invocations and holy water. Ghosts deal in the malfunction of religion. As Marshall recounts, frequently ghosts were those "for whom rites of burial or intercession had been inadequately or negligently performed," whose death was fresh and painful in the memory. Such is the case with old Hamlet. If he claims to come from purgatory it is also apparent that things in purgatory are not going according to plan.

In any case, ghost stories are always exceptional. However much it might suit the modern imagination to think that our medieval or early modern counterparts were caught up in a constant struggle with zombies, supernatural apparitions were intrinsically rare; that was what gave them power. They were also intrinsically ambiguous. Whereas witches are the occasion of legal trials, ghosts are hardly ever encountered in legal depositions, and when they are, are subject to doubt. Credence in ghosts is hedged around with incredulity, in the past as in the present. However, their intervention is also more serious than we might think. As Peter Brown has remarked in *Society and the Holy*, the supernatural is the arena for the suppressed desires and anxieties of the natural.[27] Ghosts do not act as vessels of social memory. Rather, they show the contradictory impulses of remembering the dead: the need to forget as much as the urge to recall. Never mind the zombies: it is the hold of the memory of the departed that we wish to let loose, even as we cleave to it. Just because I miss my dead father does not mean I want him back.

Old Hamlet's encounter with his son is marked less by the embodied promise of the liturgical office of the dead, than it is by a more or less desperate attempt at redemption through narrativization. He explicitly refutes the official version given of his death in the Danish court as a fabricated memory:

GHOST: 'Tis given out that, sleeping in my orchard,
A serpent stung me. So the whole ear of Denmark
Is by a forgèd process of my death
Rankly abused. (1.5.35–8)

The ghost uses a pastiche of romance language to suggest how the state has manufactured a false view of his death, an unbelievable tale of serpents in orchards. However, the language of the tale with which he then replaces false memory with true memory is equally nostalgic and romantic. First, he creates a wholly new narrative of how Claudius seduced young Hamlet's mother:

> Ay, that incestuous, that adulterate beast,
> With witchcraft of his wits, with traitorous gifts –
> O wicked wit and gifts, that have the power
> So to seduce – won to his shameful lust
> The will of my most seeming virtuous queen. (1.5.43–6)

It is tempting here to recall the definition of sacraments in *A Declaration* as "books of stories only." Memory is a competition of narrative in which one version works to press out another. Young Hamlet's vision of his mother is about to be driven out by his father's remembrance.

The ghost lingers on the outrage of his sexual betrayal before reminding the audience as well as young Hamlet of the out-of-body nature of their meeting ("But soft, methinks I scent the morning air" [1.5.58]). The line suggests how careful Shakespeare is being at this point about diegetic levels of narration. For a moment, the ghost has become an extradiegetic narrator, telling the audience not how he feels but how things really were. His effort of memory escapes from character and becomes what is conventionally known as infallible narration. The ghost's reminder that he is a specter, and cannot appear in daylight, has an effect that in narrative theory would be called metadiegetic, that is, it reveals how one narrative has become embedded within another, a story within the story. His mask having slipped, Old Hamlet quickly works to regain the narrative advantage:

> Brief let me be. Sleeping within my orchard,
> My custom always of the afternoon,
> Upon my secure hour thy uncle stole,
> With juice of cursèd hebenon in a vial,
> And in the porches of my ears did pour
> The leperous distilment, whose effect
> Holds such an enmity with blood of man
> That swift as quicksilver it courses through
> The natural gates and alleys of the body. (1.5.59–67)

Old Hamlet's story, mesmerizing though it is, can hardly be called "brief." Indeed, it draws attention to its own status as narrativization both through the consciously archaic style and its elaborate rhetorical devices of redescription.

Few watchers of the play have endorsed wholeheartedly Wilson Knight's willfully contrary proposition that it might have been better if Hamlet had forgotten the Ghost's commands to remember.[28] But Knight reminds us that it is proper to regard any infallible narrator with a degree of skepticism, and that of all narrators a ghost is perhaps the least infallible. Audiences maybe feel this skepticism towards the ghost more readily than scholarly critics. Yet a decision either way is in any case unnecessary, since the whole point of the scene is the unreliability of memory. A passage in Friedrich Nietzsche's *Also Sprach Zarathustra* may be recalling *Hamlet*. Revenge, Nietzsche wrote, is an imprisonment in the desire to undo what cannot be undone. It is *Des Willens Widerwille gegen die Zeit*, "the will's antipathy to time," a refusal to accept the *Es war* of the past.[29] Does Hamlet conclude that revenge is a task of creative remembrance?[30] However this may be, what is undeniable is that the play from this point onwards is forced to make decisive interventions in memory even when it has shown memory itself to be irreversibly undecidable.

Hamlet and the Language of Memory After the Reformation

Criticism of *Hamlet* since the "religious turn" has tended to polarize theology not so much around doctrine – which strangely enough is often placed on the periphery – but around idealized conceptions of pre-Reformation religion as a site of unified social presence and community. This is centered not only on the sacrament of the Mass, but especially on the place of memory within the Mass – the place where the living maintain an unmediated presence of the past by ritually remembering the dead. The Reformation then becomes straightforwardly the site of rupture and decomposition. Such metaphors have a strong hold even in very different interpretations of the plays. Thus, in Greenblatt's account of *Hamlet*, the dismemberment of social memory in religion allows the stage to take its place as the theater of disenchantment. In Sara Beckwith's *Shakespeare and the Grammar of Forgiveness* (2011), on the other hand, the memorial community of the medieval Mass is redeemed in Shakespeare's theater. Memory is "something shared in language, and something through which new feelings may emerge, of love, care, and tenderness."[31] This redemption takes places, she argues, in the late plays, and especially in *The Winter's Tale* and *The Tempest*. *Hamlet* plays a different role in this trajectory. Like the other tragedies, it is a place of the "interruption, suspension, or appropriation"[32] of the work of religious ritual. At the heart of this is a failed mechanism of confession and repentance.

It is the argument here that such narratives of redemption are essentially circular. They replicate the dialectical confusions that have always bedevilled accounts of Reformation history, which end up by repeating the mantras either of the Reformers themselves or of their opponents. Just as William Tyndale or Hugh Latimer are quick to endorse a theory of the disenchantment of the ritual of the Mass, so Shakespeare's Jesuit contemporaries rush to dismiss Reformed theology for its failed mechanism of repentance. This does not mean we have to take history at their valuation. Ritual was in a process of transformation everywhere in the Christian west in the sixteenth century, with the Tridentine Mass of 1570 the most significant. The watchword of the new Mass was "reform," including renewed regulation and centralization. John Bossy in a series of important essays contrasted the kinship allegiances of the pre-Tridentine Mass with the theological administration of the individual (based on hierarchy and order) favored in the new rite.[33]

Repentance is at the heart of this ritual ethic just as it is of the revised version of the Book of Common Prayer after 1552. This is not, however, a dismemberment of memory so much as a formal and theorized reconstitution of it. This formalization of memory takes place alongside the dislocation of traditional practices, and not surprisingly this leads to confusion and controversy. *Hamlet* is full of commands to remember, as well as of rememberings and misrememberings, formal and informal. As well as the unforgettable scene of the meeting of the Ghost and his son, this includes trivial occasions that are nonetheless threatening and loaded with anxiety:

LAERTES: Farewell Ophelia, and remember well
　What I have said to you.
OPHELIA: 'Tis in my memory locked,
　And you yourself shall keep the key of it. (1.3.83–6)

Correct remembering is subject to continual regulation and surveillance. This has a political dimension, but memorial acts also acquire a formal methodology, akin to a social ritual even when it is not explicitly associated (as it often is) with religious ritual. Typical of the play are enforced recitations – such as Hamlet's demand for the players to remember the lost play (2.2.396); or else parodies of such recitations, as in Hamlet's notoriously sarcastic and contrary order to Ophelia: "Nymph, in thy orisons / Be all my sins remembered" (3.1.89–90).

At a deep level, the whole of the play within a play has the status of reconstructed memory, in which the action is presented as a narrative reduplication of the past. The response of Claudius is judged on the basis of this reconstruction being correct. It is then on this basis in the following scene that Claudius is prompted to examine his conscience. Memory in this sense has been reconstituted, as it is in the liturgy of Communion in the Book of Common Prayer of 1552 and 1559, as a reflex of penitential self-analysis:

CLAUDIUS. Then I'll look up,
My fault is past. But oh, what form of prayer
Can serve my turn? (3.3.50–2)

Repentance is the corrected form of the internal narrative of the past. It is easy to align this with Bossy's assertion of the triumph of social regulation in sixteenth-century religion, Catholic or Protestant alike.[34] Young Hamlet watches him in order to peruse the performance of memory and is only inhibited from revenge because of the problem that it is not successfully externalized.

This structure is repeated in the following scene, where Hamlet examines the conscience of his mother in order to verify the truth of his father's accusation in the ghost scene. This is performed as a parody of a penitential exercise, in a catechism of question and answer:

ENTER HAMLET.
HAMLET: Now, mother, what's the matter?
GERTRUDE: Hamlet, thou hast thy father much offended.
HAMLET: Mother, you have my father much offended.
GERTRUDE: Come, come, you answer with an idle tongue.
HAMLET: Go, go, you question with a wicked tongue.
GERTRUDE: Why, how now, Hamlet?
HAMLET: What's the matter now?
GERTRUDE: Have you forgot me? (3.4.8–13)

The dialogue style is a wonderful conflation of tragic stichomythia with the liturgical formula of minister and response. The inadequacy of the dialogue as conversation is only reinforced by the macabre farce that ensues, in which Polonius the false confessor is ruthlessly slain.

All of this plays out in front of an audience that has some form of collective memory of older ways of remembering even as it learns the new ones. This is a world in which multiple and competing English Reformations had been recollected, forgotten, contested, and reinvented. Writers at the end of the century show inventive resources in apprehending this memorial detritus. Thomas Nashe, in the same decade as *Hamlet*, creates a "pleasant comedy" out of a last will and testament: "Whatever you do, *memento mori*: remember to rise betimes in the morning."[35] In *Nash's Lenten Stuff*, the penitential modes of remembering are exposed to volatile self-parody: "and to amend the matter, and fully absolve himself of this rash error of misconstruing, he commits it over to be prosecuted by a worse misconstruer then himself."[36] In *Hamlet*, the penitential structure is manifested in a game of dramatic consequences in which the past is replayed in the historic present. This is the logic of revenge, in which one thing always leads to another. This rigid narrative structure is set imperfectly against a template of memorial interpretation, in which Shakespeare works freely with material from before and after the Reformation, in such a way that the audience can never be certain of the historical context of religion.

This play of memory between old and new worlds reaches its epiphany in two marvelous scenes of the imagination, each of them somewhere between a performance and a pastiche of a funeral service. First, Ophelia "speaks much of her father" (4.5.4) in a terrifying counterpoint of madness and mourning:

> OPHELIA: There's rosemary, that's for remembrance – pray you, love, remember – and there is pansies, that's for thoughts.
>
> LAERTES: A document in madness, thoughts and remembrance fitted. (4.5.174–6)

The work of mourning cannot be completed by the attendant rituals. It is, as Derrida said, "interminable."[37] Rosemary lies somewhere between a metaphor and embodied ritual. Pansies are a scarcely sufficient (and punning) substitute for the *pensées* of memory. And yet, while this passage has been reinterpreted as carrying a nostalgic image of medieval practice from the office of the dead, in sharp contrast to the Reformed Order for the Burial of the Dead, this is not quite so clear-cut. While purgatory was abolished in the English Reformation, and tombs and charnel houses desecrated, remembering the dead continued (not surprisingly) to arouse strong feelings. Reformed funerals went beyond the strict letter of the Book of Common Prayer. Many local rituals survived the new theology. Bells continued to be tolled, and the corpse would often be met at the boundary of the church. Local rites of passage between this world and the next, like Ophelia with her flowers, continued to be closely observed.

Nowhere is this more true than in the scene at the churchyard at the opening of the final act. Juxtaposed, one scene with another, comes the aborted funeral of Polonius, and the "maimed rites" of his daughter, suspected of suicide:

> *ENTER TWO CLOWNS.*
>
> CLOWN: Is she to be buried in Christian burial, when she wilfully seeks her own salvation?
>
> OTHER: I tell thee she is, therefore make her grave straight. The crowner hath sat on her, and finds it Christian burial. (5.1.1–4)

Once again, this scene has come to be seen as a dividing line between medieval and post-Reformation theologies of death, because of the treatment of suicide.[38] Yet the refusal to bury the excommunicated that was explicit in medieval canon law was applied in just the same way in the Church of England in 1604, when the minister was forbidden to refuse burial on any other grounds, with a penalty of suspension from the ministry.[39] The word "remember" is not used once in this scene of unbearable liturgy. While Gertrude scatters flowers for Ophelia just as Ophelia did for her father before, the priest acts only in accordance with the uncompleted letter of the law:

> PRIEST: ... for charitable prayers,
> Shards, flints and pebbles should be thrown on her.
> Yet here she is allowed her virgin crants,
> Her maiden strewments, and the bringing home
> Of bell and burial. (5.1.197–201)

Chiding the hieratic liturgy ("churlish priest"), Laertes claims his sister nonetheless as "a ministering angel" (5.1.208). In this way, the fragility of ritual is acknowledged, but the work of memory is still celebrated. The devastating irony of the play's funeral rites acts all the more to preempt an acquiescence in the judicial penitentiary of the theater of revenge.

Notes

1 William Shakespeare, *Hamlet, Prince of Denmark*, ed. Philip Edwards, updated edn., *The New Cambridge Shakespeare* (Cambridge: Cambridge University Press, 2003).
2 A. C. Bradley, *Shakespearean Tragedy: Lectures on Hamlet, Othello, King Lear, Macbeth* (London: Macmillan, 1904), 25.
3 A. D. Nuttall, "*Hamlet*: Conversations with the Dead," in *British Academy Shakespeare Lectures 1980–89* (Oxford: Oxford University Press, 1993), 213–29.
4 Stephen Greenblatt, *Hamlet in Purgatory* (Princeton, NJ: Princeton University Press, 2001), 240.
5 Diarmaid MacCulloch, *Reformation: Europe's House Divided 1490–1700* (London: Penguin Books, 2004), 135.
6 See Ramie Targoff, *Common Prayer: The Language of Public Devotion in Early Modern England* (Chicago: University of Chicago Press, 2001), 1.
7 Brian Cummings, *Mortal Thoughts: Religion, Secularity and Identity in Shakespeare and Early Modern Culture* (Oxford: Oxford University Press, 2013), 224–5.
8 Brian Cummings, ed., *The Book of Common Prayer: The Texts of 1549, 1559, and 1662*, Oxford World's Classics (Oxford: Oxford University Press, 2013), 679.
9 Samuel Schoenbaum, *William Shakespeare: A Documentary Life* (Oxford: Clarendon Press, 1975), 42 and 243.
10 Bradley, *Shakespearean Tragedy*, 174.
11 Greenblatt, *Hamlet in Purgatory*, 243.
12 Eamon Duffy, *The Stripping of the Altars: Traditional Religion in England, 1400–1580*, 2nd edn. (New Haven, CT and London: Yale University Press, 2005), 404.

13 London, Lambeth Palace Library, MS 5066 ("Broughton Missal," early 15th century), fol. 2[r].
14 BCP (1549), 82.
15 Duffy, *Stripping of the Altars*, 404.
16 BCP (1559), 117.
17 *A Brief Declaration of the Sacraments Expressing the First Original How They Came Up, and Were Institute with the True and Most Sincere Meaning and Understanding of the Same Very Necessary for All Men* (London: Robert Stoughton, [1548?]), sig. B4[v].
18 Eamon Duffy, *Marking the Hours: English People and their Prayers* (New Haven, CT and London, 2006), 81–96.
19 Cambridge University Library, MS Ii.vi.2 ("Roberts Hours," Flemish, end of 14th/beginning of 15th century), fol. 109[v].
20 Christopher Haigh, *The English Reformation Revised* (Cambridge: Cambridge University Press, 1987), 176. For a critique of the "continuity" argument, see Alexandra Walsham, *Relics and Remains*, special issue of *Past and Present* 206, Supplements, n.s., 5 (2010).
21 Edwards, *Hamlet*, 24.
22 Duffy, *Stripping of the Altars*, 308.
23 Ibid., 350.
24 *Complete Works of St Thomas More*, ed. Frank Manley, Germain Marchadour, Clarence H. Miller, and Richard C. Marius, 15 vols. (New Haven, CT and London, 1963–90), 7: 196.
25 M. R. James, "Twelve Medieval Ghost Stories," *English Historical Review* 37 (1922): 413–22.
26 Peter Marshall, *Beliefs and the Dead in Reformation England* (Oxford: Oxford University Press, 2002), 16.
27 Peter Brown, *Society and the Holy in Late Antiquity* (Berkeley: University of California Press, 1982), 318.
28 G. Wilson Knight, *The Wheel of Fire: Interpretations of Shakespearean Drama* (London: Routledge & Kegan Paul, 1930), 40.
29 Friedrich Nietzsche, *Also Sprach Zarathustra: Ein Buch für Alle und Keinen*, in *Nietzsches Werke*, vol. 6 (Leipzig: C. G. Naumann, 1901), sec. ("Von der Erlösung").
30 Edwards, *Hamlet*, 77.
31 Sara Beckwith, *Shakespeare and the Grammar of Forgiveness* (Ithaca, NY: Cornell University Press, 2011), 162.
32 Ibid., 90.
33 John Bossy, "The Counter-Reformation and the People of Catholic Europe," *Past and Present* 47 (1970): 51–70; "The Social History of Confession," *Transactions of the Royal Historical Society*, 5th series, 25 (1975): 21–38; and "The Mass as a Social Institution," *Past and Present* 100 (1983): 29–61.
34 John Bossy, *Christianity in the West, 1400–1700* (Oxford: Oxford University Press, 1985).
35 *A Pleasant Comedy, Called Summers Last Will and Testament. Written by Thomas Nash* (London: Simon Stafford, 1600), sig. E2[r].
36 *Nash's Lenten Stuff Containing, the Description and First Procreation and Increase of the Town of Great Yarmouth in Norfolk: With a New Play Never*

Played Before, of the Praise of the Red Herring (London: [Thomas Judson & Valentine Simmes], 1599), sig. I3^{v}.

37 Jacques Derrida, "The Work of Mourning Learns the Impossible – and That Mourning is Interminable," in *The Work of Mourning* (Chicago: University of Chicago Press, 2001), 143.

38 Cummings, *Mortal Thoughts*, 226 and 236–8.

39 *Canons of the Church of England* (1604), in *Constitutions and Canons Ecclesiastical 1604*, ed. H. A. Wilson (Oxford: Clarendon Press, 1923), no. 68.

14

DANIEL VITKUS

Othello, Islam, and the Noble Moor: Spiritual Identity and the Performance of Blackness on the Early Modern Stage

In what sense can we talk about "An Islamic Othello"? Consulting Shakespeare's play, we find that Othello is a Christian, washed by the waters of baptism. There are hints that he is a convert (Iago scoffingly suggests that for the love of Desdemona Othello would "renounce his baptism" [2.3.310]), but this is never stated directly in the play. In any case, the Venetians would not have allowed a Muslim to lead their military forces in defense of Cyprus against an invading Islamic power like that of the Ottoman Turks. But in spite of his apparent status as a baptized Christian, whose soul is presumably washed "whiter than snow" (in the words of Psalm 51), Othello is known throughout the play as "the Moor" and remains a figure of blackness.[1] Although a Christianized Moor, he retains traces of Islamic identity and serves as a focal point for anxieties about how converts to Christianity might betray their new faith and become an internal threat to Christendom. By placing the character of Othello under the scrutinizing gaze of a color-prejudiced audience, Shakespeare's tragedy exhibits a tension between, on the one hand, the evangelistic mandate to make Christian converts throughout the world and, on the other hand, persistent ethnocentric fears of a contamination that could allegedly result from efforts to incorporate foreigners within the domestic Christian community. The Christian tradition, relying on the authority of biblical texts like the Song of Songs, sometimes declared that divine grace had the power to convert blackness to whiteness; but there was a strongly opposing idea, widely disseminated and found in texts ranging from Aesop's fables to Erasmus *Adagia* and Alciato's emblems, that the divine order in created nature was resistant to any "unnatural" attempt to "wash the Ethiope white."[2] A group of corresponding oppositions – between black and white, Islam and Christianity, evil and good, etc. – are crucial axes of orientation that establish a clear pattern of binarized meaning in Shakespeare's tragedy. The play does not, however, simply affirm these violent binaries as stable hierarchies. Othello's identity is unstable and richly overdetermined: a variety of associations are suggested by the figure of Othello in Shakespeare's text. These include Islamic identity, conversion from Islam to Christianity, ethnographic and theological conceptions of Blackness (including both the proverbial "black devil" and the washed and whitened "Ethiope" [8.26–39]), early modern notions of Moorishness, associations with the figure of the Saracen warrior from the romance tradition, and the suggestion of a noble birth somewhere in North Africa.

A number of scholars have focused their critical attention on the various pieces that make up the puzzle of Othello's identity.[3] These pieces do not come together to comprise a coherent whole: we seek in vain to uncover, via a strong reading of the text, the "true identity" of Othello. An essentializing interpretation that would fix Othello's personality or character cannot be accomplished – neither in the form of a reconstructed authorial intention nor in the shape of a distinctive identity claimed on the basis of "the text itself." Looking to various early modern contexts, however, will aid in our efforts to understand the various possibilities that the tragedy offers – in other words, the potential constructions of who Othello might be as a dramatic figure. This article will undertake a consideration of both text and early modern context in order to show how this famous character bears the imprint of religious ideology, including English Protestant views of Islam.

As a "character" in a text, albeit a theatrical script intended for live performance and embodiment, Othello should not be understood as a facsimile of any particular early modern person, whether Christian or Muslim.[4] In an important sense, all characters in plays are merely black marks on a white page. And a further reason to avoid such a characterological, art-reflects-life fallacy is the fact that the theater of Jacobean London was not a naturalistic art form. The complexity of Shakespearean drama was produced, in part, by a productive interplay between an emerging form of theatrical realism and the continuation of the non-naturalistic, emblematic performance tradition that Shakespeare and his contemporaries inherited from their late medieval predecessors. This deep source in medieval morality structure, including the personification allegory of the vice tradition, has long been recognized in *Othello*.[5]

When *Othello* was first performed, the white actor wearing black makeup was as much an embodiment of what blackness had come to mean emblematically as he was a plausible representation of a "real Moor." Today, by contrast, critics and audiences often view the performance of a dramatic role as if the actor were portraying a "real person" on a stage that looks like an actual place. And in this verisimilitudinous theater we find seated, immobile spectators silently observing the play through an unbroken fourth wall. Such a theater, which aims to produce a naturalistic dramatic illusion, is very different from that of the early modern playhouses in London. In today's living theater, where the pressing urgencies of contemporary identity politics inevitably inform our understanding of race and identity in powerful ways, black actors have taken up the role of Othello in order to create a stage character, expressed primarily through a naturalistic mode of performance, who speaks to twenty-first-century concerns.[6] This naturalistic identity takes us very far indeed from the stock type of the blackface stage Moor as Shakespeare's audience knew it.[7] Playgoers in early modern London, where there were few people of color (although more than an earlier generation of scholars had realized), saw "color" and understood "race" in profoundly different ways than they are comprehended and discussed today.[8]

Another historical contextualization that helps us to see the character of Othello more clearly is one that would place the play in the context of a traditional religious society conditioned by a Christian ideology. The post-Enlightenment secularization narrative that once prevailed has been corrected and revised under the sign of "political theology."[9] Nonetheless, we should not ignore the categorical split that began after Shakespeare and sought to drive a wedge between superstition and reason, magical thinking and unenchanted materialism, church and state, etc., in the name of "enlightenment" and of bourgeois freedom from religion as an instrument of state power and tyrannical monarchy.[10] But when *Othello* was first performed in London, it spoke to and within an early modern, pre-Enlightenment culture in which religion was still the master code. In hindsight, we see that Christianity was the prevailing, dominant discourse, although at the time "religion" was not yet conceptualized as a separate sphere of human thought or social organization. Thus, Shakespeare's play does not treat Othello's being "Black" or his status as a "Moor" as a strictly racial or national identity separate from his spiritual status.

Early modern authors of all kinds commonly employed the conventional imagery of blackness and whiteness, often associating an external with an internal condition, to affirm and enforce a hierarchy that aligned whiteness with beauty and moral purity while associating blackness with ugliness and moral depravity. In *Love's Labor's Lost*, for instance, Shakespeare's King of Navarre declares that "Black is the badge of hell" (4.3.245), and in *Othello* the language of damnation and salvation is closely tied to the imagery of blackness and whiteness. Furthermore, the non-naturalistic mode of performance helped to articulate blackness and whiteness as the signs of diametrically opposed spiritual conditions articulated through the play's emblematic language, action, and visual spectacle. After all, blackness and whiteness were understood not as mere tropes for describing the state of the soul; they were also believed to be *literal* descriptions of the soul-in-the-body as a mirror-like substance that remained white and shining (and able to reflect God's image) when pure and saintly but could easily become blackened and tarnished by the accretion of sin.

By 1603, the time when Shakespeare wrote *Othello*, the stage Moor was firmly established as a figure that reminded audiences of the damned soul from the tradition of religious discourse and drama, but Moorish characters had also begun to represent and refer to the presence of actual "Moors" and people of color in London and in those places, like Venice or Aleppo, where English merchants and seamen traveled to conduct trade. Given these two very different understandings of Moorish identity, how can we surmise what preconceptions a typical member of Shakespeare's audience might hold about Moors? And what was a "noble Moor" to the groundlings at the Globe? In fact, the word "Moor" was a rather unstable term in early modern English. It could refer to any dark-skinned person, including people from South Asia, Indonesia, or even the New World. But at the same time, the word "Moor" was frequently used as a synonym for "Muslim." And for some of the more educated or well-traveled English subjects who knew their geography, "Moor" would also be associated with Islamic North Africa or what was called "Barbary," or more precisely with Morocco or Mauritania. Thus, the word "Moor" was an overdetermined term with a range of usages: as a stage Moor, Othello would not be confined to a precise ethnic or geographic denotation or identity – he can never quite escape Roderigo's assertion that he is "an extravagant and wheeling stranger / Of here and everywhere" (1.1.135–6).

When Shakespeare composed *Othello*, he created his "noble Moor of Venice" as a version of a pre-existing stock character, the stage Moor, which had already appeared in two different forms – as a treacherous, plotting avatar of evil, and as a proud and noble, but often lustful and irascible, warrior. Such Moors are seen in plays like Marlowe's *Jew of Malta* (*c.*1590) and Peele's *Battle of Alcazar* (*c.*1591).[11] Furthermore, before penning *Othello*, Shakespeare himself had already created other Moors in earlier plays – the evil, scheming Aaron in *Titus Andronicus* (*c.*1590) and the noble warrior, the Prince of Morocco, who is one of Portia's suitors in *The Merchant of Venice* (1597). Aaron the Moor is a character who is closely connected to the earlier tradition of vice figures and stage Moors: he is amoral from start to finish, declaring defiantly that he "would have his soul black as his face" (3.1.205). In *The Merchant of Venice*, Morocco is a proud, highborn Moor, a wealthy prince of Africa who comes from a kingdom known for its gold. England had friendly relations with the Moroccan sultan at the time that Shakespeare wrote these plays, and Shakespeare's portrait of Morocco may have been influenced by the visit to Elizabeth's court of a group of noble

Moors from the court of the Moroccan ruler Ahmad al-Mansur in 1600–01, a diplomatic mission that was there to negotiate a military alliance against their mutual enemy Spain.[12] The presence of these practicing Muslims for over a year in London drew much attention, but it certainly did not deter playwrights and other English authors from continuing to perpetuate the negative image of the Moor as an infidel or even a "black devil." And it was while this Moroccan embassy was present in London that Queen Elizabeth issued a proclamation in which she complained about the "great numbers of Negars and Blackamoors which ... are crept into this realm," characterized them as "infidels, having no understanding of Christ or his Gospel," and authorized their deportation.[13] It was following these events, and perhaps (depending on how one estimates the play's date of composition) just as the vehemently anti-Muslim and anti-Ottoman James I came to the throne, that Shakespeare composed *Othello*.

As "the Moor of Venice," hired to command the Venetian defense of Cyprus, Othello occupies a place of conflict, exchange, and interaction between Christianity and Islam, a place where religious conversion was common and where many Christians "turned Turk," becoming renegades in North Africa or the eastern Mediterranean.[14] The city of Venice was a maritime center where Jews, Christians, and Turks mingled and traded – it was a kind of transnational commercial zone where identity was often unstable or hybrid. The Venetian state ruled over a sprawling maritime empire, but during the late sixteenth and early seventeenth centuries, the Venetians' empire was shrinking as the Ottoman Empire expanded and pushed the Venetians back. It was just as the Venetian empire was receding that the English arrived there and began to take on a new role as important players in the commercial environment of the Mediterranean. The Turkish invasion of Cyprus in *Othello* refers to this context of Islamic empire expanding at the expense of Christendom, a process that provoked intense concern even as far away as England. Key episodes punctuating this long struggle were the siege and capture of Constantinople in 1453 by an Ottoman army under the sultan Mehmet II, the Turkish capture of Otranto (1480–1), the taking of Rhodes from the Knights Hospitaller in 1522, and the conquest of Cyprus in 1571.

Though Islamic power dominated in the Balkans, the Eastern Mediterranean, Arabia, and North Africa during the early modern period, Muslim armies were not always victorious. Most notably, the Spanish monarch Philip II ruled over a unified Iberia that had been free of Muslim rule since the fall of Granada in 1492. The Spanish-Habsburg king Charles V and his forces had carried on the fight, conquering Tunis in 1534 and occupying the city until 1574. In 1565, the Ottomans undertook a massive invasion of the island of Malta, where the Knights of St. John had retreated after their defeat at Rhodes. This long and costly siege failed, and Suleiman the Magnificent withdrew his battered forces after suffering one of the worst military losses of his reign. After news of this victory reached England, the Archbishop of Canterbury, Matthew Parker, called for prayers of thanksgiving to be pronounced in parish churches over a period of six weeks, and accounts of the heroic defense of Malta were translated, printed, and circulated in England.[15] The Ottoman navy also suffered a major defeat in 1571 at the Battle of Lepanto where a combined Christian force, including elements from Venice, Spain, and the Papal States, destroyed an Ottoman fleet.

At the time that Shakespeare wrote *Othello*, the Turks had been in full possession of Cyprus for over twenty-five years, and conflict with Spain had led Elizabeth I to form an alliance with the Ottoman sultan and to conspire with the Turks against Spain. Beyond the expanding Ottoman Empire, there were other vast empires ruled by Muslims – most notably, the Persian Safavid Empire and the Mughal Empire in South Asia. From the 1570s on, as the English undertook more long-distance commercial ventures to the Mediterranean and beyond, they experienced the Muslim-ruled parts of the world much more directly and frequently. As Ottoman allies with trading privileges and diplomatic contacts in Constantinople, the English gained direct knowledge about Islamicate cultures, an awareness that was now based, not in crusading or waging war, but in a mutually beneficial partnership based on trade and a shared animosity toward Catholic Spain.

In early modern London, pragmatic merchants and investors, looking to their bottom line, advocated a relative openness and mutual respect for their Muslim trading partners in accordance with the requirements of a commercial working relationship. At the same time, however, the old hostility toward Islam as a religion continued, and the persistence of an ideological anti-Muslimism that harked back to earlier times was supplemented by new knowledge and new fears about Islamic power. English writers certainly felt free to demonize the Turks and other Muslims from afar, and so the anti-Muslim tradition within Christian discourse continued in spite of real-world coziness between the English and their new Muslim partners in trade.

Shakespeare's *Othello* brings together these two opposing English understandings of Islam – the practical, direct relationship, and the one constructed from a distance by a hostile Christian theology. It is a play that shows how a Moor could convert and serve the military cause of Christendom, defending Cyprus against Turkish invasion; and yet, at the same time, it is a text that insistently evokes the polarizing imagery of black versus white, and concludes by demonstrating that a Moorish Christian may be subject to a tragic relapse, one that involves a re-incorporation within an imagined Islam that was defined by irrational passion, cruel violence, and intense misogyny. There are two types, before and after, of the Moor, one a noble and assimilable servant of Christian Venice (the "all-in-all sufficient" man of valor and "solid virtue" [4.1.256–7], praised by Lodovico), and the other an essentially depraved enemy, a dark barbarian, "ignorant as dirt" (5.2.163), who will heed the white devil Iago and "put out the light" (5.2.7) of fair, innocent Desdemona.

On the early modern stage, Othello's cosmetic blackness would have been understood, not as a lifelike approximation of skin pigment, but in its emblematic and extreme dissimilarity with whiteness. This symbolic black-and-white imagery was widely disseminated: for instance, in a popular sermon that was printed seventeen times between 1593 and 1676, the English divine Henry Smith contrasted the whiteness of Christian truth with the blackness of Islam: "I think the truth of the Christian Religion will appear so much the more: for when black and white are laid together, the white carrieth the greater estimation and glory with it."[16] The meaning of a character's stage blackness drew upon a tradition of Christian iconography, religious drama, and color symbolism that predated Shakespeare but from which Shakespeare and his contemporaries derived their new forms of theater. This earlier tradition includes the religious cycle plays, the morality play tradition, folk drama, morris dancing, and courtly or civic pageantry. In such performances, blackness was associated with radical otherness, with exoticism, and frequently with damnation and sin. In his 1584 *Discovery of Witchcraft*, Reginald Scott asserted that "a damned soul may and doth take the shape of a black Moor,"[17] and his sense of the Moor as a devil damned undoubtedly derives from a long iconographic, theatrical, and literary tradition of representation. In visual art forms and in theatrical performances, extending through the medieval period and into the Renaissance, damned souls were depicted as figures of blackness. For instance, in the Coventry cycle plays, the pageant of Doomsday was presented annually (until it was discontinued in 1579), and as a part of that tradition of civic, religious theater, the Draper's Company paid for the staging of the Last Judgment. Each year, the Company hired locals who played the parts of "the saved souls" and "the damned souls," and the surviving records indicate that the latter were paid extra money for "the blacking of the souls' faces."[18] The Coventry cycle plays' employment of black face-painting as a sign of damnation was typical, not exceptional. In late medieval England, the direct experience of contact with people of color during the crusades was a fading memory, and this kind of ritual or spectacle combined medieval religious symbolism and personification allegory with a more insular sense of England as a part of the unified "world" of Christendom, far from the monsters, wonders, and exotic peoples that dwelt beyond Western Europe. An older understanding of geography and difference, taken from texts like Pliny's *Naturalis Historia* and present in Mandeville's *Travels*, is referenced in *Othello* when the Moor tells Brabantio and Desdemona the tale of his life, including his encounters with outlandish people such as "The cannibals that each other eat, / The Anthropophagi, and men whose heads / Do grow beneath their shoulders" (1.3.142–4). At the same time, Shakespeare's tragedy exhibits a newer perception of post-Reformation Christianity, divided and fighting within but simultaneously expanding outward through missionaries and colonizers as merchants from Christian Europe made contact with powerful Islamicate empires in places where multiple religions co-existed. An anxious sense that English culture and religion were being changed by that contact also informs the play.

For English Protestants, the lines were clearly drawn between, on the one hand, the faithful, the relatively small community of the saved, who declared themselves the true heirs and keepers of the "primitive church" and, on the other hand, the non-believers, the heretics, and the damned – the vast majority of humanity who did not adhere to the Protestant faith or failed to meet the test of Christian virtue. This binary, us-versus-them thinking intensified for Protestants after the Reformation, when religious war, massacre, and atrocity broke forth across Europe, and when the middle option of purgatory was eliminated, leaving an all-or-nothing binary opposition between damnation and salvation.

Shakespeare's *Othello* is replete with a language that opposes black and white, damned and saved, hell and heaven. Many of these images function to reaffirm the conventional association of black skin color with devils and damnation. For instance, early in the play, after learning of the elopement, Brabantio says to Othello, "Damned as thou art" (1.2.63). Shakespeare's tragedy repeatedly asks the audience to consider blackness as a symbol of sin: for example, when Othello declares that Desdemona's "name, that was as fresh / As Dian's visage, is now begrimed and black / As mine own face" (3.3.387–9). In the play's concluding scenes, Othello's damnation is repeatedly declared. According to Emilia, Othello's blackness is the mark of a damned devil: "O the more angel she, and you the blacker devil!" (5.2.132). This oppositional rhetoric and imagery refers, in part, to the older allegorical mode of theater and the tradition of the morality play that were still strongly felt in Shakespeare's time and in his plays. One of Shakespeare's hallmarks as a dramatist was his ability to adapt and retain elements from the old morality drama tradition while pushing his characters into a new, modern territory where they could express a more complex and naturalistic psychology. Part of what makes Shakespeare's Othello so complex is that this character was intended to be given theatrical embodiment by a white actor wearing black makeup, a cosmetic technique that we might call "blackface performance," but one that should not be confused with the sort of blackface tradition known as the "minstrel show." The strikingly anti-naturalistic effects of early modern blackface did not produce, for Shakespeare's audience, the kind of burlesque or parody that was the tendency of the minstrel shows. Nor did it refer to the identity of slaves in the system of Atlantic chattel bondage that was to arise later in the seventeenth century. What may seem thoroughly "unrelatable" to twenty-first-century audiences, who have come to expect more convincing verisimilitude and plausible visual effects, was not seen as "fake" or alienated by early modern playgoers. Early modern spectators were able to decipher the symbolic artificiality of stage blackness while at the same time they could be moved by the feelings and passions portrayed by the white actor playing the Moor. We can assume that this was the case for those playgoers who attended performances starring the reddish-blond, thin-lipped, pink-faced actor Richard Burbage, the white actor who first donned blackface makeup to play the role of Othello. Furthermore, this awareness of the actor's artifice – of his whiteness under the blackness – allowed for a complex exploration of identity as something performed and external.

According to the early modern semiotics of blackness, the stage Moor signified within the discourse of color as an emblematic figure, but at the same time he could represent more specific ethnographic identities. Early modern drama offered a ritual, carnivalesque pattern that was connected to a deep tradition, and yet it also played to English culture's newly stimulated curiosity toward foreign peoples. Shakespeare brilliantly plays the one dramatic mode against the other, producing a functional dissonance that drew power from the deep, primitive fear of alien blackness while pushing the audience to question its old, ethnocentric perspective when they identify with Othello's tragic suffering.

In Moorish characters, audiences perceived a range of meanings that drew upon the discourses of damnation, of anti-Islamism, and for some spectators, knowledge of more specific geographic information.[19] London was only beginning to become the cosmopolitan world-imperial city that it would be by the end of the seventeenth century – but it was changing. As early modern globalization developed and expanded, the old insular forms of color prejudice could no longer stand unquestioned in their crude binary opposition to English whiteness. The London theater was an important place for English subjects to confront and test new, more complex identities, encounters, and exchanges, including those between Christians and Muslims. "[A]s contact between different groups proliferated in new and often bewildering ways, so did the fear of unregulated sexuality across nations, peoples, and groups."[20] Shakespeare's tragedy is in part an expression of this fear, but that fear of sexual mixture was often connected to an anxiety about mixing with people who practiced a different religion.

Recent events in Spain, following the reconquest of Iberia and the expulsion of its Muslim inhabitants, provided a crucial model for English culture's thinking about how a person's religion was supposedly connected to their race, or even to their physical appearance. Spanish policy led to the (often coerced or forced) conversion of many Jews and Moors, who became Christians in order to retain their property and homes in Spain. But during the sixteenth century, led by the Inquisition, Spanish authorities began to accuse converted Moors, known as "moriscos" or "marranos," of continuing to practice secretly their old religion while only pretending to be faithful to the Roman Catholic Church. It was this "anxiety about 'purity of faith' that gave rise to the idea that one's faith was also an index of one's 'purity of blood,' "[21] and to the establishment of the so-called "blood laws" in Spain. Meanwhile, in England, there was a widespread conflation of "black" and "Moor," so that both dark-skinned non-Muslims and all Muslims could be referred to as "blackamoors."[22] While in principle the religious conversion of heretics and infidels was a desideratum for all Christians, in practice such absorption generated fears about such identities remaining stable and certain. According to many Christian writers in both Spain and England, conversion was not enough to erase the essential "nature" or identity of a Jew or Muslim, even if they had formally converted. This fear of false conversion is demonstrated in the following entry from Cotgrave's 1611 *Dictionary of the French and English Tongues*, where he provides a definition of the French word *marrane* (English "marrano"), a derogatory term used to refer to crypto-Jews who had been forced by the Iberian authorities to convert to Christianity: "Marrane: [m.] A Renegado, or Apostata; a perverted, or circumcised Christian; a Christian turned Turk, or Jew; also, a converted, or baptized Moore, Turk, or Jew; one that turnes Christian for feare rather then of devotion; also, a Jewish, cruell, hard-hearted, or hollow-hearted fellow."[23]

The play never explicitly states that Othello is a convert to Christianity, but as "the Moor of Venice" he would be associated with a part of the world where religious conversion between Christianity and Islam was frequent and where conversion from one religion to another was associated with "redemption" from slavery. Christian writings about Islam often asserted that Christians enslaved in North Africa or the Ottoman Empire were forced to convert to Islam. When he tells his life story to the eagerly listening Brabantio, Othello describes how he was "taken by the insolent foe / And sold to slavery; of [his] redemption thence, / And with it all [his] travels' history" (1.3.136–8). Thus Othello's oral, autobiographical captivity narrative includes his "redemption" from a captivity among Muslim masters, and his subsequent escape from bondage may account for the strong attachment to freedom that he expresses in his first long speech, where he tells Iago, "But that I love the gentle Desdemona, / I would not my unhousèd free condition / Put into circumscription and confine / For the sea's worth" (1.2.25–8). He also declares, "I fetch my life and being / From men of royal siege" (1.2.21–2), a statement that strongly implies an origin beyond Christendom. Though it was known that there were Christians native to North Africa, Shakespeare's audience would not find it easy to imagine that Othello was born "of royal siege" in any Christian kingdom. Again, we should not seek for a coherent and consistent biography here, but the text offers strong hints of an Islamic past for the play's tragic protagonist.

Before Othello arrives onstage to assert his nobility in this way, the audience hears Iago and Roderigo speak of him first – when Roderigo calls Othello "the thick lips" (1.1.67), and when Iago informs Brabantio that "the devil" Othello will make him a "grandsire" (1.1.92). Roderigo tells Brabantio that Desdemona has been "transported ... To the gross clasps of a lascivious Moor" (1.1.123–5). "Even now, now, very now," exclaims Iago, "an old black ram / Is tupping your white ewe" (1.1.89–90). Through the use of these images of animality, monstrosity, and miscegenation, Iago and Roderigo invoke in the audience their Christian-centered prejudice against Moors and Muslims. Furthermore, this was an audience that would not be as approving as we might be today of two forms of matrimony that were both considered unacceptable – interracial marriage and elopement without parental consent.

But once Othello appears onstage, his words and actions belie the negative stereotype. He is eloquent, valiant, and in control. He speaks the elegant "Othello music" with the rhetorical skill of a European courtier – a sure sign of assimilation to Christian "civilization." Initially, his loving relationship with Desdemona appears to have transcended skin color, prejudice, and cultural difference. The Venetian senators respect him and rely on him, and when Brabantio asks for Othello to be punished and the marriage prevented, Brabantio is denied by the Duke of Venice, who tells him, "If virtue no delighted beauty lack, / Your son-in-law is far more fair than black" (1.3.285–6). A virtue must be made of necessity, at the least, when the Venetians need Othello to help counter the urgent threat of Islamic power because the Ottoman Turks have mounted an invasion of a Venetian possession, the island of Cyprus.

But the Turkish threat is eliminated by a storm at sea that "drowns" the invading fleet. What happens during the rest of the play may be seen as the conversion (or reversion) of Othello back to the stereotype of the Turkish infidel or black-faced barbarian. By means of deceitful words and clever trickery, Othello's false friend Iago plays fiendishly on Othello's mind, and instigates the Moor's transformation into a monster of sexual passion, jealousy, and violence. Outward appearances and statements, including Othello's external declarations of Christian faith, loyal service, and incorruptible martial virtue, are contrasted with an internal, "Turkish" or Islamic nature, which is brought forth under Iago's malign influence and then unleashed against the innocent Desdemona. Ironically, it is a White Venetian, Iago, who appeals to the "divinity of hell" (2.3.317) and defends his slanders by saying, "Nay, it is true, or else I am a Turk" (2.1.113).

In the final scene of the play, Othello's "conversion" to the negative stereotype is fulfilled. This conversion is instigated by Iago and resolved in the demonic vow pledged by Othello and Iago at the end of 3.3; it is then substantiated in the murder of Desdemona by Othello and, finally, confirmed by Othello's suicide. In his final moments onstage, Othello becomes "Islamic," so to speak – in the sense that in the final act of the play he completes the process of reverting to the negative stereotype.

If Othello's violent jealousy, his mercilessness, and his mistaken notions of justice are understood as the defining qualities of an Islamic Moor, then the audience is encouraged to see him as such and to interpret his downfall as a reversion to such an identity. As the play reaches its climax and then draws to a close, the conventional oppositions (light/dark, white/black, heaven/hell, angel/devil, good/evil, salvation/damnation, etc.) are repeated again and again. Under the pressure of these binaries, Othello becomes a terrifying figure of darkness, of love turned, by Iago's evil, to hate and murder. Desdemona, on the other hand, is the innocent victim of that "motiveless malignity" that early modern audiences attributed to the Devil.[24] When the actor playing Othello performs in blackface, his blackness is placed in direct contrast with the cross-dressing actors in "whiteface" makeup who play the women's parts. For Shakespeare's audience, blackface impersonation and adolescent transvestitism were normal and conventional, not shocking and alienating. In mistaking the white-faced Desdemona for a "fair devil" (3.3.479), Othello draws attention to his own blackness by way of contrast with her innocent victimhood.

Our own perspective on theatrical performance technique, which has been so heavily influenced by Stanislavsky and method acting, can obscure a proper historical understanding of how characters were presented on the early modern stage. Exotic "characters" like Othello were scripted, not as naturalized or realistic "subjects," but in ways that were sometimes symbolic, allegorical, or emblematic. In his jealous rage, Othello becomes, in certain moments at least, an exaggerated, monstrous, carnivalesque figure of difference. Early modern players put on blackface in order to become a disfigured personification, an animated embodiment of blackness that was, at the same time, a figure of whiteness eclipsed and reversed. A stage Moor was seen by Shakespeare's audience through this bifocal perspective – partly in terms of a symbolic-theological ritual, and partly in terms of a naturalistic representation of North African identity. As G. K. Hunter's essay on "Elizabethans and Foreigners" has shown, "Throughout the Elizabethan period ... there seems to be a considerable confusion whether the Moor is a human being or a monster,"[25] and this view is confirmed in Karen Newman's reading of Othello as "both hero and monster."[26] He is, in fact, the Christianized hero (the "good Moor") who kills the monster (the "bad Moor"). But finally, in declaring his damnation ("damned beneath all depth in hell" [5.2.138]) and then committing suicide, Othello assumes the identity of "the Turk," which in early modern parlance was a synonym for "Mahometan" or Muslim:

> in Aleppo once
> Where a malignant and a turbaned Turk
> Beat a Venetian and traduced the state,
> I took by th'throat the circumcisèd dog
> And smote him thus.
> *He stabs himself.* (5.2.348–52)

Here, he reverts to the negative stereotype, becoming, and then killing, the Islamic enemy of Christendom. Othello presents his suicide as a reenactment of a past act, one that was a heroic defense of Christian Venice, but the pathos of this final performance lies, in part, in its futility. Othello's last-ditch attempt to recapture past "redemption" is undermined and blackened by the dramatic irony of his self-slaughter, which only insures damnation under Christian theology and displays the ferocious irascibility that was part of the anti-Muslim stereotype – an identity that "the noble Moor of Venice" seeks to evade but confirms instead. Othello attempts to regain his status as a protector of Christendom, but ironically, he can only do so by becoming, then killing, the "Turk" who threatens Cyprus. Finally, the symbolic, theological signification of blackness overtakes the sense of Othello as "whitened," redeemed, or washed by baptism. His blackness becomes the sign of the demonized Muslim Moor and of the damned soul. The fall and tragic death of the noble Moor might appear pitiable in as much as Othello is perceived as a victim deluded by Iago and driven to jealous rage, murder, and suicide; nonetheless, his death could also be interpreted as a much deserved punishment in the eyes of those playgoers who were indoctrinated with a fantastic fear of the Muslim invader or killer of innocents whose essential nature was thought to be violent and lawless. The sight of a woman-slaying warrior-Moor undoing himself willingly – and being thoroughly damned for it – might offer some sense of reassurance and satisfaction to those who feared that converts from Islam to Christianity might pose an internal threat to Christendom. If Othello's assimilation to Christian civilization taught him to be just and virtuous, led him to employ his martial ability against the enemies of Christendom, and made him acceptable to Desdemona, then it may be said that the recovery of that noble, "civilized" part of him is what moves Othello to destroy the "malignant and ... turbaned Turk." Of course, this is a significant difference from the way that Othello is generally perceived by audiences today: early modern spectators would have been much more divided in their responses to the Moor and to his death by suicide. To the degree that Othello was perceived by the audience as a unique character and not a type, he might receive sympathy; but as the symbolic avatar of un-Christian blackness and mortal sin, he would be condemned and his death applauded.

Notes

1 On the racialized signification of baptism in *Othello* and in post-Reformation English culture generally, see Dennis Austin Britton, *Becoming Christian: Race, Reformation, and Early Modern English Romance* (Oxford: Oxford University Press, 2014).

2 For a good summary of this tradition and its importance for our understanding of *Othello*, see Karen Newman, "'And Wash the Ethiop White': Femininity and the Monstrous in *Othello*," *Shakespeare Reproduced: The Text in History and Ideology*, ed. Jean E. Howard and Marion F. O'Connor (New York: Methuen, 1987), 141–62.

3 See Emily Bartels, *Speaking of the Moor: From "Alcazar" to "Othello"* (Philadelphia: University of Pennsylvania Press, 2009); Dennis Austin Britton, *Becoming Christian: Race, Reformation, and Early Modern English Romance* (Oxford: Oxford University Press, 2014); Jonathan Burton, *Traffic and Turning: Islam and English Drama, 1579–1624* (Newark: University of Delaware Press, 2005); Matthieu Chapman, *Antiblack Racism in Early Modern English Drama: The Other Other* (New York: Routledge, 2017); Jack D'Amico, *The Moor in English Renaissance Drama* (Tampa: University of South Florida Press, 1991); Jane H. Degenhardt, *Islamic Conversion and Christian Resistance on the Early Modern Stage* (Edinburgh: Edinburgh University Press, 2010); Matthew Dimmock, *New Turkes: Dramatizing Islam and the Ottomans in Early Modern England* (Aldershot, UK: Ashgate, 2005); Gerald M. MacLean and N. I. Matar, *Britain and the Islamic World, 1558–1713* (Oxford: Oxford University Press, 2011); Benedict S. Robinson, *Islam and Early Modern English Literature: The Politics of Romance from Spenser to Milton* (New York: Palgrave Macmillan, 2007); Daniel Vitkus, *Turning Turk: English*

Theater and the Multicultural Mediterranean, 1570–1630 (New York: Palgrave Macmillan, 2003).

4 For a classic account of the limitations to character-based readings of Shakespeare's Plays, see Lionel Charles Knights, *How Many Children Had Lady Macbeth? An Essay in the Theory and Practice of Shakespeare Criticism* (Cambridge: G. Fraser, The Minority Press, 1933). See also Michael Bristol, "Confusing Shakespeare's Characters with Real People: Reflections on Reading in Four Questions," in *Shakespeare and Character: Theory, History, Performance and Theatrical Persons*, ed. Paul Yachnin and Jessica Slights (New York: Palgrave, 2009) for a more recent article.

5 For two classic treatments of how the playwrights of the commercial playhouses in London build their drama on the foundation of the medieval morality tradition, see Bernard Spivak, *Shakespeare and the Allegory of Evil* (New York: Columbia University Press, 1958) and David Bevington, *From Mankind to Marlowe: Growth of Structure in the Popular Drama of Tudor England* (Cambridge, MA: Harvard University Press, 1962).

6 On the play's performance history, a good starting point is the introduction to William Shakespeare, *Othello*, ed. Michael Neill (Oxford: Oxford World's Classics, 2008), 36–112.

7 On this blackface stage tradition, see Virginia Mason Vaughan, *Performing Blackness on English Stages, 1500–1800* (Cambridge: Cambridge University Press, 2005).

8 See the attempt to make a case for a much larger Black presence in early modern England in Imtiaz H. Habib, *Black Lives in the English Archives, 1500–1677: Imprints of the Invisible* (Aldershot, UK: Ashgate, 2008). For a critical assessment of his claims and methodologies, see Daniel Vitkus, review of *Speaking of the Moor: From Alcazar to Othello*, by Emily C. Bartels, and *Black Lives in the English Archives, 1500–1677: Imprints of the Invisible*, by Imtiaz Habib, *The Upstart Crow* 27 (2008): 146–50.

9 See Carl Schmitt, *Political Theology: Four Chapters in the History of Sovereignty*, trans. George Schwab (Cambridge, MA: MIT Press, 1985); and Graham Hammill and Julia Reinhard Lupton (eds.), *Political Theology and Early Modernity* (Chicago: University of Chicago Press, 2012).

10 On the "religious turn" in early modern studies and the impact of political theology, see Jennifer R. Rust, "Political Theology and Shakespeare Studies," *Literature Compass* 6 (2009): 175–90; Hammill and Lupton, *Political Theology*; and Ken Jackson and Arthur F. Marotti (eds.), *Shakespeare and Religion: Early Modern and Postmodern Perspectives* (Notre Dame, IN: University of Notre Dame Press, 2011).

11 See D'Amico, *The Moor*, for a useful survey of these Moorish characters.

12 For a detailed, up-to-date account of this visit, see Bernard Harris, "A Portrait of a Moor," *Shakespeare Survey* 11 (1958): 89–97; and consult Jerry Brotton, *This Orient Isle: Elizabethan England and the Islamic World* (London: Allen Lane, 2016), 267–76.

13 Paul L. Hughes and James F. Larkin (eds.), *Tudor Royal Proclamations*, vol. 3 (New Haven, CT: Yale University Press, 1969), 221.

14 On early modern Venice as a cultural and commercial crossroads, see Natalie Rothman, *Brokering Empire: Trans-Imperial Subjects Between Venice and*

Istanbul (Ithaca, NY: Cornell University Press, 2011); and Eric Dursteler, *Venetians in Constantinople: Nation, Identity and Coexistence in the Early Modern Mediterranean* (Baltimore, MD: John Hopkins University Press, 2008).

15 See, for example, *A Copy of the Last Advertisement that Came from Malta, of the Miraculous Delivery of the Isle from the Turk* (London, 1665) and *Certain and True Good News, from the Siege of the Isle Malta* (London, 1565).

16 Quoted in Maclean and Matar, Britain and the Islamic World, 33.

17 Quoted in G. K. Hunter, "Othello and Colour Prejudice," *Proceedings of the British Academy* 53 (1968): 34.

18 Vaughan, *Performing Blackness*, 22.

19 See "Reading Blackness," in Neill's introduction to his edition of *Othello* (113–30) for a helpful account and synthesis of how critics have interpreted and contextualized Othello's Moorish "blackness."

20 Jonathan Burton and Ania Loomba (eds.), *Race in Early Modern England: A Documentary Companion* (New York: Palgrave Macmillan, 2007), 20.

21 Ibid., 16.

22 Ibid.

23 Randle Cotgrave, *A Dictionarie of the French and English Tongues* (London: A. Islip, 1611).

24 Coleridge first used this term to describe Iago, and his motivation to destroy Othello, as demonic and merciless, without human pity or reason – and beyond the petty motives that might be attributed to Iago as a human character (jealousy, ambition, revenge for being slighted when Cassio is promoted over him).

25 G. K. Hunter, "Elizabethans and Foreigners," *Shakespeare Survey* 17 (1964): 37–52, at 56.

26 Newman, "'And Wash the Ethiop White,'" 144.

15

KRISTEN POOLE

Poetic Creation in an Apocalyptic Age: *King Lear* and the Making and the Unmaking of the World

Today, many readers of Shakespeare's plays understand Christianity through the lens of pietism, the notion that religion is about personal morals and behavior. This emphasis on moral piety, however, is a development in the history of religion that postdates Shakespeare's lifetime. For Shakespeare and his audience, religion was not so much about the right or wrong of an individual's actions; rather, religious belief was existential, concerning questions of personal and cosmic ontology. This is not to say that morality was irrelevant (in a play like *Measure for Measure*, for instance, we witness the consequences of violating sexual mores), but on the whole "religion" in Shakespeare's time pertained to the sacred order and history of the universe, and the individual Christian's need to consider how he or she fit into that larger cosmic order and history. The existential and eschatological concerns of early modern Christianity outweighed concerns about individual behavior. Or, to put it otherwise, particular acts of wrongdoing – sins with a small "s" – were considered in the context of Sin, the ontological state of fallen humanity.

This emphasis on Sin – the general state of human alienation from God resulting from the Fall of Adam and Eve – meant that people were encouraged to understand their lives in the context of a very *longue durée* of cosmic history. While the life of Christ was naturally at the heart of Christianity, for much of the sixteenth and seventeenth centuries there was also a cultural fascination with the events understood to bookend the life of the world: the Creation and the Apocalypse. While Christ was enmeshed in these stories of cosmic origins and destruction (according to the Gospel of John, Christ is the Word through which the universe came into being, and according to the Book of Revelation, his return will bring about the final scene of judgment and earthly destruction), much of Protestant religious thought shifted attention away from the actual life of Jesus to a larger spiritual history. In part, this shift was motivated by Protestant skepticism about some of the Catholic trappings surrounding the notion of *imitatio Christi* that had been at the core of much medieval devotional practice: veneration of the cross, the crucifix, even the making of the sign of the cross all became dubious for many Protestants, who associated these actions and objects with idolatry. If the religious emphasis on cosmic spiritual history was propelled by a rejection of a particular type of medieval Christocentricism perceived as theologically problematic, it was also advanced by the rapid expansion and popularization of interest in science. Questions about the composition and operations of the natural world intersected with questions about theology. Indeed, during this time period theology and natural philosophy – the investigation of the environment and the cosmos – were essentially one and the same. Scientific study of astronomy, or chemistry, or physics (to mention just a few of the burgeoning fields of the period) were all attempts to understand how God had made the world. The making and unmaking of the world were also a favorite subject matter of artists and writers: the Creation and the Apocalypse featured prominently in sixteenth- and seventeenth-century texts. For a variety of reasons and in a variety of forms, then, Shakespeare and his audience would have been immersed in a culture that extensively considered the formation and the destruction of the universe.

In order to understand the theological and literary context of Shakespeare's *King Lear*, it is important to consider this cultural concern with the Creation and the Apocalypse. Let's start with the fascination with the Creation, the idea that God made the world in six days. In broad terms, we can think of the period of the Renaissance as framed by Michelangelo's painting of the creation of Adam on the Sistine Chapel at the beginning of the sixteenth century, and Milton's epic poem *Paradise Lost*, which tells of the Creation and Fall, towards the end of the seventeenth century. In between, one of the most popular literary texts was Guillaume de Saluste Du Bartas *La Sepmaine, ou Création du Monde* [*The Week, or the Creation of the World*] (1578) (followed by *La Seconde Sepmaine* in 1584), an extensive poem detailing the Creation. *La Sepmaine* describes in detail each day of Creation, following Genesis 1:1–8. The *Sepmaines* "intertwine poetry, classical learning, natural philosophy [science], world history, and rhetoric," in the description of Peter Auger.[1] (To this list, we might add theology, given the poems' content.) As Auger notes, "[t]his ambitious combination was both attractive and useful in the seventeenth century: Du Bartas, unlike [Francesco] Petrarch, Ludovico Ariosto, Torquato Tasso and other post-classical poets, was cited in many English-language treatises, sermons and other prose works," due in large part to King James I's admiration for Du Bartas and the many editions of Josuah Sylvester's 1605 English translation of the *Sepmaines*, *The Divine Weeks*. While Du Bartas was hugely popular in France and had a great influence on elite English poets in the late sixteenth century, Sylvester's translation propelled the poem into popular currency in England.[2] In the seventeenth century, "it was clearly reasonable to think that priests and congregations across England and Scotland would know the *Semaines* and that readers would be familiar with the work. The *Semaines* were no longer the preserve of cultured Londoners: they were known to educated readers across the country."[3] To "priests and congregations" we can add "playwrights and audiences": these influential poems about the creation of the world became part of the stable of literary sources that would shape the writing and reception of plays. We find, for instance, the character of Kate in the anonymous 1594 play *The Taming of a Shrew* very obviously translating passages of Du Bartas's *La Sepmaine*.[4]

The cultural interest in the beginning of the world was paralleled by an interest in its end. At first glance, it might seem that Reformation theology and liturgy diminished the place of the Apocalypse in the public imagination. Reformist theologians tended to be reserved about the Apocalypse and minimized the importance of the final book of the Christian Bible, the Book of Revelation (also known as the Apocalypse of St. John), which contains a vivid description of the end of days. Martin Luther doubted that the book belonged in the Bible; John Calvin wrote commentaries on the books of the Old and New Testament, but omitted the Book of Revelation, rarely even referring to it in his copious writings.[5] As Joseph Wittreich notes, "the book met with studied indifference, as in the instances of Erasmus, Tyndale, Zwingli ... or was treated with quiet disdain, as seems to have been the case with those who censured much of it both in the Book of Common Prayer and in their edicts again prophesying."[6] This reformist attitude also kept the Book of Revelation out of the lectionary, the cycle of Bible lessons that were part of church services; in the course of a year, all of the other books of the New Testament would be read through three times, but not the Book of Revelation.[7] Thus it was not only reform-minded scholars who avoided the book – the average churchgoer would not hear it being read, either.

And yet concern about the end of days persisted and even achieved a new vividness in the age of print. If the Book of Revelation was not read aloud as part of the lectionary cycle in services, it could be seen through illustrations (see Figure 15.1). Albrecht Dürer's images of the Apocalypse (published in 1498 and 1511) became an international sensation, as they were circulated and imitated widely throughout Europe. In England, the images were included in printings of the Bishops' Bible (first printed in 1568, with nineteen editions to 1606, and widely available to Shakespeare and his audience) as a series of twenty pictures.[8] Shakespeare almost certainly saw these images; in *Antony and Cleopatra*, for instance, Cleopatra's dream of Antony draws from a particular Dürer image of the Apocalypse,[9] down to

The Reuelation

Lions.
9 And they had habbergions as it were
habbergions of iron, and the sounde of
their wynges was as ẏ sounde of char-
rettes when many horses runne together to batayle.

10 And they had tayles lyke vnto scorpi-
ons, and there were stynges in their
tayles: and their power was to hurt
men fiue monethes.
11 And they had a king ouer them, which
is the angell of the bottomlesse pytte,
whose name in the Hebrue tongue is A-
badon, but in ẏ Greke tongue Apollyon,
[that is to say, a destroyer.]
12 One woe is past, & beholde two woes
come yet after this.
C 13 And the sixt angell blewe, & I hearde
a voyce from the foure hornes of the
golden aulter, which is before God,
14 Saying to the sixt angell whiche had
the trumpe: Loose the foure angels
which are bounde in the great riuer Eu-
phrates.
15 And the foure angels were loosed,
whiche were prepared for an houre, for
a day, for a moneth, and for a yere, for to
slea the thirde part of men.
16 And the number of horsemen of warre
were twentie thousand times ten thou-
sande, & I hearde the number of them.
17 And thus I sawe the horses in a vision, and them that sate on them, hauing
fierie habbergions of a iacinct colour,
and brymstone, and the heades of the
horses were as the heades of lions, and
out of their mouthes went foorth fire,
and smoke, and brymstone.
18 And of these three was the third part D
of men kylled [that is to say] of fire, smoke
and brymstone, which proceaded out of
the mouthes of them.
19 For their power was in their mouthes,
& in their tayles: for their tayles were
lyke vnto serpentes, and had heades, &
with them they dyd hurt.
20 And the remnaunt of the men whiche
were not killed by these plagues, repented not of the deedes of their handes,
that they shoulde not worship deuyls,
and idoles of golde, and syluer, & brasse,
and stone, and of wood, whiche neither
can see, neither heare, neither go:
21 Also they repented not of their mur-
ther, & of their sorcerie, neither of their
fornication, neither of their theft.

C The

Figure 15.1 *The Holy Bible: Containing the Old Testament and the New* (London: R. Jugge, 1568), fol. 149[v]. (New Testament numbered separately.) Source: Rare Books and Manuscripts, The Ohio State University.

Antony being described as "dolphin-like," a detail that is not in the Bible but clearly appears in Dürer's woodcut of the great angel.[10]

To a certain degree, these images had transferred the visual imagining of the end of days from the walls of churches to the pages of books, from communal sacred spaces to semi-private devotional texts. Medieval churches had a long and vivid pictorial tradition of Doom paintings. These depicted the judgment of the Apocalypse, with some souls being saved and ascending to heaven, and others being damned and fed by demons into the gaping maw of the hellmouth. While many of these images had been whitewashed over in the Protestant iconoclastic enthusiasm of the mid-sixteenth century, the images persisted in the cultural memory, and with time even began to return, as the paint bled through the coating of lime. Famously, the Guild Chapel in Stratford-upon-Avon is an example of the reappearing Doom. Shakespeare's father had been responsible for whitewashing the church's apocalyptic images, but the pictures almost certainly lived on in the mind's eye of parishioners who had grown up with them, and the Doom itself made a ghostly return, as the underlying layers of paint gradually became visible once more.[11]

The Apocalypse figured prominently in verbal culture as well. If Luther and Calvin had their doubts about the canonicity of the Book of Revelation, they were in agreement that the Pope was the Antichrist foretold in that book.[12] The idea of the Pope as Antichrist became a pervasive feature of the prolific outpouring of anti-Catholic polemic. And if churchgoers were not hearing the actual Book of Revelation, they certainly got a dose of Apocalypse through spoken and written sermons. John Donne, for instance, preached on All Saints' Day about the angelology and demonology of Revelation (7:2, 3).[13] George Gifford published fifty collected sermons on the Book of Revelation (1593, 1599).[14] There was, as well, a heightened poetic and dramatic interest in the Apocalypse.[15] Wittreich notes,

> The principal artists of the English Renaissance – Spenser, Shakespeare, Donne and later Herbert, Marvell, and Milton – apparently spurred by a burgeoning number of sermons and commentaries – set for themselves the task of returning the Apocalypse from exile and thrusting it into prominence. Hence the Church's, the government's, dislodgement of the Book of Revelation and dismantling of its myth is but one story; another is the resuscitation of the book by religious dissenters and later by secular artists, even by a king [James I].[16]

Shakespeare, like his contemporaries, lived in the midst of these verbal and pictorial images of both Creation and Apocalypse. His great tragedy *King Lear* appeared contemporaneously with Sylvester's translation of Du Bartas's *Divine Weekes*; his own father, as mentioned, had been involved in the whitewashing of the Doom in the Guild Chapel in Stratford-upon-Avon. Notions of the creation of the world and its destruction enter into his plays – perhaps nowhere more explicitly than in *King Lear*.[17] While *King Lear* revolves around a range of concerns – presenting, of course, a psychological study of familial relationships (which, as in other of Shakespeare's history plays, are also political relationships) – the play derives its existential heft from underlying questions about the very making and unmaking of the world.

One of the play's most famous lines – King Lear's declaration to Cordelia that "Nothing comes from nothing" (1.1.85) – positions the story within a larger context of theological debates about the cosmos.[18] Was the world created from nothing (*creatio ex nihilo* in theological terms)? Or was there some pre-existing primal matter that God used for the Creation (*creatio ex materia*)? Did the cosmos come from nothing, or from something? This was an ancient debate that made its way into early Christianity. The Bible offers no definitive explanation of the physics of creation (whether it was *creatio ex nihilo* or *creatio ex materia*), but from the second century onward, *creatio ex nihilo* became established Christian orthodoxy, and it was formulated as church dogma in the Fourth Lateran Council of 1215.[19] Major Christian theologians who shaped Reformation thought, such as Augustine and Calvin, asserted that God did create the world from nothing; *creatio ex nihilo* is a fundamental aspect of God's divinity and sovereignty. The Protestant poet Du Bartas also promotes a cosmogony of *creatio ex nihilo* in *La Sepmaine* ("This Trinity ... In the infinity of *Nothing* builded all"; "God, the Father, Son, and Holy Ghost created of Nothing the World's goodly frame"; "Nothing, but *Nothing* had the Lord Almighty, / Whereof, wherewith, whereby, to build this City").[20] On the other hand, the Roman philosopher Lucretius, newly re-discovered and popularized in the sixteenth century, maintained that the cosmos were made from a pre-existing chaos. "[N]othing's brought / Forth by any supernatural power out of naught," he writes in *De Rerum Natura*, "Nothing can be made from nothing."[21]

King Lear himself seems to adopt this pagan, Epicurean perspective of *creatio ex materia*. In case the point is lost, he even re-formulates his belief, emphasizing the idea of making: "nothing can be made out of nothing" (1.4.116). The pre-Christian setting of *King Lear* might call attention to, and even excuse, the monarch's pagan philosophical beliefs. But the play's overlay of Christian imagery produces a theological incongruity that paradoxically renders King Lear's position of *creatio ex materia* as a bleak nihilism, a sense that the world is meaningless. As with so much of religious belief, then and now, the physics of a particular worldview influence ideas about divinity and, consequently, the individual's relationship to the divine.

Creatio ex materia was understood to challenge the idea of God as supreme maker; instead of being the origin of all, God merely becomes the shaper of all. If God is a mere shaper rather than the originator, God's divine powers are lessened. God becomes less supreme.

In *King Lear*, the king's belief in *creatio ex materia* also contributes to his delusions of possessing nearly divine powers of creation. Throughout the play, King Lear presents himself as the God of the opening of Genesis, who created the world in six days. The echoes of this creation run throughout the play. King Lear's sentence of banishment on Kent, for instance, is delivered in terms that gratuitously mimic the timeline of Genesis:

> Five days we do allot thee for provision
> To shield thee from disasters of the world,
> And on the sixth to turn thy hated back
> Upon our kingdom; if on the tenth day following
> Thy banished trunk be found in our dominions,
> The moment is thy death. Away! By Jupiter,
> This shall not be revoked. (1.1.167–73)

There does not seem to be any rationale for the specific enumeration of days, other than to present something of an inverse version of creation: whereas God brings the world into beautiful order in five days and brings forth Adam and Eve on the sixth, King Lear presents the first five days of Kent's sentence to be about the "disasters of the [natural] world," and the sixth to be a day of expulsion.

We find here other instances of King Lear's habit of god-speak as well. While "dominions" literally just means territory, the particular choice of term carries overtones of "dominus" (Latin for God) and uses a charged word from Genesis, as God famously gives Adam "dominion" over the animals ("have dominion of the fish of the sea, and foul of the air, & of every living thing that moveth upon the earth"[22]). In Genesis, God creates through verbal decrees ("let there be light"), and this connection of creation and language was ingrained in Christianity through the prominence of the abstracted re-telling of the Creation in the opening of John's Gospel, which makes the creative agent a divine Word: "In the beginning was the word, & the word was with God: and that word was God … All things were made by it: and without it, was made nothing that was made." King Lear's declaration of Kent's banishment is prefaced by the accusation that Kent tried "to come betwixt our sentence and our power" (1.1.164), a formulation that emphasizes the equation of language and authority. In King Lear's summary exclamation that "By Jupiter, / This shall not be revoked," we could read the invocation of Jupiter as a mere expression (as in, "By Jove, I think he's got it!"), but the syntax seems more specific than that, actually attributing agency ("This shall not be revoked by Jupiter"): he who shall not do any revoking is the supreme god Jupiter, which, in this case, is collapsed with Lear, since, by the very definition of "revoke" (to call back) only he can recall his own decrees. In this moment of political declaration at the beginning of the play, then, King Lear reveals a speech pattern and (therefore) a thought habit that positions him as God.

Lear is not the God of creation, however, but a self-determined god of anti-creation. He is the negative inverse of the Judaeo-Christian God of Genesis. A striking instance of this is King Lear's curse on his daughter Goneril, which inverts a familiar biblical blessing into a curse. In Genesis, God creates an abundance of life, and blesses the new human couple with a dictate to "be fruitful, & multiply" (1:28). Indeed, the blessing almost serves as a type of refrain in the first chapter of Genesis, where "fruit" (in various forms) appears six times. Of the vegetation, "God said: let the earth bring forth [both] bud and herb apt to seed, and fruitful trees yielding fruit after his kind, which hath seed in itself upon the earth" (1:11). Of the fish and birds, "God blessed them, saying: Be fruitful, and multiply, and fill the waters of the sea, and let fowl multiply in the earth" (1:22). King Lear uses this biblical language of fruitful fertility in order to distort it, hurling instead a curse of sterility:

> Hear, Nature, hear, dear goddess, hear:
> Suspend thy purpose, if thou didst intend
> To make this creature fruitful.
> Into her womb convey sterility,
> Dry up in her the organs of increase,
> And from her derogate body never spring
> A babe to honour her. If she must teem,
> Create her child of spleen; that it may live
> And be a thwart disnatured torment to her. (1.4.230–8)

What might initially ring of appeal and supplication to a higher deity ("Hear, Nature, hear, dear goddess, hear") soon gives way to an appearance of divine dictate. King Lear positions himself as king of the gods (as Jupiter, as discussed above), ordering an inferior with a string of imperatives that crescendo in intensity: "Hear, nature, hear"; "Suspend thy purpose"; "Dry up in her the organs of increase": "Create her child of spleen." The twisted syntax of the final line, "a thwart disnatured torment," replicates in verbal form what King Lear is commanding of physical form. The realm of nature has been contorted into "disnature."

The apotheosis of King Lear as the anti-creator comes in the famous scene on the heath. Stripped of his authority, in a state of self-imposed exile from human society, King Lear stands in the midst of a storm and issues commands:

> Blow, winds, and crack your cheeks! Rage, blow,
> You cataracts and hurricanoes, spout
> Till you have drenched our steeples, drowned the cocks!
> You sulph'rous and thought-executing fires,
> Vaunt-couriers to oak-cleaving thunderbolts,
> Singe my white head; And thou, all-shaking thunder,
> Smite flat the thick rotundity o' th' world!
> Crack nature's moulds, all germens spill at once
> That makes ingrateful man! (3.2.1–9)

As in his curse on Goneril, King Lear's speech is saturated with powerful imperatives: "blow," "crack," "rage," "spout," "singe," "strike," "spill." These monosyllabic commands are all words of destruction; the cumulative effect is that of a god ordering the elements of nature. Lear does indeed seem to position himself as the controller of the four elements: he commands air ("winds"), water ("hurricanoes"), fire ("fires"), and earth ("nature's moulds"). In his repeated references to thunder and thunderbolts, Lear again positions himself as Jupiter. This association is enhanced by the subtle shift from the formal pronoun of "you" to the informal "thou": at the beginning of the speech he addresses the wind, "hurricanos," and fire as "you," signaling deference and respect; but he then commands the "all-shaking thunder" as "thou," demeaning the element and asserting his own superiority. Any sense of order created by the strong commands is potentially undermined, however, by the meeting of opposites that neutralize each other: water is paired with fire; "flat" with "rotundity"; creation ("germens" [seeds], "makes") with destruction ("drowned," "executing," "crack," "spill"); the Jupiter-like Lear with the pathetically old, human, and vulnerable Lear ("Singe my white head"). This sense of control balanced with chaos or destruction is reflected in the very words of the speech. A torrent of harsh c's and t's give the language a hard edge, but the sense of urgency and rage is countermanded by the aural and visual balancing of "blow" at the beginning and ending of the first line. Similarly, the repetition of "crack" at or near the beginning of lines one and eight, and the similarities of "spout" and "spill" at the end of lines two and eight, gives the speech balance and symmetry. The careful crafting of the speech is its own counterbalance to the devastation described within it. The line that falls outside of the pattern is the last one, with the introduction of the new alliteration of "makes" and "man." Although humankind is the immediate object of Lear's wrath, intriguingly the little word "man" only appears at the very end. "Man" seems to slip through the structure of the speech as well as the devastation of the elements, suggesting that for all of Lear's fantasies of power he remains impotent to affect human ingratitude. This is the culminating moment of King Lear's anti-creation, his "disnature." If the God of Genesis made man, here Lear seeks not construction but destruction, cracking the mold that made man, and replacing the "fruitful" biblical language with an image of scattered, and thus impotent, seed.

If this moment in the play presents a powerful image of a god of destruction, we should remember the important prefatory work done by the exchange between Kent and the unnamed Gentleman that opens the scene. To Kent's inquiry of "I know you. Where's the king?" the Gentleman responds:

> Contending with the fretful element:
> Bids the wind blow the earth into the sea,
> Or swell the curlèd water 'bove the main,
> That things might change or cease; [teares his white haire,
> Which the impetuous blasts with eyles rage
> Catch in their furie and make nothing of;
> Strives in his little world of man to outscorne
> The too and fro conflicting wind and raine]. (3.1.4–7)[23]

Here we encounter King Lear's rage and commanding of the elements from the point of view of an anonymous stranger, who makes the connection between Lear's actions and the events of Genesis more blatant, even as he reveals Lear's position as a deity to be a form of fantasy and self-delusion. In Genesis, one of God's first acts of creation is to separate land and water: "And God said: let there be a firmament between the waters, and let it make a division between waters and waters. And God made the firmament, and set the division between the waters which [were] under the firmament, and the waters that [were] above the firmament: and it was so" (1:6–7). By stark contrast, King Lear, from the Gentleman's perspective, "Bids the winds blow the earth into the sea, / Or swell the curlèd water 'bove the main" – either the earth can go back into the sea, or the sea can overcome the land, so long as "things might change or cease." If God initiates a beginning, Lear seeks an ending.

But the fallacy of King Lear's power to effect either change or ceasing is quickly revealed. On the heath we witnessed a King Lear who presented himself as nearly omnipotent, who commanded the fire and thunderbolts to "Singe [his] white head"; the moment is a forceful expression of bravado, and we can almost envision Lear as a god of classical myth, with flaming hair. How different is the Gentleman's description here, as Lear "teares his white haire, / Which the impetuous blasts with eyles rage / Catch in their furie and make nothing of." King Lear goes from agent to object, his old white hair now being whipped around by the eyeless wind which barely takes notice. The wind has made the something of Lear's existence into nothing ("make[s] nothing of"), reversing the process of *creatio ex nihilo*. King Lear's utter irrelevance to the workings of nature is made bitingly clear in the final lines of the Gentleman's speech: Lear "Strives in his little world of man to outscorne / The too and fro conflicting wind and raine." The wind and the rain carry on in their own realm; King Lear's "striving" and his "scorn" are minimized and rendered utterly irrelevant as they happen "in his little world of man," a phrasing that at once invokes the literal translation of "microcosm" and yet disparagingly seems to dismiss the exalted microcosm-macrocosm relationship that was the basis of Renaissance epistemology. If King Lear is a creator – it is, after all, *his* little world – he has created a world of insignificance. Elsewhere in the play, Lear speaks of "the small gilded fly [that] does lecher in [his] sight" (4.5.108–9), a reference that is almost a parody of the notion that God watches even over the sparrows (Matt. 6:26, 10:29–31). But here it is Lear that is miniscule and insignificant.

Ultimately, King Lear's own fantasy of being an omnipotent creator comes crashing down. He laments that the fawning of his followers led him to believe in a fallacy of power:

> They flattered me like a dog and told me I had the white hairs in my beard ere the black ones were there. To say "ay" and "no" to everything that I said "ay" and "no" to was no good divinity. When the rain came to wet me once, and the wind to make me chatter, when the thunder would not peace at my bidding, there I found 'em, there I smelt 'em out. Go to, they are not men o'their words. They told me I was everything; 'tis a lie, I am not ague-proof. (4.5.94–101)

The biblical resonances through here have been recognized by the play's editors. Jay Halio glosses "no good divinity" as "bad theology," and notes: "Several biblical verses are possible sources or analogues. Compare Matthew 5.37: 'But let your communication be, Yea, yea: Nay, nay. For whatsoever is more the[n] these, cometh of evil.' Compare also Matthew 5.36: 'Nether shalt thou swear by thine head, because thou canst not make one heere white or black' … and James 5.12, 2 Corinthians 1.18–19."[24] R. A. Foakes similarly notes that the passage is "probably influenced by Christ's injunction against swearing, Matthew, 5.36–37" and glosses "divinity" as "theology; suggesting they treated him as a god, and perhaps alluding to the divine right of kings."[25] These New Testament references clearly are present, but the passage also carries forward the discourse of Creation from Genesis that was so prominent earlier in the play. Lear is crushed by the fact that the thunder would not do his "bidding" – a word that brings us back to the anonymous Gentleman's account of King Lear "Contending with the fretful element: / *Bids* the winds blow the earth into the sea" (italics mine). While the visceral experience of wet and cold most physically belies his sense of superiority over the elements ("the rain came to wet me once, and the wind to make me chatter"), what gets repeated in here, and what seems like the supreme betrayal, is that the connection between language and being is not what Lear had supposed. He castigates the flattering assent – "To say 'ay' and 'no' to everything that I said" – but given the intricate connection between saying and creating in Genesis that was invoked earlier in the play, at issue here is not just run-of-the-mill sycophancy by courtiers. God brings the world into being through speech ("And God said, let there be light"; "In the beginning was the word"). This aspect of linguistic creation is highlighted if we borrow for a moment the Folio's spelling of "every thing," a common early modern spelling that allows for a recognition of the material in a way that the modern "everything" obscures.[26] "Every thing that I said," if Lear assumes the mantle of divinity, thus extends beyond mere content, to a word-matter, speech-act understanding of all Creation. And as a god-like figure, Lear is synonymous with creation: "they told me I was every thing." But, Lear recognizes in a brutally short phrase, "'tis a lie." The falsity of language severs not just the identity of Lear as "every thing," but it also cuts off the divine speech act, the efficacy of divine language to create. The God who creates something out of nothing is everything. This God is not King Lear.

The idea of Lear as Creator, and also as a negative inversion of that Creator, is grounded in language – through references to the God of Genesis creating through speech-act, through Christ as the Word, through the play's biblically resonant vocabulary, and, everywhere, through the idea that theater is a linguistic creation in and of itself. This connection of language and Creation is paired with the linguistic implications of the Apocalypse that are also present within the play. In his essay "'Image of That horror': the Apocalypse in *King Lear*," Wittreich spells out the play's echoes of the Book of Revelation:

> Besides the blaring trumpets, the play contains numerous other signatures of apocalypse: the mystery of the seven stars ... the cracking thunder and catastrophic earthquakes, the eclipse of sun and moon, the wheel of fire, the lake of darkness, the sulphureous pit, the wrathful dragon, the prince of darkness, the black angel, even the monsters of the deep and the imagery of defiled and fresh garments. The storm on the heath, which Lear refers to as "this tempest in my mind" [3.4.12], recalls what the Book of Revelation says of Armageddon ... The play is richly allusive; and some of its allusion finds conspicuous reference points in the Apocalypse: the crown of flowers, the tenth day, the wiping of eyes, the wiping away of tears, the persistent concern with

> the bestial character of man ... And there are other such instances, with the images of the earthquake, the darkened sun and moon, and the falling stars equating the Lear universe with the events that occur under the sixth seal.[27]

King Lear's fantasies of divinity and creation thus take place in a larger verbal fabric that continuously rings with references to the Book of Revelation, familiar to Shakespeare's audience members through biblical reading and sermons.

Throughout the play, we find intimations that the end of days is near. Gloucester envisions a universe that protects King Lear through the world's destruction, as "The sea ... would have buoyed up, / And quenched the stellèd fires" and "The wingèd vengeance overtake such children" (3.7.58–9, 65). Earlier, Gloucester had worried about the significance of the recent solar and lunar eclipses: "These late eclipses in the sun and moon portend no good to us. Though the wisdom of nature can reason it thus and thus, yet nature finds itself scourged by the sequent effects. Love cools, friendship falls off, brothers divide. In cities, mutinies; in countries, discord; in palaces, treason; and the bond cracked 'twixt son and father" (1.2.91–6). It is significant that "[t]hese late eclipses in the sun and moon" is, at one level, a topical reference: there were, in fact, eclipses (one solar, two lunar) in England in 1598, which prompted popular concern that these were signs of the imminent end of the world.[28]

The eclipses lead to other effects in "nature," but these turn out to be emotive, the loss of various forms of love. We find here a similar linking of physical and emotional phenomena in the idea of cracking ("the bond cracked"). References to cracking ripple throughout the play. Gloucester's observation that eclipses lead to the cracking of the bond between father and son proves prophetic; discovering Edgar's presumed betrayal, Gloucester exclaims, "my old heart is cracked, it's crackd" (2.1.89). King Lear, finding that his beloved child is dead, cries to those present, "Had I your tongues and eyes, I'd use them so / That heaven's vault should crack" (5.3.232–3). This idea of a cracked vault of heaven itself connects back to Lear's call to "Crack nature's moulds" (3.2.8). With the image of a cracked universe, we might think of *Macbeth*, a play that parallels *King Lear* in a number of ways, and Macbeth's exclamation upon learning that Banquo's lineage "will ... stretch out to th' crack of doom" (4.1.133).[29] "Crack" can be associated with the sound of trumpets signaling the end of the world as described in the book of Revelation (OED, crack, *n.* 1.a), but the cracking in *King Lear* suggests that Shakespeare also imagines the apocalypse as a process of the physical world breaking apart. And indeed, much of *King Lear* feels as if we have entered into the Apocalypse. The vivid descriptions of the storm create the climate of Revelation 11:19: "and there followed lightnings, and voices, and thundrings, and earthquake, and much hail." And as R. M. Christofides observes, the descriptions of the characters are suggestive of the dragon of the book of Revelation and the hellmouth vividly depicted in Doom paintings on church walls still visible in the sixteenth and early seventeenth centuries.[30] In the play, we encounter Lear's references to a "serpent's tooth" and a "sea-monster" (1.4.243; 1.4.216). Goneril is "serpent-like" and "a gilded serpent" (2.4.153; 5.3.78).

What is the audience to make of these apocalyptic images and invocations? This is a question that is asked within the play itself. In one of the most charged exchanges, Kent and Edgar seek to understand how to process the devastating sight of King Lear holding the dead Cordelia.

> KENT: Is this the promised end?
> EDGAR: Or image of that horror? (5.3.237–8)

The characters within the play are uncertain how to read the scene before them and can only open it up to interpretation. The intensely allusive verbal fabric of the play, one that is woven with many threads taken from the Book of Revelation, now becomes a text that the characters, audience, and scholars are pressed to interpret. Wittreich notes that these remarks "remind us that apocalypse and interpretation thereof are particular concerns for those who survive the play's catastrophe," and that, "In *King Lear*, it is true, there is all the darkness and fire and whirlwind of the Apocalypse; there is an apocalyptic encroachment on the world of the play, creating that Yeatsian sense of tragedy wrought to the uttermost. Still, the play submits to a middle ground of interpretation."[31]

This "middle ground" appears to be the space between something and nothing. The existential and linguistic status of the "nothingness" of words opens up questions about the very medium of *King Lear* itself. Jacqueline Kolosov observes that "in *Lear*, Shakespeare, the most eloquent of dramatists, stresses the inefficacy of speech to convey what lies within the human heart. 'Nothing will come of nothing' (1.1.90) and 'Nothing can be made out of nothing' (1.4.130)."[32] And yet, "The performance of *King Lear* sucks the audience inside, transforming the watcher into the witness. In such a world as Lear's and our own, not only is poetry possible, it is necessary. Perhaps this is what Shakespeare is ferrying across the wreckage of *King Lear*, a play in which the visceral reality of suffering has the final word."[33] The nothingness of the play is transformed into the shreds of a poetic something, and it is this transformation that becomes its own form of redemption, however bleak.

In a different reading, Christofides suggests that the linguistic redemption promised in *King Lear* never comes. For Christofides, the play itself is structured like a language, but one that is not anchored by a transcendent, external divine Word, or Logos. This absence is keenly felt by the characters within the play. In a powerful connection of the Apocalypse and language, Christofides unpacks the devastating implications for Kent and Edgar's brief exchange ("Is this the promised end?" "Or image of that horror?"), in which they "speculate as to whether what they see before them is the Doom or merely a replica." But the Apocalypse, which promises both heavenly salvation for the good and divine retribution for the unjust, doesn't happen. Thus,

> *King Lear* ... invokes but withholds the Doom, a traumatic reconciliation between heaven and earth preceded and set up by the Pietà. Tantalizingly out of reach, the blazing, sulphurous and apocalyptic Judgement that ends all equivocatory confusion and the tragedy it helps to bring about guarantees, by its absence, the austere, desolate outcome of the play. Earthly destruction and disaster caused by linguistic twists and turns stands unredeemed by supernatural disclosure, a ghostly coup de théâtre that holds back the end it promises – a spectral Logos that might, one day, emerge in excelsis from a fizzing portal in the clouds to deliver cloven-hoofed punishment for the wicked or winged salvation for the just.[34]

Christofides's interpretation of this scene about interpretation points to the nothingness of the something of the theater. On the stage, we are ostensibly presented with a something: the feminizing idiom of the play (which Janet Adelman so famously analyzed[35]) culminates in King Lear as a maternal body in a pose that invokes Mary holding the body of the crucified Christ. But as theater, this seeming-something and its signification are revealed, by the very nature of performance and theater, to be mere nothings. This is not reality; this is not truth. The evocation of an Apocalypse that does not come highlights absence and illusion.

But this is where we encounter a particular strain of the Shakespearean genius. Throughout the plays and sonnets, the texts paradoxically call attention to their own linguistic virtuosity, even while undermining the power of language. On a minute level, we find this paradox in Juliet's famous lines, "What's in a name? That which we call a rose / By any other word would smell as sweet" (*Romeo and Juliet*, 2.1.85–6); this moment renders the particularities and semiotic properties of language irrelevant, even as the play is one of Shakespeare's most poetically crafted, and even as words have momentous social and personal consequences. *King Lear* presents this Shakespearean paradox on a large scale: the entire play offers language as both something powerful (the action of God) and as nothing (the destruction of all, or mere illusion). In this, *King Lear* holds together opposing early modern perspectives on the relationship of human and divine creation.

On the one hand, there is the perspective of Sir Philip Sidney, author of *A Defense of Poesy* (*c.*1579), for whom a "poet's consciousness aspires to mimic both created nature (mere matter) and creating nature, and so harmonize with divine creativity."[36] On the other hand, we find William Scot, whose translation of the first two Days of *La Sepmaine* follows his *The Model of Poesy* (*c.*1599); as Auger contends, "The translation is in effect a statement that mortal creation is incommensurable with divine creation, and it provides a model for how English poets can proceed given that insight into their deficiencies."[37] One of these deficiencies is that "mortal poets cannot create all from nothing but must hitch their thoughts to fore-conceits and earlier images."[38] By accentuating the biblical images of both Creation and Apocalypse, *King Lear* manages to convey both the affinities and the distance between human and divine capabilities of making, especially through language. To return in full to our central passage:

> KENT: This is nothing, fool.
> FOOL: Then 'tis like the breath of an unfeed lawyer; you gave me nothing for't.
> Can you make no use of nothing, nuncle?
> LEAR: Why, no, boy; nothing can be made out of nothing. (1.4.113–15)

If "nothing" is "like breath" – that is, like words, language, the Word (the Hebrew and Greek word for "breath" is "spirit," an association of the Holy Spirit that runs through Christian theology and liturgy) – it is both the ultimate absence and presence. As a mere construction of spoken words, King Lear the fictional character does not exist, is nothing. As a work of art expressing complex emotional, psychological, philosophical, and theological ideas, *King Lear* is the opposite of nothing. The king's very articulation of the doctrine of *creatio ex materia* turns out, in the context of the play and the theater, to make a case for literary *creatio ex nihilo*.

Notes

1 Peter Auger, "The *Semaines*' Dissemination in England and Scotland Until 1641," *Renaissance Studies* 26, no. 5 (2011): 625.

2 Auger, "Dissemination," 628–31, 633 ff. For a summary of the *Divine Weeks* multiple editions, see 634.

3 Auger, "Dissemination," 638.

4 Richard Hillman, "'La Création du Monde' et 'The Taming of the Shrew': Du Bartas Comme Intertexte," *Renaissance and Reformation/Renaissance et Réforme* 15, no. 3 (1991): 250–1. The relationship of *The Taming of a Shrew* and Shakespeare's *The Taming of the Shrew* has long been contested; see *The Taming of a Shrew: The 1594 Quarto*, ed. Stephen Roy Miller (Cambridge: Cambridge University Press, 1998), introduction.

5 Jaroslav Pelikan, "Some Uses of Apocalypse in the Magisterial Reformers," in *The Apocalypse in English Renaissance Thought and Literature*, ed. C. A. Patrides and Joseph Wittreich (Ithaca, NY: Cornell University Press, 1984), 75.

6 Joseph Wittreich, "'Image of That Horror': The Apocalypse in *King Lear*," in Patrides and Wittreich, *The Apocalypse*, 175.

7 Helen Morris, "Shakespeare and Dürer's Apocalypse," *Shakespeare Studies* 4 (1969): 253.

8 Ibid., 253–4.

9 Ethel Seaton, "*Antony and Cleopatra* and the Book of Revelation," *Review of English Studies* 22 (1946): 219–24; cited in Morris, "Dürer's Apocalypse," 259.

10 Morris, "Dürer's Apocalypse," 261.

11 Kate Giles, "Seeing and Believing: Visuality and Space in Pre-Modern England," *Archeology* 39, no. 1 (2007): 113–15.

12 Pelikan, "Some Uses," 86.

13 Referenced in Chris R. Hassel Jr., "Last Words and Last Things: St. John, Apocalypse, and Eschatology in Richard III," *Shakespeare Studies* 18 (1986): 36. See Hassel, esp. 35–6, for references to the Apocalypse in contemporary sermons.

14 Richard Bauckham, *Tudor Apocalypse* (Oxford: Sutton Courtenay Press, 1978), 136. Cited in Maurice Hunt, "'Forward Backward' Time and the Apocalypse in *Hamlet*," *Comparative Drama* 38, no. 4 (2004–5): 386.

15 For dramatic representations of the Apocalypse, see Adrian Streete, *Apocalypse and Anti-Catholicism in Seventeenth-Century English Drama* (Cambridge: Cambridge University Press, 2017).

16 Wittreich, "'Image of That Horror,'" 175. For James's interest in the political uses of the Apocalypse, see Wittreich, 182–3.

17 It should be noted that many of Shakespeare's histories and tragedies have references to the Apocalypse. Hassel, for instance, notes that in *Richard III*, Richard "is surrounded by intimations of apocalypse and eschatology. The characters around him are preoccupied with last words and last things" (38). And *Hamlet* contains more direct references to Doomsday than any other play; see a summary of scholarly sources in Hunt, "'Forward Backward,'" 385. *Macbeth*, as discussed below, has an invocation of the Apocalypse with the reference to "th' crack of doom" (4.1.133), and the infamous gunpowder squibs used in original productions would literally have filled the air with the smell of sulfur and brimfire. But while other plays invoke an apocalyptic atmosphere, *King Lear*, as I will argue here, is most directly conceptually concerned with the making and unmaking of the world.

18 All references to the play are from William Shakespeare, *The Tragedy of King Lear*, Updated Edition, *The New Cambridge Shakespeare*, ed. Jay L. Halio (Cambridge: Cambridge University Press, 1992, 2005). At this moment in the play, the emphasis on the question of "nothing" can hardly be missed:

LEAR: What can you say to draw
  A third more opulent than your sisters? Speak.
CORDELIA: Nothing, my lord.
LEAR: Nothing?
CORDELIA: Nothing.
LEAR: Nothing will come of nothing, speak again. (1.1.80–5)

19 The theological literature on this is vast, but for orientation on the early debate, see Gerhard May, *Creatio ex nihilo: The Doctrine of 'Creation Out of Nothing' in Early Christian Thought*, trans. A. S. Worrall (London and New York: T and T International, Continuum imprint, 1994, 2004); and N. Joseph Torchia, *Creatio ex nihilo and the Theology of St. Augustine: The Anti-Manichaean Polemic and Beyond*, American University Studies, Series VII, vol. 205 (Peter Lang: New York: 1999).

20 Josuah Sylvester, *Bartas, His Divine Weeks and Works Translated* (London: Humfrey Lownes, 1605), 5, 8.

21 Lucretius, *The Nature of Things*, trans. A. E. Stallings (London: Penguin, 2007), 7, ll. 149–50, 155.

22 Citations from the Bishops' Bible are from http://studybible.info/Bishops/.

23 Only the first four lines appear in the Folio version of the play, which Halio uses for his edition; Halio includes the extended speech of the Quarto – the lines inserted here in square brackets – on page 268. While a discussion of the relationship of the Folio and Quarto versions of the play is beyond the scope of this essay, the Gentleman's lines in the Quarto, with their "make nothing of," indicate that the references to making and nothing resounds strongly in that text.

24 Halio, *The Tragedy of King Lear*, 223.

25 William Shakespeare, *King Lear*, Arden 3rd Series, ed. R. A. Foake (Walton-on-Thames, Surrey, UK: Thomas Nelson, 1997), 334n.

26 internetshakespeare.uvic.ca/doc/Lr_F1/scene/4.5/.

27 Wittreich, "'Image of That Horror,'" 189, 191, 192.

28 Hiroshi Ozawa, "'I Must Be Cruel Only to Be Kind': Apocalyptic Repercussions in *Hamlet*," in *"Hamlet" and Japan*, ed. Yoshiko Uéno (New York: AMS, 1995), 88; cited in Hunt, "'Forward Backward,'" 386.

29 Stephen Greenblatt (ed.), *The Norton Shakespeare* (New York and London: W. W. Norton, 1997).

30 R. M. Christofides, *Shakespeare and the Apocalypse: Visions of Doom from Early Modern Tragedy to Popular Culture* (London and New York: Continuum, 2012), 156–9.

31 Wittreich, "'Image of That Horror,'" 187, 188.

32 Jacqueline Kolosov, "'Is This the Promised End?' Witness in *King Lear* and Apocalyptic Poetry of the Twentieth Century," *Intertexts* 8, no. 2 (2004): 191.

33 Ibid., 195.

34 Christofides, *Shakespeare and the Apocalypse*, 182–1.

35 Janet Adelman, *Suffocating Mothers: Fantasies of Maternal Origin in Shakespeare's Plays, "Hamlet" to "The Tempest"* (New York: Routledge, 1992), chap. 5.

36 Peter Auger, "A Model of Creation? Scott, Sidney and Du Bartas," *Sidney Journal* 33, no. 1 (2015): 77, citing Michael Mack, *Sidney's Poetics: Imitating Creation* (Washington, DC: Catholic University of America Press, 2005), 189.

37 Auger, "Model," 88.

38 Ibid., 83.

16

ROBERT S. MIOLA

Immortal Longings in Shakespeare's Rome

Give me my robe. Put on my crown. I have / Immortal longings in me.
– Cleopatra (*Antony and Cleopatra*, 5.2.274–5)[1]

Shakespeare's Rome is a haunted place, dense with the metaphysical, miraculous, and mythical. There Romans (and others) dream prophetic dreams, participate in rituals and festivals, offer sacrifices, hear soothsayers, see portents and apparitions, invoke, appease, imitate, and anger the gods and God. There mortals have immortal longings: they struggle to live forever in fame or in some afterlife. They try to meet divine demands that are often uncertain, ambivalent, contradictory, indecipherable. Ever beyond human comprehension and control, the supernatural world of Shakespeare's Rome incorporates pagan and Christian texts, beliefs, ceremonies, symbols, and theologies.

Commentators have variously explored and defined this world as it appears in a narrative poem, *The Rape of Lucrece* (1594), and five plays: *Titus Andronicus* (1589–94), *Julius Caesar* (1599), *Antony and Cleopatra* (1606–8), *Coriolanus* (1609–10), and *Cymbeline* (1610–11). Many delineate the pagan ethos of honor, shame, and fame.[2] Romans adhere to a heroic, military code that demands sacrifice and offers eternal glory or infamy. Others discuss the significance of Stoicism and *constantia*, the ideal of indifference to fortune and self-mastery, including the signature motif, the pagan religious gesture of suicide: Lucrece, Portia, Brutus, Cassius, Antony, Cleopatra, and others all kill themselves as the climactic expression of their freedom and autonomy (though Cleopatra, of course, is in every way exceptional).[3] Still others focus on the Christian presences and resonances. According to these critics, Romans struggle in vain for absolutes unavailable in the fallen and unredeemed world.[4] Whether imagined as pagan or Christian or as some combination, Shakespeare's Romans long for an immortality that lies beyond their understanding and their reach. They struggle with themselves and with strange, shadowy gods, who they propitiate and personate, and who they finally encounter directly in presentation.

Divine Propitiation

In Shakespeare's early Roman works mortals express their immortal longings by offering sacrifices of themselves or others. Raped by Tarquin, Lucrece resolves to expunge the dishonor and recover her honor through suicide: "This brief abridgement of my will I make: / My soul and body to the skies and ground" (lines 1198–9). Subscribing to a ruthlessly exclusive dualism, Lucrece reasons that her dishonored body, irremediably stained, must die so that her unstained soul may live forever. None of this appears in the *Fasti*, a principal source for the poem, wherein Ovid's Lucrece, blushing and weeping, rejects her husband's and father's pardons and kills herself in shame:

> "quam" dixit "veniam vos datis, ipsa nego."
> Nec mora, celato fixit sua pectore ferro ...[5]
>
> "The pardon that you give I deny," she said. Without
> delay she stabbed her breast with the hidden blade.

Shakespeare's Lucrece, by contrast, commits suicide as an act of self-assertion and vindication, and as a means of finding eternal life.

> My honour I'll bequeath unto the knife
> That wounds my body so dishonourèd.
> 'Tis honour to deprive dishonoured life;
> The one will live, the other being dead.
> So of shame's ashes shall my fame be bred,
>   For in my death I murder shameful scorn;
>   My shame so dead, mine honour is new born. (lines 1184–90)

Despite the earlier mention of the "skies," Lucrece imagines eternal life not as the residence of her soul in heaven but as the rebirth of her honor on earth in the form of fame, the reputation for chastity and fidelity won by suicide. Lucrece thus envisions immortality as the approval of present and future mortal men and women. The gods, surprisingly, play no part in her religious reasoning, ritual, and reward; Lucrece reifies the divine as an earthly complex of values based solely on human opinion.

Shakespeare's first dramatic depiction of Rome, his and George Peele's *Titus Andronicus*, begins with another propitiation through human sacrifice. Lucius, Titus, and the victorious Romans slaughter a Goth prisoner, Alarbus, *ad manes fratrum* (1.1.98), "to the departed spirits of our brothers." The

Latin phrase attempts to valorize an invented expression of *Romanitas*, as ancient Romans generally disapproved of human sacrifice and Shakespeare and Peele could find little precedent for this ritual in classical texts. Lucius gives two reasons for the hewing of limbs and sacrifice of flesh:

> That so the shadows be not unappeased,
> Nor we disturbed with prodigies on earth. (1.1.100–1)

The "shadows," or spirits of the dead, demand the appeasement of human sacrifice, Lucius claims, and failure to comply will result in "prodigies," or portents of ill. But the play does nothing to validate these claims, presenting neither ghosts, nor visions, nor any supernatural events. The action instead seems curiously, even claustrophobically, earthbound, relentlessly natural not supernatural.

As in *Lucrece* the gods in *Titus Andronicus* are largely absent and irrelevant. Suffering an unbearable sequence of betrayals, murders, and mutilations, Titus calls upon them in English and in Latin (quoting Seneca's *Hippolytus*):

> O here I lift this one hand up to heaven
> And bow this feeble ruin to the earth;
> If any power pities wretched tears,
> To that I call. (3.1.205–8)

> *Magni dominator poli,*
> *Tam lentus audis scelera, tam lentus vides?* (4.1.81–2)

> O ruler of the great heavens, are you so slow to hear of crimes, so slow to see them?

Marcus also looks up in vain:

> O heavens, can you hear a good man groan
> And not relent, or not compassion him? (4.1.123–4)

But the pleas go unheeded. Titus even sends letters by arrow to the Olympian Jove, Apollo, Mars, Pallas, and Mercury (4.3), but the letters reach only the corrupt court of Saturninus and Tamora. The gods above, if they exist, are silent. So too the gods below. Shakespeare pointedly rejects the infernal spirits and deities of Senecan drama and, more proximately, of Kyd's prototypal *The Spanish Tragedy* (1587), which features both the Ghost of Andrea and Revenge from Hades. Instead he refashions Revenge into a role played by Tamora, accompanied by her sons presented as Rape and Murder (5.2). Titus sees through the charade. "By representing Revenge as a character's device rather than a 'reality' outside the action, as it is in Kyd's frame,"

Jonathan Bate observes, "[Shakespeare] suggests that retribution is a matter of human, not divine will. This is a world in which people make their own laws."[6] Such a world diametrically opposes that of the audiences, governed by Old Testament precept ("Vengeance is mine," says the Lord, Deut. 32:35), New Testament example, and civil laws prohibiting revenge action.

The world of Rome in *Titus Andronicus*, however, is full of horrors, as human revenge becomes the only absolute governing life and death. The sacrifice of Alarbus initiates among other atrocities a gory sequence of *kindermord* (child killing) that includes the rape and mutilation of Lavinia, the beheading of Quintus and Martius, the slaying of Chiron and Demetrius, the serving of their bodies in the Thyestean banquet, and, finally, Titus's mad stabbing of his daughter Lavinia: "Die, die, Lavinia, and thy shame with thee" (5.3.45). Unlike Lucrece, Titus cannot reify the divine into the honor-shame-fame ethos he here invokes; he has emptied that of all coherence and meaning. With no possibility of transcendence, no gods to see and hear, mortal longings for the immortal become warped and diminished into bestial instinct; Rome becomes "a wilderness of tigers" (3.1.54). The most telling and haunting evocation of the divine in the play is Titus's recognition of its absence in the Ovidian phrase, "*Terras Astraea reliquit* [Astraea [Justice] has left the earth]; / Be you remembered, Marcus, she's gone, she's fled" (4.3.4–5). The "ruinous monastery" (5.1.21) that temporarily shelters Aaron and his son, evoking the abandoned churches, chancels, and religious houses of the post-Reformation landscape, provides another poignant image of divine loss and absence.

In Shakespeare's first Plutarchan Roman work, *Julius Caesar*, the conspirators portray the assassination of Caesar, a pivotal event in human history, as divine propitiation. "Let's be sacrificers, but not butchers" (2.1.166), Brutus famously tells the conspirators,

> Let's kill him boldly, but not wrathfully;
> Let's carve him as a dish fit for the gods,
> Not hew him as a carcass fit for hounds. (172–4)

Shakespeare's conspirators intend a sacrifice not only to the gods, but also *ad manes fratrum*, in this case, to the departed spirits of brother Romans gone before. Brutus remembers another Brutus, who, outraged at Lucrece's rape, evicted the Tarquins out of Rome: "My ancestors did from the streets of Rome / The Tarquin drive when he was called king" (2.1.53–4). Cassius evokes "Aeneas, our great ancestor" (1.2.112) and the "breed of noble bloods" (151) that constitutes Rome's mythic past. "Romans now / Have thews and limbs like to their ancestors" (1.3.80–1), he reminds Casca. As in *Titus Andronicus* the shades of the dead, the conspirators claim, demand living sacrifice. To what degree this claim is true becomes the central question of the play, variously answered in various readings and productions. Often readers and audiences view the claims of divine sacrifice as merely rhetorical pretexts for brutal murder by villainous or, at best, deluded conspirators. Such interpretation restages the butchery found in North's Plutarch's account of the assassination: "he ... was hacked and mangled among them as a wild beast taken of hunters."[7]

Whatever the critical or theatrical interpretation, the intended sacrifice does not, as Lucius hopes in *Titus Andronicus*, prevent disturbance by "prodigies on earth"; instead, it evokes a terrifying sequence of omens, apparitions, and supernatural phenomena. Shakespeare presents Plutarch's portents along with additions from Ovid and Lucan: earthquakes, thunder and lightning, a fire-charged tempest, a slave with a flaming hand, men parading in fire, the bird of night hooting in the marketplace at noon, comets, a sacrificial beast without a heart, a glaring lion by the Capitol, a lioness whelping in the streets, graves opening and yielding their dead, armed warriors in the skies, a bloody rain on the Capitol, ghosts squealing and shrieking in the streets (1.3.3ff; 2.2.16ff.). He also transforms Calpurnia's prophetic dream into a vision of Caesar's statue, "Which like a fountain with an hundred spouts / Did run pure blood, and many lusty Romans / Came smiling and did bathe their hands in it" (2.2.77–9). Finally, and most spectacularly, Shakespeare stages the appearance of Caesar's ghost, who identifies himself as "thy evil spirit, Brutus," and warns, "thou shalt see me at Philippi" (4.3.282, 283).

Caesar's ghost represents a specific and revealing collision of ancient and early modern conceptions of the supernatural. What appeared to Plutarch's Brutus was not Caesar's ghost at all, but simply an ὄψιν ("vision") and a φάσμα ("apparition, phantom").[8] Plutarch's Brutus asks the supernatural visitant if he is "a god or a man" (1595, 1070). Shakespeare's Brutus expands and Christianizes the range of supernatural options, "Art thou some god, some angel, or some devil?" (4.3.279). The visitant spirit identifies itself as an evil *daimōn*: "Ὁ σός, ὦ Βροῦτε, δαίμων κακός" ("your evil *daimōn*, Brutus," *Caesar* 69.11; *Brutus* 36.7). Amyot, the basis for North's translation, renders this, "*Je suis ton mauvais ange & esprit, Brutus*" and "*Je suis ton mauvais ange, Brutus*."[9] North translates accordingly, "I am thy ill angel, Brutus"; "I am thy evil spirit, *Brutus*" (791, 1070), the last four words echoed verbatim by Shakespeare.

In Greek the untranslatable *daimōn* can mean "god, goddess, divine power, destiny, fortune, good or evil genius, tutelary divinity, lesser god, or evil spirit." Translating this spirit into Caesar's ghost, Shakespeare domesticates the alien being into a familiar figure from early modern religious culture.

He here also remembers another *daimōn* mentioned by Plutarch, "the great guardian-genius" of Caesar (trans. Perrin, *Caesar* 69.2), who pursued all the murderers and avenged the assassination. Both Amyot and North depersonalized this *daimōn* into "*celle grande fortune & faueur du ciel*" (fol. 514[v]), "his great prosperity and good fortune" (790). Shakespeare conflates the visiting phantom with Caesar's revenging guardian-genius to create Caesar's ghost. Doing so, he gets closer to Plutarch than the translators by deploying onstage the conventions of revenge tragedy descending from Seneca as well as the resources of a later supernaturalism.

The prodigies in *Julius Caesar* that culminate in Caesar's ghost, variously admonitory, threatening, and punitive, undercut or at least complicate conspiratorial claims. Suggesting supernatural protest and punishment, they cast deep shadows of doubt over the assassination and, more important, over human capacity to know and propitiate the gods. So it is that this play concludes with suicide, the archetypal Roman religious gesture, here presented as crushing personal defeat, resonant with significant ironies. Stabbing himself on his birthday with Caesar's murder weapon, Cassius concedes victory to his enemy: "Caesar, thou art revenged, / Even with the sword that killed thee" (5.3.45–6); Brutus dies similarly, with more than a hint of regret and remorse: "Caesar, now be still. / I killed not thee with half so good a will" (5.5.50–1). But as usual in Shakespeare's Roman works, the suicide also appears as Stoic triumph. Like Lucrece, Brutus expects to gain "glory by this losing day" (5.5.36), his immortal longing again expressing itself in the hope of earthly fame. This hope receives some fulfillment in the eulogies that conclude the play: *Strato*: "Brutus only overcame himself / And no man else hath honour by his death" (5.5.56–7); *Marc Antony*: "This was the noblest Roman of them all" (5.5.68); *Octavius:* "According to his virtue let us use him, / With all respect and rites of burial" (5.5.76–7).

The gods in *Julius Caesar* are not absent or irrelevant but they are distant and indecipherable; they speak a language that humans struggle to understand. Casca cannot determine if the supernatural storm betokens civil strife in heaven or impending punishment; Brutus simply reads by the exhalations whizzing in the air. Brutus believes he acts rightly and honorably, in accordance with divine wishes, but catastrophically miscalculates – he judges Antony to be harmless and allows him to speak at Caesar's funeral; he overrules Cassius's objections and leads his soldiers on to the disastrous battle at Philippi. Those who claim to see clearly, to recognize divine will here on earth, must attend Cicero's warning: "Men may construe things after their fashion / Clean from the purpose of the things themselves" (1.3.34–5). In the absence of a legible, comprehensible supernaturalism, these Romans must content themselves with fame and the consolations of human history rather than hope of eternal life. In their suicides, Gordon Braden has observed, "Shakespeare has cleanly excised the look to the afterlife that would have seemed authoritative in North and been nearly instinctive in a Christian writer, and replaced it with a foursquare bleakness: the only thing lasting forever is farewell."[10]

Divine Personation

Immortal longings in Shakespeare's Rome also take the form of divine personation, the human assumption of godly attributes or identity. In his few appearances, Caesar justifies Cassius's complaint that "this man / Is now become a god" (1.2.115–16): he speaks of himself in the third person, imperiously dismisses the soothsayer ("He is a dreamer, let us leave him. Pass," 1.2.24), and declares himself above all fear, "for always I am Caesar" (1.2.212). He ignores the warning of the portents: "Danger knows full well / That Caesar is more dangerous than he" (2.2.44–5). He fatally accepts the interpretation of Calphurnia's dream that depicts him as *mater patriae* (mother of the country) as well as *pater patriae* (father of the country), nurturer as well as protector of Rome. Denying a petition, Caesar proclaims himself above all other human beings:

> I could be well moved, if I were as you;
> If I could pray to move, prayers would move me.
> But I am constant as the northern star,
> Of whose true-fixed and resting quality
> There is no fellow in the firmament. (3.1.58–62)

Not subject to human inconstancy and mutability, Caesar proclaims himself the polestar, "unassailable," "unshaked of motion" (69, 70), shining high above mere mortals who are "flesh and blood, and apprehensive" (67). As conspirators kneel to him, he identifies himself with Jupiter and the home of pagan deities, "Hence! Wilt thou lift up Olympus?" (74).

Caesar's divine personation, of course, ill sorts with plentiful indications of human weakness and infirmity. Cassius remembers him nearly drowning and crying out for help, shaking, groaning, and growing pale from an epileptic fit (1.2.100ff.). These memories get confirmation in Casca's report that Caesar "fell down in the market-place, and foamed at the mouth, and was speechless," and Brutus's response, "'Tis very like, he hath the falling sickness" (2.4.246–8). Caesar himself admits that his left ear is deaf (1.2.213), a revealing Shakespearean invention. He arrogantly dismisses the warnings of the soothsayer and fatally postpones the reading of Artemidorus's petition. Caesar is easy prey to flattery, as Decius boasts and proves in his expounding of Calphurnia's dream. The assassination does not resolve the question of whether Caesar is a tyrant or just king, but it does prove him to be a man not a god. Human blood dramatically gushes through his white toga, spatters the stage floor, and reddens the conspirators' arms in their post-mortem washing ritual. Divine personation here appears to be merely human pretension.

So too in *Coriolanus*, where Caius Martius Coriolanus, whose very name invokes Mars, also personates a god. In battle Coriolanus appears to be a supernatural force, wielding "grim looks" and a "thunder-like percussion" that makes enemies "shake, as if the world / Were feverous and did tremble" (1.4.62–5). All Romans press to see him "as if that whatsoever god who leads him / Were slily crept into his human powers / And gave him graceful posture" (2.1.193–5). But Coriolanus scorns the "mutable, rank-scented" (3.1.67) multitude, as if he "were a god to punish, not / A man of their infirmity" (3.1.82–3). After provoking banishment, Coriolanus, as if from on high at Olympus, banishes Rome:

> You common cry of curs, whose breath I hate
> As reek o'th'rotten fens, whose loves I prize
> As the dead carcasses of unburied men
> That do corrupt my air, I banish you. (3.3.128–31)

In exile amidst the Volscians, Coriolanus still appears "as if he were son and heir to Mars" (4.5.186–7). His former enemy Aufidius "sanctifies himself with 's hand" (189–90); the soldiers "use him as the grace 'fore meat, / Their talk at table, and their thanks at end" (4.7.3–4). Cominius comments,

> He is their god. He leads them like a thing
> Made by some other deity than Nature,
> That shapes man better. (4.6.94–6)

Rejecting his former names, friends, and all pity, thrice described as a dragon (4.1.30, 4.7.23, 5.4.10), Coriolanus appears to be an angry god, sitting "in gold, his eye / Red as 'twould burn Rome" (5.1.64–5). So Menenius: "He wants nothing of a god but eternity and a heaven to throne in" (5.4.19–20).

But Coriolanus's divine personation, like that of Julius Caesar, ultimately comes crashing down to earth. Neither dragon nor deity, Coriolanus finally proves himself to be a mortal man. He cannot, as he claims, "stand / As if a man were author of himself / And knew no other kin" (5.3.35–7). Leading the deputation that convinces him to spare Rome, his own mother Volumnia forcibly represents to him his human origins, the "womb / That brought thee to this world" (5.3.124–5); she also reminds him of his human relations, his wife and son. Conquest of Rome, she argues, will destroy all his hard-won honor, bringing eternal shame and "a name / Whose repetition will be dogged with curses" (5.3.143–4). Capitulating to Volumnia, subscribing to the Roman ethos of honor-shame-fame, Coriolanus redefines himself as human being:

> O mother, mother!
> What have you done? Behold, the heavens do ope,
> The gods look down, and this unnatural scene
> They laugh at. O my mother, mother! O!
> You have won a happy victory to Rome;
> But, for your son – believe it, O, believe it –
> Most dangerously you have with him prevailed,
> If not most mortal to him. (5.3.183–90)

Speaking as a son to his mother, Coriolanus recognizes the bonds of family, reaffirms his place in the natural, social, and civic order, and ratifies his own humanity. As he recognizes, the gods, far removed from earthly incarnations and pretensions, look down on the human drama and laugh. Again, divine personation proves to be merely human pretension. Death, end of all mortals, Coriolanus here senses, will follow swiftly.

Divine personation also appears throughout *Antony and Cleopatra*, wherein the principals self-consciously play the roles of gods and goddesses. The Egyptian queen often appears to her people, Caesar reports disapprovingly, "in th'habiliments of the goddess Isis" (3.6.17). And Plutarch's account of Cleopatra as Aphrodite/Venus meeting Antony as Dionysus/Bacchus directly inspires Enobarbus's famous description in Shakespeare's play:

> The barge she sat in, like a burnished throne
> Burned on the water. The poop was beaten gold;
> Purple the sails, and so perfumèd that
> The winds were lovesick with them. The oars were silver,
> Which to the tune of flutes kept stroke, and made
> The water which they beat to follow faster,
> As amorous of their strokes. For her own person,
> It beggared all description: she did lie
> In her pavilion – cloth-of-gold, of tissue –
> O'erpicturing that Venus where we see
> The fancy outwork nature. On each side her
> Stood pretty dimpled boys, like smiling Cupids,
> With divers-coloured fans, whose wind did seem
> To glow the delicate cheeks which they did cool,
> And what they undid did. (2.2.201–15)

Surrounded by Cupids, Cleopatra presents herself as Venus. Fancy, the creative power of the imagination – Cleopatra's, the spectators', and the poet's – outworks nature and realizes the divine personation in the wondrous spectacle, at least momentarily.

Plutarch noted Antony's similar entrance into Ephesus, amidst women clothed as Bacchanals, men and children "disguised as fauns and satyrs"; "in their songs they called him Bacchus, the father of mirth, courteous, and gentle and so was he unto some" (trans. North, 978). But Shakespeare in his play chooses to focus instead on Antony's personation of his ancestor Hercules, also observed by Plutarch, who describes Antony's thick beard, broad forehead, crooked nose, and "manly look in his countenance, as is commonly seen in Hercules pictures":

> Now it had been a speech of old time that the family of Antony were descended from one Anton, the son of Hercules, whereof the family took name. This opinion did Antony seek to confirm in all his doings, not only resembling him in the likeness of his body, as we have said before, but also in the wearing of his garments. (trans. North, 970)

Accordingly, after the defeat at Actium Shakespeare's Antony delivers a densely allusive invocation to Hercules (Alcides):

> The shirt of Nessus is upon me. Teach me,
> Alcides, thou mine ancestor, thy rage.
> Let me lodge Lichas on the horns o'th'moon,
> And with those hands that grasped the heaviest club
> Subdue my worthiest self. (4.12.43–7)

Antony imagines himself in the poisoned shirt of Nessus, originally given to Hercules by a woman Deianara; the garment so maddened the hero that he threw his page Lichas into the sea and mounted his own funeral pyre. This myth was popular in the Renaissance (especially through the pseudo-Senecan *Hercules Oetaeus*) along with the legend of Hercules *furens* (told in another Senecan play), in which the hero, driven mad by another female, Hera, slaughtered his wife and children. Antony recalls both Herculean prototypes before imagining himself committing suicide with Hercules's club.

As in *Julius Caesar* and *Coriolanus*, such personation does not go unchallenged in the play. Cleopatra herself mocks Antony as a pretentious role-player: "Look, prithee, Charmian, / How this herculean Roman does become / The carriage of his chafe" (1.3.83–5). The self-proclaimed descendant of a god struts and fumes like the comic *miles gloriosus*, the bragging and blustering soldier. Remembering that she put "her tires and mantles on him" and "wore his sword Philippan" (2.5.22–3), Cleopatra continues the deflation by recalling Omphale, the Amazonian queen who enslaved Hercules, dressed him in her clothes, and wore his famous lion skin. Her reference to this Hercules myth simultaneously affirms and denies Antony's Herculean aspirations.

This paradoxical evaluation, affirmation and denial, Shakespeare writes large in a remarkable short scene (4.3), transformed magically from the *Lives*. Plutarch tells of people hearing suddenly "a marvelous sweet harmony of sundry sorts of instruments of music, with the cry of a multitude of people, as they had been dancing, and had sung as they use in Bacchus' feasts." The Bacchanalian revels leave the city at the gate that opens up to the enemy and thus signifies that "it was the god unto whom Antonius bare singular devotion to counterfeit and resemble him that did forsake them" (trans. North, 1004). Shakespeare diminishes the spectacle, makes the auditors four soldiers in the four corners of the stage, changes the music to the eerie sound of hautboys "*under the stage*" (4.3.12 s.d.), and identifies the god as Hercules rather than Dionysus/Bacchus: "'Tis the god Hercules, whom Antony loved / Now leaves him" (4.3.21–2).

On the one hand, this scene affirms theatrically Antony's Herculean personation. It gives the audience auditory evidence of divine presence, of the god accompanying, inspiring, or somehow inhabiting Antony. As Gary Taylor observes: "What the audience experiences is a sense of invisible presence, something unseen and of indefinite size and shape, which keeps shifting location, something which asserts significance but cannot be easily interpreted, something familiar but also distorted. ''Tis strange,' " indeed.[11] But on the other hand, this scene also denies the Herculean personation, depicting the very moment that the god Hercules leaves Antony. The audience consequently experiences simultaneously mystification and demystification, divine presence and absence, immanence and abandonment. Hercules's exit recalls another divine leaving, that of Astraea in *Titus Andronicus*; in both plays mortal humans are left alone, bereft, and darkling.

So abandoned, Antony must live and die on his own in a strange and hostile world. Like Shakespeare's other Romans, he commits suicide to avoid the shame of conquest and win honor and fame. "Not Caesar's valor hath o'erthrown Antony, / But Antony's hath triumphed on itself" (4.5.15–16), runs the familiar eulogy. But unlike Lucrece, Brutus, Cassius, and the rest, Antony has other immortal longings: he looks to reunion with Cleopatra, presumed dead, in the next life:

> Eros! – I come, my queen. – Eros! Stay for me.
> Where souls do couch on flowers, we'll hand in hand,
> And with our sprightly port make the ghosts gaze.

> Dido and her Aeneas shall want troops,
> And all the haunt be ours. (4.14.50–4)

Cleopatra also commits suicide to avoid dishonor, exhibition tc slaves / With greasy aprons, rules, and hammers" (5.2.208–9). S live to see "some squeaking Cleopatra boy [her] greatness / I'th a whore" (219–20). Rather she resolves to do "what's brave, what's noble," "after the high Roman fashion" (4.15.91–2). But Cleopatra also shares Antony's other immortal longings: she goes to meet him in the next life:

> Husband, I come!
> Now to that name my courage prove my title!
> I am fire and air; my other elements
> I give to baser life. (5.2.281–4)

Cleopatra dies in the robes she wore on the barge, again personating immortal Venus in the very act of proving herself a mortal woman, "commanded / By such poor passion as the maid that milks / And does the meanest chares" (4.15.78–80). Dying onstage, Antony and Cleopatra show themselves to be human, not gods. But again fancy – their imaginations, the poet's and the spectators', on and off stage – outworks nature to realize the divine personations. The theatrical experience created by the powerful spectacle and thrilling poetry moves the audience and makes possible the dream of transcendence. The lovers' immortal longings may be their final delusion or may find realization just beyond the closing moments of the play, just beyond what the audience can see and know in the theater and in life.

Divine Presentation

In modern times critics have generally and rightly regarded *Cymbeline* as Shakespeare's last Roman play. Though largely set in ancient Britain (only five scenes occur in Rome), *Cymbeline* takes place in the first century at the time of Christ's birth, after Julius Caesar's frequently recalled conquest of Britain. Augustus Caesar demands tribute, sends emissaries, and threatens offstage. Posthumus Leonatus, a main character, has a Latin name and descends from a soldier, Sicilius, who won the honorific cognomen "Leonatus" (1.1.33) in battle, just as Caius Martius did "Coriolanus." Characters frequently invoke the Roman gods, a soothsayer appears and prophesizes, Posthumus experiences a dream vision. Honor is at the stake throughout the play, here appearing in both martial and marital forms. But *Cymbeline* presents a conclusion to the Roman works by staging a Christianized resolution of earlier difficulties and tensions. Under a new dispensation the play reworks the motifs of divine propitiation and divine personation, and culminates in a theophany, the appearance of the god Jupiter. Roman immortal longings finally find fulfillment in this divine presentation, the spectacular, speaking presence onstage of a god.

The final speech of the play presents divine propitiation as the just and appropriate conclusion to the enacted struggles and wars:

> Laud we the gods
> And let our crookèd smokes climb to their nostrils
> From our blest altars. (5.4.474–6)

The sacrifice celebrates the reunification of Cymbeline's family, the rewarding of the good and punishment of the wicked, the resolution of international conflicts, and the restoration of harmony between heaven and earth. But this play ends in forgiveness rather than in human sacrifice or self-destruction: Cymbeline forgives Belarius for stealing his sons, Posthumus forgives Iachimo for the slander, Britain voluntarily pays tribute to Rome. Earlier, Innogen alludes to the archetypally Roman gesture of suicide, only to reject it explicitly. Her reputation for chastity unjustly destroyed, she considers killing herself like Lucrece; but unlike Lucrece, who regards suicide as self-validation and the means to glory, Innogen sees suicide as sin, the violation of divine order:

> Against self-slaughter
> There is a prohibition so divine
> That cravens my weak hand. (3.4.74–6)

Clearly, Innogen lives in a Christian ethical and theological universe, wherein God rules and demands obedience to clearly articulated commandments.

In this world divine propitiation must take other forms of self-sacrifice than suicide. Innogen loses her identity by putting on a disguise and searching for Posthumus, who ordered her execution. Struck with remorse, Posthumus also loses himself in disguise: donning British costume he joins the battle against Rome and resolves to die for Innogen, presumed dead by his order. Victorious in battle, he changes back into Roman garb in order to suffer capture and execution, to end his life "by some means for Innogen" (5.3.83). Although Posthumus longs for death, he never considers suicide but instead offers his life to the gods for that of his wife: "For Innogen's dear life take mine" (116). He repents, trusts in the "clement" (112) divinities above, and practices self-abnegation not self-assertion; he seeks immolation in contrition not glorification in fame.

As is clear from both Innogen's and Posthumus's attempts at divine propitiation, *Cymbeline* insists on the divide between earth and heaven, on the absolute difference between humans below and gods above. Belarius preaches on the virtue of humility: his low roof requires stooping and thus "instructs you how t'adore the heavens, and bows you / To a morning's holy office" (3.3.3–4). In this world men and women below must know their place and act humbly, not aspire to divine attributes, prerogatives, or identity. The play presents two instances of divine personation to make precisely these points. The first is Iachimo's hyperbolic description of Posthumus: "He sits 'mongst men like a descended god; / He hath a kind of honour sets him off / More than a mortal seeming" (1.6.169–71). This reported divinization, the audience knows, is an outright lie, told by Posthumus's enemy in order to seduce his wife. The second divine personation is even more absurdly false, bordering on black comedy. Innogen wakes up next to a headless corpse and identifies it as her divinely attributed husband:

> I know the shape of 's leg; this is his hand,
> His foot Mercurial, his Martial thigh,
> The brawns of Hercules; but his Jovial face –
> Murder in heaven? How? 'Tis gone. (4.2.308–11)

Here the body's godlike parts, supplied by four Olympian gods, proclaim Posthumus's identity. But the audience knows that Posthumus's earthly clothes have deceived Innogen and that the body belongs to Cloten, the boorish, decidedly earthly, suitor. In this play divine personation can only be an outright lie or a colossal mistake.

The play's insistence on the gap between earth and heaven, between mortals and immortals, sets up the extraordinary presentation of the divine in 5.3, the appearance of Jupiter onstage. Bound in chains and falling asleep, Posthumus again offers his life to the gods: "And so, great pow'rs, / If you will take this audit, take this life / And cancel these cold bonds" (120–2). The ghosts of his family, the Leonati, then enter and rebuke Jupiter, "thou Thunder-master" for not shielding Posthumus from "earth-vexing smart" (124, 130). They chant a series of questions to the god, demanding to know why he allowed the evil Iachimo to prosper and the good Posthumus to suffer. Descending in thunder and lightning upon an eagle, Jupiter hurls a thunderbolt, frightening the ghosts to their knees. After rebuking them for their presumption, Jupiter delivers the divine response:

> Be not with mortal accidents oppressed;
> No care or yours it is; you know 'tis ours.
> Whom best I love, I cross; to make my gift,
> The more delayed, delighted. (163–6)

Before reascending, Jupiter leaves a written prophesy of peace and restoration with Posthumus.

Finally, in this play a god speaks directly onstage to answer all the questions of wretched mortals, the anguished cries in *Titus Andronicus*, the earnest searching in *Julius Caesar*, the angry challenges here. This pagan god, however, gives a distinctly Judaeo-Christian answer to these questions about the problem of evil and the nature of divine justice. Proclaiming "whom best I love, I cross," Jupiter echoes no fewer than three Scriptural passages: "For whom the Lord loveth, he chasteneth" (Heb. 12:6); "As many as I love, I rebuke and chasten" (Rev. 3:19); "For the Lord correcteth him, whom he loveth" (Prov. 3:12).[12] The pagan deity here speaks as both Yahweh and the Providential God of the New Testament. Moreover, the seemingly perverse crossing of the good and beloved all belongs to a greater plan that actually serves to increase future joy, to render the divine gift, "the more delayed, delighted." This promise of reward for the good, realized in the extraordinary series of reconciliations that concludes the play, shows that the gods are not absent or indecipherable. Jupiter as the Biblical God reveals himself to be purposefully involved in mortal affairs; he is the invisible but omnipresent deity who eventually revives the stately cedar of Cymbeline's family from its lopped branches, ends Posthumus's miseries, and makes Britain flourish in peace and plenty, according to the prophecy.

So end the immortal longings of Shakespeare's Romans. In his Roman works Shakespeare explores the many-faceted and shifting relations between the human and divine. Mortals variously attempt propitiation, offering sacrifices of themselves and others. They personate the gods, assuming divine prerogatives and identities. They live by a pagan ethos of honor, shame, and fame, which the poet displays in all its barbaric grandeur. This ethos yields finally in *Cymbeline* to a new dispensation that promotes humility and forgiveness and prohibits revenge and suicide. In this dispensation humans do not propitiate or personate gods but learn to humble themselves and to be patient, meaning both to suffer earthly trial and to await divine deliverance. Above, the Judaeo-Christian God in guise of Jupiter replaces indifferent or capricious gods. This deity watches over human struggle and apportions in his own time just punishments and rewards. The Roman eagle, as the soothsayer in *Cymbeline* proclaims, finally flies westward and vanishes into British sunlight.

Notes

1 William Shakespeare, *Antony and Cleopatra*, ed. David Bevington, 2nd edn. (Cambridge: Cambridge University Press, 2005). Reference to this and the following New Cambridge editions will be cited parenthetically in the text: *The*

Poems, ed. John Roe, 2nd edn. (2006) for *The Rape of Lucrece*; *Titus Andronicus*, ed. Alan Hughes (1994); *Julius Caesar*, ed. Marvin Spevack, 2nd edn. (2004); *Coriolanus*, ed. Lee Bliss (2000); *Cymbeline*, ed. Martin Butler (2005).

2 M. W. MacCallum, *Shakespeare's Roman Plays and their Background* (London: Macmillan, 1910); D. J. Gordon, "Name and Fame in Shakespeare's *Coriolanus*," in *Papers, Mainly Shakespearean*, ed. G. I. Duthie (Edinburgh: Oliver & Boyd, 1964), 40–57.

3 Geoffrey Miles, *Shakespeare and the Constant Romans* (Oxford: Clarendon Press, 1996). Gordon Braden, "Fame, Eternity, and Shakespeare's Romans," in *Shakespeare and Renaissance Ethics*, ed. Patrick Gray and John D. Cox (Cambridge: Cambridge University Press, 2014), 37–66.

4 See J. L. Simmons, *Shakespeare's Pagan World: The Roman Plays* (Charlottesville: University Press of Virginia, 1973); Robert S. Miola, "An Alien People Clutching their Gods? Shakespeare's Ancient Religions," *Shakespeare Survey* 54 (2001): 31–45; David Kaula, "'Let Us Be Sacrificers': Religious Motifs in *Julius Caesar*," *Shakespeare Studies* 14 (1981): 197–214; Stanley Cavell, "Who Does the Wolf Love? Reading *Coriolanus*," *Representations* 3 (1983): 1–20; Sarah Beckwith, *Shakespeare and the Grammar of Forgiveness* (Ithaca, NY: Cornell University Press, 2011).

5 Ovid, *Fasti*, trans. James George Frazer, rev. G. P. Goold, 2nd edn. (Cambridge, MA: Harvard University Press, 1996), bk. 2, lines 830–1. Unless otherwise noted, all translations from Latin and Greek are mine.

6 William Shakespeare, *Titus Andronicus*, ed. Jonathan Bate (London: Routledge, 1995), 22.

7 Plutarch, *The Lives of the Noble Grecians and Romans*, trans. Thomas North (London, 1595), 789.

8 Plutarch, *Lives*, ed. and trans. Bernadotte Perrin, 11 vols. (Cambridge, MA: Harvard University Press, 1914–26), *Brutus* 36.6; *Caesar* 69.13. I cite the Greek text from this edition. For more detailed consideration of the ideas in the next few paragraphs, see my "Remembering Greece in Shakespeare's Rome," *Memoria di Roma: A Journal of Shakespeare Studies* 4 (forthcoming, 2019).

9 Plutarch, *Les Vies des Hommes Illustres, Grecs & Romans*, trans. Jacques Amyot (Paris, 1565), fols. 515^r, 697^r.

10 Braden, "Fame," 46.

11 Gary Taylor, 'Divine [ ]sences," *Shakespeare Survey* 54 (2001): 13–30, quotation on 29.

12 Naseeb Shaheen, *Biblical References in Shakespeare's Plays* (Newark: University of Delaware Press, 1999), 713.

17

TOM BISHOP

Sacred and Theatrical Miracles in the Romances

(Four thunderous chords sound, and with each chord the bedroom is saturated with colored light: first, extraordinary, harsh, cold, pale blue; then, rich, brilliant, warm gold; then, hot bilious green; and finally, spectacular royal purple. Then there's silence for several beats. Prior stares wildly around the purple-colored room.)

Prior (An awestruck whisper): God almighty.

Very Stephen Spielberg.

(A sound, like a plummeting meteor, tears down from very, very far above the earth, hurtling at an incredible velocity toward the bedroom. The light seems to be sucked out of the room as the projectile approaches. Right before the light is completely extinguished, there's a terrifying CRASH as something immense strikes earth. The bedroom shudders and pieces of the ceiling's plaster, lathe and wiring rain down on and around Prior's bed; as the room is plunged into absolute darkness, we hear the whole ceiling give way.

A beat and then. in a shower of unearthly white light, spreading great opalescent gray-silver wings, the Angel descends through the ceiling into the room and floats about the bed.)

Angel: Greetings, Prophet;

The Great Work begins:

The Messenger has arrived.

(Blackout.)[1]

Drama and religion have a complex relationship and have been entwined around one another probably for as long as both have existed. The explosive end of Part One of Tony Kushner's *Angels in America* returns to this connection, breaking apart a dramatic universe predominantly secular and realist (despite some shared hallucinations) to offer instead an irruption of supernatural forces overwhelming established conventions and announcing with apocalyptic vigor a larger order to commandeer the action. The "*angelus ex machina*" inaugurates a reshaped universe that grows, in Part Two of the play, ever stranger and more open to skyey influences. The tremendous effort required to make this transition is indexed directly in the violence of Kushner's stage direction, which I have quoted at length, as it smashes a way of urgent renovation not only into Prior's bedroom but also into a settled world and its dramaturgical norms.

Shakespeare's famous quartet of late plays – *Pericles*, *Cymbeline*, *The Winter's Tale*, and *The Tempest* – all include the intervention of such supernatural presences into the world of mortal action.[2] To register the potentially dangerous energies of these appearances, the plays employ with deliberate self-consciousness the maximum of available stage spectacle. Here, for instance, is the appearance of the goddess Diana in *Pericles*:

> PERICLES [*greeting* LYSIMACHUS]: I embrace you. Give me my robes.
> *[He is attired]*
> I am wild in my beholding, O heavens bless my girl!
> *[Music plays]*
> But hark what music? Tell Helicanus, my Marina,
> Tell him o'er point by point, for yet he seems to dote,
> How sure you are my daughter – but what music?
> HELICANUS: My lord, I hear none.
> PERICLES: None? The music of the spheres! List, my Marina.
> LYSIMACHUS: It is not good to cross him, give him way.
> PERICLES: Rarest sounds, do ye not hear?
> LYSIMACHUS: Music, my lord? I hear –
> PERICLES: Most heavenly music.
> It nips me unto listening, and thick slumber
> Hangs upon mine eyes; let me rest. *[Sleeps]*
> LYSIMACHUS: A pillow for his head. So, leave him all.
> Well, my companion friends, if this but answer
> To my just belief, I'll well remember you.
> *[Exeunt all but Pericles]*
> DIANA *[descends from the heavens]*
> DIANA: My temple stands in Ephesus, hie thee thither. (5.1.216–32)

The discontinuity between what Pericles hears (and we hear) and what the other characters cannot hear indicates that the rules of dramaturgical engagement are being radically altered. What those around him perceive as hyperbolic delusion, we greater knowers are offered instead as revelation. The sleep of the theater, a higher waking, co-ordinates enhanced theatricality with supernatural vision.

The implicit violence done to human and metaphysical boundaries by this sort of sublime revelation, here hinted at with "it nips me unto listening," also appears strongly in the account of the oracle of Apollo in *The Winter's Tale*, which, though not staged, imposes itself on the action in the form of the prophecy that controls and assures the second half of that play. Cleomines and Dion, returning from their journey to a prophetic island as Leontes's envoys, speak thus of their encounter with divinity:

DION: I shall report,
For most it caught me, the celestial habits –
Methinks I so should term them – and the reverence
Of the grave wearers. O, the sacrifice!
How ceremonious, solemn, and unearthly
It was i'th'off'ring!
CLEOMINES: But of all, the burst
And the ear-deaf'ning voice o'th'oracle,
Kin to Jove's thunder, so surprised my sense
That I was nothing. (3.1.3–11)

The combination of pomp and terror here is the striking thing. We are not told just *what* is being sacrificed, but there is a general sense of managed exposure to a revelatory and productive violence. This violence opens a special sort of space, where boundaries, like eardrums, can be burst to effect communication between nature and super-nature.[3] Here the two envoys (in Greek, *theōrói*) function for us as substitute witnesses, the spectators (another meaning of *theōrói*) of a ceremonial event that reaches out to solicit and shake their sense of who they are. It is part of Shakespeare's special tact here to keep the revelation withheld this time, controlling the temper and sense of possibility of the dramatic universe at one remove. But at the play's end, in Paulina's "chapel," the gods will be asked once more to "look down" and intervene.

Somewhere between these two instances is the descent of Jupiter in *Cymbeline*, in a prophesy likewise couched as a dream, this time thronged by family spirits half Roman lares and half Catholic intercessory dead, who invoke a grumpy god with some metrically old-fashioned complaints against his injustice:

SICILIUS: Thy crystal window ope; look out; no longer exercise
Upon a valiant race thy harsh and potent injuries.
MOTHER: Since, Jupiter, our son is good, take off his miseries.
SICILIUS: Peep through thy marble mansion, help, or we poor ghosts will cry
To th'shining synod of the rest against thy deity.
BROTHERS: Help, Jupiter, or we appeal, and from thy justice fly.
JUPITER descends in thunder and lightning, sitting upon an eagle; he throws a thunderbolt. The ghosts fall on their knees
JUPITER: No more, you petty spirits of region low,
Offend our hearing. (5.3.151–8)

The crystal window in the marble mansion along with Posthumus's prison meditation on constraint and freedom ("Most welcome, bondage, for thou art a way, / I think, to liberty" [5.3.97–8]) suggest the scene is interested in the release of what seems solidly shut up, including the dramatic world opened through the stage-roof for the spectacular appearance of the play's "eucatastrophe."[4] The thunder and lightning that accompany Jupiter's descent (possibly also masking its noise) are emblematic markers of the god, but also direct assaults on the spectators' senses that mark the irruption into our space of a divine order.

Thunder and lightning are also, of course, prominent indices of supernatural activity in *The Tempest* where they open the play with a magically induced storm and support the entrance of the magical figure of Ariel as a Harpy over the banquet in Act 3:

> *Thunder and lightning. Enter* ARIEL, *like a harpy, claps his wings upon the table, and with a quaint device the banquet vanishes.*
>
> ARIEL: You are three men of sin ... (3.3.53)

On Prospero's instruction, Ariel takes the role of the vengeful prophetic messenger, reprising in the scene several aspects of scenes from the previous plays. But thunder also appears elsewhere in *The Tempest* where it may be more innocent; the attitude of the play to supernatural visitants is complicated and will need later scrutiny.

If religion comprises the set of ideas, institutions, and practices that speak to the relations of human life with the supernatural, then these plays are clearly centrally concerned with religion, so interested are they in, so insistent on, the intersection of human suffering with divine authority.[5] And, unlike in the older romantic dramas from which Shakespeare's late works take many of their cues, such as *The Rare Triumphs of Love and Fortune* (*c.*1582; pub. 1589) or *Mucedorus* (*c.*1590; pub. 1598), deities do not appear only as framing incident-mongers governing and motivating alternations of genre or mood.[6] Rather, they break into the action at crucial moments to stage with maximum impact what revelation of the supra-human is like, when it comes, and what purposes it answers, speaks to, or fulfills. It is possible to follow the lead of Richard Paul Knowles and assimilate divine power in these plays to the shaping of dramatic narrative and the aesthetics of the creative imagination in exchanges between playwright and audience.[7] But sooner or later the issue obtrudes of what is meant by the pervasive recourse specifically to the *supernatural* as the bearer of these ideas. The plays could just as easily have avoided this move. What is the character of the religion that the plays explore? At what level and to what end are religious concepts posited and turned in them?

For a start, we might note that the worlds of the four plays are in various ways both eclectic and rather odd. John Pitcher's note that in *The Winter's*

Tale "pagan and Christian elements are often mixed" might be applied generally.[8] *Pericles* is narrated by a medieval English poet and set in a rather fuzzy Hellenistic world of the eastern Mediterranean, with knights at a tournament and shipwrecks reminiscent of the *Acts of the Apostles. Cymbeline* flaunts its Roman imperial moment, but its paganism is a strange confection and its Rome feels quite modern compared with Shakespeare's Plutarchan plays. *The Winter's Tale* opens in a Greekish Sicily but one of its kings alludes to Original Sin (the "imputation ... hereditary ours") and it concludes in a Renaissance "gallery" owned by a miracle worker named after a Christian saint, Paulina, who requires her audience to "awake your faith." Of course, this is not untypical of Shakespeare's practice, or the practice in general of contemporary English, or Renaissance, romantic narrative, which was often cheerfully promiscuous about mixing pagan deities, allegorical personifications, and Christian concepts. As far back as *The Comedy of Errors*, Shakespeare was happy to have the devil, exorcism, and Pauline theology sharing the Ephesian stage with Plautine merchants and slaves.[9] This hybridization is perhaps most striking in *The Tempest*, notionally set in a contemporary Mediterranean, which is nonetheless suffused with supernatural ideas and presences borrowed from both pagan antiquity and New World reporting. Prince Ferdinand of Naples, presumably a Christian, seems quite comfortable supposing that Miranda might be "the goddess on whom these airs attend." And Alonso of Naples has just married his daughter to the king of Tunis – not something Ferdinand I, a real king of Naples, would have considered doing.[10] In some ways, such contamination is a regular signature of Shakespeare's dramatic style, and the late plays just continue the trend. The systematic commitments to generic mixture (*genera mista*) in different inflections in Italian tragicomedy and English "mingle-mangle" popular drama, from this point of view, serve Shakespeare's poetic purposes well, and he is happy at this late stage of his career to draw from and combine both strains. But the very familiarity of this strategy in the plays means we may sometimes miss their oddness, and the extent to which Shakespeare makes efforts to create a dramatic space open to multiple lines of exploration, including in religion.

Thus, although it makes a certain amount of sense to point, as Knowles did, to the way such eclectic worlds can explore relations between levels of formal design ("the artist as maker"), and to acknowledge of course that one can't hold romance fictions to historical standards of verisimilitude, one of the advantages of such cheerful eclecticism may also be to allow commerce between humans and the divine to be opened in ways not foreclosed in advance by matters of doctrine. That is, enquiring into whether the occurrences of miracle, theophany, and apocalypse in the plays are "Catholic" or "Protestant" may be to miss the point. It is possible the ground of religious exploration being undertaken here is deliberately elsewhere, arranged to sidestep just such kinds of constraining local categories. Eclecticism allows us to keep the action in a fictive space whose religious commitments are not circumscribed in advance by historical specificity or doctrinal demands. "The poet never lieth, because he nothing affirmeth" – an old defense against partisan criticism (Philip Sidney used it a generation before), but here put to new effect by being turned on some basic phenomena of religion itself. One is used to "anachronism" being a kind of regular local effect, or even a glitch, in Shakespeare's dramaturgical machinery, but we could see it here also, even instead, as a general productive loosening of received assumptions,[11] so that in these last works Shakespeare is in effect seeking to write religious plays in an English environment where using religious texts is impossible – matters of religion proper being forbidden on the stage. To do so, therefore, he invents a series of dramatic worlds that frame and interrogate basic religious concepts, but with the liberty of using fictions freed from doctrinal or polemic foreclosure and inhabiting instead the alternative mythographies of classical antiquity, into which fundamental religious concepts common to both antiquity and Christianity – fault, sin, curse, suffering, grace, restoration, prophecy, and blessing – can be experimentally poured. We might say that the plays are carefully compounded poetic spaces of "myth and metaphor," designed so that questions of religion emerge for inspection and experience with a kind of newness or nakedness.[12]

Take *Pericles*, for instance. Shakespeare found the story in Gower's *Confessio Amantis*, and also in a minor work of Laurence Twine, *The Pattern of Painful Adventures*.[13] It is a tale of the almost unending disasters and miseries befalling the Prince of Tyre and his family over about fifteen years, presented onstage by Gower the poet. But Gower's opening lines suggest these travails also point to more general issues:

> To sing a song that old was sung,
> From ashes, ancient Gower is come,
> Assuming man's infirmities,
> To glad your ear and please your eyes. (Prologue, 1–4)

"Assuming man's infirmities" technically attaches to Gower's reincarnation for our entertainment – putting on mortality.[14] Yet we might also read it as a founding gesture of the play, pointing to the general condition of human kind as infirm and subject to capricious disaster. Gower's song is not only conveyed *through* his renewed infirmities, it both *assumes* them, in us, and *concerns* them, in the connections made between himself, wasting before us "like taper light," his story, and his audience. The play pursues these infirmities relentlessly, from the monstrous sexual and political tyrannies of Antiochus, to the bodily sufferings of the starved Tarsians and the shipwrecked Pericles, naked and "wet" ("remember: earthly man / Is but a substance that must yield to you" [2.1.2–3]), to the desires and diseases of the brothel-patrons, and above all, to the terrible vulnerability of human life to loss, death, and time: death in childbirth, death by violence, death from despair at the relentlessness of death. And for this exquisite vulnerability, the play's choice of setting very pointedly can *not* offer the reassurances or consolations made available to Christians, as in the Elizabethan "Homily on the Fear of Death":

> All those therefore have great cause to be full of joy that be joined to Christ with true Faith, steadfast Hope, and perfect Charity, and not to fear death nor everlasting damnation. For death cannot deprive them of Jesu Christ, nor any sin can condemn them that are graffed surely in him, which is their only joy, treasure, and life. Let us repent our sins, amend our lives, trust in his mercy and satisfaction, and death can neither take him from us, nor us from him.[15]

The play is quite specific about locking its world out of this sort of rescue. One of its Biblical allusions serves precisely to make this point. When Pericles's ship, sailing home to a premature happy ending with his pregnant wife Thaisa, is struck with a second violent storm, he calls out in prayer:

> PERICLES: The god of this great vast, rebuke these surges
> Which wash both heaven and hell, and thou that hast
> Upon the winds command, bind them in brass,
> Having called them from the deep. (3.1.1–4)

As Naseeb Shaheen points out, this recalls the gospel incident of Jesus calming the storm in Galilee at Luke 8:24–5:

> Then they went to him, and awoke him, saying, Master, master, we perish.
>
> And he arose, and rebuked the wind, and the waves of water: and they ceased, and it was calm. Then he said unto them, Where is your faith? and they feared, and wondered among themselves, saying, Who is this that commandeth both the winds and water, and they obey him!

Pericles, of course, has access to no such power. He is at the mercy of whatever the world of mortality throws at him. Arriving at Mytilene bereft of his wife and daughter, he is a Job without a Jahweh to lob desperate questions at,[16] sunk into the silence of dead flesh and determined to let mere nature have its will:

He swears
Never to wash his face nor cut his hairs;
He puts on sackcloth, and to sea. He bears
A tempest which his mortal vessel tears,
And yet he rides it out. (4.4.27–31)

What drags him from his despair is the re-emergence of a narrative voice, Marina's, that can reweave the past, sew the scattered fragments back together, and vindicate the ability of human life to encompass and recover the world in story.[17] The order of events is important: Marina's narration must come first. Only once this is accomplished can the theophany occur that leads him to the further recovery of his wife, Thaisa, and the reassembly of both his family and his biography as concrete and living presences. Perhaps, even, one can go further and ask whether the opening of a link to Diana's speech might be a "supernaturalizing," for this play's purposes, of the re-establishment of effective speech between humans, that is that Shakespeare is here interested in the way the dumb isolation of mortal fate is *first* overcome by the possibility of a human connectedness, and only then opened up to the revelation of gods. This revisits and revises an ancient etymology according to which "religio" derives from "ligare" – to tie together.[18] Here it is human beings that are connected first, and by their own power of storytelling, "a song that old was sung." That Gower assumed mortality for that purpose turns out to have been the point all along.

Pericles carefully avoids imputing to its title character any culpability for what happens to him. He is conspicuously innocent throughout. This makes for a fairly simple dramaturgy asking some fairly simple (but not therefore easy) questions. *The Winter's Tale* is much more complicated, and its shaping as a parable of religious experience is comparably more subtle. The play announces from very early on its strong sense that something is wrong with humanity, some "imputation ... hereditary ours" that stains human life with guilt. But the threat remains occluded and non-specific, bound up with the general condition of human life that "cannot choose but branch," until it explodes into Leontes's destructive delusion, the absence of any clear roots for this only focusing attention the more. The audience is invited and inclined to be baffled along with the characters, while Hermione, faced with her husband's murderous ferocity, can only murmur that "There's some ill planet reigns" (2.1.105). The point seems to be that this is not a tale of "sin" from a specific theological point of view, but rather from, as it were, a phenomenological one. To every man his own fault. Something has "gone wrong" with Leontes, but we are not asked to care what precisely has been the genesis or mechanism of its occurrence (as opposed to in Othello's case). It is merely, for the play, that Leontes, as all those around him vehemently and uselessly argue, is monstrously fallible.[19] His freedom to perceive, feel, and act, magnified in its effects by his royal status and power, sees and embraces profoundly evil untruths. He himself puts it in terms of the skewed perception of a once innocent experience, now taken up as fatally evil:

> There may be in the cup
> A spider steeped, and one may drink, depart,
> And yet partake no venom, for his knowledge
> Is not infected; but if one present
> Th abhorr'd ingredient to his eye, make known
> How he hath drunk, he cracks his gorge, his sides,
> With violent hefts. I have drunk, and seen the spider. (2.1.39–45)

The direction of the play is twofold – to explore this poisoned state in Leontes, a state that formal religious languages might recognize under a variety of names: hata, culpa, khati'ah, sin, pāpa – and to essay what remedies there might be for it, where they might spring from, and what they might look and feel like. If the play has, not surprisingly, Christian underpinnings, it nonetheless takes care not to flaunt them directly. And indeed it deliberately sets out to measure alternative senses of repair alongside one another, for instance in its choice and treatment of source materials.

The play's picture of remedy could broadly be assimilated to the Christian term "grace," yet to identify it so squarely risks closing down a highly flexible dramatic exploration of the concept. Certainly, the word appears frequently and in a notable range of meanings. It is a word of blessing, a word of defense, a word of love, a word of admiration. As used only of Perdita, for instance, it stretches from the perception of physical ease and beauty ("now grown in grace / Equal with wond'ring" [4.1.24–5]), to worldly fortune ("to offer to have his daughter come into grace" [4.4.739–40]), to something with quasi-theological resonance ("You gods ... pour your graces / Upon my daughter's head" [5.3.121–3]). Its mobility can be glimpsed in Leontes's simple description of Polixenes to his son, Florizel, as "a graceful gentleman," which sounds like a suitable compliment for a king, except that Leontes immediately laments that he "has done sin" against him. Or consider Hermione's hope of an unknown instance of past well-speaking: "O, would her Name were *Grace*" (1.2.98).[20] This seems to mean something like "I hope that moment was especially favoured or fortunate and brought blessing on me and those around me, even though I didn't know or intend it." But the formulation also briefly conjures a small angelic female guardian into the play, an "elder sister" named Grace, who is then formally recognized as sponsoring the beginning of her relationship with Leontes: "'Tis Grace indeed" (104).

What I would emphasize across these uses is, again, how they are not closed. Their function, indeed, seems to be precisely to *open* the concept up to as many lines of action and contemplation as possible. Where will grace come from in the play? Who may obtain it, and by what, if any, desert or authority? Is simply being young and beautiful enough? Is it, like art, something of which one says, "I know it when I see it"? Or is some disposition required in advance to receive it? These are all questions that had formal answers in doctrine and catechism of the period, of course. Yet the play also works the question in startling new ways, as in Florizel's extraordinary and ecstatic account of how he sees Perdita:

When you speak, sweet,
I'd have you do it ever. When you sing,
I'd have you buy and sell so, so give alms,
Pray so, and for the ord'ring your affairs,
To sing them too. When you do dance, I wish you
A wave o'th'sea that you might ever do
Nothing but that: move still, still so,
And own no other function. (4.4.137–43)

This is, if nothing else, a description of the experience of grace, favor, blessing, and joy all at once. And, of course, of love.[21]

As well as suffused through the action of the play, though, the interest in ideas of grace goes deeply down into its narrative shaping. Critics have often noted how composite the play is. Even by Shakespeare's standards, its sources are a heady combination of ancient and modern materials. Robert Greene's old Elizabethan romance, *Pandosto*, provides the main line of the action, but, as so often with Shakespeare, much of the key poetic material derives from what has been mixed into the basic vessel. In this case, the crucial combinant was the ancient legend of Alcestis, the wife brought back from the dead to her grieving husband by Heracles/Hercules. But even this was available to Shakespeare in a variety of versions, the relations among which are complicated and hard to reconstruct, though equally hard to deny.[22] For instance, Greene's tale bears strong resemblances to a version of the Alcestis story in an earlier set of short prose romances, based largely on French models, in George Pettie's *Petite Palace of Pettie his Pleasure* (1576). Pettie's version has nothing at all to do with antiquity, but nevertheless forms a suggestive link, as does, in another direction, the prominence of Alcestis as a leading character in the frame of Chaucer's unfinished poem, *The Legend of Good Women*, where she is a figuration both of Christ, who saves humanity by taking on death, and of the human soul, itself rescued from that same death by Christ.[23] This sense of the energies of sin and redemption is certainly in the background of Shakespeare's play, as for instance when Paulina calls to Hermione to "Bequeath to Death your numbness for from him / Dear Life redeems you" (5.3.102–3).

Euripides' play of Alcestis, meanwhile, seems likely to have been known by Shakespeare in its Latin translation by the Scots humanist, George Buchanan. Several good reasons for believing Shakespeare knew this version have been offered by critics, especially its inclusion of a hint not unlike the Pygmalion story from Book X of Ovid's *Metamorphoses*, a key precursor of the final statue scene of the play.[24] What has *not* been noticed, however, and that makes the link even more secure, is the central thematic importance to Euripides' play of the religious concept of "kharis" – in Latin "gratia" or grace, faithfully translated by Buchanan. In Euripides' play "kharis" is a principle of reciprocity – a favor or act of generosity that implies or entails a reciprocal act. It is in fact a fundamental principle of "religio" in the sense noted above, binding together alike human relations and those between mortals and gods.[25] Heracles's action in returning Alcestis to Admetus is specifically an act of "kharis/gratia," the last in a chain that began with Admetus's hosting of Apollo, exiled from heaven. The thematic working through Euripides' play of kharis/gratia, which is *not* a prominent element in Greene's romance, provides a specific model for Shakespeare's investigation of grace in his own play, and indeed opens the concept to just that interrogation which is a feature of the intermediate space of both/and noted earlier.

And there is one more possible line of development for grace in the play, perhaps even more suggestive. As T. W. Baldwin long ago showed in investigating Shakespeare's schooling, the most likely Greek text known to Shakespeare from grammar school was the New Testament, which was typically translated and worked over from Greek to Latin to English and back several times.[26] "Kharis/gratia" is, of course, a central concept of New Testament theology, especially in the letters of St. Paul, but also, less widely recognized, in 1 Peter. This is in part because in 1 Peter the term is used rather more flexibly and hence is not always translated as "grace" – in the Geneva Bible, for instance, it also appears as "thankworthy" (2.19) and "acceptable" (2.20), for human acts received *by* God as well as free gifts of favor *from* God.[27] And amid these slightly more traditional and less technical uses there also appears the following: "To whom [Christ] coming as unto a living stone disallowed of men, but chosen of God and precious, Ye also as lively stones, be made a spiritual house, an holy Priesthood to offer up spiritual sacrifices" (1 Pet. 2: 4–5).[28] Is it going too far to see in this image of a living stone receiving living stones an anticipation or analogue of the final scene in which Hermione and Leontes face one another, each offering up for inspection and abandonment, to be sure in different ways, the fact and thought of their mutual stoniness – his to her, his turning her to stone, hers to him at her death and on her tomb, hers now to him as "a rebuke for being more stone than it"? But now, at last, a "stone no more" but graspable, "living," and "warm."

The point is, nonetheless, that the play holds this scene – and those of Alcestis returned to Admetus, and of Pygmalion touching Galathea, and perhaps even of Thomas touching Jesus – strategically away from itself.[29] It is not Heracles, or Venus, or Christ, that redeems from death, but the deliberately unspecific figure of "Dear Life," a phrase neither Biblical nor classical. And yet the play's powerful, and powerfully moving, relation to currents mobilized in both classical and Christian religious traditions, and in religious myth generally, is palpable: it both is and is not a religious play. It is a play on which a religion might fasten, if one were looking to create one. Or, if that is too strong, it is the sort of text on which the characteristic hermeneutic energies of religious attention might take hold. As indeed they have done.

If *The Winter's Tale* represents Shakespeare's warmest engagement with the entwined energies of religion and drama, *The Tempest*, in many ways its dialectical twin, seems in the end more sober and skeptical about them, and this – paradoxically – despite its putting directly on display the razzle-dazzle theatricality of the supernatural. The focus of the two plays is also on different issues: though both stage tales of repentance, the former is more interested in psychological, the latter on social reconciliations. It is hardly surprising then that the primary religious text that informs the action of *The Tempest* is not evangelical but liturgical.

As several critics have noted, there is a prominent and specific reminiscence of the Book of Common Prayer in the play's vision of the reconstitution of community. Though spread more widely, this reminiscence focuses in particular on the Act 3 invitation of the Italian courtiers to the strange banquet, violently interrupted by the intervention of Ariel in the form of the accusing Harpy. As Michael Neill frames the banquet scene: "The feast is offered and then withdrawn from the 'men of sin' in a manner which immediately recalls the Prayer Book's prohibition of any 'open and notorious evil liver' from the Communion Table 'until he have openly declared himself to have truly repented and amended his former naughty life.' "[30] Neill also points out that Prospero's, and the play's, last line before the Epilogue explicitly repeats the priest's invitation to the communicants to "draw near."[31] And David Aers and Sarah Beckwith resume the point: "Here the work of theatre supports the work of the mass in a substitution of haunting power and equivocation – for the feast can only be realized in those relations of charity. Without them it is insubstantial."[32]

And yet, despite these reconciliatory allusions, which an early modern audience would likely have recognized, the play also fosters a strain of skepticism. If the Ariel-Harpy is not exactly lying in what it says to the Italians, it is certainly not telling the whole truth in calling the island spirits "ministers of fate." They are in fact ministers of Prospero – and what we make of their machinations is necessarily bound up with our judgment of him, his intentions and his procedures. And of them, the play gives us reason to be skeptical, if not suspicious.

To put it another way, the play, for all its investment in the spectacular machinery of theophanic revelation, cannot quite divest itself of the demystification of such machinery that was a major project of the Reformation. Prospero's magic may provoke repentance and reconciliation, but it also recalls such notorious frauds as the Blood of Hales and the Rood of Boxley.[33] Reports of angels appearing to urge repentance and reunion with Rome, acclaimed by Catholics but also denounced by Protestants, persisted into the seventeenth century, including one that appeared on an altar in 1601, threatening "with a naked sword in his hand."[34] Ariel positions his commination directly in this line.

While *The Winter's Tale* is careful to hold the mythic paradox of "is and is not" in relatively benign tension to entertain the question of how to interpret the stoniness of Hermione and her history, *The Tempest* takes some pains to drive in a skeptical wedge, showing acceptance and celebration on the one hand ("O brave new world!"), but distance and skepticism on the other ("Tis new to thee"). This oscillation of alternatives is sustained throughout the play. It embraces even the character and location of supernatural interventions and the extent to which they can be distinguished from an ordinary world. When Caliban complains of Prospero's spirits that,

> For every trifle are they set upon me –
> Sometimes like apes that mow and chatter at me
> And after bite me; then like hedgehogs, which
> Lie tumbling in my barefoot way and mount
> Their pricks at my foot-fall. (2.2.8–12).

it is impossible to tell whether his hurts are punishments or accidents, so saturating is his paranoid fear of Prospero's omniscient malevolence. By such means the play includes, alongside its eirenic evocations of reconciliation, the alternative of a critique of religious manipulation, recalling the reputed claim of Marlowe that "the first beginning of religion was to keep men in awe."[35] Against Paulina's invocation in *The Winter's Tale*, it is as if *The Tempest* were demanding, in one of its aspects at least, that "it is required you do awake your doubt" (5.3.94–5). No matter how hard the play tries, a suspicion haunts it that in the end the theatrical can only reveal the theatrical, even if in its bright colors it could at its best be, as Spenser put it, "shading a true case."[36] This nagging vulnerability helps account for the final decision to repudiate the project of supernatural revelation altogether as "rough magic" and to confirm humility as the ordinary lot, rebuking the charmed circles of theater.

In his third Satire, a querulous John Donne of the mid 1590s imagined the difficult search for religious truth:

> On a huge hill,
> Cragged, and steep, Truth stands, and he that will
> Reach her, about must, and about must go;
> And what the hill's suddenness resists, win so. (lines 79–82)[37]

The poem makes clear that the modern proliferation of competing doctrines requires this laborious ascent. The truth is no longer simply given. Shakespeare's late plays are written in this same environment of pervasive doubt, but the skepticism and perspectivism manifest in his earlier work here take a different form. The plays invoke religion not as truth to be sought, but as a series of open questions about what energies and needs make up religious impulses, where those impulses come from and how they may be served, expounded, or even manipulated by fiction-making, including, above all, theatrical fiction-making. Instead of climbing the hill, these plays direct attention to the character and climates of the climb itself.

Notes

1 Tony Kushner, *Angels in America. A Gay Fantasia on National Themes*, Revised Edition (New York: Theatre Communications Group, 2013), 125. See also Kushner's expansion on the technical aspects of this entrance on 318.

2 One could include also in this list the late "history" play, now known as *Henry VIII* but apparently also earlier titled *All Is True* and most likely co-authored with John Fletcher, in which a dream masque of supernatural spirits lights the final moments of Queen Katherine's life.

3 The space of the temple as a staging-place for communications with gods is important in three out of the four plays, and all of Prospero's island has a quasi-consecrated, magical ambience.

4 Tolkien coined this term, a useful one for these plays, defining it as "the sudden happy turn in a story which pierces you with a joy that brings tears." See the OED.

5 For useful discussion of complexities in the concept of "religion," see Craig Martin, *A Critical Introduction to the Study of Religion* 2nd edn. (New York: Routledge, 2017), chap. 1.

6 See G. K. Hunter, *English Drama 1586–1642: The Age of Shakespeare* (Oxford: Oxford University Press, 1997), 93–101.

7 See Richard Paul Knowles, "'The More Delay'd, Delighted': Theophanies in the Last Plays," *Shakespeare Studies* 15 (1982): 269–80; also, Kenneth Muir, "Theophanies in the Last Plays," in *Shakespeare's Late Plays: Essays in Honor of Charles Crow*, ed. Richard C. Tobias and Paul G. Zolbrod (Athens: Ohio University Press, 1974), 67–77.

8 John Pitcher (ed.), *The Winter's Tale*, Arden Shakespeare, 3rd ser. (London: Arden Shakespeare, 2010), 220 n.

9 A similar complexion makes up the world of *King Lear*, where the king swears "by Apollo" but the madman fears "the Prince of Darkness."

10 In fact, Ferdinand tried to marry his daughter to Henry VII of England.

11 On Shakespeare's use of anachronism, see for instance Phyllis Rackin, *Stages of History* (Ithaca, NY: Cornell University Press, 1990), 86–145; and Hannibal Hamlin, *The Bible in Shakespeare* (Oxford: Oxford University Press, 2013), 179–230.

12 For the fundamental importance of "myth and metaphor" to religious discourse, see Northrop Frye, *The Double Vision: Language and Meaning in Religion* (Toronto, ON: University of Toronto Press, 1991), esp. chap. 1. See also Sarah Beckwith's *Shakespeare and the Grammar of Forgiveness* (Ithaca, NY: Cornell University Press, 2011), for excellent and stimulating discussion of these plays' staging of the vicissitudes of forgiveness as a religious and philosophical concept. Beckwith provides a model for thinking through Shakespeare's handling of other religious concepts in these plays, as forgiveness by no means exhausts them, not being, for instance, a concern in *Pericles*. Beckwith, 85.

13 For our purpose, it does not matter that Shakespeare's attention may have been redirected to it by working with a presumed collaborator, George Wilkins. He knew the story from much earlier, having used it already in *The Comedy of Errors*.

14 "Infirmity" is, as Naseeb Shaheen points out, a common word for "man's frail human condition" in the Geneva Bible. See Shaheen's *Biblical References in Shakespeare's Plays* (Newark: University of Delaware Press, 1999), 687.

15 "Homily on the Fear of Death," *Renaissance English Texts*, ed. Ian Lancashire (University of Toronto, 1994), The Anglican Library, www.anglicanlibrary.org/homilies/ bk1hom09.htm.

16 Though Job is not a direct intertext for *Pericles*, the play's evident relation to *King Lear* (argued effectively by Beckwith, *Grammar of Forgiveness*, 85–92), which *is* suffused with Job, suggests a general recollection is plausible. For Job in *Lear*, see Hamlin, *The Bible in Shakespeare*, 305–33; for further exploration of Biblical texts in *Pericles*, see Hannibal Hamlin "The Acts of Pericles: Shakespeare's Biblical Romance," in *Reading Shakespeare and the Bible: Cultures of Interpretation in Post-Reformation Britain*, ed. Thomas Fulton and Kristen Poole (Cambridge: Cambridge University Press, 2018), forthcoming.

17 See Deanne Williams, "Papa Don't Preach: The Power of Prolixity in Pericles," *University of Toronto Quarterly* 71 (2002): 595–622; also see Beckwith, *Grammar of Forgiveness*.

18 See Lactantius, *Divinarum Institutionum Libri Septem* 4.28.3: "*hoc vinculo pietatis obstricti deo et religati sumus, unde ipsa religio nomen accepit*" and 4.28.12: "*diximus nomen religionis a vincula pietatis esse deductum, quod hominem sibi deus religaverit, et pietate constrinxerit.*" Lactantius, *Divinarum Institutionum Libri Septem*, ed. Eberhard Heck and Antonie Wlosok, vol. 2 (Berlin: Walter de Gruyter, 2007), 425, 427; Augustine, *De Vera Religione* 55 (113): "*Religet ergo nos religio uni omnipotenti Deo.*" Augustine, *De Vera Religione*, ed. Josef Lössl (Paderborn: Ferdinand Schöningh, 2007), 258.

19 See Paul Ricoeur, *Finitude et Culpabilité* (Paris: Aubier, 1960), 2 vols., translated separately as *Fallible Man*, rev. trans. Charles A. Kelbley (New York: Fordham University Press, 1986) and *The Symbolism of Evil*, trans. Emerson Buchanan (New York: Harper & Row, 1967).

20 The emphases (italics and capitalization) are in the Folio text here and six lines later, making the point more visible (sig. Aa1^{v}). It is surely relevant that Hermione is pregnant as she says this and thinking of her own children, and her joy in her husband, as gratuitous blessings. Latin "gratia" – like Greek "kharis" – is a feminine noun.

21 I am not, naturally, the first to point to the central importance of grace in the play. Yet most previous commentators isolate the concept, doctrinally or in some other way. What I would argue instead is the play's ecumenical interest in the concept. For various treatments, see Peter Milward, "A Theology of Grace in *The Winter's Tale*," in *Shakespeare's Other Dimension* (Tokyo: Renaissance Institute, Sophia University, 1989), 102–24. David N. Beauregard, "Shakespeare Against the Skeptics: Nature and Grace in *The Winter's Tale*," in *Shakespeare's Last Plays: Essays in Literature and Politics*, ed. Stephen W. Smith and Travis Curtright (Lanham, MD: Lexington Books, 2002), 53–72; Grace Tiffany, "Calvinist Grace in Shakespeare's Romances: Upending Tragedy," *Christianity and Literature* 49 (2000), 421–45; James Kearney, "Hospitality's Risk, Grace's Bargain: Uncertain Economies in *The Winter's Tale*," in *Shakespeare and Hospitality: Ethics, Politics, and Exchange*, ed. David B. Goldstein and Julia Reinhard Lupton (New York: Routledge, 2016), 89–111; Marion Trousdale, "The Grace of Government in *The Winter's Tale*," in *Law, Literature, and the Settlement of Regimes*, ed. Gordon Schochet, Patricia Tatspaugh, and Carol Brobeck (Washington, DC: Folger Shakespeare Library, 1990), 113–20; and Beckwith, *Grammar of Forgiveness*, 127–46.

22 For the role of the Alcestis story in the play, see Douglas B. Wilson, "Euripides' Alcestis and the Ending of Shakespeare's The Winter's Tale," *Iowa State Journal of Research* 58 (1984): 345–55, and the editions of Stephen Orgel (Oxford, 1996), 77, and Pitcher (2010), 93–4, 97–9, 446–8.

23 In Pettie, Proserpina is the divinity who restores Alcest, possibly a hint for Shakespeare's inclusion of the Proserpina myth in his play. On Alceste in Chaucer's poem, see V. A. Kolve, "From Cleopatra to Alceste: An Iconographic Study of *The Legend of Good Women*," in *Signs and Symbols in Chaucer's Poetry*, ed. John P. Hermann and John J. Burke, Jr. (Tuscaloosa, AL: University of Alabama Press, 1981), 130–78. Kolve points out that the complete *Legend* would likely have concluded with a retelling of the Alcestis story.

24 On Buchanan and Shakespeare, see Sarah Dewar-Watson, "The Alcestis and the Statue Scene in *The Winter's Tale*," *Shakespeare Quarterly* 60, no.1 (2009): 73–80.

25 In Euripides, the importance of "kharis" is emphasized by the word appearing eight times, always at the end of a line, a pattern Buchanan follows in most cases. The lines in the Greek play are 60, 70, 299, 544, 660, 840, 1074, and 1101. See Euripides, *Alcestis*, ed. J. H. Hayden (London: W. B. Clive, 1936) and *George Buchanan: Tragedies*, ed. P. Sharratt and P. G. Walsh (Edinburgh: Scottish Academic Press, 1983), where the play, untranslated, is on 209–44. Of additional interest is that both the Pygmalion and Proserpina stories in Ovid also concern themselves with "gratia" or what is "grata."

26 See T. W. Baldwin, *William Shakspere's Small Latine and Lesse Greeke*, 2 vols. (Urbana: University of Illinois Press, 1944), 2: 617–61. Baldwin concludes that "the evidence is conclusive that [Shakespeare] really did not know Greek drama" (661).

27 At 1 Peter 4:10 there is also an interesting cross-echo between a believer's "gift" ("khárisma") and "the manifold grace of god" ("poikílēs kháritos theoû").

28 The phrases are specifically reciprocal in Greek ("líthon zōnta/ líthoi zōntes") and in the Vulgate ("lapidem vivum / lapides vivi").

29 Might one even add, by contrast, the instruction to Mary Magdalene in the garden "*Noli me tangere*" (John 20:17)? Here, of course, the touch is forbidden, not bidden. I thank Hannibal Hamlin for this suggestion.

30 Michael Neill, "Remembrance and Revenge: *Hamlet*, *Macbeth* and *The Tempest*," in *Shakespeare and Jonson*, ed. Ian Donaldson (Atlantic Highlands, NJ: Humanities Press, 1983), 35–56 at 47.

31 Ibid., 49.

32 David Aers and Sarah Beckwith, "The Eucharist," in *Cultural Reformations: Medieval and Renaissance in Literary History*, ed. James Simpson and Brian Cummings (Oxford: Oxford University Press, 2015), 153–67, at 163.

33 For detailed discussion, see Colin Flight, "The Rood of Grace." www.kentarchaeology.ac/digiarchive/ColinFlight/ColinFlight.html.

34 See Alexandra Walsham, *Catholic Reformation in Protestant England* (Farnham: Ashgate, 2014), 207–15. The citation of Hall's account in note 1 on 207 should be to Hall, 159.

35 See Tom Rutter (ed.), *The Cambridge Introduction to Christopher Marlowe* (Cambridge: Cambridge University Press, 2012), 17.

36 *Faerie Queene* V.vii.2.7.

37 *John Donne: The Complete English Poems*, ed. A. J. Smith (London: Penguin, 1971), 163.

ROWAN WILLIAMS

Afterword: Finding the Remedy

Literature on Shakespeare's religious convictions or lack of them continues to grow, and essays continue to be written about how and where his vocabulary and imagination reflect the themes of classical Christian theology. In this as – proverbially – in so many other areas, he eludes categorization. When all the arguments have been made for cryptic allusions to Catholic martyrs or to the wording of the 1552 Book of Common Prayer, the plays seem neither larger nor smaller; to hear and see them as significant, as critical, challenging, and enriching, doesn't appear to depend on solving any of these puzzles. So, is the question of "Shakespeare and religion" simply a decorative excursion on the margin of Shakespeare reception and criticism?

Obviously, the authors of this book would say, No; but drawing together all these sophisticated studies and trying to find their focus is a risky task. In this brief coda to the collection, I want to draw attention to four themes in the plays that – whatever Shakespeare's personal practice or belief – leave a trail of religious or theological questioning. I am very conscious that I am largely ignoring the non-dramatic works, and that there is always a problem of selectivity in dealing with the dramas themselves. But because the plays unmistakeably talk to each other at different levels, it is not a completely artificial exercise to try and listen to some of those conversations, freely granting that there are always many others going on. Briefly, then, we shall be looking at questions around solidarity and compassion; prayer and guilt; power, including imaginative power; and gratuity, the dissolving of an economy of debt and reward. Religious issues, in the sense that they have to do with elements of human interaction and self-understanding that sit uneasily with reductive or mechanical models of human identity; in the sense that they are where the language of grace and communion comes in, whatever ontological implications we want to give to this.

The four issues are of course deeply interwoven; as soon as you start tracing one, all the others seem to arise almost immediately. *Measure for Measure* begins with what seems to be a resigning of power, but that at once appears as a straightforward exercise of it. The Duke's delegation of power to Angelo is in part to test Angelo's proverbial chilly dispassion. "Hence shall we see, / If power change purpose, what our seemers be" (1.4.54–5). Isabella's later appeal (2.2.65–7) to Angelo challenges his own use of power by appealing to a shared fragility, to solidarity: "If he had been as you, and you as he, / You would have slipped like him, but he like you / Would not have been so stern," which Angelo repudiates in the name of a wholly impersonal law: pity, for him, is pity for the imagined witnesses of an evil act who would be scandalized by forgiveness – not for the individual. Isabella's nakedly theological point – "all the souls that were, were forfeit once, / And he that might the vantage best have took / Found out the remedy" (2.2.75–7) is ignored. And at the end of the scene, Angelo admits in his agonized soliloquy that solidarity of a kind is precisely what he has discovered ("Ever till now / When men were fond, I smiled, and wondered how" [2.2.190–1]); does this then invalidate the law? But if it does, it is not simply the law of the land but the moral law itself: "We are all frail," says Angelo to Isabella, when he proposes his bargain for Claudio's life (2.4.122). The complicatedly disturbing end of the play twists around questions of justice and mercy. Like *The Merchant of Venice*, it sets a question mark against the very idea of mercy when this is itself a tool of absolute power rather than a recognition of solidarity. Angelo begs for justice rather than mercy on the Duke's terms ("I crave death more willingly than mercy" [5.1.469]), because guilt cannot be assuaged by this kind of forgiveness; Lucio is spared death and condemned to humiliation, having, in the Duke's eyes, deserved no less for his mockery of authority; Isabella is without any indication of consent declared the Duke's intended bride – and are we to say that this is a triumph for mercy? It is as though the two early refusals of authentic mercy in the play – Angelo's repudiation of Isabella's first plea and Isabella's own rounding on Claudio in 3.1.150 ("Mercy to thee would prove itself a bawd") – have closed off some possibility in the action. The characters are left with only the options of strict retribution or arbitrary and humiliating remission, and anything that might speak of a gratuitous movement towards some restoration of relation is not thinkable.

Power does indeed change purpose, it seems – both for Angelo and for the Duke. The access of power without awareness of shared humanity makes Angelo first a tyrant and then a hypocrite; but what makes the play still more complex in its moral and spiritual coloring is the Duke's resumption of power and his attempt to resolve the increasingly tangled interactions of the drama simply by fiat. Isabella's early affirmation of "remedy" as the result of sacrificing "vantage" has been lost in the panic and deceit that unfolds. "Vantage" triumphs, in the Duke's victorious casting of characters in new roles of his devising. And it is this awareness of the ambivalence of *imaginative* power that appears in Shakespeare's interrogation of the very business of theatrical representation. It is typical of his most articulate villains that they "stage" the interactions in which they are involved. Richard III is from the beginning a deviser of dramas for others, setting up the denunciation and arrest of Clarence, stage-managing the encounter with Anne and so forth. Iago again stages Othello's collapse, enticing him into the script he has prepared for him as for Desdemona and Cassio, and the unfortunate Roderigo. Edmund similarly stages his brother's treason against their father, referring to him in terms of the predictable plots of "the old comedy" (*King Lear*, 1.2.17). By the time of *The Tempest*, Shakespeare's full attention is on the conundrum of the morality of imaginative power: Prospero is supremely the magical architect of the lives and destinies of others, but at the same time somehow trapped in the very exercise of that power. The famously enigmatic Epilogue appeals to the audience, "As you from crimes would pardoned be, / Let your indulgence set me free" (19–20) – a retrieval of the theme of justice modulated by solidarity or the recognition of shared frailty, and also an acknowledgment of a certain guilt in the exercise of representing human subjects in drama, the guilt of theatrical imagination itself, the dramatist identifying with the manipulative genius of Iago or Edmund or Richard.

At the end of *The Tempest*, there is a deliberate halting of what has appeared to be a straightforward narrative resolution, Prospero's return to Milan: to the audience, he now declares that his liberty to step away from the action of the drama depends on their "good hands" – joined in applause but more importantly in prayer, a prayer that arises from the audience's recognition of complicity. They must "assault" mercy or the seat of mercy (a telling anticipation of George Herbert's bold image of prayer as "engine against th'Almighty"), so that both dramatist and audience may be absolved. Throughout the great dramas of his maturity, Shakespeare returns to the idea of theatricality as the means of discovering what is otherwise hidden (very plainly in *Hamlet*, but also in the very articulate presentations of self-dramatizing in *Julius Caesar*, or the comic manipulations of erotic passion through the theatrical and literary devices of others in *Much Ado About Nothing*, *As You Like It*, *Twelfth Night*, and so on): staging is not in itself some sort of evil. Yet staging, as a way of externalizing passion (love, fear, panic, revenge), is ultimately a very shadowed affair: it can involve a reduction in the freedom of the imagined character, sometimes a thoroughly destructive limiting of their identity and possibilities, as in *Othello* or *King Lear*, or the letter plot in *Twelfth Night*. The "remedy" that has to be sought is a remedy for the guilt involved in this enslavement of the other; readings of *The Tempest* in terms of colonial aspiration are not wrong, to the extent that colonial appropriation is a form of "staging" the history and geography of a strange territory in a self-referential shape.

Prayer features in a couple of near-contemporary passages (1599/1600) reflecting on guilt and absolution – Henry V's meditation and prayer before Agincourt (*Henry V*, 4.1.) and Claudius's soliloquy in *Hamlet* (3.3). Both wrestle with whether absolution is possible if the effect of a sin is still in force, if the usurper still enjoys the power that has been unlawfully seized. Henry promises maximal *external* reparation, through the approved ritual means, but also acknowledges (with an echo of the Book of Common Prayer's Collect for Quinquagesima Sunday) that what he can do is "nothing worth, / Since that my penitence comes after all" – i.e. (probably; it is an enigmatic text) since his personal or interior repentance is the least of his responses, and he can only ask forgiveness for his lukewarmness in asking forgiveness. If the echo of the Prayer Book is significant here, what he in fact lacks is "that most excellent gift of charity." His reparation is without love; and so it fails to remedy or repair what was broken in his father's usurpation and the killing of Richard II. Claudius likewise tries to kindle a repentance that is more than self-disgust: like Henry, he knows that what matters is the interior change effected by "charity," and that words alone, like rituals alone, will not bring healing. In a starkly counterintuitive move, Shakespeare shows us, with these two prayers, two deeply intelligent figures who plumb their interior depths to find not the simple inner truth of their being but an ineradicable division and falsehood. Interiority does not uncover sincerity but represses it afresh by focusing our attention on the need out of which our self-images arise. The simple exposure of what is hidden – as with Malvolio's obsession with Olivia – only compounds the deceits and self-deceits. And from yet another point of view, Macbeth's desire to find out the hidden future leads not to the vision of a neutrally describable truth but to the exposure of guilty desires that seize on the idea of a fated future as a moral alibi – the exposure of a self-creating self. "Prophecy" becomes another kind of moral test: *all* futures are imagined futures, so the search for foreknowledge does not remove the challenge about how power will be enacted. Foreknowledge is a temptation not an absolution.

The more these dark themes come into focus, the clearer it is that the challenge of the drama is in part to reacquaint us with our vulnerability to the seductions of drama, the re-creation of self and others as players in a controlled script. When we imagine, we cannot truly imagine freedom, which is a way of saying that we cannot imagine the *person*. Or at least not consistently: Shakespeare's drama shows us, if anything can, just how far imagination can go in constructing persons out of words and conversations, and it is a bit of a cliché to say that the highest points of his drama are in the creation of utterly distinctive individuals (Falstaff, Hamlet). But before we start enthusing romantically about this, we need to be equally attentive to what Shakespeare shows us of the danger of imagining in this way or on this scale, and the limits of what can be imagined. Ultimately (as with Prospero) the creator is trapped in relation to the created figures by the inescapable logic of control that is bound to be at work somewhere in the process. Hence the prayer for liberation that Prospero urges on his audience. One of the central paradoxes of Shakespeare's drama is that in the very depth and abundance of his creativity, his capacity to show how much we can imagine of another human subject, he reminds us that this very skill is what we use to imprison or destroy others (Ariel; Othello at the hands of Iago), and so to destroy ourselves. Imagination is – to use a familiar trope – the *pharmakon* that may be cure or poison. It is itself to some degree its own antidote, but also its own recurring seduction. It both evokes and dissolves the remedy for our self-imprisoning violence.

It would be ridiculous to say that Shakespeare consciously sets out to present any such picture of his own craft, yet as we trace what is being said and asked in his words about solidarity, guilt, power, and gratuity, something like this is what comes together. The theme of how some kinds of renunciation of power are subtle bids for power is sharply delineated again and again, in *Richard III*, *Julius Caesar*, *Measure for Measure*, *King Lear*; the punishment for failures in solidarity in terms of captivity to illusion is as potent in *Twelfth Night* or *All's Well That Ends Well* as in *King Lear* ("Expose thyself to feel what wretches feel!" [3.4.34]) or *The Merchant of Venice* (where Shylock's refusal of mercy is pitilessly mirrored by the cruelty of his Christian judges; as in *Measure for Measure*, it is as if the earlier refusals of grace and reductions of relations to transactions of profitable exchange have already closed certain doors, leaving only destructive polar alternatives). The failure of the language of debt to cope with the reality of love or human fidelity is again a central concern in *King Lear* ("No cause, no cause!" [4.6.74]). And as Shakespeare moves into the last phase of his dramatic development, he seems to become more fascinated by this breakdown of the categories of debt and merit. Most markedly in *The Winter's Tale*, he sidesteps questions of guilt and punishment – or rather, relativizes them: Hermione's "resuscitation" is being prepared virtually from the moment of Leontes's most open and violent repudiation of her. It is not his penitence that earns her renewed life, but something more like a sense of a new configuration of possibilities with the reappearance of Perdita. Morally, the play jars in any number of ways; imaginatively it does exactly what it sets out to do, to "awake faith" in life beyond violence, rejection, and betrayal. It is a sort of reversed image of what *King Lear* does. There, the reconciliation of Lear and Cordelia is fully achieved, and then simply allowed to be destroyed; it has not "earned" visible success or sustainability, and the catastrophe overtaking the king and his daughter is nakedly unjust in any obvious terms of transcendent justice. But it is *there*, real and achieved, independently of how any ending turns out. In *The Winter's Tale*, the unforgivable, unhealable catastrophe comes first; and the reconciliation of 5.3 is as disconnected from "justice" as is the apocalyptic dreadfulness of the end of *King Lear*. Behind and beyond the plots of power unrecognized or misrecognized, guilt and desperation and the plea for release, the belated understanding of the cost of refusing solidarity and compassion, there is a pointing to the fundamental insight: neither appalling suffering nor intense joy is earned, they are not rewards and punishments in the usual sense. And this means that the valuation of who we are and what we do is removed from success and failure as we commonly understand them – and so removed from the contest of power, the contest as to whose *will* shall prevail.

Shakespeare, then, is inviting his audience to look past a moral economy of debt and desert. "Grace," the advent of unplanned and uncontrolled insight, healing, or restoration, is not invalidated if it fails to bring victory and security. It is not earned, and it does not have to earn, to justify itself by success: it is what it is. Recognizing it is recognizing the presence of a certain *freedom* at the center of the human world that is very different from a mere freedom of choice, something more like an inexhaustible possibility that humiliation and pain are not final, necessary, imprisoning. But – and here is the relevance for the dramatist's own labors – the nature of that freedom is such that it is stifled or distorted by an authorial will determined to stage it adequately, to *produce* grace and remedy. The imagination of the dramatist works on the knife-edge between control of what is created and the letting-grace-happen that articulates the freedom that the imagination intuits. So the dramatist who wants to avoid mechanical, moralistic staging is driven to dramatizing the crises of self-deceit and the cunning of imaginative power, driven, finally, to dramatize prayer for release. The dramatist, like the abdicating monarch, acknowledges a solidarity that is both threatening and releasing, deathly and life-giving. The deeply uncanny, *unheimlich* playing with death and life, dead and dismembered bodies, suspended lives and absurd resurrections in *The Winter's Tale* and *Cymbeline* and, to some extent, *Pericles* is the work of a writer who has recognized this sometimes-grotesque interweaving of things dying and things newborn, who is exploring an increasingly uncontrolled imaginative world, in the sense of a world where the conventional plots of merit and reward have dissolved.

Part of the narrative into which we are invited as a Shakespearean audience is a story about power abandoned so that life may happen, about the discovery of how resourceful and persistent the power of a carefully managed and imaged self can be, about the evasions of solidarity and the unexpected saving pain of compassion. To put it at the most minimal, this is a narrative that would be very different without the story Isabella sums up in terms of vantage and remedy; it is permeated by the conviction that the release that imagination promises comes by finally releasing the imagination itself from controlling and edifying purpose. Ariel is set free, and Prospero too must find his freedom in the wake of that abdication of control. Thinking about "Shakespeare and religion," specifically about the Christian narrative that he inhabited (with whatever degree of "personal" conviction), needs finally to look not so much at this or that specific echo and allusion, but at what the underlying myth of loss, falsehood, sacrifice, and remedy uncovers about the human imagination itself. And the theologian is left asking about the way in which this imagination can be read as the finite imprint of a free, creative intelligence of a quite other order.

GUIDE TO FURTHER READING

Shakespeare and the Bible or Religion

Adelman, Janet, *Blood Relations: Christian and Jew in "The Merchant of Venice."* Chicago: University of Chicago Press, 2008.

Batson, Beatrice (ed.), *Shakespeare's Christianity: The Protestant and Catholic Poetics of "Julius Caesar," "Macbeth," and "Hamlet."* Waco, TX: Baylor University Press, 2006.

Shakespeare's Second Historical Tetralogy: Some Christian Features. West Cornwall, CT: Locust Hill P, 2004.

Battenhouse, Roy W., *Shakespearean Tragedy: Its Art and Christian Premises.* Bloomington and London: Indiana University Press, 1969.

(ed.), *Shakespeare's Christian Dimension: An Anthology of Commentary.* Bloomington: Indiana University Press, 1994.

Bearman, Robert, "The Early Reformation Experience in a Warwickshire Town: Stratford-upon-Avon, 1530–1580." *Midlands History* (2007): 68–109.

"John Shakespeare: A Papist or Just Penniless?" *SQ* 56, no. 4 (2005): 411–33.

Beauregard, David N., *Catholic Theology in Shakespeare's Plays.* Newark: University of Delaware Press, 2008.

Beckwith, Sarah, *Shakespeare and the Grammar of Forgiveness.* Ithaca, NY: Cornell University Press, 2011.

"Stephen Greenblatt's *Hamlet* and the Forms of Oblivion." *JMEMS* 33, no. 2 (2003): 261–80.

Belsey, Catherine, *Shakespeare and the Loss of Eden.* New Brunswick, NJ: Rutgers University Press, 1999.

Betteridge, Thomas, *Literature and Politics in the English Reformation.* Manchester and New York: Manchester University Press, 2004.

Bishop, Tom, *Shakespeare and the Theatre of Wonder.* Cambridge and New York: Cambridge University Press, 1996.

Bloom, J. Harvey, *Shakespeare's Church.* London: T. Fisher Unwin, 1902.

Boitani, Piero, *The Gospel According to Shakespeare.* Trans. Vittorio Montemaggi and Rachel Jacoff. Notre Dame, IN: University of Notre Dame Press, 2013.

Britton, Dennis Austin, *Becoming Christian: Race, Reformation, and Early Modern English Romance.* New York: Fordham University Press, 2014.

Brockbank, Philip, *"Upon Such Sacrifices," British Academy Shakespeare Lecture.* London: Oxford University Press, 1976.

Brownlow, F. W., *Shakespeare, Harsnett, and the Devils of Denham*. Newark, NJ: University of Delaware Press, 1993.
Bryant, J. A, *Hippolyta's View: Some Christian Aspects of Shakespeare's Plays*. Lexington: University of Kentucky Press, 1961.
Buccola, Regina, and Lisa Hopkins (eds.), *Marian Moments in Early Modern British Drama*. Aldershot and Burlington, VT: Ashgate, 2007.
Cavell, Stanley, *Disowning Knowledge in Seven Plays of Shakespeare*. Cambridge and New York: Cambridge University Press, 1987.
Coodin, Sara, *Is Shylock Jewish? Citing Scripture and the Moral Agency of Shakespeare's Jews*. Edinburgh: Edinburgh University Press, 2017.
Coursen, Herbert R., Jr., *Christian Ritual and the World of Shakespeare's Tragedies*. Lewisburg, PA: Bucknell University Press, 1976.
Cox, John D., *The Devil and the Sacred in English Drama, 1350–1642*. Cambridge: Cambridge University Press, 2000.
Seeming Knowledge: Shakespeare and Skeptical Faith. Waco, TX: Baylor University Press, 2007.
Cummings, Brian, *Mortal Thoughts: Religion, Secularity, & Identity in Shakespeare and Early Modern Culture*. Oxford: Oxford University Press, 2013.
DeCook, Travis, and Alan Galey (eds.), *Shakespeare, the Bible, and the Form of the Book: Contested Scriptures*. New York: Routledge, 2012.
Devlin, Christopher, *Hamlet's Divinity and Other Essays*. Introduced by C. V. Wedgwood. London: Rupert Hart-Davis, 1963.
Dollimore, Jonathan, *Radical Tragedy: Religion, Ideology, and Power in the Drama of Shakespeare and his Contemporaries*. 3rd edn. Durham, NC: Duke University Press, 2004.
Dutton, Richard, Alison Findlay, and Richard Wilson (eds.), *Region, Religion, and Patronage: Lancastrian Shakespeare* (Manchester and New York: Manchester University Press, 2003).
Theatre and Religion: Lancastrian Shakespeare. Manchester and New York: Manchester University Press, 2003.
Elton, William R., *"King Lear" and the Gods*. San Marino, CA: Huntington Library, 1966.
Espinosa, Ruben, *Masculinity and Marian Efficacy in Shakespeare's England*. Farnham, UK, and Burlington, VT: Ashgate, 2011.
Fernie, Ewan (ed.), *Spiritual Shakespeares*. London and New York: Routledge, 2005.
Fisch, Harold, *The Biblical Presence in Shakespeare, Milton, and Blake: A Comparative Study*. Oxford: Clarendon Press, 1999.
Foulkes, Richard, "William Shakespeare: The Model Victorian Protestant." *Shakespeare* 5, no. 1 (2009): 68–81.
Freinkel, Lisa, *Reading Shakespeare's Will: the Theology of Figure from Augustine to the Sonnets*. New York: Columbia University Press, 2002.
Frye, Roland Mushat, *Shakespeare and Christian Doctrine*. Princeton, NJ: Princeton University Press, 1963.
Fulton, Thomas, and Kristen Poole (eds.), *The Bible on the Shakespearean Stage: Cultures of Interpretation in Reformation England*. Cambridge: Cambridge University Press, 2018.
Graham, Kenneth J. E., and Philip D. Collington (eds.), *Shakespeare and Religious Change*. Basingstoke, UK and New York: Palgrave Macmillan, 2009.

Greenblatt, Stephen, *"Hamlet" and Purgatory*. Princeton, NJ: Princeton University Press, 2001.

Shakespearean Negotiations: The Circulation of Social Energy in Renaissance England. Berkeley and Los Angeles: University of California Press, 1988.

Will in the World: How Shakespeare became Shakespeare. New York: W. W. Norton, 2004.

Groves, Beatrice, "Shakespeare's Sonnets and the Genevan Marginalia." *Essays in Criticism* 57, no. 2 (2007): 114–28.

Texts and Traditions: Religion in Shakespeare 1592–1604. Oxford: Clarendon, 2007.

Hamilton, Donna B., *Shakespeare and the Politics of Protestant England*. New York and London: Harvester Wheatsheaf, 1992.

Hamilton, Donna B. and Richard Strier (eds.), *Religion, Literature, and Politics in Post-Reformation England, 1540–1688*. Cambridge: Cambridge University Press, 1996.

Hamlin, Hannibal, *The Bible in Shakespeare*. Oxford: Oxford University Press, 2013.

Psalm Culture and Early Modern English Literature. Cambridge: Cambridge University Press, 2004.

Hassel, R. Chris, Jr., *Faith and Folly in Shakespeare's Romantic Comedies*. Athens: University of Georgia Press, 1980.

Renaissance Drama & the English Church Year. Lincoln: University of Nebraska Press, 1979.

Hirschfeld, Heather, *The End of Satisfaction: Drama and Repentance in the Age of Shakespeare*. Ithaca, NY: Cornell University Press, 2014.

Holland, Peter (ed.), *Shakespeare and Religions*. Shakespeare Survey 54. Cambridge and New York: Cambridge University Press, 2001.

Hunt, Maurice, *Shakespeare's Religious Allusiveness: Its Play and Tolerance*. Aldershot, UK, and Burlington, VT: Ashgate, 2004.

Shakespeare's Romance of the Word. Lewisburg: Bucknell University Press, 1990.

Hunter, Robert G., *Shakespeare and the Mystery of God's Judgments*. Athens: University of Georgia Press, 1976.

Jackson, Ken, *Shakespeare and Abraham*. Notre Dame, IN: University of Notre Dame Press, 2015.

Jackson, Ken, and Arthur F. Marotti, "The Turn to Religion in Early Modern English Studies." *Criticism* 46, no. 1 (2004): 167–90.

(eds.), *Shakespeare and Religion: Early Modern and Postmodern Perspectives*. Notre Dame, IN: University of Notre Dame Press, 2011.

Jenson, Phebe, *Religion and Revelry in Shakespeare's World*. Cambridge: Cambridge University Press, 2008.

Jones, Emrys, *The Origins of Shakespeare*. Oxford: Clarendon Press, 1977.

Jorgensen, Paul A., *Redeeming Shakespeare's Words*. Berkeley and Los Angeles: University of California Press, 1962.

Kastan, David Scott, *A Will to Believe: Shakespeare and Religion*. Oxford: Oxford University Press, 2014.

Klause, John, *Shakespeare, the Earl, and the Jesuit*. Madison, WI: Fairleigh Dickinson University Press, 2008.

Knapp, Jeffrey, *Shakespeare's Tribe: Church, Nation, and Theater in Renaissance England*. Chicago and London: University of Chicago Press, 2002.

Knight, G. Wilson, *Shakespeare and Religion: Essays of Forty Years*. London and New York: Routledge & Kegan Paul, 1967.

The Wheel of Fire: Interpretations of Shakespearian Tragedy. London: Methuen, 1930.

Kronenfeld, Judy, *King Lear and the Naked Truth: Rethinking the Language of Religion and Resistance*. Durham, NC: Duke University Press, 1998.

Kuchar, Gary, *The Poetry of Religious Sorrow in England*. Cambridge: Cambridge University Press, 2011.

Lewalski, Barbara K., "Biblical Allusion and Allegory in *The Merchant of Venice*." *SQ* 13, no. 3 (1962): 327–43.

Loewenstein, David, and Michael Witmore (eds.), *Shakespeare and Early Modern Religion*. Cambridge: Cambridge University Press, 2015.

Lupton, Julia Reinhard, *Citizen-Saints: Shakespeare and Political Theology*. Chicago and London: University of Chicago Press, 2005.

Malin, Eric S., *Godless Shakespeare*. London and New York: Continuum, 2007.

Marshall, Cynthia, *Last Things and Last Plays: Shakespearean Eschatology*. Carbondale: Southern Illinois University Press, 1991.

Marx, Steven, *Shakespeare and the Bible*. Oxford and New York: Oxford University Press, 2000.

Mayer, Jean-Christophe, *Shakespeare's Hybrid Faith: History, Religion, and the Stage*. Basingstoke, UK and New York: Palgrave Macmillan, 2007.

McCoy, Richard C., *Faith in Shakespeare*. Oxford: Oxford University Press, 2013.

McEachern, Claire, and Debora Shuger (eds.), *Religion and Culture in Renaissance England*. Cambridge and New York: Cambridge University Press, 1997.

Milward, Peter, *Biblical Themes in Shakespeare: Centring on "King Lear."* Tokyo: Renaissance Institute, Sophia University, 1975.

The Catholicism of Shakespeare's Plays. London: Saint Austin Press, 2000.

Miola, Robert, *Shakespeare's Reading*. Oxford and New York: Oxford University Press, 2000.

Montrose, Louis, *The Purpose of Playing: Shakespeare and the Cultural Politics of Elizabethan England*. Chicago: University of Chicago Press, 1996.

Morris, Ivor, *Shakespeare's God: The Role of Religion in the Tragedies*. London: Allen & Unwin, 1972.

Noble, Richmond, *Shakespeare's Biblical Knowledge and Use of the Book of Common Prayer*. London: Society for Promoting Christian Knowledge; New York: Macmillan, 1935.

O'Connell, Michael, *The Idolatrous Eye: Iconoclasm and Theatre in Early Modern England*. New York: Oxford University Press, 2000.

Pinciss, Gerald M., *Forbidden Matter: Religion in the Drama of Shakespeare and his Contemporaries*. Newark: University of Delaware Press; London and Cranbury, NJ: Associated University Presses, 2000.

Poole, Kristen, *Radical Religion from Shakespeare to Milton: Figures of Nonconformity in Early Modern England*. Cambridge: Cambridge University Press, 2000.

Reed, Robert Rentoul, Jr., *Crime and God's Judgment in Shakespeare*. Lexington: University Press of Kentucky, 1984.

Richmond, Velma Bourgeois, *Shakespeare, Catholicism, and Romance*. New York: Continuum, 2000.

Rosendale, Timothy, *Liturgy and Literature in the Making of Protestant England*. Cambridge: Cambridge University Press, 2007.

Rust, Jennifer R., *The Body in Mystery: The Political Theology of the Corpus Mysticum in the Literature of Reformation England*. Evanston, IL: Northwestern University Press, 2014.

Sautter, Cia, *The Performance of Religion: Seeing the Sacred in the Theatre*. Abingdon, UK and New York: Routledge, 2017.

Shaheen, Naseeb. *Biblical References in Shakespeare's Plays*. Newark: University of Delaware Press; London: Associated University Presses, 1999.

Shapiro, James, *Shakespeare and the Jews*. New York: Columbia University Press, 1996.

Shell, Alison, *Shakespeare and Religion*. London: Arden Shakespeare, 2011.

Shuger, Debora, *Habits of Thought in the English Renaissance: Religion, Politics, and the Dominant Culture*. Berkeley: University of California Press, 1990.

Political Theologies in Shakespeare's England: The Sacred and the State in "Measure for Measure." Basingstoke, UK: Palgrave Macmillan, 2001.

Siegel, Paul N., *Shakespearean Tragedy and the Elizabethan Compromise*. New York: New York University Press, 1957.

Sims, James H., *Dramatic Uses of Biblical Allusions in Marlowe and Shakespeare*. Gainesville: University of Florida Press, 1966.

Sohmer, Steve, *Shakespeare's Mystery Play*. Manchester and New York: Manchester University Press, 1999.

Sokol, B. J., *Shakespeare and Tolerance*. Cambridge: Cambridge University Press, 2008.

Sterrett, Joseph, *The Unheard Prayer: Religious Toleration in Shakespeare's Drama*. Leiden and Boston: Brill, 2012.

Stockton, Will, *Members of his Body: Shakespeare, Paul, and a Theology of Nonmonogamy*. New York: Fordham University Press, 2017.

Streete, Adrian, *Protestantism and Drama in Early Modern England*. Cambridge: Cambridge University Press, 2009.

(ed.), *Early Modern Drama and the Bible: Contexts and Readings, 1570–1625*. Basingstoke, UK; New York: Palgrave Macmillan, 2012

Swift, Daniel, *Shakespeare's Common Prayers: The Book of Common Prayer and the Elizabethan Age*. Oxford: Oxford University Press, 2013.

Targoff, Ramie, *Common Prayer: The Language of Public Devotion in Early Modern England*. Chicago: Chicago University Press, 2001.

Posthumous Love: Eros and the Afterlife in Renaissance England. Chicago: University of Chicago Press, 2014.

Taylor, Dennis, and David N. Beauregard (eds.), *Shakespeare and the Culture of Christianity in Early Modern England*. New York: Fordham University Press, 2003.

Vitkus, Daniel, *Turning Turk: English Theatre and the Multicultural Mediterranean*. Basingstoke, UK: Palgrave Macmillan, 2008.

Walsh, Brian, *Unsettled Toleration: Religious Difference on the Shakespearean Stage*. Oxford: Oxford University Press, 2016.

West, Robert H., *Shakespeare and the Outer Mystery*. Lexington: University of Kentucky Press, 1968.

White, Paul Whitfield, *Drama and Religion in English Provincial Society, 1485–1660*. Cambridge: Cambridge University Press, 2008.

Wilson, Richard, *Secret Shakespeare: Studies in Theatre, Religion, and Resistance*. Manchester and New York: Manchester University Press, 2004.

Wilson, Robert F., "God's Secrets and Bottom's Name: A Reply." *SQ* 30, no. 3 [1979]: 407–8.

Wittreich, Joseph, *"Image of that Horror": History, Prophecy, and Apocalypse in "King Lear."* San Marino, CA: The Huntington Library, 1984.

Womersley, David, *Divinity and State*. Oxford and New York: Oxford University Press, 2010.

Woods, Gillian, *Shakespeare's Unreformed Fictions*. Oxford: Oxford University Press, 2013.

Wright, Daniel L., *Anglican Shakespeare: Elizabethan Orthodoxy in the Great Histories*. Vancouver, WA: Pacific-Columbia Books, 1993.

Young, Alan R., *The English Prodigal Son Plays: A Theatrical Fashion of the Sixteenth and Seventeenth Centuries*. Salzburg: Institut für Anglistik und Amerikanistik, Universität Salzburg, 1979.

Zysk, Jay, *Shadow and Substance: Eucharistic Controversy and English Drama Across the Reformation Divide*. Notre Dame, IN: University of Notre Dame Press, 2017.

History of the Bible, the Church, and Religion

Crockett, Bryan, *The Play of Paradox: Stage and Sermon in Renaissance England*. Philadelphia: University of Pennsylvania Press, 1995.

Daniell, David, *The Bible in English: Its History and Influence*. New Haven, CT: Yale University Press, 2003.

Darlow, T. H., and H. F. Moule, rev. A. S. Herbert, *Historical Catalogue of Printed Editions of the English Bible 1525–1961*. London: The British and Foreign Bible Society; New York: The American Bible Society, 1968.

Dimmock, Matthew, and Andrew Hadfield (eds.), *The Religions of the Book: Christian Perceptions, 1400–1660*. Basingstoke and New York: Palgrave Macmillan, 2008.

Duffy, Eamon, *Reformation Divided: Catholics, Protestants and the Conversion of England*. London: Bloomsbury, 2017.

The Stripping of the Altars: Traditional Religion in England, c.1400–c.1580. 2nd edn. New Haven, CT and London: Yale University Press, 2005.

Green, Ian, *Print and Protestantism in Early Modern England*. Oxford: Oxford University Press, 2000.

Haigh, Christopher, *English Reformations: Religion, Politics, and Society under the Tudors*. Oxford: Clarendon Press; New York: Oxford University Press, 1993.

The Plain Man's Pathways to Heaven: Kinds of Christianity in Post-Reformation England, 1570–1640. Oxford and New York: Oxford University Press, 2007.

Heal, Felicity, *Reformation in Britain and Ireland*. Oxford and New York: Oxford University Press, 2003.

Hunt, Arnold, *The Art of Hearing: English Preachers and Their Audiences, 1590–1640*. Cambridge: Cambridge University Press, 2010.

"The Lord's Supper in Early Modern England." *Past and Present* 161 (1998): 39–83.

Kauffman, Peter Iver, *Religion Around Shakespeare*. University Park, PA: Pennsylvania State University Press, 2013.

Killeen, Kevin, Helen Smith, and Rachel Willie (eds.), *The Oxford Handbook of the Bible in Early Modern England, c.1530–1700*. Oxford: Oxford University Press, 2015.

Lake, Peter, *Moderate Puritans and the Elizabethan Church*. Cambridge and New York: Cambridge University Press, 2004.

with Michael Questier, *The Anti-Christ's Lewd Hat: Protestants, Papists and Players in Post-Reformation England*. New Haven, CT: Yale University Press, 2002.

Maltby, Judith, *Prayer Book and People in Elizabethan and Early Stuart England*. Cambridge and New York: Cambridge University Press, 1998.

Marshall, Peter, *Beliefs and the Dead in Reformation England*. Oxford: Oxford University Press, 2002.

McCulloch, Diarmaid, *The Later Reformation in England, 1547–1603*. New York: Palgrave, 2001.

Narveson, Kate, *Bible Readers and Lay Writers in Early Modern England: Gender and Self-Definition in an Emergent Writing Culture*. Farnham, UK and Burlington, VT: Ashgate, 2012.

Norton, David, *A History of the Bible as Literature*. Cambridge and New York: Cambridge University Press, 2000.

Questier, Michael, *Catholicism and Community in Early Modern England: Politics, Aristocratic Patronage and Religion, c.1550–1640*. Cambridge and New York: Cambridge University Press, 2006.

Ryrie, Alec, *Being Protestant in Reformation Britain*. Oxford: Oxford University Press, 2013.

Shagan, Ethan. *Catholics and the "Protestant Nation": Religious Politics and Identity in Early Modern England*. Manchester: Manchester University Press, 2005.

The Rule of Moderation: Violence, Religion and Politics of Restraint in Early Modern England. Cambridge and New York: Cambridge University Press, 2011.

Walsham, Alexandra, *Church Papists: Catholicism, Conformity, and Confessional Polemic in Early Modern England*. Woodbridge: Published for the Royal Historical Society by Boydell Press, 1993.

Providence in Early Modern England. Oxford; New York: Oxford University Press, 1999.

The Reformation of the Landscape: Religion, Identity, and Memory in Early Modern Britain and Ireland. Oxford: Oxford University Press, 2011.

White, Peter, *Predestination and Polemic: Conflict and Consensus in the English Church from the Reformation to the Civil War*. Cambridge: Cambridge University Press, 2002.

Wooding, Lucy, *Rethinking Catholicism in Reformation England*. Oxford: Clarendon Press; New York: Oxford University Press, 2000.

INDEX

Cambridge Companions To ...

AUTHORS

Edward Albee edited by Stephen J. Bottoms
Margaret Atwood edited by Coral Ann Howells
W. H. Auden edited by Stan Smith
Jane Austen edited by Edward Copeland and Juliet McMaster (second edition)
Balzac edited by Owen Heathcote and Andrew Watts
Beckett edited by John Pilling
Bede edited by Scott DeGregorio
Aphra Behn edited by Derek Hughes and Janet Todd
Walter Benjamin edited by David S. Ferris
William Blake edited by Morris Eaves
Boccaccio edited by Guyda Armstrong, Rhiannon Daniels, and Stephen J. Milner
Jorge Luis Borges edited by Edwin Williamson
Brecht edited by Peter Thomson and Glendyr Sacks (second edition)
The Brontës edited by Heather Glen
Bunyan edited by Anne Dunan-Page
Frances Burney edited by Peter Sabor
Byron edited by Drummond Bone
Albert Camus edited by Edward J. Hughes
Willa Cather edited by Marilee Lindemann
Cervantes edited by Anthony J. Cascardi
Chaucer edited by Piero Boitani and Jill Mann (second edition)
Chekhov edited by Vera Gottlieb and Paul Allain
Kate Chopin edited by Janet Beer
Caryl Churchill edited by Elaine Aston and Elin Diamond
Cicero edited by Catherine Steel
Coleridge edited by Lucy Newlyn
Wilkie Collins edited by Jenny Bourne Taylor
Joseph Conrad edited by J. H. Stape
H. D. edited by Nephie J. Christodoulides and Polina Mackay
Dante edited by Rachel Jacoff (second edition)
Daniel Defoe edited by John Richetti
Don DeLillo edited by John N. Duvall
Charles Dickens edited by John O. Jordan
Emily Dickinson edited by Wendy Martin
John Donne edited by Achsah Guibbory
Dostoevskii edited by W. J. Leatherbarrow
Theodore Dreiser edited by Leonard Cassuto and Claire Virginia Eby
John Dryden edited by Steven N. Zwicker
W. E. B. Du Bois edited by Shamoon Zamir
George Eliot edited by George Levine and Nancy Henry (second edition)
T. S. Eliot edited by A. David Moody
Ralph Ellison edited by Ross Posnock
Ralph Waldo Emerson edited by Joel Porte and Saundra Morris
William Faulkner edited by Philip M. Weinstein
Henry Fielding edited by Claude Rawson
F. Scott Fitzgerald edited by Ruth Prigozy
Flaubert edited by Timothy Unwin
E. M. Forster edited by David Bradshaw
Benjamin Franklin edited by Carla Mulford
Brian Friel edited by Anthony Roche
Robert Frost edited by Robert Faggen
Gabriel García Márquez edited by Philip Swanson
Elizabeth Gaskell edited by Jill L. Matus
Edward Gibbon edited by Karen O'Brien and Brian Young
Goethe edited by Lesley Sharpe
Günter Grass edited by Stuart Taberner
Thomas Hardy edited by Dale Kramer
David Hare edited by Richard Boon
Nathaniel Hawthorne edited by Richard Millington
Seamus Heaney edited by Bernard O'Donoghue
Ernest Hemingway edited by Scott Donaldson
Homer edited by Robert Fowler
Horace edited by Stephen Harrison
Ted Hughes edited by Terry Gifford
Ibsen edited by James McFarlane
Henry James edited by Jonathan Freedman
Samuel Johnson edited by Greg Clingham
Ben Jonson edited by Richard Harp and Stanley Stewart
James Joyce edited by Derek Attridge (second edition)
Kafka edited by Julian Preece
Keats edited by Susan J. Wolfson
Rudyard Kipling edited by Howard J. Booth
Lacan edited by Jean-Michel Rabaté

D. H. Lawrence edited by Anne Fernihough
Primo Levi edited by Robert Gordon
Lucretius edited by Stuart Gillespie and Philip Hardie
Machiavelli edited by John M. Najemy
David Mamet edited by Christopher Bigsby
Thomas Mann edited by Ritchie Robertson
Christopher Marlowe edited by Patrick Cheney
Andrew Marvell edited by Derek Hirst and Steven N. Zwicker
Herman Melville edited by Robert S. Levine
Arthur Miller edited by Christopher Bigsby (second edition)
Milton edited by Dennis Danielson (second edition)
Molière edited by David Bradby and Andrew Calder
Toni Morrison edited by Justine Tally
Alice Munro edited by David Staines
Nabokov edited by Julian W. Connolly
Eugene O'Neill edited by Michael Manheim
George Orwell edited by John Rodden
Ovid edited by Philip Hardie
Petrarch edited by Albert Russell Ascoli and Unn Falkeid
Harold Pinter edited by Peter Raby (second edition)
Sylvia Plath edited by Jo Gill
Edgar Allan Poe edited by Kevin J. Hayes
Alexander Pope edited by Pat Rogers
Ezra Pound edited by Ira B. Nadel
Proust edited by Richard Bales
Pushkin edited by Andrew Kahn
Rabelais edited by John O'Brien
Rilke edited by Karen Leeder and Robert Vilain
Philip Roth edited by Timothy Parrish
Salman Rushdie edited by Abdulrazak Gurnah
John Ruskin edited by Francis O'Gorman
Shakespeare edited by Margareta de Grazia and Stanley Wells (second edition)
Shakespearean Comedy edited by Alexander Leggatt
Shakespeare and Contemporary Dramatists edited by Ton Hoenselaars
Shakespeare and Popular Culture edited by Robert Shaughnessy
Shakespeare and Religion edited by Hannibal Hamlin
Shakespearean Tragedy edited by Claire McEachern (second edition)
Shakespeare on Film edited by Russell Jackson (second edition)
Shakespeare on Stage edited by Stanley Wells and Sarah Stanton
Shakespeare's First Folio edited by Emma Smith
Shakespeare's History Plays edited by Michael Hattaway
Shakespeare's Last Plays edited by Catherine M. S. Alexander
Shakespeare's Poetry edited by Patrick Cheney
George Bernard Shaw edited by Christopher Innes
Shelley edited by Timothy Morton
Mary Shelley edited by Esther Schor
Sam Shepard edited by Matthew C. Roudané
Spenser edited by Andrew Hadfield
Laurence Sterne edited by Thomas Keymer
Wallace Stevens edited by John N. Serio
Tom Stoppard edited by Katherine E. Kelly
Harriet Beecher Stowe edited by Cindy Weinstein
August Strindberg edited by Michael Robinson
Jonathan Swift edited by Christopher Fox
J. M. Synge edited by P. J. Mathews
Tacitus edited by A. J. Woodman
Henry David Thoreau edited by Joel Myerson
Tolstoy edited by Donna Tussing Orwin
Anthony Trollope edited by Carolyn Dever and Lisa Niles
Mark Twain edited by Forrest G. Robinson
John Updike edited by Stacey Olster
Mario Vargas Llosa edited by Efrain Kristal and John King
Virgil edited by Fiachra Mac Góráin and Charles Martindale (second edition)
Voltaire edited by Nicholas Cronk
David Foster Wallace edited by Ralph Clare
Edith Wharton edited by Millicent Bell
Walt Whitman edited by Ezra Greenspan
Oscar Wilde edited by Peter Raby
Tennessee Williams edited by Matthew C. Roudané
August Wilson edited by Christopher Bigsby
Mary Wollstonecraft edited by Claudia L. Johnson
Virginia Woolf edited by Susan Sellers (second edition)
Wordsworth edited by Stephen Gill

W. B. Yeats edited by Marjorie Howes and John Kelly

Xenophon edited by Michael A. Flower

Zola edited by Brian Nelson

TOPICS

The Actress edited by Maggie B. Gale and John Stokes

The African American Novel edited by Maryemma Graham

The African American Slave Narrative edited by Audrey A. Fisch

African American Theatre edited by Harvey Young

Allegory edited by Rita Copeland and Peter Struck

American Crime Fiction edited by Catherine Ross Nickerson

American Gothic edited by Jeffrey Andrew Weinstock

American Literature of the 1930s edited by William Solomon

American Modernism edited by Walter Kalaidjian

American Poetry Since 1945 edited by Jennifer Ashton

American Realism and Naturalism edited by Donald Pizer

American Travel Writing edited by Alfred Bendixen and Judith Hamera

American Women Playwrights edited by Brenda Murphy

Ancient Rhetoric edited by Erik Gunderson

Arthurian Legend edited by Elizabeth Archibald and Ad Putter

Australian Literature edited by Elizabeth Webby

The Beats edited by Stephen Belletto

British Black and Asian Literature (1945–2010) edited by Deirdre Osborne

British Literature of the French Revolution edited by Pamela Clemit

British Romanticism edited by Stuart Curran (second edition)

British Romantic Poetry edited by James Chandler and Maureen N. McLane

British Theatre, 1730–1830 edited by Jane Moody and Daniel O'Quinn

Canadian Literature edited by Eva-Marie Kröller (second edition)

Children's Literature edited by M. O. Grenby and Andrea Immel

The Classic Russian Novel edited by Malcolm V. Jones and Robin Feuer Miller

Contemporary Irish Poetry edited by Matthew Campbell

Creative Writing edited by David Morley and Philip Neilsen

Crime Fiction edited by Martin Priestman

Dracula edited by Roger Luckhurst

Early Modern Women's Writing edited by Laura Lunger Knoppers

The Eighteenth-Century Novel edited by John Richetti

Eighteenth-Century Poetry edited by John Sitter

Emma edited by Peter Sabor

English Literature, 1500–1600 edited by Arthur F. Kinney

English Literature, 1650–1740 edited by Steven N. Zwicker

English Literature, 1740–1830 edited by Thomas Keymer and Jon Mee

English Literature, 1830–1914 edited by Joanne Shattock

English Melodrama edited by Carolyn Williams

English Novelists edited by Adrian Poole

English Poetry, Donne to Marvell edited by Thomas N. Corns

English Poets edited by Claude Rawson

English Renaissance Drama, second edition edited by A. R. Braunmuller and Michael Hattaway

English Renaissance Tragedy edited by Emma Smith and Garrett A. SullivanJr.

English Restoration Theatre edited by Deborah C. Payne Fisk

The Epic edited by Catherine Bates

Erotic Literature edited by Bradford Mudge

European Modernism edited by Pericles Lewis

European Novelists edited by Michael Bell

Fairy Tales edited by Maria Tatar

Fantasy Literature edited by Edward James and Farah Mendlesohn

Feminist Literary Theory edited by Ellen Rooney

Fiction in the Romantic Period edited by Richard Maxwell and Katie Trumpener

The Fin de Siècle edited by Gail Marshall

Frankenstein edited by Andrew Smith

The French Enlightenment edited by Daniel Brewer

French Literature edited by John D. Lyons

The French Novel: from 1800 to the Present edited by Timothy Unwin

Gay and Lesbian Writing edited by Hugh Stevens

German Romanticism edited by Nicholas Saul

Gothic Fiction edited by Jerrold E. Hogle

The Graphic Novel edited by Stephen Tabachnick

The Greek and Roman Novel edited by Tim Whitmarsh

Greek and Roman Theatre edited by Marianne McDonald and J. Michael Walton

Greek Comedy edited by Martin Revermann

Greek Lyric edited by Felix Budelmann

Greek Mythology edited by Roger D. Woodard

Greek Tragedy edited by P. E. Easterling

The Harlem Renaissance edited by George Hutchinson

The History of the Book edited by Leslie Howsam

The Irish Novel edited by John Wilson Foster

Irish Poets edited by Gerald Dawe

The Italian Novel edited by Peter Bondanella and Andrea Ciccarelli

The Italian Renaissance edited by Michael Wyatt

Jewish American Literature edited by Hana Wirth-Nesher and Michael P. Kramer

The Latin American Novel edited by Efraín Kristal

Latin American Poetry edited by Stephen Hart

Literature and Disability edited by Clare Barker and Stuart Murray

Literature and Science edited by Steven Meyer

The Literature of the American Renaissance edited by Christopher N. Phillips

The Literature of Berlin edited by Andrew J. Webber

The Literature of the Crusades, Volume 1, edited by Anthony Bale

The Literature of the First World War edited by Vincent Sherry

The Literature of London edited by Lawrence Manley

The Literature of Los Angeles edited by Kevin R. McNamara

The Literature of New York edited by Cyrus Patell and Bryan Waterman

The Literature of Paris edited by Anna-Louise Milne

The Literature of World War II edited by Marina MacKay

Literature on Screen edited by Deborah Cartmell and Imelda Whelehan

Medieval English Culture edited by Andrew Galloway

Medieval English Literature edited by Larry Scanlon

Medieval English Mysticism edited by Samuel Fanous and Vincent Gillespie

Medieval English Theatre edited by Richard Beadle and Alan J. Fletcher (second edition)

Medieval French Literature edited by Simon Gaunt and Sarah Kay

Medieval Romance edited by Roberta L. Krueger

Medieval Women's Writing edited by Carolyn Dinshaw and David Wallace

Modern American Culture edited by Christopher Bigsby

Modern British Women Playwrights edited by Elaine Aston and Janelle Reinelt

Modern French Culture edited by Nicholas Hewitt

Modern German Culture edited by Eva Kolinsky and Wilfried van der Will

The Modern German Novel edited by Graham Bartram

The Modern Gothic edited by Jerrold E. Hogle

Modern Irish Culture edited by Joe Cleary and Claire Connolly

Modern Italian Culture edited by Zygmunt G. Baranski and Rebecca J. West

Modern Latin American Culture edited by John King

Modern Russian Culture edited by Nicholas Rzhevsky

Modern Spanish Culture edited by David T. Gies

Modernism edited by Michael Levenson (second edition)

The Modernist Novel edited by Morag Shiach

Modernist Poetry edited by Alex Davis and Lee M. Jenkins

Modernist Women Writers edited by Maren Tova Linett

Narrative edited by David Herman

Narrative Theory edited by Matthew Garrett

Native American Literature edited by Joy Porter and Kenneth M. Roemer

Nineteenth-Century American Women's Writing edited by Dale M. Bauer and Philip Gould

The Novel edited by Eric Bulson

Old English Literature edited by Malcolm Godden and Michael Lapidge (second edition)

Performance Studies edited by Tracy C. Davis

Piers Plowman by Andrew Cole and Andrew Galloway

Popular Fiction edited by David Glover and Scott McCracken

Postcolonial Literary Studies edited by Neil Lazarus

Postcolonial Poetry edited by Jahan Ramazani

Postcolonial Travel Writing edited by Robert Clarke

Postmodern American Fiction edited by Paula Geyh

Postmodernism edited by Steven Connor

The Pre-Raphaelites edited by Elizabeth Prettejohn

Pride and Prejudice edited by Janet Todd

Renaissance Humanism edited by Jill Kraye

Robinson Crusoe edited by John Richetti

The Roman Historians edited by Andrew Feldherr

Roman Satire edited by Kirk Freudenburg

Science Fiction edited by Edward James and Farah Mendlesohn

Scottish Literature edited by Gerald Carruthers and Liam McIlvanney

Sensation Fiction edited by Andrew Mangham

Sherlock Holmes edited by Janice M. Allan and Christopher Pittard

The Sonnet edited by A. D. Cousins and Peter Howarth

The Spanish Novel: from 1600 to the Present edited by Harriet Turner and Adelaida López de Martínez

Textual Scholarship edited by Neil Fraistat and Julia Flanders

Theatre History by David Wiles and Christine Dymkowski

Transnational American Literature edited by Yogita Goyal

Travel Writing edited by Peter Hulme and Tim Youngs

Twentieth-Century British and Irish Women's Poetry edited by Jane Dowson

The Twentieth-Century English Novel edited by Robert L. Caserio

Twentieth-Century English Poetry edited by Neil Corcoran

Twentieth-Century Irish Drama edited by Shaun Richards

Twentieth-Century Russian Literature edited by Marina Balina and Evgeny Dobrenko

Utopian Literature edited by Gregory Claeys

Victorian and Edwardian Theatre edited by Kerry Powell

The Victorian Novel edited by Deirdre David (second edition)

Victorian Poetry edited by Joseph Bristow

Victorian Women's Writing edited by Linda H. Peterson

War Writing edited by Kate McLoughlin

Women's Writing in Britain, 1660–1789 edited by Catherine Ingrassia

Women's Writing in the Romantic Period edited by Devoney Looser

World Literature edited by Ben Etherington and Jarad Zimbler

Writing of the English Revolution edited by N. H. Keeble

The Writings of Julius Caesar edited by Christopher Krebs and Luca Grillo